MW01074612

The Dreadful History
and Judgement of God on
Thomas Müntzer

The Dreadful History and Judgement of God on Thomas Müntzer

The Life and Times of an Early German Revolutionary

Andrew Drummond

VERSO

London • New York

First published by Verso 2024
© Andrew Drummond 2024

1 3 5 7 9 10 8 6 4 2

Verso
UK: 6 Meard Street, London W1F 0EG
US: 388 Atlantic Avenue, Brooklyn, NY 11217
versobooks.com

Verso is the imprint of New Left Books

ISBN-13: 978-1-83976-894-1
ISBN-13: 978-1-83976-896-5 (UK EBK)
ISBN-13: 978-1-83976-897-2 (US EBK)

British Library Cataloguing in Publication Data
A catalogue record for this book is available from the British Library

Library of Congress Cataloging-in-Publication Data

Names: Drummond, Andrew, 1952– author.
Title: The dreadful history and judgement of God on Thomas Müntzer : the
 life and times of an early German revolutionary / Andrew Drummond.
Description: First edition hardback. | London : Verso, 2024. | Includes
 bibliographical references and index.
Identifiers: LCCN 2023037921 (print) | LCCN 2023037922 (ebook) | ISBN
 9781839768941 (hardback) | ISBN 9781839768972 (US EBK) | ISBN
 9781839768965 (UK EBK)
Subjects: LCSH: Münzer, Thomas, approximately 1490–1525. | Peasants' War,
 1524–1525. | Reformation – Germany – Biography.
Classification: LCC BX4946.M8 D78 2024 (print) | LCC BX4946.M8 (ebook) |
 DDC 284/.3092 – dc23/eng/20231016
LC record available at https://lccn.loc.gov/2023037921
LC ebook record available at https://lccn.loc.gov/2023037922

Typeset in Sabon by MJ & N Gavan, Truro, Cornwall
Printed and bound by CPI Group (UK) Ltd, Croydon, CR0 4YY

Contents

CONTENTS

THE WETTIN FAMILY IN THE EARLY SIXTEENTH CENTURY

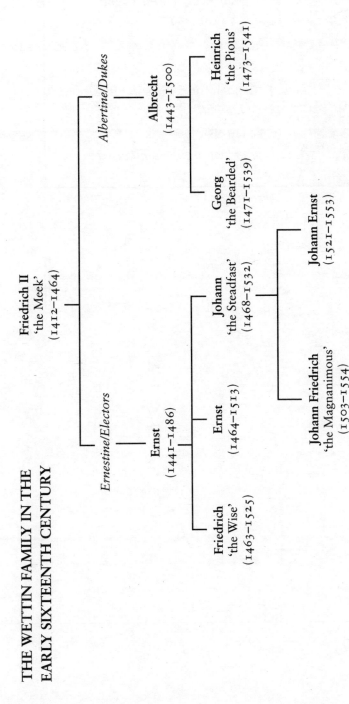

Ernestine/Electors

Albertine/Dukes

Friedrich II
'the Meek'
(1412–1464)

Ernst
(1441–1486)

Albrecht
(1443–1500)

Friedrich
'the Wise'
(1463–1525)

Ernst
(1464–1513)

Johann
'the Steadfast'
(1468–1532)

Georg
'the Bearded'
(1471–1539)

Heinrich
'the Pious'
(1473–1541)

Johann Friedrich
'the Magnanimous'
(1503–1554)

Johann Ernst
(1521–1553)

The Albertine line was staunchly Roman Catholic during the Reformation period, and the Ernestine moderately to fiercely reformist or Lutheran. Duke Georg resolutely defended the Roman Church; on the reforming side, Prince Friedrich and his brother Duke Johann shared the responsibilities of government until Friedrich's death in 1525. Duke Johann was largely responsible for the implementation of Luther's reforms throughout Saxony.

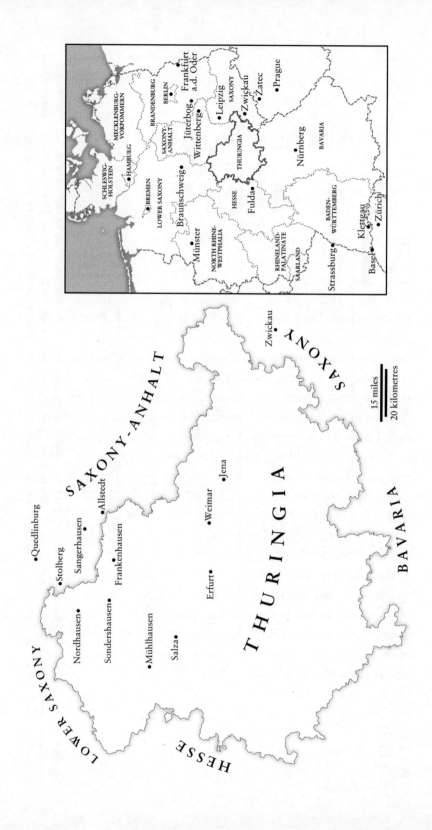

Acknowledgements

My thanks to the following people who have, over the years, helped me in the writing of this book: the late John L. Flood of the University of London; Peter Matheson, of Otago University, New Zealand; Doug Miller, of Northumberland University; Lyndal Roper, of Oxford University; the late Tom Scott, of St Andrews University. All of the above have kindly offered advice, facts, opinions and thoughts. I owe a particular debt to Professor Roper, who bravely volunteered to read through my manuscript and then furnished me with a more than adequate number of corrections and suggestions. I have not always paid attention to all these advisers – so any fault lies entirely with me. The many essays and articles by Professors Scott and Matheson have proved invaluable; and without the body of work by Thomas T. Müller, Günter Vogler and the late Siegfried Bräuer, little of this book would have been possible. From an earlier generation, I owe a large debt to the studies of Bob Scribner, as well as those of the East German historians Max Steinmetz, Martin Bensing and Gerhard Zschäbitz. Finally, my gratitude to Leo Hollis and John Merrick at Verso for their faith in this book and their guidance towards a finished product; and to Tim Clark, my copy-editor, whose outstanding work and attention to detail has saved me – thus far – from several embarrassments.

Notes on the Text and
Some Helpful Remarks

All quotations in the text have been rendered into English. This has been done to save the reader the pain of translating modern German – or, what is infinitely more painful, highly eccentric sixteenth-century German or Latin. Despite the fact that most of Müntzer's writings have been translated into excellent English by others (first and foremost Peter Matheson), I have chosen to provide my own translations, which are based on the principal modern German edition of Müntzer's works: the three-volume *Thomas Müntzer: Kritische Gesamtausgabe* (for more details on the German and English editions, see the bibliography at the end of this book). My translated titles of Müntzer's pamphlets are similar to, but not always the same as, those given by Peter Matheson.

Notwithstanding that laudable goal of saving the reader pain, I have retained the German rendering of personal and town names. Thus, we refer to 'Friedrich' and not 'Frederick', to 'Georg' and not 'George'; similarly to 'Braunschweig' and not 'Brunswick', 'Nürnberg' and not 'Nuremberg'. However, compromising this principle, I have rendered wider geographical names in their English format: so, 'Thuringia' and not 'Thüringen', 'Saxony' and not 'Sachsen'.

Monetary values are occasionally mentioned – specifically the 'guilder' (or gulden, also known as a 'florin'). As a rough guide to its value in 1525, an army company captain received forty guilders per month, while a lowly foot soldier would earn four guilders.[1] Müntzer received an annual stipend of thirty florins/

guilders when engaged as preacher in Zwickau. You could buy a fine pig, or a good pair of riding boots (with spurs), or thirty-five gallons of ordinary wine, for one guilder; more expensive, at six guilders, would be a cart, fully equipped and road-ready.[2] A 'groschen' (groat) was a small denomination – twenty-one of these to the commonly used 'Schneeberg' guilder. Your average lower-class labourer might hope to earn about four groschen each day. However, since currency units and values varied widely across Germany – and their value also varied depending on whether they were made of gold, silver or copper – exact values are hard to determine.

To provide some assistance to the reader in coming to terms with the somewhat confused politics of Saxony, a very sketchy family tree of the main Saxon nobility is provided above (with thanks to Tom Scott). The Wettin House of Saxony was divided into the 'Albertine' branch and the 'Ernestine' branch after the Treaty of Leipzig in 1485, which gave (roughly speaking) the south of Saxony to Albrecht and the north to his brother Ernst.

Introduction

A Most Useful Lesson

The History of Thomas Müntzer, the Fomenter of the Thuringian Tumult; a Most Useful Lesson

Philipp Melanchthon (1525)

O n 15 May 1525, Thomas Müntzer found himself surrounded by the ranks of the rebel peasant army on a hill in central Germany, exhorting the soldiers to victory over the godless. Ranged against them were the combined armies of the princes of the German nation, both Lutheran and Catholic. Before much time had elapsed, most of the rebel army lay dead on the ground, the rest fleeing and scattered, with Müntzer himself captured, soon to be executed.

So, who was this Thomas Müntzer? And why should anyone be interested in him today?

Who was Thomas Müntzer? Simple: he was a Devil, he was Satan, he was a Ravening Wolf and a False Prophet, who stirred up murder, rebellion and bloodshed. Or so, at least, said Martin Luther, the theologian whose posting of ninety-five theses to the doors of a church in Wittenberg in 1517 opened the floodgates to the Reformation movement. He and his colleagues had much more to say about our man; none of it good. Almost all of the chapters in this book are headlined with quotations from the many contemporary tracts, letters and pamphlets which condemned Müntzer. But hopefully what emerges from these chapters is that much of what was said and written about Müntzer was simply untrue. One of the aims of this book is to show how Müntzer's reputation languished for several centuries – and in some circles, still languishes today – in the darker recesses and slanderous footnotes of history books.

Writing a biography of Müntzer is fraught with danger and excitement. Despite the very best efforts of several generations of historians and archivists, the documentation that is available today only illuminates his life for less than thirty months of his first thirty years. Even though he only lived to be thirty-five, this is not a lot. Large gaps will have to be filled in, largely – but not entirely – by inspired guesswork.

By contrast, plenty of Müntzer's own words, expressions and opinions have survived – none of which help much in establishing his biography, but all of which help in understanding his mind. Those of his writings which have come down to us were, rather ironically, preserved by his enemies, who scarcely imagined that later generations might not be so condemnatory of Müntzer. Perhaps if we take one of his more resonant calls to the common people of Germany to take up arms against their rulers, we will understand why his contemporaries did not much approve:

> On, on, onwards, for the fire is hot! Do not let your sword grow cold, do not let it hang loose in your hands! Smite cling clang on the anvil of Nimrod and cast down their towers! As long as they live, it is not possible to be emptied of the fear of man. You can be told nothing about God as long as they rule over you. On, onwards, while you have daylight. God marches before you, so follow, follow![1]

But, against that admittedly provocative battle-cry, we have also this from Thomas Müntzer, clergyman and religious reformer:

> But I have no doubts in the common people. Oh, you poor, pitiable little band, how you thirst after the word of God! For it is quite clear that no one or almost no one knows where they stand or what group they should join. They . . . are frightened by the spirit of the fear of God to such a degree that in them is truly come

to pass what was prophesied by Jeremiah: 'The young children ask for bread and no man breaketh it unto them.' Oh, oh, no man broke it![2]

Or how about this:

> Therefore it is still my firm intention to assist poor, downtrodden Christianity with German [Church] offices, be they Masses, Matins or Vespers, so that any good-hearted man will see, hear and understand how the desperate Papist evil-doers have stolen the holy scriptures from poor Christianity, to its great injury, and have prevented true understanding.[3]

Perhaps, then, this radical reformer was not a ravening wolf and a bloodthirsty devil, but a man dedicated to improving the spiritual position of the common people? Perhaps we will find, behind the slurs and epithets, a man of considerable learning and principle, a man deeply sympathetic to the misery of the peasantry and the poor, a man of complex character?

If asked to identify who the Lutherans saw as their deadly enemy, the average scholar would name the Pope and the Roman Church. If we could consult Luther himself, though, he would surely add the name of Müntzer to that list. Yet, although Müntzer was an implacable enemy of the Lutherans, he was no friend or admirer of the Roman religion either. He was in fact, at one time and briefly, a colleague of Luther. As we shall see, the vitriol poured upon him by Luther and his party was supplied by their need to distance themselves, as reputable and loyal reformers, from the thoroughly disreputable and disloyal rebels of the German Peasants' War of 1525 – a huge, popular and lower-class uprising in which Müntzer took the side of the peasantry against the feudal authorities. Their view of Müntzer's untimely end was quite straightforward:

> So we should learn from this how severely God punishes disobedience and tumult against our rulers, for God has commanded that we should honour our rulers and obey them. God will not leave unpunished anyone who goes against this command.[4]

From our relatively smug twenty-first-century position, the idea that our rulers are ordained by a god to govern us, honoured and unchallenged, is fanciful, even disturbing. So the opinions of Müntzer's enemies alone should pique our interest in the man. What on earth did he do to upset them so much? Did he really call for murder and bloodshed? Why, in the end, did the rulers of the lands of Germany feel the need to cut off his head?

The life of Thomas Müntzer was brief. He was born in late 1489, in Stolberg in the Harz mountains of central Germany, possibly the son of a coin-maker. When he died on the executioner's block in 1525, he was only thirty-five years old. His active role in the religious reform movement in Germany spanned the last eight of those years, and for just the last four of these can he be considered a determinedly radical opponent of Martin Luther. And yet his activity has always been of crucial importance in the historiography of the 'German Reformation'; there is not one book of value on the subject which does not make some mention of him, and there are many which attempt to analyse his role.

Müntzer was educated at the universities of Leipzig and Frankfurt an der Oder. As the reform movement in Wittenberg gained traction, he was, like many of his contemporaries, swept up by the intellectual frenzy of the period. He was soon involved in debate on the nature and role of the established Church. His earliest interventions for reform were made in the same spirit as those of Martin Luther, although some of his arguments were self-evidently not 'Lutheran'. However, as the revolutionary movement developed and provided the tidal flow to the reforms, with urban and rural protest becoming the normal manifestation of reform, so Müntzer elaborated his own theological and political positions. These gradually came so much into conflict with Luther's basic teachings that an open split was inevitable. This occurred between the years 1520 and 1522, when Müntzer was preaching in towns and cities in Saxony and Bohemia; by 1523, after he had taken up a post in the small Saxon town of Allstedt, his proposed reforms were very different from – indeed contrary to – those of the movement led by Luther.

Let us be quite clear, here and for the rest of this book: it is impossible to understand the motivations of anyone in sixteenth-century Europe without acknowledging that their underlying worldview was anchored by a belief in a high divine authority, personified by the Christian God. This God ruled the fate of individuals and the world in general. God ordained military victories and defeats, natural and unnatural disasters, drought, starvation and times of plenty. God established civil authority and justice. A belief in the divinity underpinned every philosophy and every justification, from civic by-laws to an Apocalyptic call to arms. To imagine otherwise is to do the sixteenth century a gross injustice and to completely misunderstand our ancestors. It is therefore necessary for us to make some analysis of Müntzer's stated theology, a task to be undertaken in more detail later in this book.

The essential difference in theology between Luther and Müntzer, though, can be summarised as follows: Luther believed that the earthly power of the secular authorities was immutable, that the territorial princes of Germany should be encouraged to embrace reform, but that it was the task of all Christians to achieve personal salvation within whatever constraints were imposed by their rulers. Müntzer, on the other hand, believed that the powers of the State and of the Church actively obstructed the acquisition and spread of faith, and that it was the task of the 'Elect' to help God destroy those barriers. To defend his own position, Luther maintained that the words of the scriptures must be obeyed, while Müntzer proposed that individual spiritual experience framed the only law of any importance. From these two positions, and from the social forces which supported them, two utterly opposed socio-political strategies developed. Luther decided on a 'slow' process of reform, whose pace and direction were determined by the secular authority; Müntzer on a swift and all-consuming Apocalyptic revolution triggered by God, led by the Elect and propelled forward by the common people.

Between 1523 and 1525, throughout south and central Germany, pressure was building towards the eruption of a widespread Peasants' War. In this 'war' – arguably the greatest popular uprising in Europe until that time, and sometimes described as a revolution – the religious demands of reformers combined explosively with the social and economic demands of the peasantry and urban plebeians. The build-up of pressure was also reflected in the politics of the religious reformers, some of whom went over to the side of the territorial princes, fearing the overthrow of God's order, while others threw in their lot with the insurgents. In May 1525, Müntzer, despite hopeless odds against him, attempted to lead the peasants of Thuringia in central Germany against the armies of the principalities of Saxony and Hesse. His subsequent capture and decapitation served two purposes for the victors: firstly, it rid them of a dangerous troublemaker; secondly, it was a warning to all the other radicals of the time of the likely consequence of their actions. But this 'Judgement of God upon Thomas Müntzer', as the Lutherans saw it, failed to prevent the radical reform movement from developing. A sizeable proportion of the later Anabaptists – small communities which rejected both the Lutheran and Catholic churches in favour of a more individual form of worship – drew their inspiration and doctrines directly or indirectly from Müntzer and carried his legacy forward beyond 1525.

A study of Müntzer's life and thought brings us into rather intimate contact with the labels commonly attached to this period, so we must seize this opportunity to define our terms of reference more closely.

The term 'Reformation' itself is a rather cloudy and confusing concept. Everyone knows what we mean by it, but . . . what do we actually mean by it? It has been pointed out that the term did not appear until the seventeenth century, and that even then it was intended to describe only Luther's activities.[5] The reformers themselves did not regard their cause as 'the Reformation'; the term 'Lutheran' or 'Martinian' was current at that time, usually applied by the opponents of reform, often without great perception and rarely distinguishing between different flavours. But since the reform movement embraced a very wide spectrum of opinion and motivation, is it fair or even helpful to stamp 'Lutheran' on the forehead of everyone with a will to reform the Church? Proposals for reform were, after all, put forward by territorial princes, Imperial nobles, urban patricians, burghers, academics and theologians, artisans, peasants and plebeians – even indeed by some adherents of Papal authority. If there was such a thing as a 'Reformation' in Germany, then it was a very broad social and religious movement covering several decades from the mid-fifteenth century through to the mid-sixteenth century. Of course there was a period which can with hindsight be labelled 'the Reformation', but it neither began with Luther's famous theses of 1517, nor ended with his death in 1546.

To add to the confusion, it is clear that the commonly recognised core period of the German Reformation was a game of two halves: an early one from around 1517 to 1521, and a later one, which continued throughout the sixteenth century. The dividing line between the two was the point at which Luther himself decided that the motive power of reform lay with the political rulers alone. As if all that were not bewildering enough, there was an earlier reform movement in Bohemia – the Hussite reforms, beginning around 1420 – and a contemporary one in Switzerland, beginning around 1519, led by Zwingli. Both of these geographical areas lay just across the borders from what is loosely described as 'Germany', but those borders provided no barrier to radical religious ideas.

The few years between 1517 and 1525 were ones of tremendous excitement and activity in Germany, the like of which were not seen for 400 years thereafter, until perhaps the chaos and creativity of the revolutionary years immediately after 1918. It was a period when the floodgates of the national intellect were thrown open. Ordinary people finally found expression for long-suppressed hopes and fears; they strove in all manner of ways to set to rights the injustices of society. The Humanists, the Wittenberg reformers, the radicals, the political leaders of local and national uprisings, early capitalists and entrepreneurs, even individuals among the nobility, all struggled to come to terms with their past and their present, aspiring to build a new future in their own image. In this confusion, quite bizarre things were said and done, out of naivety or pure enthusiasm. Realistically, no secular or religious authority could properly function in such an atmosphere and still maintain power over the labourers and producers of wealth, and so order had to be restored in town and country – through the political control of religious affairs, and through naked physical repression.

The 'failure' of Müntzer and his fellow thinkers in 1525 is not the important feature of the radical reform movement; what is important is the fact that there were any radicals at all, and that they scored some significant points before being defeated, for this signals to us that 'the Reformation' was not a monolith, nor a juggernaut heading along one straight road, but a living, contradictory movement which provided hope for all classes of people by promising a better and fairer life. Any study of the Reformation period must take notice of the losers, for the seed of future events resided as much in them as in the victors.

If the relatively simple concept of 'the Reformation' begins to get a little muddy, that is as nothing compared to trying to paint a clear picture of the 'also-rans' – those groups of radicals who wanted to push the boundaries of religious reform much further, and who challenged the sacred domains of economic activity, property relations and civil authority. Since the radical reformers were hounded and – after 1525 – physically purged from the surface of German society, the ability of those radicals to express themselves in writing or print was severely limited. For the most part, their doctrines have only come down to us through the kind consideration of their torturers, jailers and executioners. In such an atmosphere, the accused sometimes opted for self-preservation and confessed whatever was asked of them; sometimes they stood defiant, and their doctrines were then publicised posthumously in the most lurid light. The Lutherans wrote whatever they liked about the radicals, and they would get away with it – who, after all, was going to complain?

Biographical details of the radicals are extremely scanty, because they were men and women of low birth who only stepped into public view immediately before their deaths. Of those who lasted for a relatively long time – like Müntzer – details of their early life were not in great demand at the time of their death, and can now only be pieced together out of scraps; many gaps exist, and sometimes creative thinking has to stand in for evidence. In our particular case, Müntzer's life before 1523 is adequately

TOMAS MVNCER PREDIGER ZV ALSTET IN DVRINGEN.

Portrait of Müntzer, etched and published by Christoffel van Sichem in 1608.
This is the most reproduced portrait although, given its date, it is questionable
if it bears any resemblance to the living Müntzer. Behind him on the left is
probably the tower of Heldrungen castle where he was held captive, and on
the right is a depiction of his beheading.

documented only for the eleven-month period of his residence in Zwickau. We are forced to make stabs at the biographical record for most of the first thirty-three years of his lifespan, and a significant period of his last two years as well. We are not certain of his year of birth, nor of his family, nor of his education. It is a most embarrassing position for any biographer to be in.

We certainly do not know what Müntzer looked like. Sure enough, there is a persuasive portrait of him, an engraving by the Dutch artist Christoffel van Sichem, who created a series of likenesses of heretics and Anabaptists. Sichem's portrait shows a rather surly, heavy-jowled man in a thick coat, looking sideways and rather distantly towards the artist, his hands leafing through the Bible. In the background, a hilly rural scene and the tower of a castle are shown, conceivably the locations of Müntzer's last battle and his imprisonment: a dim figure can just be seen behind the iron-barred window of the tower. But this image, a surprisingly non-judgemental one, dates from 1608. It is possible that it was based on an earlier portrait done by someone back in – let us suppose – 1524, when Müntzer was in Nürnberg (home town of the 'three godless painters', of whom more later). Significantly, the explanatory text below the portrait reads: 'Thomas Müntzer. Preacher of Allstedt in Thuringia'; this description could suggest that it was a portrait executed before Müntzer became famous in Mühlhausen in 1525. Or not. We have no idea. (However, it is probably a better image to have before us than the sixteenth-century woodcut showing a preacher holding forth to a small assembly of engrossed and plainly dressed listeners; this is annotated 'This prophet looks like Thomas Müntzer.' Given that the woodcut is the frontispiece to a book of prophecies by an astrologer who died in 1503, the suggested likeness seems both fanciful and totally irrelevant. But such wild inaccuracy has never stopped commentators with an axe to grind.)

If the contemporary reports on Müntzer and his fellow radicals were bad, their effect on historiography for the next five centuries was even worse. Many of the descriptions of Müntzer's life and doctrines which were published by his bitterest opponents in the year of his death have been accepted quite uncritically right up until the present century. The purpose of this book, then, is to cut through the myths and to tear off the labels which serve largely to obscure the view of what really happened in the early German Reformation and of who that bloodthirsty, rebellious and murderous man, Thomas Müntzer, really was.

1

The End of the World

Historical and Religious Background to the German Reformation

The Day of the Lord is at hand, when the Man of Sin and the Son of Perdition will be revealed. For we are those who have reached the End of the World.

Nikolaus von Amsdorf (1521)

Thomas Müntzer was born – as far as can be determined – in 1489. And having brought him into the world, let us immediately abandon him there for the duration of his childhood, for we must make a brief attempt to comprehend the world into which he was born.

Not long after Müntzer's birth, a writer later dubbed – a little arbitrarily – the 'Revolutionary of the Upper Rhine' set out his predictions for the coming decade:

The Lord will come after seven thousand years and will pass a mighty judgement over Man and punish us for our evil . . . The peasant will rise up against his masters and even his spiritual leaders . . . and the common man will cast down the high and mighty.[1]

The *Book of One Hundred Chapters and Forty Statutes* of this 'Revolutionary' is a curious one, full of wild predictions, astro-logical terminology and warnings of the imminent end of the world; for the end was indeed nigh, and could be expected some-where around 1500 (which is announced as the year marking the end of the mystical seventh 'Chiliade' or millennium). Although the author was in fact an Austrian nobleman – whose aim was to promote a reformed Empire with governing structures which would improve the lot of the peasantry, while keeping them in their place: in short, a reformist, not a revolutionary[2] – his book was by no means an outlier when it came to the popular thought of the fifteenth century. A few decades earlier, in 1440, another work entitled *The Reformation of the Emperor Sigismund* had appeared, in which similar predictions were made: 'The time is now come when we must awake', its author wrote, 'stand up, acknowledge God, and prepare the way which is that of God and righteousness . . . for you will clear the path for He who will come next.'[3] The book clearly struck a chord with the intellectuals of the time, being reprinted in 1476, and several times more in the first two decades of the sixteenth century. Even as late as 1521, Martin Luther and his colleagues were themselves not averse to imagining that something rather Apocalyptical was about to happen.

For many intellectuals, then, there was something important about the numerically significant year of 1500. Just as in the late twentieth century, when people looked to the year 2000 as some kind of watershed, albeit with a fair degree of pessimism (quite unjustifiably as it turned out: the Apocalypse did not come until a little afterwards), many late fifteenth-century Europeans attached their hopes and fears to the turning of the century.

Millenarianism is the expectation of the Second Coming of Jesus Christ, and the consequent establishment of a 'Kingdom of God'; it had been a feature of the preceding centuries, and by the late fifteenth century it was breaking forth once more in the German-speaking territories. Discontent was also stalking the lands in more potent form in the guise of rural and urban revolt. In 1476, for example, there was a powerful but short-lived revolt by thousands of peasants in the Tauber valley in Franconia, led by a man known as the 'Drummer of Niklashausen'. The revolt had shown that resentment in matters social and economic among the poor was at boiling-point, likely to spill over into popular revolt at any moment. This was to be the first in a series of such sporadic and localised uprisings – generically grouped together as the 'Peasant's Shoe' (*Bundschuh*) movement, from the symbol they adopted on their banners – that would culminate in the great German Peasants' War of 1525.

Nor was it just the lower classes who revolted: the Imperial aristocracy, too, felt downtrodden, and were in constant conflict with the territorial princes as their traditional power was slowly eroded by land-purchase and political manoeuvring. The Holy Roman Empire, which had held sway across much of central Europe since the tenth century, was gradually seeing its power slip away into the hands of its electoral college, the local principalities and territories. The knights of the Empire clung desperately to their ever-diminishing estates and privileges, but theirs was a struggle against the tide. By contrast, in the flourishing towns, the burgher classes, the more well-to-do artisans and the intellectuals were beginning to scratch the itch of independence, seeking to sever feudal relationships and cut loose from the Church in Rome. Some towns and cities had effectively become independent political and economic units, having only nominal feudal lords; they were doing quite nicely on their own, despite an economic downturn towards the end of the fifteenth century.

In the religious sphere, matters were no calmer. Seventy years before Müntzer's birth, the Hussite reforms in Bohemia had inspired an entire nation to rise up and challenge the might of the Papal Church, and this reform movement had infected parts of Germany over several decades. So now the Bohemians and Germans knew that it was at least possible to question the spiritual authority. Having taken that step, they found the courage to ask more, and more penetrating, questions about the role and status of the Church – any Church – in the life of a nation.

The late fifteenth century in central Germany, then, was something of a leaky powder-keg. There was unrest in towns and villages, and there were people openly questioning the basic tenets of the Papal Church. The combination of social and political unrest with the intellectual and religious debate was to provide the fuse which lit the powder.

Suffering under the entire weight of the feudal burden, it was primarily the peasant or disenfranchised lower-class town-dweller who participated in religious heretical movements or in rude and untrammelled riot. None of this was new. All the countries of Europe had been affected at one time or another, with the fourteenth-century Peasants' Revolt in England and the Jacquerie in France being just two obvious examples. And even before that, between the eleventh and thirteenth centuries, there had been popular crusades and a whole host of colourful and tragic heresies involving the lower classes, all cruelly suppressed. Closer to our subject, the Hussite and subsequent Taborite rebellions in Bohemia in the early fifteenth century provide another example, as do the popular uprisings in Hungary and Slovenia in 1514–15. Without exception, the expression of this discontent and rebellion was a religious one. Social analysis and class politics were several hundred years into the future. Religious disagreement, frequently termed 'heresy', was almost the only way in which unrest could manifest itself.

But these radical religious movements were not simply links in an eternal chain of heresy. Of course, they have striking and persuasive similarities over time. Almost every heresy one cares to uncover has a doctrinal element that could well have been lifted from some previous one. But great care is required before supposing any kind of genetic inheritance: firstly, because many of the European millenarian doctrines relied on the only intellectual 'authority' of those times, the Bible (specifically those Apocalyptic books which had most to offer the oppressed), and coming from a single source the variations in doctrine were of necessity limited; secondly, because the heretical movements were spread out widely across the continent, and the opportunities for transmission over distance were limited; and thirdly, because descriptions of heretical doctrine were provided very often by Church inquisitors or by hostile observers who, just like those claiming to see 'Marxism' or 'Communism' nestling in any left-wing group today, tended to suspect anyone exhibiting the merest spot of erroneous doctrine of being utterly infected by the rampant plague of some vile heresy.

These revolts were signs of a deeper development. The Middle Ages had seen the rise of the merchant and early capitalist class in Europe. The Crusades of the twelfth and thirteenth centuries had prised open many of the trade routes across and out of the continent and created the conditions for highly profitable mercantile activity. The Crusades also dealt a hefty blow to feudal relationships between serf and lord, and to the aristocracy itself. Estates were lost when their lords died in foreign lands, and serfs were freed for military service and subsequently perished or settled elsewhere. In turn, the opening of the trade routes led almost directly to the great plagues that swept into Europe, killing hundreds of thousands and leaving land untilled and obligations unfulfilled. It took until well into the fifteenth century for the European economies to stabilise after these heavy blows. But as the old fabric of society slowly fell apart, the chances for rich and powerful people to further enrich and empower themselves multiplied. Estates were joined end to end, and widely distributed land changed hands to improve cultivation or to consolidate political alliances, or simply for cash. This was a very gradual process: looking at a map of Germany of that period, you are struck by the intricate and patchwork nature of territorial holdings, ranging from the very large to the tiny. There are small, scattered islands of land belonging to a single lordship, whose main territory might be hundreds of miles away. Even in a single village, different people might have allegiances and obligations to a variety of different landowners and feudal lords. But regardless of which lord they belonged to, peasants had an almost universal legal duty to provide unpaid labour; they were also heavily taxed when a head of family died, denied the right to move to another part of the country or into town, and banned from accessing the basic necessities of life: timber for building and fuel, water for power and fish, and game for eating. For a rural population which was extremely susceptible to the catastrophes of poor harvests, such access was of paramount importance. Quite naturally, then, this led to those very sources of food and fuel being enclosed by estate owners. Meanwhile, any income or possessions a peasant might have would be steadily eaten up by taxes and tithes; it has been calculated that as much as 40 per cent of production was transferred from the peasantry to their lords, and then there was a 10 per cent tithe on grain on top of that (not to mention the 'smaller tithe', the wine tithe and a tithe on livestock – schemes by which value was skimmed off lesser items of production); to finish them off, taxes of up to 5 per cent were also imposed.[4] And it must not be forgotten that many of the landowners were in fact representatives of the Church: the estates of wealthy abbeys, monasteries and nunneries were just as adept as their lay equivalents at squeezing the last drop of blood from the peasantry – perhaps more so, since some of the worst of them were known to threaten their peasants with excommunication if they refused to pay their taxes or perform their labour duties.[5] Excommunication, it should be remembered, was considered a fate worse than death itself. And it was the Church lordships in particular which began to re-impose basic serfdom during the fifteenth century.

After the economic slump of the fourteenth and fifteenth centuries, the recovery was led by the urban communities, in particular the town merchants and patricians, and the vast fortunes they accumulated began to rival and even outshine the splendour of the late-medieval courts. Outstanding among these were the several branches of the Fugger family, based in Augsburg, who had been accumulating wealth through weaving, mining, trade and land deals since the beginning of the fifteenth century. By the start of the sixteenth, they had become the wealthiest family in northern Europe, investing in all aspects of cloth-making, and in copper, silver and gold mines, while also managing transactions for the Church in Rome and lending money to the landed nobility. In their accumulation of capital, merchants like the Fuggers presented both a status to be aspired to and the means – through financial loans – by which it might be achieved. The feudal lords could raise money either by mortgaging lands or by squeezing their dependants, and preferably both. All of which made the life of the peasant almost unbearable.

It was in the fifteenth century that German merchant capital found under its very own feet the commodity that was its lifeblood: gold and silver. The mines of Saxony had been worked for 200–300 years before they began to be exploited in earnest, but by the end of the fifteenth century Saxony had become one of the richest states in Europe, yielding huge amounts of metals, precious and otherwise. Silver coins from Saxony were renowned for their reliability as currency. By the end of the sixteenth century, Saxony and Bohemia were producing up to 4,000 tonnes of raw copper from their mines, and Saxony alone produced 30 tonnes of refined silver. By its very nature, ore extraction and processing demanded huge capital investment, and it was this which attracted, then enriched, the more astute merchants of the time. The Fugger family, for example, established a huge smelting-works not far from Erfurt, to which copper ore from as far afield as Upper Hungary was brought, processed and then redistributed across Germany and Europe.[6] The Fugger family also intervened at critical points in the German Peasants' War – in March 1525, for example, they lent the Swabian League, then gearing up to suppress the peasantry, the sum of 10,000 florins; and in a series of complaints raised by Tirolean miners in 1525, the Fuggers were specifically mentioned for their exploitative practices.[7]

Wellcome Trust (CC by 4.0)

Miners prospecting near Zwickau. From Georg Agricola's book, *De re metallica* (1556).

The forests and rivers of southern Saxony made the region ideal for the development of early industry, providing fuel, motive power and transportation options. As soon as the merchants and princes realised the potential of this yield for German trade, the mines were opened up for exploitation. The wealth of Saxony spread out over Germany. And yet, by the beginning of the sixteenth century, the mines were beginning to run into difficulties – seams were proving harder to access, mining technology was not far advanced, and loans had to be repaid. Investors sought other means of getting rich. By 1540, for example, the major silver seams around Schneeberg in Saxony had been completely exhausted, and by then the importation of cheap silver from the New World had already begun. By the time Luther and Müntzer emerged onto the historical stage, the Saxon economy was entering something of a decline.[8]

Economic development gave rise to changes in political structure, as well as being subject to them. It led steadily to the longer-term undermining of the authority of the Holy Roman Empire in German territories and to the collapse of the smaller feudal estates. While the Imperial Diets and the bureaucracy of Empire still performed a useful and necessary political function in Germany, the trend lay towards the political independence of the larger territories such as Saxony, Württemberg, Brandenburg, Hesse and the Palatinate. Even those towns and cities that were designated 'Free Imperial', i.e. legally subject only to the Emperor, were obliged to make alliances with the territorial powers for protection. The lesser aristocracy was squeezed out; for a long time, their main source of income was either banditry – at which they excelled – or war, but in the latter their age-old skills were already becoming outdated. By 1522, the year that the German knights, under the leadership of Franz von Sickingen, made one last effort to postpone the inevitable, they were complaining that many of them had been prevented by 'various princes and nobles' from attending the Imperial Diets, 'either by force or by threat of force'.[9] This miserable spectacle, of a once-brilliant class reduced to quixotic poverty and impotence, was the comic side of historical development. Far more tragic was the lot of the peasantry.

The efforts of the feudal powers, both secular and religious, to accumulate wealth and land – and with the land, serfs and tenants – resulted in an increasingly severe and arbitrary imposition of financial, legal and social demands on the labouring classes. Serfdom – either in the form of farm tenancies with accompanying duties and taxes or the older 'bodily' serfdom which went back several centuries – was widespread and manifestly unjust. As returns from land investment diminished, landowners attempted to impose the more rigorous types of serfdom on their tenants – a tactic adopted by the Church in particular.[10] The peasantry, despite gallant efforts to argue their rights through all the courts available, and despite isolated and abortive attempts to make their point by force, gradually found their condition worsening. The few who could escape to the towns found that trade and manufacture had developed to the point where pre-learned skills were essential, so most of the migrants ended up among the disenfranchised and impoverished urban poor. Not that there were many large towns for them to go to: in Germany, only twenty-eight towns had a population greater than 10,000, and the vast majority had fewer than 2,000.[11] As a result of the economic pressures at the end of the fifteenth century, many towns were already beginning to forbid entry to rural immigrants. For those who remained in the village or on the farm, in a period when the rural population was growing apace, the divide between rich and poor simply increased.[12] To add to the problems, landowners were concerned to retain 'their' peasants on the land, in order to squeeze the last drops of labour and money from them. It has been calculated that before 1600 80 per cent of Germany's population lived and worked on the land – any deterioration in rural social conditions, therefore, had a massive effect on the politics and economics of the region.

All of these changes, as might be expected, were given complete justification by law. Where a relevant law did not exist, a new one was conveniently created or justification was provided by the lawyers, against whom it was always difficult to argue. Many of the peasants' complaints harked back to the 'old laws' and the 'old ways', and in the second and third decades of the sixteenth century those with real grievances began to talk up

'Divine laws' – the laws and morality set out in the Bible. In the late fifteenth century, the author of the *Book of One Hundred Chapters and Forty Statutes*, that Revolutionary of the Upper Rhine whom we met earlier, was adamant that the world had begun to go downhill once the German lands had been occupied by 'Romans' with their Roman law, and that in the long-gone Golden Age those lands had been ruled by different, faultless and home-grown German laws. This work, appetisingly bizarre though it is, is a good barometer of the feelings generated by the changes in society, law and politics in that century. The later and more famous millenarian work, *The Reformation of the Emperor Sigismund*, echoed these sentiments. This book promoted a kind of democratic Empire, led by an Emperor (a real one as it happens, Sigismund, who reigned from 1433 to 1437) who – unlikely as it might seem – was to display all the moral goodness of a poor and modest Christian. Under his guidance, feudalism was to be abolished, governing bodies would be democratically elected, private property communised, and physicians and magistrates made accessible to the common people – for 'the time is now come that we must awake'.

The spiritual and intellectual response to these economic and social changes was multi-faceted. There were those who turned to heresy, such as the Flagellants of Thuringia in the fourteenth and fifteenth centuries. Others – the Humanists – turned to the legacy of Ancient Rome and Greece, and others again to alchemical thought and practice, to religious mysticism or to millenarianism expressed in astrological terms. Our ill-named Revolutionary of the Upper Rhine predicted the arrival of the messianic 'Friedrich' by his observations of the stars and planets: 'Now when the sun is in the sign of Aries, the masters of astrology call this a "Chiliade"; and this brings a change in the whole world.' The eighth Chiliade was to bring the Emperor Friedrich, who would perform all kinds of miracles on behalf of the German nation, not least the slaughter of 2,300 clerics each day for forty-two months. (The magic figure of forty-two months comes from, among other biblical references, the Book of Revelation; it is also rendered more poetically as 'a time, times and half a time', i.e.

one year, plus two years, plus half a year. During this three-and-a-half-year period, great Apocalyptic events and massacres were predicted, ushering in the Second Coming.) For those modern readers easily seduced by predictions, a cautionary note: the method of the author of this work was not faultless. Not only did he vary the length of a 'Chiliade' – sometimes 1,000 years, sometimes 960 – but, computing on the basis of a 'cycle' – half of a Chiliade – he also managed to predict the Second Coming for the years 1500 (twice), 1509 (four times), 1521 and 1528. It might also have been expected in 1596. Luckily for everyone, and especially some 3 million nervous clerics, it never happened.

Anti-clericalism has scarcely been uncommon anywhere in Europe, in any century. The local representatives of the Church, as well as the bishops and others in the higher echelons, rarely covered themselves in Christian glory, and their misbehaviour had been legendary for centuries, deeply embedded in popular culture. Anti-clericalism was given added impetus by the fact that German-speaking regions regarded themselves as almost a national confederation (although 'Germany' did not become a political entity until 1871). The economic and political strength of central and south German territories gave birth to perfectly valid questions: Why were hard-won German finances being transferred over the Alps into the gaping maw of the Papal state? Why should perfectly good estates in German lands be under the control of abbeys and other religious institutions, when they could so easily be transferred to non-religious landowners? Why should the richest country in Europe submit to a foreign power which was manifestly rotten, and why should a foreign Emperor dictate the politics of taxation, economy and finance? Rome, with its Church and allied Empire, became the usurper, not just in the eyes of the poor who suffered at a local level, but now also in the eyes of those who wielded real power over huge territories. Indeed, even the established (i.e. Roman) Church in Germany had for years been grumbling bitterly about the insatiable greed of Rome.[13]

New modes of thought were on the agenda – heresy, mysticism, the study of the Roman and Greek civilisations. The spread of these ideas was aided by the introduction of moveable type to Europe by Johannes Gutenberg around 1450, even if it can be argued that, because printing spread ideas only among those who could read, its overall importance has been overrated. While newly printed material helped diffuse the doctrines of Humanism beyond its interested circle, slowly easing mind-sets away from religion and superstition, the Bible still remained the most widespread source of ideas and doctrines. Even before our period, the Bible was already partially available in translation; it was expounded daily in some form or other – although not necessarily accurately – from the pulpit in the meanest villages of the land; while others, like the secretive bands of heretics, passed their own interpretations of the scriptures down from generation to generation. Depending on your status in life and your inclinations, you could turn to the Old Testament prophets, the Gospels or the Book of Revelation, and in them find precisely the justification you needed for whatever aspirations you had. It is perhaps difficult to talk of original modes of thought when most thinking centred around the Bible and its interpretation, but people nevertheless found new ways to express their feelings about everyday life through examples plucked from the scriptures. Some turned to mysticism, imitating Jesus as he is described in the New Testament; some turned to millenarianism, following the lead set by the twelfth-century Italian Apocalyptic thinker Joachim de Fiore;[14] while others tried to fashion a new relationship between humanity and God by melding the Old and New Testaments. In all of these efforts, the language of thought was that of the Bible itself.

This turn towards new modes of expression was largely an urban phenomenon. It was only in the towns and universities that literacy had reached a level where books could be easily accessed and read, let alone written. Despite the fact that many of the revolts of the period took place in the countryside, it was from the towns and universities – such as Wittenberg – that the reforms were promoted, and it was initially in the towns that they were enthusiastically taken up.[15]

❧

So what was this German Reformation, this movement that emerged fully armed from the mind of Martin Luther of Wittenberg in 1517? At the risk of seeming to dodge the question, we need to retrace our steps to Bohemia and the Hussite reforms of the late fourteenth and early fifteenth centuries. Here we find similar economic and political developments to those described above for Germany. In the reign of Karel IV, from 1346 to 1378, Bohemia flourished intellectually and economically. Aided not a little by the fact that Karel was made Holy Roman Emperor in 1355, and that Prague thereby became one of the most important cities in Europe, the Bohemian economy was booming. It was based on a strong mining industry, centred around the silver mine at Kuttenberg (Kutná Hora, sixty kilometres east of Prague); in addition, there were flourishing weaving and brewing industries, and the country was crossed by two major trade routes to east and west, north and south. In this environment, a burgher culture thrived and there arose a growing nationalism, which in 1409 led to the expulsion of Germans from the University of Prague. The national aristocracy came often and dramatically into conflict with king and Empire – King Wenceslaus IV of Bohemia, for example, was arrested and imprisoned by his own nobles, on several occasions, between 1394 and 1404.

Under these conditions, the reform of religion was an imperative. Bohemians had to come to terms with their new material conditions and erect political structures to match their economic and social status. In the late fourteenth century, reformers of the Church in Bohemia set in motion a popular movement which demanded the reform of religious practices and the improvement of the ill-educated and corrupt clerical body. Around the same time, the so-called Lollards, who came to Bohemia around 1395, began to spread the dissenting and reforming doctrines of the English cleric John Wycliffe. The main features of his theology were: reliance on the Bible alone for spiritual enlightenment, thus dispensing with the need for all the apparatus of Canon Law and Scholasticism; the resulting establishment of a direct relationship between believers and God, mediated through local scriptural interpretation; and the view that the Church should return to its 'original' position as spiritual leader, unencumbered by material wealth – and therefore that the Church should be disendowed and its estates and wealth transferred to secular ownership. Such ideas were taken up by both the lower urban strata and the solid citizenry around the theologian Jan Hus, not least because they helped express the desire to establish sovereignty in both town and nation and to oust the foreign Church and its foreign – mostly German – clergy.

Jan Hus (1372–1415) was a theologian and a committed Bohemian nationalist; most of his sermons and writings were composed in Czech, and only as an afterthought translated into Latin or German. Like Luther a hundred years later, he found almost immediate widespread support among the burghers and the poor, as well as among the nationalist aristocracy. One of the demands of the Hussite tendency was that the Mass be celebrated 'in both kinds' (Utraquism), meaning that both wine and bread were given to everyone taking communion, not just the priests. It was therefore a more democratic religious rite, and one which immediately challenged the superiority of the officials of the Church. In 1414, Hus was summoned to the Council at Constance, which had been convened by the Pope in an attempt to restore some unity to the massively fractured Roman Church, and there he was made to pay a price for this unity. Hus was charged with heresy and expeditiously burned at the stake. But his ideas and his cause were taken up more practically by the social forces he had helped to set in motion: the Hussite Reformation girded up its loins.

It was now open season for attacks on the Papal Church. The landowning nobility saw their chance to annex the astonishingly rich Church estates; the burghers saw their chance to remove the restraints of feudalism from their towns and trade; the intelligentsia saw their chance to clear away the detritus which medieval thinking had piled up to support a rotten institution; and the poor saw their chance to lighten their own heavy burdens. When the lower classes, under Jan Zelivsky and Martin Huska, began to make threatening noises, King Wenceslaus IV, who had previously sided with Hussitism, started to backtrack with all speed, even to the extent of restoring the old Church authorities. One thing led to another, and in 1419 the radical

Hussites carried out the first 'Defenestration of Prague', resulting in the deaths of several town councillors. (Throwing people out of windows became something of a fashion among enraged Bohemians – the third defenestration, in 1618, precipitated the Thirty Years' War.)

The death of Wenceslaus in 1419, and the political crisis which resulted from the succession of his decidedly anti-Hussite brother Sigismund (the eponymous Emperor of the aforementioned 'Reforms' programme), led in short order to the so-called 'Hussite Wars', in which the supporters of the Papal Church and the forces of the Holy Roman Empire lined up against the Bohemian Hussites. This in turn triggered a reaction among the more radical wing of the Hussites, who, in expectation of an imminent Apocalypse, issued a 'call to the mountains'. By 1420, their citadel at Hradište (eighty kilometres south of Prague) had become their 'Tabor', the hill on which to await the Apocalypse; it was named after the mountain in the Book of Judges (4:6) on which the Israelites camped before routing their oppressors. Having thus secured themselves, the 'Taborites' pronounced upon their fellow citizens and awaited the end of time:

> In our time there shall be an end to all things, that is, all evil shall uproot on this earth . . .
> Everyone who will not go to the mountains shall perish amidst the towns, villages and hamlets by the blows of God . . . we shall see Christ bodily descend from Heaven to accept his Kingdom here on earth.[16]

Eventually the mainstream Hussites made their peace with the Papal Church, and a compromise form of Utraquist Catholicism was introduced to Bohemia; but the more radical factions separately continued their own traditions.[17] Although this reform movement peaked well before Müntzer's birth and the German Reformation, Hussitism was by no means just another heresy, passing grey in the medieval night. It had a significant influence on Luther, Müntzer and other German reformers.

The Taborite movement, which began in 1419 and was not suppressed until at least 1452, laid the basis for a later underground radical tradition in south and west Bohemia, one that crept over the border into Saxony. In the early sixteenth century, this tradition was still very much alive. Although many of its precepts were drawn from earlier millenarian tendencies, it was far broader and better known than many of the odd local heresies which had burst into brief life during the preceding centuries.

The main Hussite movement itself also began to spread beyond the boundaries of Bohemia. In the 1420s, one Johann Drändorff took the cause to Heidelberg, where, for his pains, he was burned at the stake; armies of Hussites and Taborites penetrated as far as Bamberg and Nürnberg in 1430, there to be welcomed by the lower classes who took the opportunity to expel their own patrician authorities; Hussite preachers were arrested in towns right across Germany. In 1447, 130 Hussites were burned in the valley of the Tauber. In 1462, more were burned in Zwickau, a flourishing mining and weaving town close to the border with Bohemia, and a town which was to be Müntzer's home for a crucial year; the grisly fate of their predecessors did not prevent more Hussites from turning up there in 1475. In the first large-scale German peasant rebellion of 1476, under the Drummer of Niklashausen, there is arguably evidence of Bohemian involvement. Even Martin Luther saw much to admire in the Hussite Reformation, to the extent of proclaiming in 1520 that 'we are all Hussites' (perhaps more of a slogan of solidarity, along the lines of John F. Kennedy's 'Ich bin ein Berliner', than an unconditional agreement on theology), and he encouraged Emperor and princes to go to Bohemia to see for themselves how difficult it would be to put a reforming genie back in its bottle.[18] Hussitism, perhaps disadvantaged a little by being foreign, nonetheless offered a concrete precedent for Germany of what could be done to dislodge the parasite of the Papal Church. It was a precedent which Müntzer also admired.

With the Hussite movement, the first bell was tolled for the end of the hegemony of the Papal Church in central Europe. Hussitism went far beyond the bounds of a 'heresy'. A heresy is simply a set of ideas which, to a greater or lesser extent, conflicts with the religious dogma of a predominant religion. Crucially, however, a heresy remains a heresy by losing the battle with its opponent. Neither the Hussite nor the Lutheran 'Reformations' was a heresy any more – each of them succeeded in establishing its own institution.

What we have set out above is a necessarily short and broad-brush sketch of the political, social and economic background of central Europe at the end of the fifteenth century. It goes without saying that things were far more complex and nuanced than this sketch suggests. As one historian has warned of this period in Germany: 'To look for monocausal explanations is to embark on a fool's errand.'[19] Everywhere, there were exceptions: in some places, feudal relationships were sharper and more oppressive than in others; some towns and cities embraced radical religious fervour, while others studiously avoided it; the peasants of some rural areas took up weapons and marched out upon brief rebellions, while others kept quiet. But the overall tendency was a steady growth in the influence of the urban merchants and early capitalists; there was a gradual transfer of power from the Holy Roman Empire to the larger territories; hand in hand with this, since Empire and Church were intimately connected, the authority of the Pope began to diminish. This permitted heretical thoughts to gain a foothold and become reforming thoughts. Precursors of revolution and reformation had burst sporadically upon the scene for decades before the sixteenth century. In Saxony in 1489, the year of Müntzer's birth, we had not yet come as far as a German Reformation – but it was not far off.

2

The Devil Sowed His Seed

Müntzer's Early Years

After Doctor Luther had been preaching for several years, and had taught the Gospel purely and clearly, the Devil sowed his own seed alongside, and awakened many false and harmful preachers.

Philipp Melanchthon (1525)

Thomas Müntzer was born in 1489. Or perhaps not. He was born in the small town of Stolberg in the Harz Mountains. Or so we believe.

We have already hinted at the lack of hard evidence for long periods of Müntzer's life. Sadly, the very question of his birth and early upbringing is one example of this. The complete absence of verifiable documentation before 1514 permits a variety of chronologies and theories about his life. Different historians have come up with various suggestions as to Müntzer's date of birth, ranging from 1467 through to 1490. Faced with such uncertainty, all we can do is look at the scant and circumstantial evidence and then make a wild stab at a scenario which seems to fit most of the facts.

The present consensus, that he was born in 1489, is based on the record of a 'Thomas Müntzer of Quedlinburg' in the matriculation lists of Leipzig University in October 1506. On the assumption that this Thomas was sixteen or seventeen years old at the time (the norm for a new student), and that he was born around St Thomas's day (21 December) – the nearest appropriate saint's day being the traditional basis for naming children – you could arrive at a plausible date of birth in late December 1489.

However, the attentive reader will already have spotted that Müntzer was believed to have been born in Stolberg, not in Quedlinburg, which lies about thirty kilometres to its north: similar area, different town. Luckily, at a later date, Müntzer himself mentions the two places in one sentence, implying that he regarded both as home.[1] Of course, there is no guarantee that the 'Müntzer of Quedlinburg' registering at Leipzig was in fact our man; the surname (meaning 'coin-minter') was not uncommon in that region of mining and metal processing; neither was the forename unusual. It does not necessarily help that, when Thomas matriculated at Frankfurt University in 1512, he registered himself as being 'from Stolberg'. (Assuming, of course, that this student from Stolberg was also our man.) However, further evidence – such as the fact that Thomas became a priest in May 1514, at a time when a priest had to be at least twenty-four years old – should bring us back to the years 1489 or 1490.

That is one possibility. Another, far less likely, is based on records of a Thomas Müntzer being fined for 'misbehaviour at the dance-hall' of Stolberg in 1484 – this would put his year of birth back to around 1467, and hence require us to believe that his prime activity between 1521 and 1525 took place when he was in his mid-fifties.[2] While it is tempting to imagine youthful shenanigans on a Saturday night out, nothing else about this desperate reveller would fit. A further possibility, from evidence of Müntzer's university education and subsequent activity in Braunschweig, is that he was born no later than 1482, and attended an unknown university at the turn of the century.[3] However, although the evidence for these earlier dates has almost as much validity as the traditional date, two questions would remain unanswered: firstly, why do we have no correspondence to or from Müntzer before the year 1515 – if he was by then in his thirties, one might expect some earlier letters; secondly, if he was born in, say, 1482, why do we have no documentary evidence of his education before 1506?

So, for no better reason than that a university education at Leipzig (1506) and Frankfurt (1512–14) seems to fit a young man, and that a career peak (1521–5) in his early thirties feels right, we shall stick with 1489. We shall also stick with Stolberg:

Müntzer himself names it as his home town several times, not least in the very first words of his 'Prague Manifesto' of 1522: 'I, Thomas Müntzer, born in Stolberg'. (Martin Luther, incidentally, was born in 1483 only forty kilometres to the east of Stolberg, in Eisleben – two local Harz boys made good.)

Although precise information on the Müntzer family is scant, the family name suggests a link with the profession of coin-making. It is possible that his father was one Matthes Müntzer, who was a town councillor in Stolberg in 1491 and master of the mint there in 1497. The fact that Matthes died in 1501 – here we have at least one sure fact to grasp tightly – could invalidate the theory of him being Thomas's father, since the son was writing a letter to his 'father' in 1521; or it might not, if we suppose that Müntzer's mother remarried. And if she did, then it is not impossible that the family moved to the larger town of Quedlinburg. Other historians have speculated that Müntzer senior was a goldsmith, or even a long-distance trader, but the evidence is weak. Friedrich Engels, relying on earlier historians, proposed that Thomas's father died in 1505 'on the scaffold, a victim of the obduracy of the Count of Stolberg'.[4] Attractive though it is to suppose that the death of Müntzer senior impelled young Thomas towards a career as a revolutionary, the idea has no solid basis whatsoever. And in any case, there were far stronger forces around to drive Müntzer to open rebellion in later life. Regrettably, despite there being absolutely no evidence to support this colourful legend, it persists even to the present day.[5]

So, yes: everything about Thomas's birth and family is, rather awkwardly, obscure.

His parents were probably of middling financial means; in a letter, Thomas notes that his mother had brought a significant dowry to her marriage.[6] Certainly, if the 'Thomas Müntzer' enrolling at the University of Leipzig in 1506 was our man, then his parents had managed to scrape together enough to send him there, although not quite enough to muster the full fee for the semester. This financial shortfall was not altogether unusual, and did not prevent Thomas from matriculating; but it may have prevented him from taking any exams.

The University of Leipzig was founded in 1409, initially to accommodate the German academics and students who had been forced to flee Prague during the initial stages of the Hussite reforms. At Leipzig, Müntzer enrolled on a course to gain a degree as Bachelor of the Arts, which covered the three basic subjects of grammar, logic and rhetoric – but not theology. Religion and theology were not far from the arts, however, and such an education did not exclude one from advancing to a career in the Church. He might have been expected to complete his course and graduate as 'Baccalaureus' in 1509; but there is a deafening silence in the graduation lists. No record of a pass or a fail. Either the record is faulty (not impossible – see below) or he dropped out of Leipzig in 1507 or 1508, either out of disenchantment or for financial reasons – not entirely an uncommon upset in a young person's education, then as now.

We are thus confronted with a gap of two or three years in the documentary record. If he did drop out, then what did he do between 1507 and 1510, when he is next heard of? One theory suggests that he attended a completely different university – possibly Erfurt, or even Wittenberg. This idea would handily resolve the knotty problem of where Müntzer acquired his university degrees. It would also conveniently explain how he first became acquainted with a number of people across Germany with whom he corresponded in later years. But the records of many German universities from those days are extremely patchy – some have been lost, others destroyed in the numerous wars since, none ever perfect. The absence of an official record from the era means nothing, one way or another.

In the intoxicating realm of absolute certainty, however, we know that, around 1510, Thomas was appointed to a post as 'collaborator', equivalent to a curate or assistant priest. This was a common enough career move for a young man with a university education. For part of the time he was resident in both Halle and Aschersleben, a smaller town about forty-five kilometres to the north-west of Halle. However, our only record of this period comes from Thomas himself. After his arrest in 1525, he confessed that: 'in his youth, when he was a "collaborator" in Aschersleben and Halle . . . he organised a league . . .

which was against the Bishop Ernst'.[7] There are two ways to interpret this confession. On the one hand, we can suppose that, like many a reckless youth, he had enmeshed himself in plot and intrigue against the bastions of the Church, as personified by Ernst, Archbishop of Magdeburg (d. 1513). On the other hand, it might have been an attempt to smudge the facts about a more recent plot. We know that Müntzer was involved in disturbances in Halle in 1523, and it could well be that his confession was an amalgam of fact and fiction, designed to protect his comrades from that time. There is no evidence from other sources of any such plot during the period around 1510. We may have to accept the confession as that of a man unburdening his soul before death, and assume that the plot actually existed – not altogether implausible, given the Archbishop's low popularity among the people of Halle – but was perhaps some wild and youthful scheme that never reached fruition.

Our next piece of solid evidence of Thomas's activity comes when he enrolled at the University of Frankfurt an der Oder in October 1512, this time being in a position to pay the entire fee – which suggests that he had found gainful employment in the meantime – and this time also declaring that he was 'of Stolberg', rather than Quedlinburg. (At some later date in the sixteenth century, another hand carefully inscribed the word *'seditiosus'* – rebel – alongside Müntzer's name in the matriculation list: the rebellious undergraduate's further career had not gone unnoticed.)

As – yet again – no record of his graduation from Frankfurt has been preserved, there remains some question about the degrees and qualifications Müntzer actually possessed. From the greetings and signatures on a variety of letters, both formal and informal, over the following years, we can conclude that he held a master's degree in the arts (*artium magister*), which implies that a bachelor's degree in the same subject had already been gained. But there was also talk of him holding a bachelor's degree in theology (*baccalaureus biblicus* – Bachelor in the Holy Script): there is one letter addressed to him in this way, and a scrap of paper written in 1521 by Müntzer himself also states that he was a *'sancte scripte baccalaureus'*. Two degrees are not impossible, although he would have had to engage in a longer university career than is documented; three degrees is a more tricky proposition, although again not out of the question. But 'Master' is at least a reasonable certainty: in August 1524, Luther wrote a letter to the authorities in Mühlhausen warning them against a certain 'Magister Thomas Müntzer'; it is extremely unlikely that Luther would have attributed a formal qualification to his deadly enemy if there had been any doubt about it. But since there is no extant record of his graduation with any degree at all, let alone both a master's and a bachelor's, the intriguing question remains: did he attend another university between Leipzig and Frankfurt, and there gain a degree in theology?

The answer is distressing: we have no idea.

Meanwhile, in May 1514, the town council of Braunschweig provided Müntzer with a benefice at the Michaelskirche (St Michael's Church), looking after the altar of the Virgin Mary. In the 'presentation' document (a copy of which Müntzer still had in his possession in 1525), Thomas is described as living in the diocese of Halberstadt; from other evidence, we know that an old family friend named Hans Pelt, a merchant, also lived in that town, which lies not far from Stolberg. For Müntzer to have been considered for this post suggests not only that his education was proceeding satisfactorily, but also that he had had some experience outside the university, perhaps as sub-deacon. This benefice in Braunschweig, where the duties were far from onerous, gave him an income of five guilders per annum (as a measure of its value, this was the amount required to lodge a pupil at one of the town's schools for a year),[8] and he continued to benefit from it until late 1521, when he finally renounced it. At or before his appointment in Braunschweig, he must have left Frankfurt University with – we are to assume – an MA degree.

Around May 1514, therefore, he moved to Braunschweig, where he lodged with his friend Ludolf Wittehovet, a graduate of Wittenberg University who also had a benefice at the Michaelskirche. There was another person in the town at that time who would play an important role in the early reform movement – Johannes Agricola, later a close colleague of Luther – and it is likely that their paths would have crossed. But Müntzer's most interesting contact was with the rector of St Martin's school in Braunschweig, Heinrich Hanner, an educated man who had gained an MA in Paris. Hanner and Müntzer evidently engaged in theological discussions with each other for it was to Müntzer that Hanner turned for theological advice in 1517, when the long-simmering controversy over indulgences, fuelled by Martin Luther's famous ninety-five theses, boiled over. (The Church promoted the sale of indulgences which effectively bought forgiveness for sins committed; in Germany specifically, indulgences were sold so that Church debts could covertly be repaid to the Fuggers.) Just how long Müntzer remained in Braunschweig is unknown; the benefice itself did not oblige Müntzer to reside in the town, a widespread practice that was a common cause for complaint among reformers. But his five guilders would not suffice to cover all the expenses he incurred, which included his lodgings and a cook whom he shared with Wittehovet. Unhappily, there was conflict between the two men, and it involved a woman. In a letter to Müntzer, Wittehovet complains that 'your cook' had been intriguing to gain possession of Wittehovet's precious heated room, and had been accusing him of spreading certain rumours about her and Müntzer. Although the complaint is worded discreetly, it seems clear that 'the cook' may have been Müntzer's lady-friend: 'you should know better than to fall in love with women', Wittehovet cautions. Cook or girlfriend or both? Either way, this letter is to be treasured as one of very few which give us a sidelong view of Müntzer as a young man in his twenties.[9] We do not have much material illuminating his relationships with women, and Müntzer himself gave few clues.

To supplement his income, Müntzer went to the Cistercian nunnery in Frose, about seventy-five kilometres south-east of Braunschweig. Here, probably in the spring of 1515, he was appointed 'prefect' responsible for the education of the inmates and for tutoring the sons of richer Braunschweig citizens. The abbess, Elisabeth von Weida, was later to declare herself for the reforms championed by Wittenberg; evidently the young Müntzer made a good impression on her. It was probably here, as the dialectic of teaching required him to question what he taught, that he first began to formulate his own doctrines. We know also that, among Müntzer's other activities, he began to work on his own liturgies – hymns and services in song – an activity to which he would return in earnest in 1523. There is a Latin manuscript written by him in 1516 or 1517, a few years after his arrival in Frose, entitled the 'Office of St Cyriacus'. There is no doubt that he became familiar with the breviaries of Magdeburg, missals or liturgies from Halle, Erfurt, Halberstadt, and others of the late fifteenth century.[10]

For two years, then, Müntzer divided his life between Frose and Braunschweig, undertaking his duties within the Church, while possibly also spending time in Halberstadt with Hans Pelt. Halberstadt lay near Frose, about halfway between Halle and Braunschweig, and so provided a suitable base for a young and mobile intellectual. Müntzer saw nothing untoward in being an 'absent beneficiary'; surprisingly, it was only in the summer of 1521, after his expulsion from Zwickau, that he initiated the process of disengaging himself from the benefice in favour of another 'reformed' preacher. For those entire seven years, most of which he spent elsewhere, he continued to receive the income from the Virgin Mary's branch office in Braunschweig.

In June or July 1517, Hanner wrote to Müntzer to pose a series of theological questions on the role of the Pope and bishops, and on sin and justification, all of which were evidently part of some long-standing debate.[11] The letter was addressed to Müntzer 'at the house of Hans Pelt', and contains two words that describe the relationship between the men: one was 'pupil' (*discipulus*) which Hanner applies to himself; the other was 'father' (*pater*), applied to Müntzer. Perhaps this was merely Hanner indulging in some semi-serious banter with his friend. The tone of the letter alternates between jocularity and urgent questioning, and the address may simply be another element of that, with Hanner acknowledging that Müntzer was at least his equal in theology, despite being the younger. But the questions posed by the Braunschweig schoolmaster relate very obviously to matters which were then disturbing Saxon intellectuals, not least of whom was Luther. There were nine points in his letter demanding serious explanation, and all were posed in the hope that Müntzer would be able to reply simply and openly. They relate to the question of indulgences and to the authority of the Pope in carrying out the work of God on Earth. Hanner asks how prelates, who were also men, could forgive or give forgiveness for sins against God; how simple folk could give any more credence to the Gospels if the apparent defence of indulgences in these books was called into question; whether indeed faith could be drawn from the Gospels; and whether the saints were as valuable to the Church as the Passion of Christ. He asked Müntzer to explain 'as briefly as he could' his position on indulgences. In the summer of 1517, Johannes Tetzel, a Dominican friar now notorious due to the bitter conflict between him and Luther, was in the Braunschweig area on an indulgence sales campaign, and his presence was inviting not a little discussion.

While all this theological stuff may seem a little irrelevant today, the significance of Hanner's letter lies in the implication that Thomas had already been defending doctrinal positions close to those of Luther in 1517. As a young intellectual eager for new ideas, Müntzer would have been very sensitive to the noises emanating from Wittenberg, and it was most likely his public position on such matters that finally led to his expulsion from Braunschweig in 1518, presumably after a public condemnation of Tetzel. There is an official Church report from 1519 stating that Thomas 'had not long previously been expelled by the citizens of Braunschweig, to whom he had been preaching'.[12] Johann Agricola also noted with some glee in 1525 that Müntzer had 'fled from Braunschweig'[13] – but his satisfaction was a little misplaced, since Duke Heinrich of Braunschweig was no great friend of Church reform and had come down heavily on any and all reform-minded clergy.

From Braunschweig and Frose, Müntzer retreated initially to the house of his friend Hans Pelt, and for a while he is lost from sight. But it seems that he spent some time in Wittenberg between 1517 and 1519, attending lectures at the university when he could and soaking up the stimulating atmosphere in the fortress of reform, where he would have met and talked to Luther and other members of the inner circle of reformers. It is even possible that he delivered informal lectures himself.[14] In December 1524, Müntzer, countering an accusation by Luther, stated that he had not seen Luther for 'six or seven years', which dates a meeting to 1517 or 1518. He also paid a very brief visit to Rothenburg on the Tauber, in Franconia, in 1518/19.[15] But our next definite sighting comes in a letter, dated 11 January 1519, from Christian Döring to Müntzer at an inn in Leipzig, mentioning that there was a post available as chaplain to the provost of Kemberg, near Wittenberg, should Müntzer care to apply. Döring was an eminent goldsmith (and entrepreneurial printer) in Wittenberg, and was by then acting as a kind of broker for the appointment of reforming clerics. For him to have written to Müntzer can only mean that the two had met previously, or that men of some authority in the reform movement had recommended the young cleric. That Müntzer was staying at an inn in Leipzig is interesting: Luther – possibly accompanied by Melanchthon – was also in the town at the very same time, arranging matters for the Leipzig Disputation later in the year; evidently, Müntzer was there, if not as a member of the inner circle, then at the very least as a tolerated supporter.[16]

The post proposed by Döring would have been vacant in Easter of that year, which fell on 24 April. But instead of going there, our man next turned up in the town of Jüterbog, about thirty kilometres north-east of Wittenberg. (Jüterbog was a town frequented by none other than Tetzel in early 1517; today its main claim to fame is a gigantic skate-park.)

In Jüterbog, the reforms were being spearheaded by the preacher Franz Günther, who, according to reports (admittedly those written by his opponents), had argued that: (a) there was no need to confess, since confession was not mentioned in the scriptures; (b) there was no need to fast, since Jesus had done that for the faithful already; (c) prayers should not be offered to the saints; and (d) the Bohemians were better Christians than the Germans. Günther had plainly been heavily promoting the Wittenberg cause, and thereby fallen foul of the Franciscans. By May, however, he felt in need of some support. Müntzer arrived to provide it.

There exists a report on Müntzer's activities in Jüterbog, written by the Franciscan priest in the town, Bernhard Dappen, to his bishop in Brandenburg on 4 May.[17] In his letter he describes the uproar being triggered by Günther's sermons, and provides a rather colourful picture of life in the early Reformation years. 'At this point,' he writes, 'on whose authority I do not know, there arrived another master of that sect by the name of Thomas, who had not long previously been expelled by the citizens of Braunschweig.' Dappen proceeds to describe in some detail Müntzer's preaching in favour of fundamental reforms to Church governance, and his characterisation of bishops as 'tyrants' and 'adulterers'. 'And he said not once, but often that the Holy Word had lain under a bushel for more than 400 years, and now several men wished to risk their necks in changing that.' Dappen's report finishes peevishly: 'I will remain silent about the insults which I, as a brother of the Minorite Order, personally suffered in that sermon before the whole populace.'

The local church evidently provided a very lively forum for public debate and fierce controversy. That it was possible for Günther and Müntzer to pursue their activity openly and without hindrance speaks volumes for the popularity of reformed doctrine in the town. But Dappen's outraged report also raises an interesting question: 'on whose authority' did Müntzer come to Jüterbog? There was no shortage of towns for reformed preachers to visit, and Günther had apparently not been unsuccessful so far. We know of no previous contact between these two reformers, although they may have met in Wittenberg; if this was the case, then perhaps Günther had specifically asked for Müntzer to be sent. Alternatively, it is possible that Müntzer was despatched by Wittenberg to bring the reforms in Jüterbog rapidly to a successful conclusion.

The swift and widespread adoption of reforming religion, as exemplified by events in Jüterbog, may seem startling to us today. Did all this suddenly result from one man, Martin Luther, posting some theses on a church door in 1517? Sadly, cause and effect are never quite so simple. For a proper understanding of this rapid push for change, it is necessary to examine the early years of the German Reformation. The first decades of the sixteenth century saw many social groups undertake a closer examination of their position within the universe, an examination which took place within the already-familiar theological framework, most often in the form of a critical analysis of Papal doctrines and the resulting Church practices. Although Humanism may have represented a higher intellectual level than the strictly religious and clerical view, it did not contain that coarse spark of life which grabbed the imagination of the illiterate and the superstitious; nor was it ever intended to do so. Since social order and the Church were so closely intertwined – since, indeed, one of the major contributors to the crisis was the Church itself, through its social institutions, political influence and enormous wealth – any solution to the problem had first to challenge the Church. The Papacy, so long despised and feared by the common people of Germany and other European countries, so blatantly corrupt, was nevertheless the weakest link in the chain of the feudal order. It was therefore the easiest and first target for any movement questioning social relationships. And, precisely because it was the Church, it was also the most critical target: remove the divine justification for this institution, and very little justification remained. But there was more than just God at stake here: of the seven influential electors of the Holy Roman Empire, three were archbishops of the Papal Church in Germany; if the Papacy were to lose its influence there, what would happen to the Empire? The proposals coming out of the circle of reformers in Wittenberg coincided both in form and content with the aspirations of the German nation, dressing a theoretical representation of the crisis in familiar religious garb. This in turn allowed many intellectuals to come to terms with the perceived problems and attempt to work out practical solutions using whatever tools they had mastered.

The tumultuous years between roughly 1470 and 1560 form what we now term the 'German Reformation'. Yet the term should not be limited to the reform school of Luther alone, for the intellectual Reformation was a very catholic, inclusive church. And what of the term 'Lutheran'? The adjective is freely used to describe anyone who had any ideas at all about reforming the Church. Most opponents of reform tended to lump all reformers together in order to smear each trend with the worst faults of every other. On the other hand, those concerned to ensure that Luther's robe was not dirtied by the less pristine aspects of the reform movement denied that any of the more radical reformers could possibly be 'Lutheran'. In the years 1516 to 1520, however, almost all reformers considered themselves to be either fellow thinkers or, at least, distant comrades of Luther. But as the practical consequences of reform came into focus, that united front began to fracture: Müntzer and Karlstadt are two outstanding examples of reformers who quite soon no longer considered themselves fully paid-up 'Lutherans'; Johann Agricola fell out with Luther on the question of sin and faith in the 1530s; and there were many more (among the Humanists as well as the radical and less radical wings of the Anabaptist movement) who consciously diverged from Luther's reforms. It is fair to say that Luther was not the 'father' of reform, but rather a figure through whom many trends were channelled. Many reformers owed much to Luther for allowing them to reach a tenable position from which to advance; but, that position reached, there was frequently a parting of the ways. Despite being a supporter of Luther between 1517 and 1521, Müntzer never considered himself in any way inferior to the man of Wittenberg, and even less an unquestioning devotee.

In Jüterbog then, the actions of Günther and Müntzer might have been seen as 'Lutheran' by the Franciscans, but it is clear that both men were pursuing generic reform strategies in their own way. It would be unwise to rely on the affronted Dappen's say-so for an accurate picture of Müntzer's arguments. But it has been suggested that there were critical differences between Müntzer's reported thoughts and those of Günther.[18] The fact that Müntzer did not call upon the Gospels or the Bible to act as witness, while Günther did, indicates an early divergence between Müntzer and the official Wittenberg line.

The actions of the two reformers in Jüterbog did not require Luther's blessing; indeed, the latter had no detailed knowledge of what was happening there, having at that time no need to micro-manage the pair. The doctrines expounded were similar to those of Luther, expressed for example in his pamphlet *To the Christian Nobility of the German Nation* of 1520 – specifically, the demand that Councils of the Church could be convoked by authorities other than the Pope alone. (This pamphlet contains an early statement by Luther of his willingness to place religious reforms under the direction of the secular princes.) But, at length, Luther was obliged to become involved in the controversy at Jüterbog after complaints had reached his ears of the activities of his colleagues. In a letter to the Franciscans of 15 May 1519, he stated that he did not know precisely what 'Thomas' had been preaching in the town, but implied that he had sufficient confidence in the preacher not to care.[19] Indeed, he defended Müntzer against the *'calumniatores et detractores'*, and demanded that the Franciscans apologise for their accusations and insinuations. But by then, his task completed, Müntzer had once more left Günther in full charge at Jüterbog. He had moved on.

Among the collection of Müntzer's letters and documents confiscated in 1525 was a list of errands for Müntzer, prepared by Konrad Glitzsch of Orlamünde, the parish of the other leading reformer, Andreas Bodenstein von Karlstadt.[20] Although given the benefice of Orlamünde in 1510, Karlstadt had never taken up the post – a dedicated townie and follower of fashion, he preferred to stay in Wittenberg, where he lectured at the university and, as was customary, paid someone else to do the job in the sticks. Since farming – an essential survival skill in Orlamünde – was not for him, he enrolled Glitzsch as his semi-permanent stand-in. Glitzsch's document in itself is unimportant, detailing a variety of purchases to be negotiated. (It was a challenging shopping list nevertheless: a selection of the latest books by reformers, various vegetable and herb seeds – beetroot, marjoram, hyssop – a measure of saffron, some assorted nails and screws and, of course, two sows and one uncastrated boar – the latter reflecting Glitzsch's pressing need to get to grips with husbandry.) It was written at the end of June 1519, and its significance lies in the fact that the errands were to be carried out in Leipzig at the time of the Disputation there between the Papal representative Johann Eck, on the one side, and Karlstadt and Luther, on the other. It is not clear whether Müntzer had been in Orlamünde (which lies some 100 kilometres south-west of Leipzig) or, if not, how or why Glitzsch appointed him as his personal shopper.

But the shopping list suggests that Müntzer at least intended to be present at the famous Disputation. Glitzsch also asked him for news of the leading reformers, and to be remembered to them. Müntzer cannot have played a prominent role in Leipzig, for there is no other report of his visit. But there was probably a personal interest: Eck had in his possession the reports on the recent events in Jüterbog, to use as ammunition against the Lutheran camp.

There is another interesting aside on this period in Müntzer's life, namely the strange affair of Glitzsch's cook. This woman was reported to have harboured spiritualist beliefs and appears to have been greatly interested in the fourteenth-century mystic Johannes Tauler (1300–61). She is said – by Martin Glaser, a Lutheran preacher writing in 1529 – to have exercised undue influence over both Karlstadt and Müntzer, and misrepresented to both of them the nature of Tauler's doctrines.[21] Glaser added the intriguing remark that she 'had such an air about her in Leipzig that she was considered to be holy'. Whether or not she was a cook, in Orlamünde or not, we cannot ignore the possibility that it was she who prompted the young Thomas to a deeper study of Tauler and the mystics; the mere hint that a woman could exert spiritual or theological influence in that male-dominated period is a fascinating one. And evidently Müntzer himself was quite ready to listen to her, regardless of her gender or education.

The shopping done, attendance at the Disputation in Leipzig would surely have strengthened Müntzer's resolve as a reformer. These were thrilling times. The fate of the Church in Germany hung in the balance and, between the might of Rome on the one side and the reformers on the other, a titanic battle for the very soul of Christianity was about to kick off. But Müntzer's next move seems odd. After the Disputation ended in July, he headed off to a Cistercian nunnery at Beuditz, near Naumburg (forty kilometres south-west of Leipzig), to take up a post as Father Confessor. What at first may look like a return to the deepest folds of the Church is not as eccentric as might be thought. In the first place, the 'Reformation' was for several years something of a 'long march through the institutions', and often took the form of the gradual conversion or self-persuasion of the inmates of ecclesiastical institutions. Secondly, Müntzer apparently wished to spend some time in peace and quiet, pursuing his studies of late medieval theologians like Tauler who offered some kind of alternative to Papal doctrine – and where better to do that than in the tranquillity of a nunnery? Thirdly, the person most likely to have got him the post was none other than the abbess Elisabeth, earlier encountered at Frose. She was the sister of the leading Dominican in Naumburg, and her interest in Müntzer may have been piqued by his reaction to the events of 1517; conversely, she would definitely have vetoed his appointment had she had any doubts about his doctrines. This was not the only time that Müntzer's career was advanced by a woman of standing.

His life in Beuditz seems to have been pleasantly undisturbed and productive. In January 1520, he wrote to Franz Günther describing his studies, mentioning particularly the histories of the Church written by St Augustine, Hegesippus and Eusebius.[22] Perhaps stirred up by the holy cook of Orlamünde, he also made a study of Tauler and Heinrich Suso (1295–1366), both of whom wrote much on the nature of spiritual suffering, along the same lines as Thomas à Kempis's *Imitation of Christ*. (A rather coy letter written to Müntzer by 'Sister Ursula', a nun at either Frose or Beuditz, gently flirts with him on the matter of the mystics: 'I cannot imagine that you learned from your Tauler or Brother Suso', she writes, 'that you should buy presents for pretty girls at the fair. But keep on doing this – it will do you no harm.'[23] In those days, as now, a passing reference to the mystics could be a good chat-up line. That a nun should be teasing him in a letter – and that Müntzer should have retained it – reminds us that he was, after all, just another young man. Ursula also sent him five small loaves of bread; what Müntzer had sent her as a present is, alas, unknown.) There is evidence, too, in a letter he sent to a bookseller in Leipzig, that he read widely on Canon Law and Jewish history, in the works of St Jerome, and on other Church historical matters, as well as some of the recent works by Luther.[24] His proposed reading list is quite long, and strengthens the idea that he retired to Beuditz in order not to be drawn too closely to Wittenberg, but to try to work out for himself the meaning of the reform of the Church.

That January letter to Günther also presents us with some interesting pointers to Müntzer's preoccupations. He wrote: 'I have turned over certain volumes of history: this is a cross for me in the Lord Jesus, and bitter besides, because I cannot get hold of several authors who are necessary for my studies. I do not seek this knowledge for myself, but for the Lord Jesus.' The Father Confessor obviously felt a calling to the reform, one that he took very seriously. His mission was for God, and his quest for answers was frustrating – a frustration which he expressed in the language of the mystics.

Turning back to the works of the past, either to scholars who did not openly defend the status quo within the Church, or even further back, as with the Humanists, to Classical Roman and Greek writers, was characteristic of the intellectual movement both before and during these years. In this context, many of the mystics of the preceding centuries, such as Joachim de Fiore, Tauler and Suso, were receiving renewed attention. Tauler had based his doctrines on the idea that 'God was the foundation of the soul', and so was present as much 'within' as 'above'; the divinity also existed in opposition to the worldly 'creature' in humans. Mortals had to overcome their own worldliness and sinfulness to reach a state of grace, and this was achieved by spiritual suffering and torment. Suffering was, however, not self-induced, but imposed by God: a person was helpless against this 'darkness', 'thirst', 'burden' and 'death'. It was, in a sense, an abandonment by God. But, in order to attain grace, the sufferer had to welcome the torment – one of Tauler's famous and less cheery phrases was 'God greet you, bitter bitterness full of all grace.' Tauler declared himself opposed to the 'Pharisees', the Church scribblers who wrote so much on sin and grace while knowing nothing of the subject. Suso had very similar ideas; his writings read like a gloomy jeremiad, an itinerary of the soul through the appalling sins and crushing despairs of the world, searching for the key to unlock the door to faith. The selfish nature of Man would be expelled by a 'higher suffering', imposed by God: 'the release from worldliness at first causes pain, as is right and just; but then one acts in joy, and so that kind of pain disappears'.[25]

Many were the reformers who studied Tauler, Suso and the popularisation of their doctrines in the mystical treatise *Theologia Deutsch* – promoted and translated, incidentally, by Luther in 1518. Many indeed were the monks, nuns and scholars of the fourteenth to sixteenth centuries who had read these works, so Müntzer's researches here were by no means singular. There was no direct evidence of Müntzer promoting the mysticism of the Cross or inner suffering in the reports from Jüterbog, nor in any other source up until then. But, by the time he began to formulate his theology in the summer of 1520, he was already making heavy use of the language of mysticism. And he drew different conclusions from 'inner suffering' than those drawn by Tauler and Suso.

We have no immediate access to Müntzer's thinking in this period. He may have written other letters to his contemporaries, but these have not been preserved. We can only make some general suppositions based on his activities and his lists of books. What we do know is that he had flung himself wholeheartedly into the reform movement led by Wittenberg, and was questioning the whole structure of the late medieval Church, its institutions and its main doctrines. For whatever reason, he did not wish to stay in Wittenberg to pursue his studies, but preferred to seek some answers of his own. He turned back to the mystics of the fourteenth century, and to the writings of the early medieval Churchmen, in an attempt – surely – to gain his own perspective on the decline of the Church.

Only when Müntzer settles into his next post after Beuditz do we discover how far he had progressed. The place to which he moved, after about nine months in Beuditz, was the town of Zwickau. It was here that Thomas, now aged thirty, made perhaps the greatest leap in his understanding of his world. And he did so not by pursuing his studies in theology, but by engaging with the ordinary people of the town.

3

Murder and Riot and Bloodshed

Preacher in Zwickau (1520–1521)

Please guard yourself diligently against this false spirit and prophet, who goes around in sheep's clothing, but underneath is a ravening wolf. In many places now, but especially in Zwickau, he has shown beyond all doubt what kind of tree he is, for he bears no other fruit than incitement to murder and riot and bloodshed.

Martin Luther (1524)

We have documented the first three decades of Müntzer's life in a rather haphazard manner. Very little can be said with certainty about his birth, his parents or his education. Gradually, however, the picture becomes less patchy, and we find Müntzer firmly set on a career within the Church. There are still huge holes in the record, but the patient reader will doubtless be pleased to learn that, for the next eleven months of his life, more adequate documentation is available.

The town of Zwickau is located on the western edge of the Erzgebirge (literally, the 'ore mountains'), which formed the physical border between Saxony and Bohemia. Described by Prince Friedrich of Saxony as 'the pearl in the land', in 1520 it boasted a population of around 7,000 souls – as many as there were in, for example, Leipzig – and its taxable wealth was four times that of Dresden.[1] As a measure of the town's prosperity, it is recorded that, in 1514, 777 brewings took place in Zwickau and its dependent villages, representing around 1.25 million gallons of beer.[2] In 1527, 4,000 hundredweight of wool was transformed into 12,000 pieces of cloth. And at the beginning of the sixteenth century, Zwickau was close to the centre of the German iron, gold and silver mining industries. Both Schneeberg (not far from Zwickau) and Annaberg were home to mints which gave their names to well-respected silver coins of the era. In the 1520s and 1530s around 85 per cent of Europe's silver production came from Germany, and around a quarter of that from the Erzgebirge. There was also a mint in Zwickau, and one of the richest men in richest Saxony was the Zwickau citizen Martin Römer, a merchant with a finger in every pie. The town, in short, was a flourishing example of Saxon trade and industry. (In later years, it became the centre of production of the late-lamented East German Trabant car, whose body made very little use of the ore of the surrounding mountains.)

To cater for the spiritual and corporeal health of the town's citizens, there were eight churches and six chapels, several monastic institutions and four hospitals. The main church, the Marienkirche, boasted twenty-three altars; the next largest, the Katharinenkirche, had ten. There were schools with a combined roll of around 900 pupils, including a Latin school, founded by the Church, and a Greek school, founded by the Humanists – the first schoolmaster of which was Georg Agricola, who went on to establish the science of mineralogy.

This, then, was a town in which a massive influx of capital from trade and mining contributed to a rapid growth in industry and population. As a result, the burghers of Zwickau exhibited a highly independent attitude towards the Papal Church, and numbered among the very first conquests of the Wittenberg reform movement: in late 1520, Luther dedicated his famous pamphlet *Concerning Christian Freedom* to Hieronymus Mülphordt, the bailiff of Zwickau. In 1523, the town council helped to establish a printing works in the town, specifically for the printing of works by Luther and his colleagues. (By some managerial oversight, this printery was also churning out Hussite and radical works in the mid-1520s. That was soon stopped.)

The presence of such industry and wealth inevitably gave rise to vociferous groups of artisans and poor craftsmen and women, each demanding a say in the democratic management of town affairs. The lower classes had contacts with the miners from the surrounding area, and the weavers had contacts with their brothers over the border in Hussite Bohemia. In the mid-fifteenth century, Zwickau played a role in the spread of Hussitism and Taboritism into Germany. In 1462, Hussites were burned there, in 1475 the presence of Bohemian preachers was reported, and at the beginning of the following century the town had links with the town of Žatec, once a citadel of the Taborites, and never free of that heresy. Around 1520, followers of Niklas of Vlásenice (a village some eighty kilometres south-east of Prague), an uneducated peasant who believed in real and direct revelations from God to the laity, were active in Zwickau, under the leadership of a weaver named Nikolaus Storch. This was fertile ground indeed for the reform movement.[3]

This busy town and surrounding countryside, then, was subject to the same economic and political pressures that determined the development of the Reformation across Germany, and perhaps more so, due to its advanced stage of economic development. The organisation of industry in Zwickau meant that three sections of society were in conflict: the burghers coveted municipal power, the patrician and rich families wished to retain and increase their monopoly of power and wealth, and the lower artisans and craftspeople – often relegated to lower positions by the influx of the new wealth of the mining magnates – strove for a general improvement in their condition. Sometimes this conflict was sublimated into religious disputes between the followers of Rome and the followers of Wittenberg, or into a three-cornered fight between Hussite-like radicals, Romans and Wittenbergers; at other times it burst out violently in riot with or without political overtones. The weavers in particular, always the most coherent grouping of the Middle Ages, were to be found proposing concrete social reforms – the establishment of schools and hospitals for the poor, the care of children, the statutory provision of poor funds and similar. During the riotous events of 1520 and 1521, which we shall soon observe, it was the weavers who were to the fore, and who were the first to be arrested. And religious dissent was not restricted to Zwickau itself: in nearby Schneeberg in 1524, a radical preacher named Georg Amandus was found to have been stirring up 'the common man against authority'; he 'was an enemy of Latin, makes no reference to the Bible ... and mocks the sacrament, baptism, images, and ceremonies'.[4] The miners of Saxony, despite their small numbers and status – somewhere between a proto-proletariat and the self-employed – were frequently to be found supporting peasant and urban rebels.

Müntzer could scarcely have chosen a more suitable place in which to pursue his search for the true Church and to advance the cause of reform. But, in the event, he did not choose it for himself. He was selected – by men who later had cause to regret their choice.

The incumbent preacher at the Marienkirche (St Mary's Church) of Zwickau was Johann Wildenauer of Eger, a reformed preacher and a supporter of Wittenberg who had come to the reforming movement from Humanism (his Latinised professional name, from his hometown, was 'Egranus'). As events were to prove, he remained very much a Humanist, something of a dilettante intellectual who had a measure of academic agreement with Luther's theology. Egranus was present at the Disputation of Leipzig (between Eck and Luther) in June 1519, and Luther had apparently recommended Müntzer to him as a man who could help the cause of reform. In 1520, Egranus wrote to Luther about 'Master Thomas whom you commended to me in Leipzig'.[5] And indeed Luther himself praised Müntzer as 'the very best of men' in a letter of May 1520.[6] Evidently Müntzer's performance in Jüterbog had been seen as a promising start to his reforming career. In 1520, Egranus asked the town council of Zwickau for sabbatical leave, so that he could pursue his Humanist studies in Nürnberg and Basel; although the benefice at the Marienkirche was nominally in the hands of the canon of Naumburg Cathedral, the council had effective management of the position. Egranus's request was granted and, at his recommendation, the temporary post was offered to Müntzer, at that time in Beuditz.

But the decision to go to Zwickau was not straightforward, for Müntzer received another offer that same month. In April 1520 an old friend, Heinrich von Bünau, in his capacity as Archdeacon in Elsterberg (a small town not far from Zwickau), wrote to Müntzer to ask him urgently to come and take up a post as vicar.[7] Bünau was aware that 'the people of Zwickau' had already made him an offer, but pressed him nevertheless to think carefully before coming to a decision.

In the event, Thomas opted for Zwickau, no doubt because it was a large town which had already demonstrated its strategic importance as a centre for reform. Eager to get to work, he arrived there in early May, and on the 17th of that month he was preaching before the well-to-do congregation of the Marienkirche. Despite the many assertions that Müntzer entered Zwickau as a confirmed radical, his first public sermon since Jüterbog was not enough to have the congregation trembling with indignation in the pews. Although he preached passionately, and more loudly than Egranus, against the manifest abuses of Rome and the Franciscan monks – who, he said, a little tactlessly, 'have mouths from which you could cut a pound of flesh and still leave a good enough mouth'[8] – he said nothing that was not music to the congregation's ears: the rich were only too eager to remove their religious rivals in richness, and the less rich were quite content to hear lively criticism of the discredited clergy. The only people he angered were the Franciscan monks. (Müntzer's second sermon, a few days later, was briefly enlivened by the collapse of a roof-rafter. Fortunately it was prevented from falling on the heads of those below by becoming jammed in a window niche. Franciscans and their critics alike might have seen in this event an act of God.)

The Franciscans were by no means a defeated force, and they protested vigorously against Müntzer's spirited attacks. Although Egranus had promoted the reform movement in Zwickau since 1517, the controversy had been conducted at a more elevated level: the monks had suffered no gross insults from him. Their leader was Tiburtius of Weissenfels, who began a series of counterattacks (or 'noisy positions', as Müntzer preferred to describe them), stoking up a campaign which had been smouldering genteelly for three years. One criticism suggested that Müntzer was encouraging the 'common man to anger, rather than improvement'.[9] The controversy rapidly became a popular one, and news of the very public denunciations soon reached Wittenberg. By 13 July, the town council felt that the time had come for authoritative intervention from the outside. They wrote to Johann, Duke of Saxony, asking him to intervene: to be quite clear, Johann was asked to intervene against the Franciscans and other representatives of the Bishop of Naumburg, and not against Müntzer. Müntzer himself delivered copies of his sermons to the bishop, and then wrote a long letter (in Latin) to Luther explaining the situation as he saw it.[10] 'The town council has advised me, most sweet father,' he began, 'to seek your advice in the fight against my accusers'; he then goes on to detail the attacks on him by the 'hypocritical monks'. He asks Luther not to believe what he may have been told: 'You are my patron in the Lord Jesus. I ask you not to listen to those who talk about me. Do not believe those who defame me as inconstant and virulent and six hundred other names. I do not care a fig for them, for all others are grateful to me for my Christian teaching.' He ends with this remarkable view of his own mission:

> I believe most surely that I have been freed from the greatest dangers in order to fight for another, desirable world. [God] will pluck me from the most deadly mire, He will deliver me from the claws of the beasts and lions and dragons, so I am not afraid, even if I walk in the valley of the shadow of death, for the Lord is with me as a mighty, terrible one. He Himself gave me speech and wisdom which none of our enemies can withstand. What more can I desire? Farewell in Christ, model and lantern of the friends of God.

The letter was signed: 'Thomas Müntzer whom you brought to life through the gospel'. Oddly, a later attempt seems to have been made to physically erase these last words from Müntzer's copy of the letter. By Müntzer himself? By a nervous Lutheran archivist? Either might have been anxious to excise any suggestion of dependency.

The first and most obvious point arising from this letter is Müntzer's apparent desire to remain a colleague of Martin Luther. He states that Luther first inspired him to join the reform movement; he recognises him as a leader of the movement, one to whom he can turn for support; he regards Luther's activities as consistent with his own. But he does not ask for any doctrinal assistance. He has no doubts that what he has been preaching is correct, and he sees no need for further justification. Although he writes that 'I put my trust in God to be guided by you alone', the 'alone' is immediately qualified: 'and by the advice of all Christians'. So while Müntzer regards himself as a 'Wittenberger', he places himself on an equal footing with Luther as far as doctrinal authority goes. What he asks of Luther, in a flattering way, is additional political support.

The other outstanding feature of the letter is Müntzer's view of his own divine role in the reform of the Church. He regards himself as a mouthpiece of God, and his persecution as entirely consistent with the 'mortification' of the soul. This should not be regarded as some form of megalomania, since he was simply expressing what most reformers – and especially Luther – believed of themselves.

In the letter, Müntzer also set out the Franciscan 'noisy positions' as he saw them: that the Church had always had the right to make its own laws; that there is no such thing as a 'living' Gospel, which is perpetuated in men and women today; that the suffering of Jesus should not be imitated; that the Gospel does not condemn the power of kings; that if riches are to be condemned for priests and bishops, then princes and kings would also have to become beggars.

This letter, then, summarised how Müntzer regards the process by which people are saved or damned. He argues that the work of God did not stop when Jesus died, but that it continued and continues in the spirits of true Christians. These Christians perpetuate the 'living Gospel' in themselves, as people predestined to execute the will of God on earth. These people are 'elected' by God to do his work. It is their fate to suffer in this world. Opposed to the Elect are the rich and the powerful, who do not live by the word of God, and the priests who love their comfort and perpetuate it by keeping the common people in ignorance. By arguing that 'good works' will lead to faith, and that these good works generally increase the bounty of the Church, the representatives of the Church oppress the common people. This last argument would probably have found Luther's favour, since it was his teaching that 'good works' flowed from belief, and not vice versa. What Luther would have made of the other points is less certain.

Müntzer had begun to draw his conclusions from Tauler and Suso and to apply them to the contemporary religious situation. Even the language he uses to describe his own position in the controversy indicates his view of the role of the Elect. And now he was also drawing social and political conclusions – however tentatively – from his interpretations of the mystics and the Gospels.

We have no record of Luther ever replying to Müntzer's letter, nor of any intervention of his in the furious debate in Zwickau. It is quite possible that he did intervene, but evidently not to condemn his colleague. In any case, he had his own problems to worry about: the Papal Bull of Condemnation of Luther was issued on 15 June 1520, threatening him with excommunication and ordering his submission to Rome. In response, Luther turned to the German ruling class, appealing for help in defeating the machinations of the Pope in his pamphlet entitled *To the Christian Nobility of the German Nation*, which was printed in August. His assertions here were not particularly new, but the conclusions he now drew were important for the Reformation. He argued that 'Papal tyranny' was buttressed by three claims: that spiritual power was greater than temporal power; that the Pope had sole authority on interpretation of the scriptures; and that only the Pope could call a council. Arguing that secular power was a gift of God, Luther proposed that a 'Christian magistrate' had sufficient authority to intervene to protect those Christians who made a correct interpretation of the scriptures. This was not yet *carte blanche* for the nobility to direct the Reformation, since Luther still argued that they had to be 'true Christians', but it was obviously a major step on the way.

During the late summer and into autumn, Luther's works and the teaching of his doctrines were banned in various parts of Germany – those areas where the Emperor Charles or his allies had unchallenged authority. In further efforts to gain wide support, in November Luther published his other famous pamphlets of that year, *On the Babylonian Captivity* and *Concerning Christian Freedom*. The former was addressed to the educated middle layers of society, clerics and Humanists, and provoked something of a stir among them by arguing for the Hussite tradition of 'Utraquism' (offering both cup and bread to the laity during Mass, something Luther had already initiated in 1519). The latter was a tract aimed at the general public, praising the joys and spiritual freedom arising from true faith.

By July 1520, Müntzer's head was up, and he launched into the fray with a great deal of enthusiasm. Although it was probably not a conscious change of direction, he was now finding the confidence to pursue radical religious reforms not in the works of the mystics or the histories of the Church, but in the living voices, concerns, hopes and – above all – the support of ordinary people. The next few months saw him achieving two great feats. The first was to entirely upset the Wittenberg apple-cart in Zwickau, opening up 'the Reformation' to many kinds of interpretation; the other was to stimulate the lower classes in Zwickau to such a pitch that within eighteen months they themselves were causing all manner of confusion in the leading minds of Wittenberg.

On 18 July, the town council of Zwickau registered a vote of confidence in their reforming preacher, and requested him to stay on at the Marienkirche. Disconcertingly, and somewhat contradicting this vote of confidence, a month earlier, in mid-June, the council had already invited Egranus to return. (Egranus, for his pains, had been named in the same Papal Bull as now threatened Luther; he cannot have been best pleased.) Egranus replied to the invitation in September with a list of conditions for his return, which were discussed by the council in session. To the modern reader, these demands seem quite exotic, but no one except Müntzer seems to have batted an eye. Egranus demanded the right to be given his meals in the house of some respectable citizen, instead of the presbytery, and to be excused early morning Mass on weekdays in the winter months, 'most particularly during Advent'. Mid-winter was not a time for any self-respecting gentleman to be out of doors or standing about in a draughty church. He also wanted assurances that he would be protected against any and all enemies. Happily for him, the council acceded to all these demands, and Egranus found himself able to return to the Marienkirche at Michaelmas.

On 1 October, two days after Egranus had returned, Müntzer took up the permanent post of preacher at the Katharinenkirche (St Katharine's Church) in Zwickau. It was a step upwards, not least in financial terms: he now received a salary of twenty-five florins per annum, where previously, as a 'locum' at the Marienkirche, he had received only fourteen and a half. While it would not be accurate to depict Müntzer's new parish as one inhabited solely by 'the poor', it did encompass much of the more volatile lower-class district. The church was used by many of the weavers, who had their own altar there; one of the most famous of the weavers was a man named Nikolaus Storch.

In the historiography on Müntzer much has been made of his relationship with Storch, the general implication being that

The Katharinenkirche in Zwickau, where Müntzer preached in 1520–21.

the chemistry between them set Müntzer on the pitiless path of radicalism from which he never strayed.[11] In this narrative, the unfortunate town of Zwickau acted as midwife to a monster of the Reformation, and in turn spawned the worst of the Anabaptists, those dissenting and radical religious communities established from around 1524 onwards. Thus the town was the junction where Müntzer was seduced away from reform and propelled towards revolution. This assumption, if it is to be founded on anything at all, must be based on an analysis of Storch's teachings, of Müntzer's doctrines, and of the documented relationship between them during the pivotal years of 1520 and 1521.

As we have previously noted, among the weavers in Zwickau were many followers of German and Bohemian spiritualism who drew their inspiration from the Taborite wing of the Hussite Reformation. These traditions had been suffused with new life after Luther issued his call for reform, and it was Storch who led the radical movement in the town. Despite the generally lower status of weavers in sixteenth-century Germany, Storch himself was by all accounts in quite a stable economic position; in addition, he was remarkably well read in the Bible, having been taught by the rather ominously named Balthasar Teufel ('Devil'), erstwhile schoolmaster of Zwickau. Storch had made several trips to Bohemia in the line of business, and had been in discussion with the radicals of Žatec. In Zwickau he now conducted 'corner sermons' – private sermons – in the houses of other weavers.

Storch left behind no personal record of his doctrines; we are obliged to his opponents among the Lutherans for descriptions of what he taught and thought. These are of necessity somewhat disjointed, and should not be given total credence. It would be pleasant to find any comparison between what Storch taught '*ante* Müntzer' and what '*post* Müntzer'; but this is impossible, since every report which does exist originates in the period after Storch had been in close contact with Müntzer, a fact which in itself strongly suggests where the dependency lay.

On 18 December 1521, a rather worried letter reached Duke Johann of Saxony from the citizens of Zwickau. Most likely written by Nikolaus Hausmann, the Lutheran preacher who had by then succeeded Egranus at the Marienkirche, the letter confided that

> some men doubted whether the belief of the godfather can be of use in the baptism. And some think that they can be blessed without being baptised. And some state that the Holy Bible is not useful in the education of men, but that men can only be taught by the Spirit, for if God had wanted to teach men with the Bible, then he would have sent us a Bible down from heaven ... And suchlike horrible abominations which are giving your Lordship's town an unchristian and Picardish name.[12]

Hausmann also reported on some of the riotous behaviour that accompanied such ideas. Whether his use of the word 'Picardish' – referring in a roundabout way to the Taborites – indicates some knowledge of the Bohemian connection, or whether it was just a general pejorative term, is uncertain. But from this brief description it seems that the Storchites believed in some form of divine 'election' to faith, and that the principles of Christianity could be learned from sources other than the Bible. Horrible abomination indeed, and very reminiscent of Müntzer's doctrines.

A summary of Storch's doctrines, composed much later in 1596, confirmed Hausmann's opinion and added some more points for good measure.[13] The Lutheran Markus Wagner listed eight articles of faith, which included: a condemnation of the 'Christian' institution of marriage, while propagating the idea that 'anyone can take women whenever his flesh commands him ... and live with them promiscuously as he wishes'; a call for the communisation of property; an invective against secular and ecclesiastical authorities; arguments against infant baptism – but not, it should be noted, in support of adult baptism; condemnation of the ceremonies of the Church; and a proclamation of free will in matters of faith.

Wagner's report is to be handled with protective gloves; the intervening seven decades had witnessed the brutal repression of radicals and Anabaptists of all shades, which was given justification by all manner of scandal and libel – referencing in particular the 'Kingdom' of Münster in the years 1533 to 1535: there, radical Anabaptists took control of a large town and polygamy had been instituted for a few months, allowing the enemies of Anabaptism to point to promiscuity as the inevitable outcome of dissension. In 1531, Luther discussed Müntzer during one of his 'table-talks' (informal but documented discussions over suppers shared with colleagues), accusing him of using his visions to assist in the seduction of a young girl in Zwickau.[14] This slanderous story has no foundation in any documented fact, and we can be reasonably sure that Wagner's later attempt at titillation has none either. The other articles of faith, by contrast, seem quite plausible.

A rather more valuable report on Storch was written in late 1521, by none other than Luther's lieutenant, Philipp Melanchthon. Melanchthon, only twenty-four at the time, was bravely holding the fort at Wittenberg. Luther was by then in the Wartburg castle, whither he was spirited in April 1521 after the Imperial Diet at Worms. While Luther was developing his ideas, translating the New Testament into German, fighting off attacks from legions of devils, or engaged in struggles with black sows and constipation, young Melanchthon was swaying pilotless in the stormy sea of reform, pitched hither and thither by rebellious monks, by Karlstadt, and now by Storch. In mid-December 1521, Nikolaus Storch, Markus Stübner (also known as Markus Thomas: as we shall discover, he had just returned from accompanying Müntzer on a journey to Prague) and Thomas Drechsel turned up in Wittenberg to argue for their interpretation of religious faith before the leading reformers. Melanchthon's immediate reaction was one of excitement, a feeling shared by several of his colleagues. However, caution reared its ugly head, and he decided to seek advice from Prince Friedrich and from Luther. He wrote to the prince on 27 December about the meeting he had had with the three men:

> I have listened to them; it is a wonder, but they sat down to preach, and said clearly that they had been sent by God to teach, that they spoke familiarly with God, that they could see the future; in short

that they were prophets and apostles. How much I was moved by them, I cannot easily express. Certain things persuade me not to condemn them.[15]

In a covering note to Friedrich's chaplain, Georg Spalatin, Melanchthon added: 'the Holy Spirit is in these men'. The reaction in the university town of Wittenberg was all the more interesting given the innate feeling of intellectual superiority of most of the reformers; anyone without the 'proper' training or education was generally given short shrift. In later years, most unordained reformed preachers were regarded as 'Anabaptists'.[16] But in the last months of 1521, radicalism was rampant, and Melanchthon listened open-mouthed.

Friedrich's very sensible reaction was to despatch Spalatin to Wittenberg post-haste, to interview the three 'prophets' and warn Melanchthon against Storch. Melanchthon immediately changed his tune, and expressed an interest only in the question of baptism; Storch's views on this had already been reported by Hausmann. In 1529, Melanchthon looked back over these years and further described Storch's doctrines:

> God had shown him [Storch] in dreams what He wanted. He claimed that an angel had come to him and had said that he would sit upon the throne of the Archangel Gabriel, and would thus be promised mastery over all the earth. He also said that saints and the Elect would reign after the destruction of the Godless, and that, under his leadership, all the kings and princes of the world would be killed and the Church would be cleansed . . . He simply laughed about Mass, baptism and communion. He invented certain worthless tricks with which he intended to prepare men for the reception of the Spirit: if they spoke little, dressed poorly and ate poorly and together demanded the Holy Spirit of God.[17]

The doctrines Melanchthon reported bear more than a passing resemblance to the Taboritism of the fifteenth century, and to early Anabaptism after 1525, so it is possible that his retrospective description was coloured by the events of intervening years.

From these various reports we can distil three doctrines that are also found in Müntzer's theology: firstly, millenarianism, a belief in the Second Coming of Christ; secondly, the insistence on subjective, individual paths to God; and thirdly, the belief in the divine provenance of dreams. Of these three, only the last might be considered a 'Storchite' influence on Müntzer. As we have seen, millenarianism was by no means uncommon in the period, and we shall see later that Müntzer's conception of history was significantly different from Storch's. Müntzer had already established his doctrine of the Elect, and therefore of individual communication with God, and he never shared Storch's vivid and ambitious picture of that relationship. But the significance of dreams is something we have not yet encountered in Müntzer's doctrine. This element in his theology is not to be ignored, nor is it regrettable that it appears to have been borrowed from Storch (the unstated view in most historiography). Dreams, of course, were regarded by everyone in that era – including Luther – as worthy of note and of supernatural origin. But the interpretation of dreams was arguably an activity allowing most scope for the individual interpretation of the material world – which was precisely the freedom demanded by all dissenters in the reform movement.

The charge that Müntzer ditched all his previously held doctrines and gave himself up to Storch, however, must be rejected. That a man such as Müntzer, trained and trained again in reading and careful study, should cast aside all his circumspection on contact with a man who, even by contemporary accounts, he supported from a critical distance, is less than credible.

Nonetheless, Storch and Müntzer certainly had an effect on each other. Thomas probably saw in Storch and the weavers of Zwickau a confirmation of his view, already hinted at in Jüterbog, that the motive power of the reform movement lay in the common people. This would have predisposed him to listen seriously to what Storch had to say. And undoubtedly Müntzer now came into closer contact with the traditions of Hussitism and Taboritism. But such a serious student as Müntzer would have sifted out from this new material whatever was promising for a development of his own ideas; the fruit of this contact would emerge later in 1521, in Prague.

A defamatory account of April 1521 gives us some idea of the non-dependent relationship between the two men. In it, Müntzer was depicted thus:

> at that time [the] preacher at St Katharine's made them [the Storchites] his supporters, won over the weavers, particularly one named Nichol Storch, whom he praised so mightily from the pulpit, raised him above all other priests as the only one who knew the Bible better and who was highly favoured by the Spirit . . . Storch dared to give corner-sermons beside Thomas . . . Thus this Nichol Storch was favoured by Master Thomas; who recommended from the pulpit that laymen should be our prelates and priests.[18]

Although this same report talked of the 'Storchite sect', there is no indication that this included Müntzer; indeed, the highly hostile account goes on to describe the '*secta Storchitorum* . . . [which] conspired and gathered together as Twelve Apostles and Seventy-Two other Disciples [and were] reinforced by Master Thomas and his followers', which strongly suggests that there were two separate groupings. Not exactly a picture of blind and reckless devotion by a united sect.

The alliance between Storch and Müntzer was to be short-lived. Following his departure from Zwickau in April 1521, Müntzer had no more to do with Storch. In June 1521, he wrote to Markus Stübner wondering why Storch had not written to him, but his question was not shaded with any emotion or disappointment. His only other reference to Storch in later days was in a letter to Luther of July 1523,[19] in which he indicates his doubts about Storch and Stübner, obliquely suggesting that they were hypocrites and fearful of debate.

How then did Müntzer's ideas develop in 1520 and 1521? The available evidence indicates that contact with Egranus was more important in this matter than contact with Storch. Egranus excited in Müntzer an ardent personal hatred and a desire to see real reforms in Zwickau. For the more radical man, the Humanist tendencies of the other were contrary to the ideals of reformed religion – in this, Müntzer's conflict with Humanism pre-dated Luther's with Erasmus by five or six years. The public debate on Egranus was the cause of regular disturbances, in which Müntzer was always implicated one way or another. Not long after his transfer to the Katharinenkirche he divided his criticisms between the Franciscans, the old-style priests of outlying villages, and Egranus.

He imparted his doubts about Egranus in letters sent to Wittenberg. A reply from Johann Agricola, dated 2 November 1520, makes reference to now-lost correspondence, and starts off thus:

> in the first place I implore you by the sacred name of Christ not to act publicly in hatred against Egranus, nor to undertake any-thing against him. We know how unreasonable he is, and how inconstant in spirit, and without the least glimmer of learning.[20]

The rest of this letter expands on the theme, advising the preacher not to offend any of the allies of Wittenberg by rash undertak-ings. In October, Egranus was already in dispute with Luther, who now suspected him of being of Johann Eck's party at the Disputation in Leipzig. On 4 November, Luther wrote to Spalatin to denounce Egranus. This did not, however, prevent Luther from mentioning Egranus uncritically in the dedication to his pamphlet of that same month, *Concerning Christian Freedom*. What precisely Müntzer had said to those in Wittenberg about Egranus in October is unclear, but it was undoubtedly related to Egranus's love of material comforts and to his rejection of the idea of salvation through spiritual pain.

On the other front, Müntzer thrust a spear ever deeper into the body of the Papal Church, leading to some scandalous acts. With a passionate sermon on the 26 December 1520, Müntzer

> stirred up the populace . . . so that they chased a priest, Nikolaus Hofer, priest at Marienthal [a western suburb of Zwickau], threw mud and stones at him, threw him out of St Katharine's churchyard, chased him through the castle and the moat, so that he scarcely escaped alive, because he had apparently accused

Müntzer of lying. He finally got away by entering Peter Kolbe's house and getting out through the back garden.[21]

There was inevitably an inquiry into these goings-on by the town council, and the evidence indicated that the immediate cause had been an intervention by Hofer in the Katharinenkirche, when he ill-advisedly called the preacher and all his followers an 'heretical rabble and rascals'.[22] Small wonder there was a riot. The inquiry also determined that the congregation's reaction was spontaneous, and that the incumbent preacher had no part in it. Sure enough, on 29 December, Hofer's actions were condemned by the town council.

The dramatic events in December soon reached the ears of the Bishop of Naumburg, whose chancellor resided in Zeitz, some forty kilometres north-west of Zwickau. Müntzer was summoned to Zeitz on 16 January to explain himself, but the council chose to send a deputation in his place (no fewer than ten officials made the journey – which smacks somewhat of an expenses-paid jolly). The delegation's explanation was accepted and, by 6 February, the unfortunate Hofer was out of a job. Müntzer had repeated his call for the extirpation of 'false preachers' on the very day in January that the officials set off for Zeitz. In retaliation, supporters of the old Church regime daubed graffiti on Müntzer's house.

Two developments in December 1520 gave Müntzer increased confidence in his divinely inspired battle against the old Church and its representatives. On the 10th of that month, Luther had burned copies of the Canon Law of the Church and the Papal Bull which had been issued against him by Pope Leo X. News of Luther's courageous defiance reached Müntzer about ten days later. Luther's justification for the burning was that he had a duty to uproot 'false, misleading and unchristian doctrine'. In Müntzer's eyes, such an action can only have strengthened his belief that the reform movement had taken a giant step forward. It was also in mid-December that Egranus finally tendered his resignation from the pulpit of the Marienkirche, apparently disenchanted with the direction taken by Luther – most probably after the publication of the latter's pamphlet *On the Babylonian*

Captivity, with its support of Utraquism. A more immediate cause for Egranus's resignation was his desire to move to Joachimsthal, a mining village then transforming itself into a boom town after the discovery of a rich new silver seam. (Barely four years later, Egranus might have had cause for regret: Joachimsthal was by then a highly radicalised area, with miners up in arms to assist the peasants' rebellion in 1525; scarcely a peaceful retreat for contemplation.) The town council did not hesitate to accept the resignation, which was agreed for the following Easter, and within days had requested that Franz Günther – he of Jüterbog – be appointed as successor, almost certainly at Müntzer's suggestion. Günther, however, was unavailable, having already taken up a post elsewhere.

The events of December and January brought Müntzer's argument with Egranus to a head. Thomas saw in Egranus not just a weak-willed academic and a dilettante Humanist, but the worst personification of godlessness and blasphemy, both resulting from false doctrine. Yet his opposition to Egranus was not an opposition to Lutheranism; although Müntzer may not have been defending the doctrines of Luther in this fight, he was still far from consciously opposing them. Instead, Egranus's position, in Müntzer's view, was dangerously close to that of the Franciscans and of the richer citizens. In mid-February, Egranus had written to Müntzer, complaining that he had called him a 'devil'. 'Perhaps', he continued, 'it is your Spirit that taught you this, the one you boast about and which you – as I have heard – have fished from the waters.'[23] Note here the mocking reference to the 'Spirit', and how Müntzer came by it. 'The waters' are the waters of the soul, the torrent of bitter mortification in which the faithful drown before attaining faith. From Egranus's description, Müntzer had evidently been teaching the lessons he had learned in Tauler and the *Theologia Deutsch*, and had not been reticent about his belief in 'election'.

On 16 February, the town council was obliged to intervene in the hostility between the two men, and a temporary truce was effected. Towards the end of the month, however, Müntzer composed his 'Propositions of the Virtuous Man, Doctor Egranus', a parallel to his 'Propositions' of the Franciscan Tiburtius.[24] These

comprised twenty-six 'statements' written in Latin and supposedly made by Egranus, from which we can work out Müntzer's
positions. They included:

> 5. The Passion of Christ was not bitter, as many noisily proclaim,
> nor does it bear any other fruit except a disposition to good works.
> 6. The remission of sins may take place without any pain; for
> contrition in the heart is sufficient.
> 7. There can be no experience of faith in the world except through
> books. Therefore neither a layman nor the uninitiated, however
> tempted, can judge on matters of faith.
> 15. The fear of God should not be instilled in the human breast,
> for the New Testament is silent on sin, and perfect love drives
> out fear.
> 21. In four hundred years, no one has been more learned than
> Egranus. He is the first apostle to the town of Zwickau.
> 22. In a thousand years, no man has had the Holy Spirit, nor has
> the Church been governed by it . . .
>
> I will dispute these axioms against the whole world, and espe-
> cially against that ass Thomas Müntzer. Written in Joachimsthal.

Aside from the rather bitter and heavy-handed satire, the value
of these axioms lies in their portrayal, through negation, of
Müntzer's own beliefs. Thus, Müntzer believed that there are
'Elect' souls, throughout history, who have suffered great pain
and torment to come to their faith; that God's law is to be feared;
and that human reason and book-learning are of secondary
importance in the acquisition or clarification of faith.

These are the keys to Müntzer's doctrines – and therefore to
his later activity. From the belief in the Elect who undertake
the will of God, regardless of their level of education or their
surroundings, comes the conviction that the ways of men are
to be challenged and overturned if they are not in accordance
with God's will. From the 'fear of God', in opposition to the
'fear of Man', comes the strength to proceed in the face of civil
authority to perform God's work. Any individual could now
attempt to justify his or her social actions by calling on God's
law. The path is opened for the layman, the uneducated and the

radical reformer to proceed against all forms of spiritual and social oppression, in the sure knowledge that inner conviction is justification enough. To be sure, this is not how Müntzer would have expressed his theology, but these are the logical conclusions which could and did flow from it.

His running battle with Egranus, which raised a few eyebrows in Wittenberg, was set against a background of rising unrest in Zwickau. On 12 February 1521, supporters of the Papal Church contrived to smash the windows of Müntzer's house. The town council was overwhelmed with complaint and counter-complaint. Nine days later there was another disturbance, led by the weavers, in support of Müntzer against his enemies. On 7 March, the council intervened yet again, but to no avail. At Easter, 29 March, Egranus was to be found preaching that the suffering of Jesus was not as important as people were led to believe, a sermon which can only have confirmed the worst suspicions of the radical party in Zwickau.

In January or February, Müntzer had received another letter from Wittenberg, again from Johann Agricola. It seems to have been prompted by an approach from certain citizens of Zwickau – most probably the town council, whose enthusiasm for Müntzer was cooling rapidly – to the perceived reforming 'authorities' in Wittenberg. Agricola gives hesitant encouragement to Müntzer, but takes him to task on tactical matters:

> I have said nothing about that immodesty which you have shown towards Egranus. For I agree not a little with you in this matter, that Egranus does not understand anything of Holy Scripture . . . But to say it straight out, they claim that YOU HAVE BREATHED ONLY THREATS AND BLOODSHED . . . Those who only wish to correct you have written to me.[25]

(The words in capitals are so in the original – it is a quote from the Book of Acts, citing Saul's threats against the other apostles. Agricola clearly wanted to make a point.) The gist of Agricola's message was still that Müntzer should proceed with his reforms, but not annoy too many people as he did so. The advice fell on deaf ears, and can only have raised in Müntzer's mind the sharpest doubts about Wittenberg's ability to carry through the task of reforming the Church.

It was in April 1521 that matters finally came to a head. The crisis was preceded by confrontations between social and religious groupings. The conservative intellectuals and Lutherans began to close ranks against Müntzer, and the town council now joined them, most likely with some encouragement from Wittenberg. This reorientation of forces was accelerated by the death on 2 April of Dr Erasmus Stüler, a leading Zwickau councillor and a firm supporter of Müntzer. The rebellious parties, including Storch, the weavers and other townspeople, swiftly formed an alliance with Müntzer and his supporters. In the first two weeks of April, these opposing fronts became sharply defined, and there were provocations and defamations from both sides. On the night of 10 April, Müntzer was heard crying 'Fire! Fire!' in his sleep, perhaps evidence of the enormous stress on him in that period. A few days later, on 14 April, a 'Letter of the 12 Apostles and 72 Disciples' was posted up across town, addressed to Egranus as the 'desecrator and slanderer of God . . . a heretical rogue . . . who hounds God's servant'. The letter enumerated, in verse, all the false doctrines of Egranus, his denial of the suffering of the soul, his worship of the 'world' and of money, and his preference for the company of 'bigwigs' and fine ladies:

> And you seek mere chattels, cash and praise,
> But that's the last thing you'll get from the 72 Disciples,
> And just watch what you'll get from the 12 Apostles,
> And then even more from the Master . . .
> And we will prove in writing that you're an arch-heretic.[26]

(The 'Master' in this context is probably Müntzer, although it might have referred to God; in the ninety-odd rhyming lines, Müntzer's person is hinted at several times, but never named.)

This public vilification of Egranus caused a furore. A lengthy charge sheet was composed in reply (also in verse) by the supporters of 'the honourable Egranus', in which 'that holy man' Müntzer was denounced as 'bloodthirsty'.[27] On the same day – although Müntzer had probably had nothing to do with the 'scandal-sheet from the Twelve Apostles' – the town council suspended the preacher from his post on the recommendation of the commissioner of Johann of Saxony, who had understandably been taking a keen interest in the continuing disturbances. All that day there were demonstrations. Müntzer himself seems to have kept a low profile; in a letter to Luther two years later, he even claimed, possibly a little disingenuously, that he had been in the bath at the time.[28] Although this picture might seem a touch too cosy, it may not have been untrue, and in any event he would have been busy packing up his belongings. The scurrilous 'Letter of the 12 Apostles' was just not Müntzer's style. It is more than likely that the riot was another of those spontaneous events, egged on by Storch, with a benevolent blind eye turned by Müntzer.

But on 16 April Müntzer conceded defeat. During the day he was formally advised by the town council that he had been relieved of his position at the church. He was paid the outstanding amount of his stipend, and in a last act of defiance signed the receipt as 'Thomas Müntzer, who fights for truth in the world'. The weavers gathered en masse to give him a guard of honour on his way out of town. But things got out of hand; a riot ensued, in the course of which an impressive total of fifty-five weavers were arrested and held in prison overnight; and in the end Müntzer had to leave under cover of darkness.

In an historical irony, on that very same day, 16 April 1521, on the other side of Germany, Martin Luther, well protected by his aristocratic supporters, had entered Worms to appear before the Emperor Charles V and the Imperial Diet.

4

He Ran Away like an Arch-villain

A Visit to Prague (1521)

It is well-known how he behaved wherever he spent time, in
Braunschweig, Zwickau, Prague in Bohemia, in Halle and in many
other places, and he ran away from each one like an arch-villain.

Johann Agricola (1525)

The coincidence of dates in Luther's famous arrival in Worms and Müntzer's less famous departure from Zwickau is striking; one could almost suppose that the sacking of the radical was hastened by those who wished to provide a calm political background for the Diet of Worms. Even the Catholic Duke Georg of Saxony was in favour of some reforms in the business of the Church in Germany and was prepared to convince the newly elected Emperor, Charles V, that the power of Rome had to be reduced. The last thing the principal supporters of Luther would have wanted was a major town in Saxony embroiled in civil dissent and violence, incited by those publicly identified as his followers. Setting aside any conspiracy theories, however, the simple facts are: Luther arrived in Worms on 16 April 1521 to face his Papal accusers, and in early May was spirited off for safe-keeping, by agents of Friedrich of Saxony, to the fastness of the Wartburg, disguised as 'Junker Jörg'; Müntzer left Zwickau on 16 April, and by mid-June had returned from an exploratory journey into Bohemia, specifically to the Taborite base at Žatec. The diverging geographical paths

Metropolitan Museum, New York (Open Access Public Domain)

Martin Luther disguised as 'Junker Jörg' when hiding
at the Wartburg, Lucas Cranach the Elder, 1522.

of the two reformers reflected their diverging theological and
political paths – the one into the protection of the ruling class,
the other into the historical territory of lower-class rebellion.

Quite what the good people of Zwickau thought of Müntzer's
rather abrupt departure is indicated in a letter from a supporter,
Hans Sommerschuh, written on 31 July. Sommerschuh writes
that 'those who also persecuted your Reverence say that you have
been poisoned and are very ill; others say you are dead, and suchlike'.[1] He asks Müntzer to write regularly so that his supporters
do not despair. The shocking tenor of the rumours reflected the
still-volatile situation in Zwickau after those rousing April days
(they echo similar rumours then doing the rounds about Luther).
It had taken Sommerschuh more than two months to write to
Müntzer, but he explained that the delay was partly down to a
miscommunication between Müntzer's 'servant' – referring to
his '*famulus*' or secretary, Ambrosius Emmen (of whom more
later) – and the people of Zwickau. In any event, we know that

Müntzer was alive and kicking, despite the hopeful fantasies of his opponents. He had merely crossed the border into Bohemia on a scouting mission.

We now slip again into a period of Müntzer's life where third-party documentation of his activities is virtually non-existent. To compensate, however, we do have a fair number of words from Müntzer himself, such as the letter he wrote in June 1521 to Egranus's successor in Zwickau, Nikolaus Hausmann, in which he professes to 'have visited Bohemia, not for my own glory, not for the love of money, but in the hope of my future death'.[2] This 'future death' should be understood as referring to the necessity of suffering in the cause of faith. By the suffering of one 'Elect' person, the mystery of the Cross would not be lost to humanity. The hint that the trip to Bohemia could prove dangerous prompted another letter to Michael 'Ganssau' – this was Michael Claussbeck, a well-to-do citizen of Jena – in which Müntzer undertook to pay him a visit in the coming winter, and in the meantime consigned to his safe-keeping all manner of documents. He promised that, in the event of his martyrdom, the documents would become Ganssau's property 'by a testament in my own hand'. This letter ended with the words: 'I myself will wander over all the earth on behalf of God's word which guards us all.'[3]

In the meantime, after his appearance at the Diet of Worms, Luther had disappeared and was presumed dead by many in the wider reform movement.

It is in this context that Müntzer's letter to Hausmann must be understood. Following Luther's disappearance, a major crisis engulfed the movement, and many reformers expected to see the Apocalypse – the retribution of God brought summarily upon the world. As Müntzer wrote: 'Now is the time of the Antichrist, as Matthew 24 said clearly: since the Gospel of the Kingdom will be preached throughout the earth, you will see the abomination of desolation.' The rest of this letter, which was written from the spa town of Elsterberg, dealt with Hausmann's unwillingness to condemn Egranus, a man 'full of blasphemy', and warned him that such inactivity constituted a failure to serve God: 'As Paul himself showed: "If I sought the favour of men, then I would not be a servant of Christ."' By contrast, Müntzer stated that 'I desired nothing other than my own persecution' in order to be able to teach the people.

Although there is no direct evidence, it seems that from Zwickau Müntzer went immediately to Žatec (also known as Saaz), a centre of Taboritism, around 100 kilometres over the mountains from Zwickau. On this trip he may even have gone as far as Prague, although that is unlikely.

Since Luther's disappearance the region seemed even less safe than before. There was no saying whether or not some kind of Papal or Imperial counterstrike might soon be unleashed upon the German reformers. Against this, Bohemia offered new possibilities, not least with its long history of religious reform. Müntzer's contacts from Hussite Prague must have given him a favourable impression of the climate there, one in which a thoroughgoing reform might succeed, and on his return to Saxony he immediately began organising an 'embassy' to go to Prague. He even went so far as to draft a sketchy proclamation 'to the most praiseworthy councillors of all Bohemian towns', introducing himself as an ally in their fight against 'the baneful Roman tyranny'.[4]

Following his return from this first trip to Bohemia, Müntzer travelled to Elsterberg, some twenty-five kilometres south-west of Zwickau, where his immediate material needs were catered for by his friend Heinrich von Bünau, then the town's pastor and archdeacon. It was from here that, in the middle of June, Müntzer wrote to Markus Stübner, the erstwhile student at Wittenberg whom he first met in 1518. Stübner, whose father owned the public bath in Elsterberg, had himself only just returned from Wittenberg. Melanchthon in January 1522 stated that: 'I had a disputation with this Markus six months ago, but at that time he said nothing about conversations with God.'[5] In his letter of June, Müntzer wondered why 'Nikolaus has not written or returned'.[6] This is something of a puzzle. The Nikolaus in question would be Storch, and there is no indication in the records that Storch had ever left Zwickau. The fact that he had not written to Müntzer is not necessarily odd, given what we have learned about their relationship; the fact that he had not 'returned' from somewhere is more intriguing. Had he perhaps also been in Wittenberg with Stübner? As we shall see, the pair were there later, in December 1521, to throw Melanchthon into a spin. Wherever he had been, Storch had evidently lost touch with Müntzer. But this rather swift loss of contact is further indication that, despite a common conviction, the two men were not at all close friends.

Another man whom Müntzer contacted around this time was Hans Lebe, 'the Bohemian' of Zwickau, who had a great deal of respect for Müntzer. 'You have asked me to come to see you,' Lebe replied to Müntzer, '[and] it is right that I should follow you like a son, as I respect God's law, but I cannot do it just now.'[7] He then promised to follow as soon as he was free from his other heavy responsibilities, such as 'reviling and shaming priests, who have had to learn from one who had never had the faith before' – a glorious picture of how the radical laymen of Zwickau bullishly approached the task of reform. Lebe mentions two other comrades who also hoped to join Müntzer: one named Klapst – possibly a Bohemian – who would have been useful for interpreting, and 'Hans of Freistadt', a cloth-worker from Austria who had been active in the recent disturbances, achieving the laudable feat of being expelled from Zwickau twice.[8]

Something was happening in Prague that prompted Müntzer's trip back to Bohemia so soon after the first. And there was obviously some urgency to it. As Müntzer explained in his letter to Stübner, the trip 'cannot be delayed any more . . . Be here tomorrow, for I need to discuss a great deal with you, so that Satan does not prevent our journey.' Although it is unclear what exactly these events were which made a journey so urgent, we do know that in Prague at this time the radical Hussite movement was undergoing something of a regeneration, doubtless partly due to the events taking place in neighbouring Saxony. The radical Hussites, under Burian Sobek and Matej Poustevnik – the former a graduate of Wittenberg who had had several of Luther's tracts translated into Czech, the latter a man of Žatec, and both stout defenders of Utraquism – had begun organising a series of open-air gatherings and public demonstrations that led in the summer of 1521 to outbreaks of iconoclasm, the storming of monasteries, and other riotous scenes. But the reform movement in Bohemia was fractured and split into warring factions – conservatives and radicals, burghers and plebeians – all vying for ascendancy. (Only six years later, under the rule of the Catholic Habsburgs, the power of Hussitism in Bohemia was to be dismantled.) On top of this, the bloody divide between Hussite and Taborite was still alive, long after the great dramas of the Bohemian Reformation a century earlier.

In that same letter to Stübner, Müntzer also refers to his mother's recent death. A slightly earlier and undated letter, addressed 'to my dear father', is also preserved.[9] The letter is written in somewhat strained tones; his father (perhaps stepfather?) had evidently been attempting to deny him some portion of his mother's estate: 'I had not expected you to behave so unfairly to me,' it begins, 'just as if I was a whore's bastard or a heathen.' This seems a little strong, but evidently Müntzer had no great respect for a man who 'had for long not been able to support yourself . . . despite what my mother brought to you' – presumably as part of her marriage dowry. 'Many people in Stolberg and Quedlinburg have told me this', he scolds. There was probably much more scolding in the letter, but the surviving fragment, on a rather scrappy piece of paper, breaks off in mid-sentence. But the complaint seems to have done the trick: in June, the almost-disinherited son was able to advise Stübner that he now had many household goods left to him after his mother's death.

All preparations now complete, in the second or third week of June Müntzer and Stübner set off for Prague, which they would have reached within a week. Müntzer's hopes for a larger party had been reined in – two or three of his friends from Zwickau were unavoidably detained (Lebe et al.). Nonetheless, there were now three travellers, the 'servant' Ambrosius Emmen being the third. We know very little about Emmen. He appears once or twice in Müntzer's correspondence – very specifically in a letter to Emmen in Allstedt, written in September 1524, asking him to come to Mühlhausen and bring with him 'father and the piglet' – an interesting combination.[10] A rather excitedly maternal letter from Emmen's mother to her son, dated sometime

around the autumn of 1520, notes that Ambrosius had, against
his father's wishes, gone to the 'Greek school' – very likely the
one in Zwickau.[11] This could be where Emmen and Müntzer
came into contact, since, to supplement his income in Zwickau,
Müntzer had acted as landlord to some school pupils. (Among
Müntzer's collection of letters, there is one from a supplier of
bedlinen, making pretty lame excuses for the poor quality of
the sheets delivered for Müntzer's lodgers.[12] Every so often,
real mundane life pokes its quivering nose out of the archives.)
Emmen's family came from Jüterbog, however, so an earlier
acquaintance is another possibility. His employment by Müntzer
would have been partly for financial reasons (like most mothers,
Emmen's was very worried about her son's lack of funds – she
sent him 12 groschen for his purse), but the fact that he remained
as secretary and servant for another three years, through thick
and thin, strongly suggests that the young Ambrosius was also
an admirer of Müntzer's religious enthusiasm.

Müntzer took with him a short handwritten document listing
a number of points of religious significance.[13] These were not
Müntzer's own thoughts, however: they were in fact bullet-points
from the bachelor's thesis presented by Philipp Melanchthon,
dating from September 1519. What was Müntzer doing with
these? Most likely, they were intended as a sort of doctrinal passport to the reform-minded intellectuals of Prague. He would not
have attempted to pass them off as his own – more plausibly they
were just as described: 'Questions for Master Thomas Müntzer
to dispute', and they may have been acquired for Müntzer by
Stübner while he was in Wittenberg. But for a couple of weeks,
at least, this passport seemed to ease the party into Prague theological circles.

There were reports that Müntzer preached a sermon in Prague
on 23 June, and two weeks later, on 7 July, the Germans found
themselves in a procession held in memory of Jan Hus, which,
through no fault of theirs, turned into a riotous assembly. Over
the next few months, possibly masquerading as a follower of
Martin Luther, but certainly in the guise of a representative of
the German reform movement, Müntzer was permitted to preach
in a variety of chapels and churches, even in the great central

Týn Church. His lodgings were initially within the university, which gave him access to certain audiences and facilitated heated discussion with the academics; however, he seems to have been ejected from this comfortable accommodation after the university authorities realised that their guest was not necessarily a respectable 'Martinian'.

Unfortunately, we have few details of the activities of either Müntzer or Stübner in Prague. A couple of contemporary Bohemian documents indicate that Müntzer was preaching and officiating at Mass – one reported that he was distributing the bread and the wine 'in both kinds, to both sexes'.[14] A letter from Hans Pelt, written to Müntzer in September 1521,[15] gives us another second-hand report of what had been going on. Pelt had initially sent his letter to Zwickau, but on its way through Naumburg it was 'returned to sender' because someone there knew that Müntzer had already gone off to Prague. Pelt added a postscript and then sent it on to Prague; the postal service may

Part of a panorama of Prague, made in 1606 by Johannes Wechter. The Týn church is the twin-spired building depicted on the right-hand side.

Metropolitan Museum, New York (Open Access Public Domain)

have been slow, but it was efficient. He writes that a contact (described in the letter as 'this Jew', possibly a colleague in the mercantile or import trade) had informed Pelt that he had 'seen you [Müntzer] given a splendid welcome in Prague and that you had two learned Bohemians with you who tell the people [i.e. translate] what you say about the gospel of Christ'. (These learned Bohemians may have been Sobek and Poustevnik.) Pelt goes on to write that he understood 'there were better Christians [in Prague] than here' and that he wanted to hear more about Müntzer's activities there. We share his desire – but in vain. In a rather touching sign-off to the letter, Pelt writes that 'my wife and children wish you a thousand peaceful nights' and advises that 'the Jew' would be back in Braunschweig in November, so that Müntzer could send a reply by him. No such reply is preserved.

What we do have, from Müntzer himself, is a notable piece of writing from November 1521, the so-called 'Prague Manifesto'. This was Müntzer's clearest and fullest declaration of his theology up until 1521, and remained so until mid-1523. As such, it is essential that we examine it to determine how Müntzer viewed the crisis of his epoch, and what he intended to do about it. The next three years of Müntzer's life cannot be understood without this pivotal document.

The work was never printed. It only survives in four handwritten versions, each one different. One of them bears the title 'A Protestation Concerning the Bohemian Matter', but the work is commonly known under the more attention-grabbing title of the 'Prague Manifesto'. Of the four versions, the first, dated 1 November, is a fairly short text in German; the second, dated 25 November, is a much-extended German version, bearing the title noted above; the third is in Czech, and is undated, and the fourth in Latin, dated simply '1521'; these last two are free translations of the longer German version, although there is a reasonable suggestion that the Latin version preceded all the others. The Czech version, which is in Emmen's handwriting, remains largely incomplete. The pieces of paper on which they were written, however, are suggestive: both the Latin text and the shorter German text are set down on large sheets – the Latin one is about 35cm wide and 50cm tall, the shorter German one about 33cm by 43cm. This has led to speculation that Müntzer had intended, in emulation of Luther and his ninety-five Wittenberg theses, to paste them to a church door – although Luther's bill-posting itself may well be apocryphal. Unhappily, two things militate against this idea: firstly, the German version is written on both sides of the paper, making it a little inconvenient for a poster; secondly, the writing would have been extremely hard to read when it was stuck up on the outside of a door. It is not impossible that the Latin or Czech version, or a copy thereof, was indeed pasted up – but actual evidence is non-existent.

We shall take all of our quotations from the longer German version.[16] 'I, Thomas Müntzer,' the text begins,

> born in Stolberg and resident in Prague, the town of the dear and saintly fighter Jan Hus, propose to fill the resounding and moving trumpets with the new praise of the Holy Spirit. With my whole heart I bear witness, complaining bitterly to all the churches of the Elect, and to the whole world, wherever this letter may reach. Christ and all the Elect, who have known me from my youth, strengthen such a resolve.

Straightaway, then, a reminder of the struggle of Hus, and a direct statement of Müntzer's own position, intentions and beliefs. He presents himself as one of God's Elect, effectively equal with Jesus and the Apostles, who had themselves been 'Elect'. With his position thus fixed, he goes on to accuse and to expose the errors of the existing Church, in language colourful throughout:

> I make so bold as to declare truthfully that no self-absolved priest and no spirit-claiming monk has ever been able to show the basis of faith in even the smallest degree. I state freely and briskly that I have not heard one donkey-farting doctor whisper the least fraction or trace of the order of God and all creatures, let alone proclaim it out loud. Even the most illustrious Christians (by which I mean the priests who are firmly rooted in Hell) have never once had an inkling of the whole and undivided perfection of it all . . . Ever and again have I heard them spouting mere Scripture

which they have stolen archly from the Bible like spiteful thieves and horrible murderers.

This paragraph recalls Müntzer's earlier 'Propositions of Egranus', where he condemned the use of objectified belief – scripture – as a substitute for the living, subjective spirit. The teachings of the old Church, the imposition of its own sterile doctrines upon the people to the detriment of progressive forces and of the developing belief, had been an integral part of its oppressive regime – 'For they deny that [God's] spirit talks with people.'

Such a criticism of the Church was no mere theological disagreement or disputation. Müntzer made it quite clear that the degradation of the Papal Church had led to a global crisis of Apocalyptic proportions, in which only the Elect could change the course of history.

> God will pour his insurmountable anger over such proud, wooden men, who are impervious to all good, Titus 1:7, for they deny the basic healing of faith ... Yes, they are not insignificant, they are greatly damned villains who have existed in all the world since the beginning, here to plague the poor people who are thus so benighted.

The 'poor people' – and this is not a sociological term, but must be understood as 'the poor in spirit', even though, in practical terms, this was precisely the poor and the lower classes – had been kept in mortal ignorance by the Church; at the Apocalypse, they would be damned unless the Elect could re-educate them in the true faith.

The word '*arm*' (poor) in German has the same double meaning as in English – either lacking in money or possessions, or lacking in good fortune or spirit. In Müntzer's writings we find that the adjective was applied not only to people, but also (and indeed more so) to 'Christianity', the religion and the Church; and in these cases, clearly, the second meaning applies – Christianity was in a pitiable state. We should therefore approach with some caution any mention of 'poor man' or 'poor people' –

according to context, the adjective can have one or other or both meanings.

Müntzer was to develop this theme of re-education in later years, but in Prague in 1521 he was content to describe the education of the Elect alone:

> Where the seed falls on good ground, that is in the heart which is full of the fear of God, that is then the paper and parchment upon which God writes the real spiritual word, not with ink, but with His living finger . . . And there is no more certain testimony which proves the Bible than God's living word, which the Father speaks to the Son in the hearts of men. All the Elect can read this word.

God speaks directly to his chosen people. There is no need of mediation by scholars or priests. The finger of God writes on the individual spirit of the Elect. And the damned are those who are unable, either through miseducation or attitude, to hear this direct communication from God. God's people do not have to be learned or well read to hear the Word, only prepared according to a mystical process of 'emptying'. The spirit of the individual was thus freed from the power of the Church.

The Elect were to re-educate the people by explaining the Bible according to their own spiritual experiences; mere imposed belief is not education. 'But I do not despair of the people', Müntzer writes.

> Oh, you really poor, pitiable little band, how you thirst after the word of God! For it is quite clear that no one, or almost no one, knows where they stand or what group they should join . . . The prophecy of Jeremiah was fulfilled in them: 'The young children ask for bread and no man breaketh it unto them.' . . . Oh, oh, no man broke it! There were plenty of money-grabbing knaves who threw down before the poor, poor, poor people the papish, unexperienced texts of the Bible, just as one tosses bread to the dogs. But they did not break it for them in the knowledge of the Holy Spirit, that is, they did not open their understanding . . . They are like the stork which fishes up frogs in meadows and swamps and then feeds them quite raw to its young ones in the nest. So

also are the usurious and tithe-stealing priests, who swallow the dead words of the Scriptures and then disgorge the letter and the unexperienced faith (which is not worth one louse) over the truly poor, poor people.

Opposed to this method of lumpish indoctrination was the method of the initiate Elect, which was to impart knowledge from living experience. Note, too, the optimism in Müntzer's view of the present state of Christianity: 'I do not despair of the people.' Those words arguably directed his life over the next four years. The common people required leadership. As Müntzer writes, 'The office of the real shepherd is this, to lead all the sheep thither and to refresh them with the living voice, for knowledge of God is taught by a master.' Again and again Müntzer returns to the basic opposition of subject and object, of subjectified living experience and objectified reported belief, stressing the primacy of the first in all its independence:

I affirm and swear by the living God: whoever does not hear the real living word of God from the mouth of God, and does not distinguish between Bible and Babel, he is nothing more than a dead thing. But God's word, which penetrates heart, brain, skin, hair, bone, marrow, juice, strength and power, must come to us differently, and not in the way our foolish, scrotal doctors babble about.

Here the opposition is between 'living voice' and 'dead word', present and past. This opposition was the most basic dialectic in Müntzer's thought, and from it can be traced much of his other philosophy. It reflected, in distorted manner, the need of the epoch for a new set of ideas, ideas which were not the child of an age of exploitation and oppression, which permitted the assimilation of immediate and new experience in order to throw off all the burdens of the past.

Müntzer's anger against the priests and academics ('*schrifft-gelerten*' – those learned in scripture) was quite uninhibited; he attacked them for their doctrines, using words absolutely calcu-lated to offend:

Oh woe, woe unto the preachers who teach like Balaam, who speak the word through their snouts, but whose hearts are more than one thousand times one thousand miles away . . . It would be no great marvel if God brought us all, Elect and damned together, to dust and ruin in body and soul with a far worse Deluge than before . . . All other nations call our faith a burlesque: and we have given them an answer from our hen-coop, proudly scribbled great books full of blots and scorings-out, saying: we have written this and that in our law, and Christ said this, Paul wrote that, the Prophet predicted such and such, such and such was decreed by the madam (in the brothel), the Holy Church, oh yes the Holy Nero, our utterly wooden Pope and chamber-pot in the Roman coal-shed has ordered such and such a great thing, and truly he has sent out an excommunication which, as our little straw doctors tell us, cannot be ignored for the sake of our conscience.

Müntzer, in quite extraordinary language, opposes his basic tenet to all the abuses and monolithic judgements of the Roman Church: all the accepted doctrines, all the books of the Scholastics, the Canon Law and the Bulls were as nothing beside the living and perpetual experience of the faith. Müntzer, like Luther, created the priesthood of the layman, but went one step further – to the priesthood of the untrained layman, the freedom of opinion for all. And any failure to deal with the old ways, he insisted, would lead to Apocalyptic punishment.

But Müntzer quite clearly saw hope for the future:

All villainy must urgently be brought to light. Oho! how ripe are the rotten apples! Oho! how ripe are the Elect! The time of the harvest is here! For this, God has sent me to his harvest. I have made my sickle sharp, for my thoughts are eager for truth and my lips, skin, hands, hair, soul, body and life curse the faithless.

He ends with a warning and a firm prediction:

Whoever despises this advice is already in the hands of the Turks. And then the raging heat of the true Antichrist will reign, he who is the real opponent of Christ; Christ will shortly give the kingdom of this world to his Elect for all eternity.

The signature is as follows: 'Thomas Müntzer wishes to pray to no dumb God but to a speaking God.'

The basic maxims of this remarkable document, then, are: that faith comes not through the reading of the scriptures, or from the books of learned professors of theology, but from a real and living experience 'written in the heart'; that the acquisition of this living voice, or word, is not an easy experience, but rather one that is bitter and painful; that the suffering of belief can only take place in the souls of those who have the 'fear of God', allowing the Elect to communicate directly with God; and that the crisis in the Church had by now reached such a stage that an Apocalyptic event was virtually certain. Finally, the practical conclusion to be drawn from all this – although one which Müntzer himself did not expressly assert – was that the Elect must strip all power from the centralised religious apparatus (the chamber pot in the coal shed), from its academic support (the hen-coop full of chicken shit) and from the Papal court (the brothel with its courtesans). Against all this would be posed the common people, the members of the Elect and the heretofore ignorant masses, a combined force with its own ultimate justification for its social and political aspirations.

Alas, whether as a result of his teaching, or simply because, by preaching, he attracted the attentions of the authorities, Müntzer had no sooner set down his thoughts on paper than he had to leave town. There were reports that he had been placed under house-arrest, or put in prison for four days, or had fled or been expelled. Stübner reported later in December that they were pelted with stones and forced to flee. (Better that than being defenestrated, perhaps.) But Müntzer may well have decided for himself that there was no point in remaining in Prague since he was getting nowhere in his mission. Whatever the case, it is certain that the radical faction in the city had lost a great deal of ground, and on that ground Müntzer had built his hopes.

From Prague there was nowhere to go but back to Germany. Müntzer had kept himself informed of events there through his friend Hans Pelt, who reported on the Edict of Worms which had condemned Luther and banned the printing of his works; Müntzer was thus well aware of the dangers involved in returning and the likely opportunities offered.

Back to Germany they went. Stübner probably headed directly to Zwickau, and there met up with Storch, before the pair set off for Wittenberg to unnerve Melanchthon. It is unlikely that this course of action was at Müntzer's suggestion: he had, as his 'Manifesto' seems to make clear, virtually ruled out any further cooperation with the academics of Wittenberg.

Thomas himself returned to Thuringia, probably in the company of young Ambrosius. But, for the moment, he had run out of options.

5

Satan Wandered in the Wilderness

Erfurt, Nordhausen and Halle (1522–1523)

Satan was expelled and wandered in the wilderness for one year or three, seeking rest but finding none.

Martin Luther (1524)

While Müntzer was away in Bohemia, the situation in Wittenberg had been heating up in a distinctly radical manner.[1] Luther had been closeted away in the Wartburg since early May 1521, and although he monitored the progress of the reform movement by letter, he was unable to prevent all manner of questionable developments. The day-to-day business of the Wittenberg movement was now in the care of Melanchthon and Justus Jonas. From around October, events in the town escalated rapidly. Early that month, Luther announced that he no longer celebrated private Mass. This announcement was echoed by a campaign in Wittenberg to start celebrating Mass in the Utraquist fashion, offering both wine and bread to the laity as a symbol of their equality with the clergy. In mid-October, Karlstadt, seizing the opportunity to give leadership to the reform movement, presided over a commission of Church and university members in Wittenberg, to debate in public and agree to major reforms of the Mass. Meanwhile, in the Augustinian cloister in the town, the monk Gabriel Zwilling was energetically encouraging his fellow monks to abandon their calling and take up a useful trade. These developments were most unwelcome to the electoral prince, Friedrich the Wise, who, though he had stuck his neck out for Luther, was not in favour of anything that would aggravate his cousin, the Catholic Duke Georg or, indeed, the Emperor. But the reform movement was now entering a phase which could not so easily be stopped. The proposed changes to the Mass won ready and extensive support, and by early December the students and populace – who had been accustomed to rioting both for and against the reforms since the summer of 1520 – were disrupting any Masses celebrated in the old fashion. Priests were mocked, threatened and stoned, altars overturned. On 25 December, things came to a head when Karlstadt, who had by now assumed effective leadership of the Wittenberg reforms, celebrated a public evangelical Mass, reciting the sacraments in German and offering both bread and wine.

Luther had secretly visited Wittenberg in the early days of December – indeed, he was there while Masses were being disrupted – and stated that what was being done in the town met with his full approval. His only doubts were expressed in an open letter, an *Earnest Exhortation to All Christians to Avoid Uproar*, in which he warned his followers not to go too far lest they force the Papal authorities into oppressive measures; but he stopped short of condemning the reforms then being pushed through. So in January 1522, the changes proceeded inexorably. Karlstadt became betrothed and quickly married, moving into a house in the town, all with Luther's approval. On 11 January, the Augustinian monks led by Zwilling destroyed images and altars in their own chapel; on 24 January, the town council issued the 'Wittenberg Ordinance', which approved the reform of the Mass, promoted iconoclasm, abolished begging, closed the town brothel and established a 'poor chest' funded by the discontinued religious endowments. This programme was drawn up jointly by the council, Karlstadt and other reformers. At the start of February, the townspeople were to be found destroying altars and graven images in various churches.

In the middle of all this, three prophets from Zwickau turned up and created a new crisis for the leadership.

The deputation from Zwickau comprised Storch, Stübner and a man named Thomas Drechsel, of whom we know very little, other than that he was an educated weaver like Storch. Stübner had only just returned from Bohemia, and had probably met up with Storch in Zwickau. The three had good reasons for coming to Wittenberg, not only because of the radical reforms on the agenda there, but also because Storch and his closest companions had been obliged to leave Zwickau.

The troubles in Zwickau had not ceased with Müntzer's departure in April 1521, and were only curbed eventually by some hard work on the part of the town council and the Saxon authorities. In May 1521, a cleric was chased through the streets while on his way to early Mass, and the reforming priest Nikolaus Hausmann was publicly accused of being too soft. In November, Duke Georg reported to Duke Johann that 'in Zwickau a priest carrying the Holy Sacrament was stoned', and that 'there are ruffians there who have no belief, but imagine that when they die, both body and soul die too'.[2] Ruffianly behaviour indeed, and Georg suspected Luther of being behind it all. By December, however, the authorities had managed to order all the Storchites to submit to a theological disputation; Storch and his inner circle refused to comply and left the town.

On 26 December, the three arrived in Wittenberg. Storch and Drechsel began to frequent the inns and houses of the lower classes and conduct 'corner sermons'. Stübner was already known to Melanchthon, and turned up at his house, where he examined the study and remarked, a little snippily, that 'There are a lot of Bibles here, but only outwardly, not within, in the soul.' By the following day, Melanchthon was panicky; he wrote a letter to Friedrich the Wise, asking for his advice on how to deal with the 'Zwickau prophets'.

Georg Spalatin was despatched to sort things out and arrived on 29 December. Spalatin was Friedrich of Saxony's secretary and chaplain, and the man of choice when it came to negotiations between the electoral prince and Wittenberg. Over the following three days, Spalatin sat down with Melanchthon, two other leading reformers – Martin Borrhaus (aka 'Cellarius') and Nikolaus von Amsdorf, the Canon of Wittenberg – and the 'prophets' themselves. Pointing to the riotous events in Zwickau over the past year, Spalatin's main argument against the three radicals was that the situation in Wittenberg, already volatile, might spin completely out of control if too much credence was given to Storch and Stübner. During the meetings it emerged that Amsdorf's first reaction had been similar to that of Melanchthon. He had initially urged Spalatin to take the issue very seriously, warning that 'This is truly a matter which one should not despise. The day of the Lord is at hand, when the Man of Sin and the Son of Perdition will be revealed. For we are those who have reached the end of the world.'[3]

By the end of a gruelling session with Spalatin, however, Amsdorf had changed his tune and was no longer prepared to listen to the radicals. Melanchthon, too, altered his stance somewhat, stating (a little disingenuously) that 'I was not particularly moved by their claims to divine revelation and so on . . . But the question of baptism interested me.'[4] This was a rather rapid retreat from his earlier enthusiasm, and it is not without significance that the question of baptism had been discussed by Stübner, while Storch had concentrated on revelation – Stübner was after all the Wittenberg-trained academic, he spoke the same language as Melanchthon, and the baptismal rite was high on the reformers' agenda.

By 13 January 1522, Luther had been made aware of the arrival of the 'prophets'; he wrote to Melanchthon advising,

> The spirits are to be tested. If you cannot test them . . . postpone judgement . . . Inquire whether they have experienced spiritual distress and the divine birth, death and hell. If you should hear that all their experiences are pleasant, quiet, devout . . . then do not approve of them.[5]

Here Luther was drawing upon the ideas of Tauler and the *Theologia Deutsch*, ideas he had clearly not abandoned. His letter also discussed infant baptism and the vexed question of whether faith can be sprinkled upon babies, coming down firmly on the fence. 'Who can see faith?' he wrote. 'To present a child for baptism is nothing else than to offer it to Christ.' His argument, like many of his other positions on sacraments and religious traditions, was that if some practice was not expressly denied in the scriptures, then it should continue.

While our knowledge of the beliefs of Storch and Stübner is sketchy, the real importance of their visit to Wittenberg was its timing. The developments in the town in December 1521 seemed to be heading inexorably towards a radical solution, and the intervention of the three 'prophets' would only have given encouragement to Karlstadt, which in turn contributed to Luther's decision to return to Wittenberg in early March 1522.

The Ordinance issued by the town council on 24 January, although popular with the laity, caused a rift among the academics. The Ordinance gave legal authority to a number of reforms that had already been instituted by Karlstadt, with the enthusiastic support of many of the citizens and the student body. But they challenged established political authority. Under pressure, Melanchthon began to set out arguments for revoking or delaying the proposed innovations. In mid-February, Friedrich of Saxony made clear his opposition to the Ordinance, seeing in it a political precedent for devolving major decisions from prince to town. He himself was under pressure from the Imperial rulers, who had issued a mandate in late January which effectively made all Church reforms illegal. At length, the more radical reforms began to be rolled back. A compromise agreement was reached in mid-February, placing a moratorium on the changes; as a result, Karlstadt was left high and dry, with, as he later put it, 'his head in the noose'.

In early March, on his own initiative, Luther emerged from the Wartburg. Various theories have been proposed for his return at this precise point, the least charitable of which suggests that he simply wanted to wrest leadership of the reform movement back to himself. Perhaps, just as simply, he had picked up the strong message of disapproval from Friedrich and saw that only he could put the movement back on the straight and narrow.

Two tasks faced Luther on his return to the imperilled town of Wittenberg. The first was to execute Friedrich's decision to reverse the Ordinance. Under Luther's supervision, images were reinstated, Utraquist practices abandoned, and services

Friedrich the Wise, engraving by Albrecht Dürer, 1524.

conducted in the old way with the proper vestments and the use of Latin. In so doing, Luther reversed rapidly away from the very positions he had been promoting only two months earlier. He now insisted that 'the weak' should not be driven pell-mell towards reform, but should be led slowly and gently. The man with his head in the noose, Karlstadt, was forbidden to preach anywhere and was swiftly removed from any position in which he might do damage. By May, the self-appointed censoring committee of Wittenberg went so far as to destroy Karlstadt's tract against Dr Hieronymus Dungersheim von Ochsenfart, professor of theology at Leipzig and a fierce Catholic critic of Luther. (This man with such a splendid and sonorous name is a flitting shadow across Müntzer's biography: from 1501 to 1505, he was the priest at Zwickau's Marienkirche, fifteen years before Müntzer; in late 1525, he turned up in Mühlhausen, to oversee the reinstatement of the Papal ceremonies.[6])

Luther's other task was to interview Stübner and Drechsel. On 17 March, he wrote to Hausmann in Zwickau to say that 'the "prophets" who came from your town are ... pregnant with monstrosities which I do not like ... their spirit is extremely deceitful and specious'.[7] To confirm this belief for himself, he summoned Stübner for a meeting in late March, reporting afterwards that 'I have had a look at these new prophets and found that, in his wisdom, Satan has shat himself'.[8] This somewhat uncouth summary of the interview was expanded upon some years later in remarks over the supper table to the effect that Stübner had spoken in Taulerian terms of the path to faith, much as Müntzer did; how accurate this is, we cannot now tell.[9] But Stübner himself soon made his peace with Wittenberg and caused no further trouble.

In April it was Drechsel's turn – but he rather ruined his credibility by talking of a small cloud he had seen in the sky when entering Wittenberg, adducing this as proof of his revelations from God. Finally, in September, Storch was brought before Luther to talk about baptism. He was quickly dismissed and thereafter wandered from town to town before being implicated in riots in south Germany in 1524 and 1525. He died, as far as is known, in Zwickau sometime around 1536.

Despite these rapid and decisive strokes against the more radical wing of the Wittenberg movement, Luther was now obliged, during a grand tour of his principality, to spend several days in Zwickau itself from 28 April to 2 May 1522 in an attempt to repair the damage inflicted on the reform movement by Müntzer, Egranus and Storch. But despite some measure of success, the radicals did not disappear from the town.

The early months of 1522 were arguably the turning point for Luther – the point at which he abandoned any thought of reforming the Church from below, or of giving radical ideas free rein. Instead he opted to place the reforms effectively in the hands of civil authority, and to ensure that he had the backing of at least one branch of the House of Saxony. It might be argued that this was a case of realpolitik – that he recognised that Wittenberg was too small a place to be able to maintain radical reforms for very long.[10] At the time, however, for people like Karlstadt and Müntzer, it looked very much like betrayal.

For Müntzer, 1522 was a year of wandering – but, as usual, there is no conclusive evidence about the exact route and timetable of his travels. He may conceivably have been in Wittenberg in January, though the evidence is sketchy at best.[11] We can, nevertheless, at least establish a tentative itinerary. His embassy to Prague had failed; so too had Stübner's embassy to Wittenberg. After two unsuccessful attempts to influence the course of the reform movement, Müntzer's immediate problem at the end of 1521 was to find a home for the winter. His first port of call would have been Jena, to visit his contact, the magistrate Michael Ganssau. How Ganssau was known to him remains something of a mystery. It is not impossible that they had met in Leipzig – Ganssau had graduated from the university there in 1505, the year before Müntzer matriculated; or perhaps Müntzer had been in Jena during one of those early 'missing' periods of his life; but evidently they were well enough acquainted for Müntzer to entrust his collection of letters to him, the previous June, just before setting off for Prague. Müntzer's most precious possession throughout his life was his satchel full of letters. It was his possession of a bundle of such letters which betrayed his identity after the fateful battle of Frankenhausen four years later, in 1525.

Müntzer's homelessness reinforced his belief that he was one of the Elect. Behind all of his actions and writing was a very real desire to force through changes. He was convinced that he was living in a time of great existential crisis for humanity, that the wrath of God would be poured out upon the world, and that he, along with the other Elect, had to prepare the ground for this final act. But at the same time he must have felt that he was almost alone in his beliefs. Despite the heartening support in Zwickau and an initially warm reception from the radicals in Prague, things had not gone the way he had hoped. Evangelical crusades did not work. He had returned to German lands where the future of the reform movement was in real danger. And he had no job and no home. Other men might have given up, found a safe place within the institutions of the Church, and waited to see how the historical dice fell. Müntzer did the next best thing: he turned his attention to finding a job – but in the hope of continuing his reforming work. His very first task on reaching Saxony was to sit down and write letters to all his contacts across central and south Germany, asking them for recommendations to suitable posts.

And gradually the replies came back. A letter dated 25 January 1522, from his friend Franz Günther (by now in Lochau, the location of Prince Friedrich's principal castle), noted that Müntzer had been driven from Bohemia and that they 'say that you now live in Thuringia'.[12] Günther's source of information was Spalatin, who by then had talked with Stübner. Unfortunately, Thuringia is a big place, and we do not know which part of it is here being discussed.

In another letter, dated late in the preceding month, a group of dissident Benedictine monks at Petersberg near Erfurt wrote to Müntzer describing 'very great dissent' in their monastery and controversy over his letters.[13] Two of these monks – Gentzel and Goldschmidt – were natives of Stolberg, and it is conceivable that they knew Müntzer personally from his youth; Goldschmidt was evidently a dissatisfied man, for in 1527 he was obliged to swear a lengthy 'oath of truce' with both his monastery and the town of Erfurt.[14] Their letter indicates that Müntzer had already been in touch with the monks, most likely after the offer of a post in the monastery sent to Zwickau in the summer of 1520. Doubtless he had turned to that still-open offer in desperation. And he was in luck, for the monks offered him a post as teacher, with 'expenses and board covered, up to thirty florins'. Were they actually authorised to do this? There seems to have been considerable argument with the abbot about the propriety of inviting a reformer into their midst.

We have no idea whether Müntzer took up the monks' offer, but it does seem possible that he stayed in Erfurt, if only for a short time. In late March, he wrote a momentous letter to Melanchthon, to which a postscript was attached. 'Do not inquire after the god of Ekron, your Lang,' wrote Müntzer, 'for he is despicable, he has persecuted the servant of the Lord through his immortal pride.'[15] Ekron was a great Philistine city, its god none other than Beelzebub; Johann Lang, on the other hand, was the representative of Wittenberg in Erfurt. For Müntzer to speak of Lang in this way suggests that the latter had in some way engineered his enforced departure from Erfurt, and the 'your' suggests that Müntzer was aware of hostility from Wittenberg, and therefore of the fate of Stübner's initiative. By the time of this letter, Luther had returned from the Wartburg, hot on the trail of radicals, and Lang's intervention may have been part of the subsequent purge of radical dissenters.

This letter to Melanchthon draws the Church-political conclusions from the 'Prague Manifesto' and applies them to the German reforms. Effectively, Müntzer announces his intention to part company with Wittenberg. Apart from one letter to Luther in 1523, this was also his last major letter in Latin, the language of the academics; but the final sentence, the conclusion in both senses of the word, was in German. The letter began promisingly: 'Greetings, instrument of Christ, I embrace your theology with all my heart, for it has saved many Elect souls from the snare of the fowlers.' Just how little Müntzer embraced Melanchthon's theology soon becomes apparent.

> But I reproach you in this, that you worship a dumb God, without knowing whether you are elect or damned . . . It is indeed your error, dearest, that everything has been undertaken in ignorance of the living word . . . Man does not live by bread alone, but in all the words which proceed out of the mouth of God: you see – 'out of the mouth of God' and not from books.

Müntzer then set out the doctrines he had developed and defended in Zwickau and Prague. To Melanchthon they must have sounded uncomfortably close to those of Storch and Stübner. Müntzer also, for the first time, accused the Wittenbergers of the very faults he had earlier found in the defenders of Rome, in the Humanists and in the Hussites; there could be no further agreement on principle with them.

The 'living word', Müntzer writes, must enter the hearer, the individual must dictate the view of the world. 'The wisdom of

God speaks to you, orders you, advises you that you might know more surely when you pay regard to the Elect.' Müntzer then refers to the events in Wittenberg of the past winter, specifically in relation to the Mass: 'I commend the hatred of Papal ceremonies . . . The tribute of wine and bread is obvious to men, for they are . . . given the knowledge of the testimonies of God, not from dead papers but from the living promises.'

Turning to Luther's management of the situation, Müntzer goes on: 'Our dearest Martin acts in ignorance in not wishing to offend the poor in spirit, for those are the children who, being a hundred years old, shall still be accursed.' The accusation that 'our dearest Martin' was holding back from reforms in order not to give offence, or to avoid driving away the as-yet-unreformed, is one of the main criticisms levelled by Müntzer in his three-year campaign against Luther. The news of Luther's role in reversing the Wittenberg Ordinance had obviously reached him. But there was more to this complaint than a mere disagreement on tactics:

> Indeed, the distress of Christians is imminent . . . Dear brother, stop your delays, it is time![16] Do not delay, the summer is nigh. Do not reconcile with the damned, for they will prevent the word from acting with great strength. Do not seek admiration from your princes, for then your audience will be subverted.

Müntzer's advice to proceed at full speed with Church reform is triggered by his belief that some Apocalyptic event is close – the summer is nigh; any concessions or delays act only against reform.

And finally, he issues a warning on Melanchthon's denial of purgatory, arguing that purgatory is part of the process of acquiring faith:

> No one can gain peace unless the seven stages of the mind are opened to the seven spirits. The error of denying purgatory is abominable, beware! If you wish, I will corroborate this from the Scriptures, from God's order, from experience, and from the express word of God.

Müntzer's generous offer to explain things further was, needless to say, not taken up. And he signs off in German at the end: 'You dainty scribes, do not be indignant: I cannot do it otherwise.' The use of the word 'you' in this phrase sets the critical distance between Müntzer and Wittenberg. The split was proposed, on the basis of a profound disagreement on the goal of reform and on the strategy for attaining that goal.

If Müntzer had been in Erfurt, then he left it hurriedly in March possibly with some encouragement from Johann Lang. After this, we have a report of him preaching in his home town of Stolberg at Easter 1522 (13 April), 'despising Luther and other Christian teachers, thinking more of himself, and on top of that provoking a most damaging unchristian uproar'.[17] In June or July, Müntzer turned up in Nordhausen, barely fifteen kilometres from Stolberg, where he remained until September or October. This was a medium-sized town of about 5,000 inhabitants. His stay was of short duration, firstly because he had no steady employment, only temporary teaching posts; and secondly because his conflict with the followers of Luther in the pulpit and on the town council followed the same pattern as in Zwickau and Prague – he was soon in a defeated minority.

The main feature of his months in Nordhausen seems to have been his involvement in social unrest, iconoclasm, riots and attacks on the established Church. Here the principal representative of Luther, after the reform movement had been initiated in the town by Justus Jonas in late 1521, was Lorenz Süsse. Süsse had been at Nordhausen since the spring of 1522, and probably had standing orders from Luther to keep any radicals at bay – Luther himself was even then touring Saxony to consolidate his position and combat 'false doctrine'. That Müntzer clashed with Süsse is clear from later statements. In a letter to the Nordhausen town council, written in April 1525, Müntzer denounced their imprisonment of an iconoclast: 'Dearest brothers, who has misled you so, that you imprison someone because of a picture? Thus your teacher [Süsse], even if he were an angel, is damned and worthy of death . . . according to the law he should be stoned.'[18] We must suppose, then, that Müntzer and Süsse had not hit it off. This is also clear from a pamphlet against Luther, written in October 1524, in which Müntzer wrote: 'You know very well with your uncooked Lorenz of Nordhausen how the evil-doers are rewarded in wanting to kill me.'[19] The 'uncooked Lorenz' is an underdone version of the St Lawrence who suffered martyrdom by being roasted on a gridiron. The accusation, however, is startling. Did Süsse really pursue his task of keeping the radicals at bay to such a degree that he planned to have them assassinated? If so, then the controversy in Nordhausen must have reached an extraordinary pitch. A memorial plaque to Süsse erected shortly after his death made the point clearly: 'exosus monachis ... exosus Papae ... exosus Thomae' – detested by the monks, the Pope and Thomas.[20]

What form the arguments took is hinted at in a letter from Müntzer to an unknown critic in Nordhausen, in July:

> The windbags are lying when they babble that I have revoked the doctrine of Christ ... What does it matter that they complain that men's spirits will be confused and made insecure; more dangerous times lie ahead for these godless men ... who know as much of divine grace as a goose of the Milky Way ... Therefore keep quiet from now on, lest they find some trickery in your statements, as they are accustomed to do: Müntzer shuns scribes, Pharisees and hypocrites ... At first they talked about abandoning the Mass. But now they want to bring it back, as soon as the people shout: 'This is right, this is right!' They have started something here that they would not be able to continue.[21]

In almost every town affected, the refreshing breeze of religious reform after 1517 breathed new life into religious demands, expressing the needs of every class which had an interest in reform. There was a 'Reformation' among the nobility, offering mutual support for the 'Reformation' of the patricians; there was a 'Reformation' championed by the quixotic Imperial knights around Hutten and Sickingen; there was a 'Reformation' of the artisans and middle strata; and there was a 'Reformation' of the plebeians and peasants. While support for a 'Reformation' came from every class, the direction of the reforms themselves reflected different social goals. Thus, when the Wittenbergers found that their proposals were being adopted with unbridled enthusiasm by the lower social groups, who had quite different social and economic aspirations from the authorities, they tended to row back.

At the end of September, Müntzer was still in Nordhausen, but obviously not in a happy situation. On the last day of the month he received a letter from Johann Buschmann, another friend of his to whom he had written earlier enquiring about any posts that might be available. In reply, Buschmann advised that a pulpit at Sooden in Hesse – a town with a large population of salt-miners, about sixty-five kilometres to the west – had become vacant, but that 'our prelates judge you as a Martinian and worse', and so there was nothing to be offered.[22] Müntzer was evidently acquiring something of a reputation in Church circles, both Roman and Lutheran.

Another contact of Müntzer's at this time was a Flemish monk named Jan van Esschen. Esschen was a brother in a monastery in Antwerp whose residents had come out en masse in favour of Luther's reforms. For this, they were locked up in October 1522 and forced to recant. Two who did not recant – Esschen being one of them – were subsequently burned to death in Brussels, making them among the very first martyrs of the Reformation. For its heretical role, the monastery itself was demolished. At the time of his reply to Müntzer, Esschen was behind bars; but he penned an enthusiastic and supportive letter: 'You know better than anyone how the Elect of God walk amongst lions, snakes and scorpions.'[23] Quite how the pair knew each other is, as usual, a bit of a mystery; Esschen had been in Eisleben in Saxony in 1521, and Müntzer may well have been there after his return from Prague.

By October, Müntzer had had enough. He left Nordhausen, once more embarking on his endless travels. Whither next? In his confession of May 1525, Müntzer is alleged to have stated that he had spoken to Dr Jakob Strauss in Weimar, when Strauss was disputing with the Franciscans.[24] A well-documented disputation between Lutherans and Franciscans took place in Weimar in the late autumn of 1522, under the chairmanship of the reformed preacher Wolfgang von Stein. There is a record of Müntzer's attendance here in a note by Spalatin, on the 'Conversation between Master Wolfgang Stein of Zwickau and Thomas'. Strauss, however, was not there in 1522. A meeting with Strauss, who was something of a firebrand himself, took place in Weimar in August 1524, but on that occasion the Franciscans were not involved. Müntzer's confession thus seems to fuse two quite separate events, intentionally or not, as with the case of the mysterious youthful plot in Halle, mentioned earlier.

According to Spalatin's report of the Weimar meeting, Müntzer had again expounded on the necessity of suffering to come to faith, and on the source of knowledge in the 'spirit'.[25] Without mincing his words, Müntzer attacked Luther: 'Ha! My friend,' he is reported to have said, 'I shit on your Scripture and Bible and Christ unless you have the knowledge and spirit of God. He [Müntzer] thinks and speaks badly of the Wittenbergers, calling Dr Martin Luther, Dr Karlstadt, Phil. Mel[anchthon] and Dr Lang all doltish.' From what we know of Müntzer in his 'Prague Manifesto' and in later published works, the direct and unrefined language bears the stamp of authenticity. (Neither Luther nor Müntzer beat about the bush when it came to insults. Scatological language was perfectly normal; Luther was a master of it.) After that episode, there cannot have been much left to discuss. Whether Spalatin's record is accurate cannot now be determined.

Included in Müntzer's alleged pantheon of dolts was Karlstadt. By May it was clear that Karlstadt was out in the cold as far as Luther was concerned, and it seems inconceivable that this news had not reached Müntzer by the autumn, when the Weimar disputation took place. Perhaps Müntzer had made an approach to Karlstadt in the summer, but had received no reply – and perhaps there was no reply because Karlstadt did not wish to undermine his own position further by contacting another known dissenter. Müntzer and Karlstadt shared many ideas in common at that time – both promoted 'inner revelation' as a source of faith, although Karlstadt came out more strongly than Müntzer for a radical reform of the sacraments and other religious practices. However, on 21 December, Karlstadt did write to Müntzer, who by then was in Halle, mentioning 'your letters' which indicated that 'you are swimming in stormy waters' (these were letters, now lost, Müntzer had recently written to him, probably enquiring after employment).[26] Karlstadt also chastised him for cursing and for being arrogant. While urging caution and humility, however, Karlstadt pronounced himself 'greatly pleased that certain actions displeased the people of Zwickau' but also gratified that Müntzer had distanced himself from Storch. He now issued an open invitation for Müntzer to come and visit him in Wittenberg, and thereafter 'to my new home which I have acquired in the country. I think and hope that you will not regret taking the trouble.' Karlstadt had just acquired a small farm at Wörlitz, not far from Wittenberg. Müntzer may indeed have paid a flying visit to Karlstadt for a morning's discussion on 24 December, but the evidence is circumstantial, and the chances are slim that Müntzer – who was no country boy – made a special journey in mid-winter with the prospect of staying on a farm.

In any case, the day before Karlstadt's letter was written, Müntzer had taken up a post as chaplain at St Georg's church, attached to a nunnery in the Halle suburb of Glaucha. The previous chaplain had been so taken with the continuing reforms that he had in short order resigned his post, got married and hurried off with his new wife to Wittenberg. In Halle, Müntzer is reported to have given communion in the Utraquist fashion to a rich widow of reform persuasion, Felicitas von Selmenitz; it was probably this lady who had arranged for Müntzer's appointment. His salaried activity in the town was restricted to conducting various divine services. His more private and personal religious crusade was continued among a small circle of friends, embracing such men as the goldsmith Hans Huiuff, who later joined the Swiss Anabaptist Conrad Grebel, and other lesser-known radicals who were later caught up in the central German Anabaptist movement. Another follower was one Engelhardt Mohr, who later wrote on 31 March 1523: 'you led your life with us, dear Thomas, and you explained the various hidden inspirations of God in the inmost part of men and such that you led me from suffering . . . I ask that you explain to me about the Eucharist . . . [since] all the little priests just prattle away . . . and buy themselves a comfortable perch on the dung-heap.'[27]

But luck was not on Müntzer's side. Although he kept a low profile in Halle, on 27 January 1523 a riotous assembly of 400 reform-minded townsfolk stormed the nearby monastery at Neuwerk. Our Thomas was probably not involved, but the town council, in relentless pursuit of justice, discovered him. Events took their almost inevitable course, and towards the middle of March Müntzer was expelled from town. Apart from anything else, this new blow left him virtually destitute, in possession of two guilders, one of which was owed, the other of which was given to his servant and companion Ambrosius Emmen, who had accompanied him for these past several months. But Müntzer managed to rationalise his situation. On 19 March, he wrote to his supporters back in Halle:

I beg you not to be angered by my expulsion, for the abyss of the soul is emptied in such assaults, so that it becomes even clearer and recognises how to drink from the inexhaustible witness of the Holy Spirit. No one can find God's mercy without being forsaken . . . So let my suffering be an example for yours. Let all weeds blossom as only they can, for they must come under the flail along with the wheat; the living God is sharpening his scythe in me so that later I may cut down the red poppies and blue cornflowers.[28]

Nothing that Müntzer had experienced during this year and more of wandering had in any way shaken his self-belief. If any-thing, his confidence had been strengthened. He had suffered, he was of the Elect, and God would wreak vengeance on his persecutors. His concern in this letter was to raise an immediate experience to the level of theological theory, and not to engage in petty polemic.

Despite which, he stood once more expelled, penniless and homeless.

6

Satan Made Himself
a Nest in Allstedt

A Fruitful Year of Activity
in Allstedt (1523–1524)

*Satan set himself down in Your Highness' principality and made
himself a nest in Allstedt, and now thinks that he can attack us
from under the shield of our peaceful protection.*

Martin Luther (1524)

U p until this point in his life there had been very little to
indicate that Müntzer might be worthy of independent study. He had as yet achieved nothing to warrant
special consideration, significantly less than Luther, Karlstadt or
Melanchthon, or a host of other contemporaries. His activities
in Jüterbog and Zwickau were impressive, but not enough to
generate more than passing interest. His brief flash of brilliance
in the 'Prague Manifesto' had barely reached an audience in
Bohemia, let alone Germany. His several clerical appointments
dotted about Saxony had all ended in failure, in so far as he had
always been obliged to abandon them. But he had learned from
his failures – and not simply that the Elect must suffer. More
importantly, he had begun to learn new tactics, in particular how
to bring people over to his way of thought and how to establish small networks of friends and supporters. These new skills
proved very useful.

❧

Just two weeks after his expulsion from Halle, Müntzer was firmly installed in the pulpit at the Johanniskirche in the small Saxon town of Allstedt. It was his patroness in Halle, Felicitas von Selmenitz, whom he had to thank for this. Her late husband, Wolf von Selmenitz, was the respected electoral official of All-stedt until his retirement in 1513, and his widow evidently still retained some influence in the town. With this new move began an extraordinarily rich and fulfilling period for the reformer.

Müntzer's stay in Allstedt during the years 1523 and 1524 was to prove one of the two great periods of success for the 'radical Reformation' in central Germany before 1525 – the other coming in the winter of 1521/2 in Wittenberg under Karlstadt. In his seventeen months in Allstedt, Müntzer implemented practical Church reform; he exchanged numerous letters with like-minded colleagues all over Saxony; he introduced reformed evangeli-cal Masses and liturgy; he composed, printed and re-printed a number of powerful pamphlets outlining his doctrines; and he participated in political activities aimed at hastening the intro-duction of God's kingdom on earth. Much has been written about this period, and Müntzer's activities during it are – as a pleasant change for reader and biographer alike – quite well documented. One area where much critical discussion is still aroused is in the interpretation of Müntzer's motives in this activity – which peaked in the summer of 1524 – and for that reason we will initially look at his writings and examine his own interpretation of the events, before we move on to the events themselves.

The driving force behind Müntzer's actions was his convic-tion that he personally was continuing the work of Jesus and the Apostles and 'all the Elect'. This motivation was now being explicitly stated in a number of his pamphlets and letters. But fuelling this system of ideas was the gathering storm of social and political crises whose rumblings were felt several times in Allstedt during these months. Subtle changes of emphasis crept into Müntzer's basic theories as a direct result of these external events, and some of his ideas were forced out of the realm of religious doctrine into the arena of political action. The culmina-tion of this process is to be found in his famous 'Sermon to the

Princes' of July 1524, in which theology combined with political demands to create a powerful programme for radical action.

The Saxon town of Allstedt lies about fifty kilometres west of Halle, and when Müntzer arrived in 1523 it was neither large nor important. Its population at this time is estimated to have been somewhere between 600 and 900 souls. It was just a sleepy market town, with two churches which provided for the spiritual needs of the townspeople and those living in the half-dozen surrounding villages. There was no concentration of manufacturing activity, nor, consequently, was there any of that burgher culture apparent in other, larger towns. Neither was there any monastic institution in the town – although a good twenty nunneries were scattered within a thirty-kilometre radius. As a result, Allstedt remained something of a peaceful backwater.

Allstedt was one of those tiny 'exclaves' of a much larger territory some distance away; it was a small patch belonging to the Ernestine branch of the nobles of Saxony, surrounded by extensive lands governed by the Count of Mansfeld and by the Archbishop of Magdeburg. Since both of the latter held resolutely to the Papal Church, while the elector of Saxony inclined strongly to reform, it was an interesting geographical anomaly. Despite it being a small place, there was quite a large castle up on the hill, used infrequently by the Saxon princes. Duke Johann also had one of the two Allstedt churches in his gift – the Johanniskirche, to which Müntzer now came. That no one apparently asked the prince for permission to make this appointment highlights the spirit of independence on the town council.

The peasants in the locality had until this point been unaffected by the restlessness of their brothers to the south and west in the intermittent flashes of revolt before 1525. Much of Müntzer's support in the town came from the artisans and townspeople. The incumbent preacher of Allstedt's other church, St Wigberti's, was Simon Haferitz, an ex-monk and so far unexceptional priest tentatively looking towards Wittenberg. The pulpit here was supposedly in the gift of one of the local nunneries, but not much attention was paid to that formality either, when Haferitz was appointed to the post.

It was, however, precisely this seeming calmness which led to the intense excitement that gripped the townspeople in 1523. Nothing had changed for decades; the surrounding country was governed by a nobility stolidly of the old faith, or by the Papal Church itself; the reform-minded Saxon princes were notable by their absence. This ensured that there were no precedents when reform-fever finally hit town. Most of the force of reform in Allstedt was directed against the more manifest abuses in the Church, with no safety valve: the Catholic nobility was easily wound up into adopting an uncompromising stance which did them no good at all. To make matters worse, Wittenberg had no eyes and ears on the ground here, so Luther was largely unaware of any attempts for or against reform in Allstedt – unaware, that is, until Müntzer began to make waves.

Müntzer's first actions on becoming established in a permanent post at the Johanniskirche were a little out of the ordinary. From the very start, he began a major reform of the services and Masses conducted there. In the same way as Karlstadt had reformed the divine offices in Wittenberg over a year earlier, so Müntzer began a thoroughgoing reform of the public celebration of Mass in Allstedt. It might seem unexpected that Müntzer should suddenly launch into this kind of activity; there had been no real sign of it before March 1523, even though we have handwritten fragments of liturgies from earlier days. There was nothing to indicate such a turn in the 'Prague Manifesto', nor in any of Müntzer's letters from 1522. It is not only unexpected, but, to the modern lay mind, perhaps also slightly unwelcome: liturgical matters are an arcane irrelevance to most lives these days. Why should we now spend time looking at them?

The answer is quite simply this: that church services constituted the one forum in which the main body of the populace encountered theological ideas. Academic debate on the rights and wrongs of 'good works', or the provenance of belief, would pass far above the heads of uneducated people, but participating in church services had some immediate bearing on their lives. It was the sole occasion on which any message concerning the works of God might be transmitted. Up until the 1520s it would have been impossible to exploit such an opportunity for education, because much of the business of celebration was conducted in Latin, or in whatever might pass for Latin in the mouth of some half-educated cleric. The sacraments and rites were simply so much necessary magic, and incomprehensible to the people. In the preceding centuries, the divine office had fallen into disrepute: the services were often incomplete or garbled; the priests themselves often ignorant or untrained, sometimes illiterate; the congregation had long since given up any pretence at worship, to the extent that pet dogs roamed the church during services while their owners gossiped; the priests had adopted the practice of charging for special (optional or votive) Masses, a practice which occasionally spread to even the standard ones. The magical powers ascribed to Mass included relief from punishment for sin, improvement of the digestive system, increasing the longevity of the lives of the congregation, and easing the labour of pregnant women. Local variations on these benefits abounded, as did other superstitions relating to life, death and torment. (There was a popular belief that, on Sundays, the dead in purgatory could sleep in peace, but that as soon as the living returned to work on Monday, the torment of the dead recommenced. It therefore became a sin to go to work too early on Monday – an attractive thought.) By the fifteenth century, things had got so out of hand that German bishops were obliged to issue official instructions to reduce the number and importance of votive Masses; some even went so far as to introduce minor reforms, although without much success. For ordinary people, by the start of the sixteenth century, the divine office in Germany hovered somewhere between a mystery and a burden. Thus, to reform the Mass in such a way that the congregation actually participated and understood what was going on would be a major breakthrough.

It should be understood, then, that these reforms constituted the gearing mechanism between Müntzer's revolutionary theology and the forces of social revolution. And if nothing else, the reaction of the civil authority to his reforms should alert us to their importance. When Müntzer introduced his reforms, Luther had long since rolled back the earlier changes to church services championed by Karlstadt. The Latin Mass had been reintroduced to Wittenberg in 1522, and in 1523 Luther was defending the use of Latin and the retention of old practices, mostly for fear of upsetting Friedrich of Saxony.[1] It was not until 1526 that Luther finally published his own German Mass, and even then he was still promoting Latin on the grounds that it educated young people in the Classics. Indeed, in 1528, Luther actually reintroduced the Latin litany for a while, in place of his own German one. Müntzer's reforms, however, were introduced as early as April 1523, and appeared in printed form at the end of that year. His changes revolved around, firstly, the exclusive use of German instead of Latin and, secondly, his own translations of scriptural texts to carry his unique message. The tactic was both simple and blindingly obvious.

Why did he choose to begin his campaign in Allstedt in this manner? Obviously he wanted to re-educate the people, as was hinted at in the 'Prague Manifesto'. But Müntzer was quite clear about his intentions. The very title of his first liturgical work was

> a German Church Office, composed in order to raise the treacherous cover under which the light of the world was concealed, and which now shines forth with these songs of praise and godly psalms to teach the growing force of Christianity according to God's unalterable will and bring about the downfall of the lavish mimicry of the Godless.[2]

And that was just the title. This statement of aims is further developed in the preface:

> It can no longer be tolerated that men attribute some power to Latin words, as if they were the words of magicians, nor that the poor people should leave the church even more ignorant than when they entered . . . So I have brought improvement in a German way and in German form, and translated the psalms more according to their meaning than their words, in the undeniable mystery of the Holy Spirit.[3]

In the autumn of 1523, Müntzer published a longer explanatory tract on the liturgical reform in his pamphlet *Order and Account of the German Church Service in Allstedt*, which became his most sought-after publication, being reprinted twice in 1523 and again in 1525.[4] Here, he presented the reforms as an educational tool, both in the purely formal aspect of liturgy – the communal singing of psalms and hymns – and in its content, with the recommendation that:

> We must always read an entire chapter of an Epistle or a Gospel, instead of just scraps here and there, so that the people get to know the holy scriptures; indeed, the superstitious ceremonies or dumb-shows will become useless through the continual hearing of God's word.[5]

The reforms, then, were intended to educate the populace after centuries of being kept in ignorance by the clergy, and they would lead the people to true belief. The means by which this was to be achieved was the German language; for the same reasons, Luther had already translated the New Testament in 1522, and was then engaged in working his way through a translation of the Old. Müntzer judged that the use of Latin was no longer to be tolerated, since, as he explained in this pamphlet, 'it is the task of a servant of God to conduct the divine office publicly, and not to mumble it like some hocus-pocus, but rather so that it will enlighten and educate the whole community'.[6]

A closer examination of the German text of the liturgy shows how this bringing of the 'poor in spirit' closer to the ways of God was to be achieved. Much of the liturgy was based on the local 'missal' (a book containing all the instructions for Mass, ceremonies, etc., throughout the Church year), the *Breviarium Halberstadtiensis*, which was widely used in both Halle and Allstedt. The music was in the very simple Gregorian style, and might well have been composed by Müntzer himself, working from existing melodies. What was finally published under the title of *German Church Office* contained the five main offices of the Church year: Passion-tide, Easter, Whitsun, Advent and Christmas. But the intention, later explained, was for these five to become models for the remaining forty-seven weeks of the year, in the course of which 'the whole Bible will be sung instead of read out'.[7] Thus, in a full year, much of the Bible itself should become familiar to regular churchgoers, and the process of their education begin.

In the structure of the *German Church Office*, Müntzer introduced no startling deviations from the traditional form of service. The sequence of worship follows the orthodox sequence of the three offices of Matins, Lauds and Vespers, and the music and texts themselves are drawn from a specific set of known sources. The only changes introduced to the form were aimed at reducing the length of the services. However, Müntzer's use of Gregorian music has caused a fair amount of heated debate among historians. Luther, too, was enraged by it. Some claim that Müntzer's choice of music meant that none of his parishioners could possibly sing along; others that it indicates Müntzer was, underneath his revolutionary gloss, profoundly conservative. But the simplest reason of all for choosing the Gregorian mode was that this was exactly what the parishioners were used to hearing. The participation of the congregation in some of the more complex arrangements was not, to be sure, indicated in the text for the *German Church Office*, but the hymns and psalms would have been well within their capabilities. And, for once, the parishioners would actually be participating and understanding the words, not just looking on and thinking of their Sunday dinner. By providing a highly familiar vehicle for the new texts, Müntzer was able to make the transition to the new doctrine as painless and uncontroversial as possible.

Müntzer's liturgical work, in both the *German Church Office* and his later *German Evangelical Mass*, possesses a powerful artistic force. It has even been convincingly argued that his psalms and hymns influenced Luther, and forced the latter into his hymn-writing activity of 1523 and 1524.[8] But there is no doubt that Müntzer's reforms of divine service were among the first attempts to break away from the Latin and Papal Mass of the late Middle Ages.

If the structure of Müntzer's new liturgy was already familiar to his audience, for most of them the content would have been completely new, since they had no real knowledge of the Latin original. Here the strength of his translations becomes important, for this is the point at which he could exercise full control over the education of his parishioners. And some of the translations are quite revealing; as an example, look at the accompanying translation of Psalm 140, verses 9 to 14, and compare it to Luther's version (here translated into English) and, for reference, the 'standard' King James text – which, to be quite clear – is not necessarily authoritative.

Luther's version	Müntzer's version	King James version
Lord, do not let the godless have their desire; do not strengthen their wantonness; they wish to overcome it.	O Lord, do not let the godless have their way, for their misdeeds blind the whole world, over whom they have set themselves in honour.	Grant not, O Lord, the desires of the wicked: further not his wicked device; *lest* they exalt themselves. Selah.
The misfortune which my enemies encourage shall fall upon their heads.	When I sit with them at table, then I am forced to eat in their godless manner.	*As for* the head of those that compass me about, let the mischief of their own lips cover them.
He will pour a blinding light upon them; he will smite them so deep into the pit with fire, that they will never raise themselves up again.	O God, give them the temptation of faith, test them like red gold in the glowing coals, then they must fall into a ditch from which no one can help them.	Let burning coals fall upon them: let them be cast into the fire; into deep pits, that they rise not up again.
An evil mouth will have no good fortune upon Earth; a sinful and evil person will be chased away and destroyed.	The untested man who chatters merrily of God will find no blessings in his demise.	Let not an evil speaker be established in the earth: evil shall hunt the violent man to overthrow *him*.
For I know that the Lord will champion the miserable and give justice to the poor.	God nurtures the cause of the needy and impartially judges the poor.	I know that the Lord will maintain the cause of the afflicted, *and* the right of the poor.
And the righteous will praise your name, and the pious will remain forever in your sight.	The Elect seek only the name of God and the righteous do not fear His face.[9]	Surely the righteous shall give thanks unto thy name: the upright shall dwell in thy presence.

Müntzer's translation really was 'according to the meaning of the words' – i.e. a free reinterpretation – and clearly reflected his theological concerns. While much of his liturgy contains non-contentious translations, time and time again it startles in both vocabulary and symbolism. The Elect, for example, figure prominently in the texts: verse 2 of Psalm 93 is rendered as: 'Because you are a changeless God, you have brought the Elect to your throne',[10] which bears barely even a passing resemblance to the original ('Thy throne is established of old; thou art from everlasting'). But this is a valid translation if we remember that Müntzer's fundamental doctrine was that the scriptures were not sacred texts where 'the word' was fixed for all eternity, but simply historical reports of past events – events of spiritual significance which were still happening to the contemporary Elect. The translation 'Elect' (*ausserwelten*) covers a variety of Latin originals, including the words for 'saint', 'the people', 'pious', 'the soul'. Conversely, the translation 'godless' (*gotlos*) is applied to 'wicked', 'heathen' and other enemies of God. It is quite clear from any study of these liturgical texts that Müntzer's translations of the Latin originals take their inspiration from his theology. This established a solid, mutual relationship between God and the Elect, a relationship born of the suffering of the spirit and nurtured by direct spiritual communication, the aim of which was to overcome the godless world of godless men.

The dominant tone of almost all these texts is one of strength through pain, ultimately promising victory over the heathen; this is particularly evident in the offices of the Passion, where the number of references to suffering is quite overwhelming. Even in the Advent and Christmas offices, where you might expect the tone to be one of cheer and festive positivity, there are prayers quite openly calling for the destruction of the godless and the raising up of the poor. It was, indeed, quite extraordinary that the common people of Allstedt and its environs were every week standing up in church and singing songs about the overthrow of the oppressors.

Thus, Müntzer's *German Church Office* was not just one of the first German reformed liturgies, but a liturgy with specifically revolutionary intent. When it was published in its complete form, probably in early 1524, it comprised some 204 pages of both words and music. The printer, Nikolaus Widemar of Eilenburg, must have had some difficulties with it, being a tradesman of very modest means indeed: he was apprenticed to the Lutheran printer Stöckel of Leipzig, of whom it was lamented on occasion that he had no Greek or Hebrew letters (and even lacked Roman capitals). That the apprentice managed to collect a full set of print characters is awesome. Even more so for the 'square' musical notation, which needed to be cut on over 700 separate wooden blocks, a long and fraught exercise in printing craftsmanship. All this would have cost a pretty penny – to the extent that the Allstedt town council had to subsidise the costs. It is obvious from the complexity and length of the text that Müntzer could not have prepared the new liturgy just in his first few months in Allstedt. He must have arrived with the bulk of the completed work in his satchel.

At the same time as he developed his Church Office, Müntzer was also working on a version of the Mass. Both of these new liturgies may have been introduced to the parishioners of Allstedt at around the same time, although the Mass was not printed until the summer of 1524. The Mass was a far simpler rite, comprising twenty-four short sections for each of the five principal annual festivals, while the Office was almost three times as long, being subdivided into Matins, Lauds and Vespers. The *German Evangelical Mass*, then, was a model for daily use, the *Office* for special occasions. It follows the same format as the standard *Missale Romanum* and the local *Missale Halberstadtiensis*; the translations of the text, although distinctly Müntzerian in places, are generally quite sober. Again, the examples given by Müntzer relate to the five main celebrations of the church year, but are to be used as models for any other Mass. Some of the directives provided in the text are significant; from these we see that Müntzer was determined that the officiating preacher should celebrate with – and not merely in front of – his parishioners: the instructions for the celebration of communion ensured that the preacher was facing the congregation and not, as had hitherto been the case, turned away from them; the sacrament was also to be given 'in both kinds', in the Utraquist manner.

Müntzer's liturgical reforms had a particular durability. In 1533, a church inspection led by the Lutheran Justus Jonas was

One of the elaborately printed pages from Müntzer's *German Church Office* of 1523.

appalled to find in Allstedt that 'the present priest came after Thomas Müntzer, and found that the altar in the church was so placed that he had to stand behind it and turn his face towards the people; we ordered that this altar be changed'; Jonas also demanded that 'all songs which were composed at the time of Thomas Müntzer should be banned forthwith'.[11] Notwithstanding the well-publicised execution and official condemnation of its author, the liturgy for the *German Evangelical Mass* was reprinted in 1525, 1526 and, with some revisions and liberal additions, in several editions up until 1543. During 1524, there were attempts in Nürnberg to reform the liturgy, and several of the resulting texts appear to steal heavily and unashamedly from Müntzer's works. Individual hymns and translations of psalms were lifted verbatim out of the two liturgical works and made appearances in other collections, for example in the 'Salminger' hymnary issued by the Anabaptists in 1537. Incredibly, parts of

Müntzer's Church Office and later Mass were still being used or appearing in print as late as 1612.

In autumn 1523, Müntzer's pamphlet *Order and Account of the German Church Service in Allstedt, recently introduced by the Servants of God* was printed. This explained the rationale behind the introduction of the liturgical reforms, and its title suggested that the reformed church services had been rolled out not only in Müntzer's own church but also in that of Haferitz. The pamphlet makes mention of the various sacraments as they appear in both major liturgies, and describes special offices for baptism, marriage, last rites and burial. Interestingly, adult baptism (or '*ana*-baptism' – baptism again) is not even hinted at here, much less championed. At this time, Müntzer was happy to inject the old traditions and practices with the new blood of the German language. Some further explanation was provided on the significance of certain points in the Office or Mass; for example, when the preacher says 'The Lord be with you' and the congregation replies 'And with your spirit', Müntzer explains as follows: 'This is so that this same needy congregation do not have a godless man as preacher. For anyone who does not have the spirit of Christ is not a child of God, so how can he then know God's work which he has never suffered?'[12]

Similar points are made about the Eucharist, the sermon, the readings and other rites:

> Finally, let no one be astonished that in Allstedt we celebrate the Mass in German ... We are German people in Allstedt and not Italians, and we want to find a way through the turmoil so that we know what to believe ... If only every servant of God had the power to teach his flock so that they might be instructed with psalms and hymns from the Bible.[13]

The continuity of tradition in the form of the local breviaries, the popularity of the liturgical reforms in the summer of 1523, the repressive measures undertaken by all of Müntzer's opponents, the reprinting of parts and whole sections of the liturgical works, and the almost incredible survival of his reforms in Allstedt for eight years after his execution – all these, if nothing else, give the lie to any idea that the liturgies were 'too difficult' for, or irrelevant to, the common people. They also indicate just how important an appreciation of Müntzer's liturgies is for an appreciation of Müntzer himself.

While Müntzer was consolidating his position in Allstedt and setting out his reforms in a very practical manner, far away on the other side of Germany other commotions were in train. The so-called 'Knights Revolt', a last and desperate throw of the dice by the Imperial nobility of Germany to regain their former glory, had begun in the autumn of 1522. A haphazard alliance of knights who were of either a Humanist or Lutheran tendency, led by Ulrich von Hutten and Franz von Sickingen, had resolved to push through social and religious reforms in the hope of shoring up their own position in German society. Sickingen, who made his living by an edifying mixture of banditry, plunder and extortion, alternating with bouts of mercenary service, had already offered refuge to Luther after the Diet of Worms – but Luther was not daft: he opted for the more reliable protection of Friedrich of Saxony. In September 1522, Sickingen and a band of fellow knights declared war on the Archbishop of Trier, a staunch opponent of Luther. The intention was to dispossess the Archbishop and hand over his vast estates to some form of secular and democratic government. They duly laid siege to Trier, near the border with Luxembourg, but no assistance from other Imperial forces was forthcoming. Sickingen's troops were rapidly driven off by the mercenary forces of the Archbishop and his allies. The group disbanded for the winter, and Sickingen retreated to his castle at Landstuhl (in south-west Germany), while Hutten did the only sensible thing and fled to Switzerland. Sickingen's plan to spend winter at home was not such a good one: the lords of the Palatinate and Hesse laid siege, the castle was stormed and Sickingen died of his wounds in May 1523. Thus ended the first military engagement of the German Reformation.

Closer to home, sporadic unrest flared up. While Müntzer, in this period of creativity and development, was embarking on a programme of steady but radical change inside his church, some of his previous comrades were proving less patient. He had last seen the people of Stolberg around Easter 1522, when he preached some sermons there ('provoking', as we recall, 'a most damaging unchristian uproar'). In July 1523, however, a report had reached him that his eager audience in Stolberg, frustrated at the very slow pace of reforms, had taken matters into their own hands. There are no details of what they had got up to, but it probably involved a bit of iconoclasm, chasing monks and clerics through the streets, smashing windows – the traditional sport of the lower classes of Germany. A little unexpectedly, Müntzer now wrote to them advising them to bide their time:

> It is an overweening madness for many of the elect friends of God to imagine that God will alleviate the miseries of Christianity and come swiftly to their aid, because then no one is keen or strives to become poor in spirit through suffering and perseverance . . . There is much to be done if we are to let God rule over us: we must know for certain that our faith does not deceive us, by suffering the effects upon us of the living word; we must know the difference between the work of God and the work of creatures . . .
>
> When we become aware of the power of God passing through us . . . [only] then will the whole circle of the earth be granted to the congregation of the Elect, and a Christian government will be founded which no barrel of gunpowder could ever overthrow.[14]

Müntzer spared no one here: his followers had to steel themselves for suffering and the loss of faith; they had to realise that their own conduct would shape the destiny of the future. Before signing off, he censured them for lust, gluttony and drunkenness, for neglecting the need for pain: 'I am told that . . . when you are in your cups, you spout great words about our cause, but when you are sober, you are frightened poltroons. So improve your lives, dearest brothers, and avoid high-living.' For Müntzer, then, this was not yet the time for public bravado. It was a time for preparing the Elect, building a firm foundation for God's intervention. Until they disciplined themselves, the only thing that was certain was an escalation in the tyranny of their oppressors.

His letter probably did not go down well with the Stolberg comrades. But the importance which Müntzer attached to his intervention can be gauged from the fact that he had it printed almost immediately as *A Sober Epistle to his Brothers in Stolberg, to Avoid Untimely Commotion* – his first foray into publishing. Tellingly, he did not tell them to avoid any other type of commotion, just the untimely kind. Nonetheless, the message was clear: fighting for God's justice was not an easy option.

This letter bears comparison with Luther's similarly titled exhortation of January 1522, *A Sincere Admonition by Martin Luther to all Christians to Guard Against Insurrection and Rebellion*, aimed at Karlstadt, students and iconoclastic monks.[15] Müntzer scolded the brothers of Stolberg for not submitting to the inner suffering which would ultimately allow God to overthrow the tyrants and establish an unassailable Christian government. But for Luther, the matter presented itself quite differently: God would deal with the wicked priests of Rome and establish a reformed Church; the faithful need not intervene. He scolded his followers in Wittenberg for being over-zealous; the best way to convince ordinary people was not by hectoring or bullying them, but by writing and preaching, 'kindly and gently'. Above all, Luther's Christians were not to disobey the secular authorities in an attempt to force through reforms: rebellion and violence are never justified under any circumstances – 'God', he wagged his finger at them, 'has forbidden insurrection.' And if anyone was to suffer, then it was the evildoers under the punishment of God, and not the faithful in acquiring faith.

The ruling class had their own take on Müntzer's reforms. Much of Thuringia was still governed by a nobility loyal to the Papal practices, and the course of the reforms did not run as smoothly as Müntzer would have liked. While – indeed, one should say 'because' – his reformed services aroused great enthusiasm among the people of Allstedt and its surrounding districts, and while these were tolerated and even actively supported by the town council, the feudal authorities were determined to prevent the rise of alternative rites in their jurisdiction. In the summer of 1523, news of the liturgical changes and sermons in the

Ernst von Mansfeld, depicted in pious mood on his tomb (c. 1531).

Johanniskirche had spread over a wide area, and people came each Sunday from neighbouring towns and villages to hear what Müntzer had to say. They even trekked from the mining area of Mansfeld, over twenty kilometres to the north. Some reports speak convincingly of up to 2,000 people flocking to Allstedt. For Count Ernst of Mansfeld, this was a step too far: his miners were known as a surly group of malcontents at the best of times, engaged in strikes and fostering rebellious thoughts; neither did he wish to see his peasantry imbibe dangerous ideas along with new-fangled bread and wine. In that summer he therefore let it be known that no one was to go to Allstedt, and began to organise road-blocks to turn back the weekly pilgrimage.

When news of Ernst's attempted blockades reached Müntzer in September, he was swift to react. He regarded these manoeuvres as an attack on God and preached against the count from the pulpit. On 22 September, he wrote a singular letter to the Mansfeld castle at Heldrungen:

The electoral official and town council of Allstedt have shown me your letter, according to which I am supposed to have called you 'a heretical scoundrel' and 'a curse upon the people'. This is quite true, for I am well aware – indeed, it is common knowledge – that you have strictly forbidden your people with a public proclamation from attending my heretical services and sermons. To this I have said – and I will denounce you before all Christian people – that you have had the insolence to ban the holy gospel, and if (God forbid) you persist in such raging and insane bans, then from today onwards, for as long as my blood still pulses in my veins, I will name you on paper a deranged madman – and not only before all Christendom, but I will also have my books translated into many tongues and scold you before the Turks, the Heathens and the Jews. And you should know that I do not fear you or anyone in the whole world in these great and just matters, for Christ cries 'Woe unto you!' at those who remove the key to the knowledge of God . . . Do not tug, or the old coat will rip the way you don't want . . . If you force me into print, I will deal with you a thousand times worse than Luther did with the Pope.[16]

The letter was signed: 'Thomas Müntzer, a destroyer of the faithless'. (For good measure, Simon Haferitz also wrote to Ernst, advising him not to 'strive against God . . . I will call those people heretics who describe the Holy Gospel as heresy.'[17])

The letter was a quite extraordinary attack on civil authority. Müntzer respected no social differences when it came to defending the word of God. Not content with attacking Ernst himself, he also wrote to Friedrich the Wise, on 4 October. This letter was more respectful – slightly – but the gist was the same, that Christian practices were to be defended against the faithless:

To conduct such a religious service in the church, so that no time is wasted in vain, but instead strengthening the people with psalms and hymns: these are the basic principles of the German Mass . . . But all my speeches and protests counted for nothing, when the well-born Count Ernst of Mansfeld spent the entire summer forbidding his subjects from attending my services, even before the edict of the Emperor had even been published . . . I ask Count Ernst of Mansfeld to appear here along with the ordinaries of the diocese and to prove that my teaching or office is in any way heretical . . . Princes should not terrify the pious. But if that does happen, then the sword will be taken away from them and given to the zealous people to destroy the godless.[18]

Müntzer did not propose to take any of this lying down. He demanded that his enemies prove that what he had been doing was against the laws of the Church, or against the message of the Bible; and he was not going to debate on their home-ground – they had to come to Allstedt. Count Ernst, it goes without saying, did not respond, but he did complain bitterly to Friedrich. Friedrich's only real reply to all this came in a letter he wrote to the count in early October in which he promised to investigate, and suggested that Müntzer would agree to abide by the Imperial mandate. As such a suggestion is indicated nowhere else, we can assume that this was Friedrich's somewhat insouciant interpreta-tion of the episode. Given what Müntzer had just written to him about the 'sword of the princes', his attitude was perhaps a little too relaxed; he did wonder idly who had appointed Müntzer to the pulpit in Allstedt, but did not follow up the thought. Müntzer had won the first round.

The Imperial mandate mentioned by Müntzer and Friedrich was issued in Nürnberg in March 1523, after a months-long discussion on the crisis in the German Church. It was a very temporary agreement by which the status quo was to be strictly maintained until the Papal authorities had taken a decision on the reforms in Germany: any church or town not yet reformed was not to be reformed, while any church or town so far reformed was to be allowed to retain its new rites. Additionally, in a futile attempt to prevent the mass exodus from cloister and church, priests were forbidden to marry, and monks and nuns forbidden to leave their cloisters; the proverbial stable-doors were, however, not mentioned. (By July, Müntzer had neatly managed to defy this Imperial instruction to the full by also marrying a runaway nun.) The mandate was issued in March, but only published in Saxony in May; Count Ernst had begun his campaign almost as soon as Müntzer had begun his reforms. So, in theory, Mansfeld was within his rights. Müntzer begged to differ.

What did Luther think? One year later, in his diatribe against Wittenberg in the pamphlet *Highly Provoked Vindication and Reply*, Müntzer charged Luther himself with complicity in Count Ernst's actions:

> The truth is quite simply ... that all the roads were full of people from many places, who came to hear how the Allstedt Office permitted the singing and preaching of the scriptures. And even if he [Luther] were to burst, he could not do this in Wittenberg ... which irked him so much that he persuaded his princes to prevent my Office from being printed. But when the Wittenberg Pope's edict was not heeded, he thought: 'Ho! I will arrange it so that the pilgrimage will be broken up.'[19]

While we know that Luther was no friend of Müntzer's reforms, there is no evidence to suggest that Müntzer's accusations here were true. But they cannot be rejected as entirely unlikely, given Luther's history of dealing with his opponents.

There are two ironical twists to this whole episode. In 1525, Count Ernst asked the composer Christoph Flurheym to compile a 'first popular missal', a German version of the Roman Mass, which was duly published in Leipzig in 1529, and hailed as a major attempt at modernisation by the Catholic Church. Was the idea suggested to Ernst by Müntzer's obvious success? In 1525 again, when Müntzer's liturgies were reprinted in Erfurt (Müntzer by then being dead), Luther gave them his approval – in total ignorance of their origins.[20]

The new technology of printing using moveable type became one of the sharpest weapons in the armoury of the German reformers.[21] Even if the vast majority of the population could not read, far less afford to buy even a modest number of books, if you wanted to get the message out into the world in the six-teenth century then you needed ready access to a printer. Which is precisely what Müntzer set about securing in the summer of 1523.

Between July 1523 and August 1524, Müntzer arranged the printing of no fewer than six documents, ranging in length from four pages to over 200. His printer, as we have noted, was Nikolaus Widemar, apprentice to Stöckel of Leipzig. In 1522, after Duke Georg placed a ban on the printing of Lutheran works in Leipzig by Stöckel, the latter promptly moved this part of his business to Eilenburg and placed it under the supervision of Widemar. Eilenburg lies some eighty kilometres to the east of Allstedt; between the two towns lie the cities of Halle and Leipzig; most importantly for Stöckel, Eilenburg lay in Ernestine Saxony, out of Duke Georg's reach. Widemar's printing establishment was hardly convenient for Müntzer. But it might well have been all he could get at the time. On the other hand, having a printer so far away may have helped to obscure the source of pamphlets which did not always meet with approval in government or ecclesiastical circles. The Eilenburg print shop was unquestionably busy: in its eighteen months of existence, some thirty pamphlets of varying length were printed, all of the reforming tendency – including titles by Luther, Melanchthon, Hans Sachs and others.[22]

Widemar was perfectly competent as a printer, as is clear from the products themselves. Several of them bear a frontispiece containing the Allstedt coat of arms, in recognition of the town council's financial support. At some point in the early summer of 1524, however, Widemar's works closed down; perhaps Stöckel was finding the arrangement too awkward for his business model. By then Müntzer had already sent his manuscript of the *German Evangelical Mass* to Eilenburg, and some of the typesetting had already been done. Müntzer took this closure in his stride: he arranged for everything – the galleys for the text and the wooden blocks with the musical notation – to be brought back to Allstedt, where a basic printing press was hurriedly set up and the printing completed by the end of the summer. This was no mean task. Further use was made of this new arrangement in July 1524, when Müntzer's next publication, the so-called 'Sermon to the Princes', was also printed in Allstedt.

∾

By the early autumn of 1523, for once, all was going well for Müntzer. He was confident of the success of his reforms. Yes, there had been a stand-off with Mansfeld, but in Allstedt no one had complained, and, as in Zwickau, Müntzer found support among the ordinary people and ready allies among the members of the town council – and even in the local representative of the Saxon authorities, the electoral official Hans Zeiss. His relationship with Zeiss, who was patently open-minded on the subject of religious reform, was relatively friendly. Müntzer exchanged several letters with him, debating some of the finer points of religion.

In these early years of the Reformation, the inhabitants of monasteries and nunneries were abandoning their institutions in numbers. Some of the monks threw in their lot with the Wittenberg movement and became preachers or teachers; others more radically inclined wandered the land, causing trouble with their ad hoc sermons and agitation. For nuns, the options were more limited. Some ended up marrying ex-monks or other reformed preachers. One such was Ottilie von Gersen, who was possibly of noble birth, and may have been one of a group of sixteen nuns who deserted the Dominican nunnery at Wiederstedt – a tiny place about thirty kilometres north of Allstedt. Escaping from a nunnery was a fraught affair, since it was a punishable offence. Eleven of this group sought protection with Zeiss in Allstedt, while the other five were taken in by Count Albrecht of Mansfeld (Ernst's brother, but a supporter of reform). In 1523, possibly in April – the date is very uncertain – Ottilie married Thomas Müntzer. Unfortunately, beyond this, we know very little else about her. As a woman, and then as the wife of a bloodthirsty radical, she herself was never going to be the subject of any biographical study written in the sixteenth century, when the facts might still have been available. And Müntzer unhelpfully told us nothing whatsoever about her.

Ottilie only appears three times in the historical record thereafter – once when she bore a son in Allstedt the following year; later when she was identified among a party of women disrupting prayers in a convent; and finally when she begged for charity from the authorities after her husband had been executed. It is not at all unusual for women of the time – either singly or in groups – to be completely ignored in the historiography of the male-dominated Reformation. And historians are not much helped by the attitude of the husbands and partners of those women. Müntzer himself, like many of the leaders of the German Reformation, was rather ambivalent towards relations with the opposite sex. At least before his marriage, in the heady days of early 1522 when reformed preachers were busily marrying, Müntzer wrote to Melanchthon to issue an acutely embarrassing condemnation of the new fashion of priestly matrimony; he described it as 'a Satanic brothel', since it prevented men from receiving the living word of God; further, that 'we should make use of wives as if we did not have them' – a quotation from the First Book of Corinthians on the question of devotion to the cause. It is not entirely clear what Müntzer meant by all this; but surely, on any interpretation, his was not a modern view.[23] Oddly, though, he begins this same letter by commending the fact that priests are marrying, as they thereby avoided the hypocrisy of living in sin with, say, a housekeeper. Later, in July 1523, around the time that he himself married Ottilie, he wrote to Karlstadt – one of those men whose marriage had prompted Müntzer's tirade against the 'Satanic brothel' – and signed off his letter by offering greetings to Karlstadt's wife. But even as late as the summer of 1524, Müntzer was prepared to chide Johann Lang for his recent marriage to a rich widow; Lang, he thought, had been 'swept away by passion' and was in danger of neglecting his calling as a preacher.[24] It is not entirely clear why Müntzer, now a married man and preacher himself, had so taken against Lang's marriage – but it may well have been precisely because the new Frau Lang was a rich widow; he returned to the theme later, in a general condemnation of priests who 'woo old ladies with great wealth'.[25] Another consideration, of course, is that Müntzer and Lang had history, arising from events in Erfurt in 1522 when Lang allegedly had a hand in Müntzer's expulsion from the town.

Müntzer's attitudes to matrimony in general, and the marriage of priests in particular, as well as his decidedly old-fashioned views on sex, are of interest since they shed a sideways light on his otherwise good relationships with women. It is almost as if, while he objected to sex and marriage on principle, in his own specific case he was quite happy with both; there is an undeniable measure of hypocrisy in all this. However, by late 1523 he and Ottilie had quite the regular household in Allstedt, since Ambrosius Emmen, his long-suffering 'servant', also lived with them. Emmen's duties included that of secretary – some surviving notes for Müntzer's sermons are written in his hand.

In this atmosphere of continuing success, Müntzer decided to approach Wittenberg again. On 9 July 1523, he wrote a letter to Luther, describing Allstedt as 'a calm refuge'.[26] Now he wrote not as a renegade seeking forgiveness or a pupil seeking approval, but rather as an equal seeking dialogue. However, he was anxious to clear the record and to give the true facts about past activities. Addressing 'the most sincere father among many', he defended himself against 'the most pestilential Egranus' and all his other enemies in Zwickau (here is that pleasing story about having been in the bath at the time of the final riot) and proclaimed that he had 'made strong walls for the glory of the name of God'. He advised Luther not to be influenced by rumours, and not to think badly of those who experienced 'living' revelation.

> I recognise the divine will by which we are filled, through Christ, with knowledge and infallible spiritual wisdom . . . No mortal knows the doctrine of Christ . . . unless previously the floods have lifted him up . . . and they are uprooted anew in pain by the hoarse roaring of wild beasts . . . One may rely with great certainty on divine revelation to distinguish the work of God from that of evil spirits . . . Dearest protector, you know Thomas by sight and by name, I do not counterfeit either visions or dreams; unless God gives them to me, I do not believe them unless I see their work.

(One of the problems facing those who regarded dreams, or visions, or strange events, as messages from God was the simple counter-argument: that they could just as well be messages from the Devil. It was a tough position to defend. Luther himself had faced deep and continuing doubts when he explained his decision, after a violent thunderstorm, to become a monk: was the storm really a sign from God, or was it a trick of Satan?)

The letter finished with greetings to Melanchthon, Karlstadt, Lang and Agricola, and the hope that Müntzer and Luther might 'proceed together on the road of affection'. But such a hope was far removed from reality. It was clear that Müntzer had no intention of throwing away his principles in some alliance with the movement which, fifteen months previously, he had condemned for relying exclusively on book-learning and objectified belief. And Luther, for his part, had long since passed any point which might induce him even to tolerate Müntzer. The latter had evidently not yet heard that Karlstadt had renounced his academic titles and retired to Orlamünde in April 1523, there to reform the Mass and adopt – by necessity – a simpler rural lifestyle as a farmer/preacher, even allegedly preaching while dressed in a peasant's smock. He was no longer a colleague of Luther. But the news did eventually filter through to Allstedt: at the end of July, Müntzer wrote to Karlstadt, addressing his letter to 'Andreas Karlstadt, farmer at Wörlitz'; he went on to complain about the lack of communication and announced that he was sending a certain Nikolaus to bring news from Allstedt: 'Believe this man. He is sincere in God's spirit.'[27] This news was probably related to the unilateral decision of the townspeople of Allstedt to withhold the tithe from the Cistercians at Naundorf; Karlstadt's 'Wittenberg Ordinance' had proposed something similar in a reform of Church finances. Of the identity of this envoy, nothing is known – it could have been the Allstedt magistrate Nickel Rucker (or Rückert); nor is there any record of Müntzer's initiative bearing fruit; indeed, when Karlstadt replied almost a full year later, he was more than a little critical of Müntzer.

The introduction of the new liturgy, as a means of re-educating the people of Allstedt, was a resounding success, but it also stirred up a hornets' nest and brought Müntzer's opponents out into the open. With the summer now over, Müntzer learned that he still needed to fight for his cause. Not only must his supporters be strengthened in questions of theology, but he himself had to be prepared to defend them against attacks. In November, he received a reply to his letter to Luther which served to strengthen his belief in Luther's active opposition. The reply did not come directly. Before Prince Friedrich and his secretary Spalatin stopped off in Allstedt in November 1523, en route to the Imperial Diet at Nürnberg, Luther had provided them with a list of very basic doctrinal questions to pose to Müntzer. A meeting took place at the castle between Müntzer, Haferitz, Spalatin and Johann Lang – the man who allegedly had Müntzer expelled from Erfurt – along with a couple of Count Ernst's representatives. (It seems to have been a productive meeting: expenses were recorded for about 180 litres of wine; a follow-up meeting in March of the following year made inroads into even more. The Allstedt castle accounts show the consumption of two and a half and three and a half *eimer* – literally: buckets or pails – respectively; by Weimar's official standards, each *eimer* contained around seventy litres.)[28]

Luther's eleven questions concerned the nature and provenance of belief, its characteristics and powers. We have no record of how the actual debate might have gone in Allstedt castle. But we do have, almost immediately, another pamphlet from Müntzer's pen. This was the *Protestation or Proposition of Thomas Müntzer of Stolberg in the Harz, now pastor at Allstedt, concerning his doctrine and the beginning of the true Christian belief and of baptism.*[29] This new work was an attack on those who defended the old beliefs, and was written in much the same tenor as the 'Prague Manifesto'. The difference in approach of the two men to the discussion is characteristic – Luther pushed for a very private, and proxy, debate in the castle; Müntzer replied with a full and very public exposition in print. It is a typical Müntzer production, couched in colourful and lively language. It talks of the Elect, it emphasises the necessity of spiritual suffering, and it fiercely attacks the priests who dismiss suffering with a few ignorant words:

> An eager expectation of the word is the first stage in becoming a Christian. This same expectation must first suffer the word and there must be no comfort in being promised eternal forgiveness because of our works. It is then that a person thinks he has no

faith at all. And finally he has to break out and say: 'Oh, how miserable I am, what is going on in my heart? My conscience is devouring my juices and my strength and everything that I am. Oh, what am I supposed to do? I am losing my mind, I have no comfort from either God or creature. God tortures me with my conscience, with disbelief, with despair and I blaspheme against him. Outwardly I am assailed by sickness, poverty, distress and every kind of need, by evil people, etc. And inwardly it is even worse than that.'

And then along come the pious scholars, if ever such dismal folk come at all . . . and get really annoyed that they have to open their mouths, for every word should cost a tidy sum, they say: 'Ha, my dear man, if you cannot believe, then go to the devil!' And then the poor creature replies: 'Oh, most learned doctor, I would really like to believe, but my lack of faith overwhelms all my intentions. What in the world am I supposed to do?' But then the scholar says: 'Well, my dear fellow, you should not bother yourself with such lofty things. All you need do is believe. Put those thoughts away. That is all idle fantasy. Run along home and be cheerful – that's the way to forget all these cares.' See, dear brother, that is the kind of comfort which has prevailed in the Church.

This lengthy and heartfelt denunciation of the 'objectified' belief of the old religious practices – and, by implication, of the Wittenberg flavour of religion – formed the central pillar of the pamphlet. From its tone and almost from the very phrases used, it is identifiably a pamphlet in which the 'Prague Manifesto' came of age, representing the most important work so far of Müntzer's Allstedt period: he now had a clear picture of his readership, and a clearer picture of those who constituted the 'academics'.

Here Müntzer again addresses the perilous situation of 'the poor' – in the sense of the spiritually poor – and castigates the academic theologians for their high-handed neglect of ordinary people:

If we scholars are to pursue such things, then we must make better use of our heads. So the neglectful scholar says: 'Yes, well, if you present such lofty doctrine to the people, then of course they will go mad and lose their senses.' They then say: 'Christ says that one should not cast pearls before swine. What use is such splendidly spiritual teaching to the poor coarse people? That is something only for scholars to know about.' Oh no, no, no, dear sir! St Peter tells you who the fatted pigs are: they are all the disloyal, false scholars, regardless of which sect they belong to, who consider it right to stuff themselves with food and make themselves drunk and who follow all their lusts in high living and gnash their sharp teeth like dogs if anyone says a word against them.

Finally, Müntzer addresses the question of baptism, coming as close here to the doctrine of adult baptism as he ever did. But his concern with baptism is in the context of the academics' lack of comprehension. Baptism, he says, has become 'a bestial mimicry'. Although the academics quote from the Gospel of John, concerning baptism in water, they have not understood that the water is the 'motion of our spirit in God's spirit'. The baptising of uncomprehending children condemns them to perdition. 'Our ignorance about baptism', he concludes, 'arises because we are concerned only with ceremonies and church-rites.'

Müntzer's ideas on baptism flowed naturally from his doctrines on the origins of belief. If belief comes through doubt and despair, and is fed by spiritual experience, then infants cannot possibly be brought into Christianity through external rites. Nor could the practice of allowing godparents to take up the burden of religious supervision be accepted, since this simply implied an external sacrament, shifted in time. While this argument today, like that over the sacrament of wine and bread, may appear a little esoteric, the question of whether the baptised individual should understand her or his baptism is one which leads directly to the central point: the need of the individual to experience true belief, and the freedom of the individual from the rites and ceremonies of the Church.

Müntzer closes his work with an offer of debate – in public, not closeted away 'in a corner without sufficient witnesses, but in the light of day'. Here was a thinly veiled criticism of Luther, whose reaction to Müntzer's approaches was somewhat underhand. In 1524, Luther was again to attempt to persuade

Müntzer to engage in a disputation behind closed doors. But Müntzer was not to be drawn; his belief that the people had to be educated permitted no secrecy. To Luther was addressed this remark: 'he who takes no insult from this should write as a friend, and I will reply to him in full, so that neither can judge the other unjustly'.

The end of 1523 was a busy time for Müntzer – and for his printer. In December, Widemar printed the *Protestation*; in either December or January he also printed a new (third) edition of the *Order and Account* and was finalising the proofs for the *German Church Office* – a task which in itself had taken about four months from start to finish. For good measure, over in St Wigberti's, Simon Haferitz, who had been working closely with Müntzer, also kept Widemar busy by publishing in January his sermon 'On the Three Kings', in which tyrants, the Elect, and dreams featured prominently; it was a booklet which leaned heavily on Müntzer's doctrines and vocabulary.[30]

Over the New Year period, Müntzer contrived to add to Widemar's workload by writing a new pamphlet, entitled *On Fraudulent Faith*. This seems to have been well received, since it was reprinted twice in 1524 and again in 1526. In format, it comprised fourteen paragraphs, and practically every single line has a reference in the margin to some passage of the Bible – perhaps a little ironic, when Müntzer was attempting to move away from reliance on the scriptures.[31] Müntzer builds up his picture of the old, 'counterfeit' belief, contrasting it with the faith of the Elect, which is only attained after much suffering, doubt and torment. The task of a 'righteous preacher', he argued, was to destroy the old belief and prepare people's hearts for God's living word. Müntzer firmly rejects the easy and sweet acceptance of belief:

> My elect brother, just have a good look at all the words in Matthew chapter 16! There you will find that no one can believe in Christ unless he has become formed like him beforehand. In the midst of unbelief, the Elect person will find that he will cast off all the fraudulent faith which he has learned, heard or read

in the scriptures; then he will see that no outward testimony can create anything of essence inside him . . . Therefore he is eager for revelation.

Appended to the pamphlet in its printed form was a letter written to Hans Zeiss in early December 1523, in which Müntzer argued that the suffering of the Elect effectively completed the suffering of Jesus – that the Elect and Jesus were therefore complementary. But here he also explained why he was proposing to present his arguments with so many scriptural references: 'I need to explain the scriptures in all those places where I have not referred to the scriptures . . . otherwise my book will be published without being armed against the weapons of the fleshly academics.'[32]

The year 1523 closed as positively as Müntzer would have wished. He had consolidated his position in the community, and had demonstrated that he had a valuable and positive contribution to make. In carrying out his practical preparations for reform, he had forced his Catholic and Wittenberg opponents to show their hands.

The following year began in similar style. Müntzer spent the early months of the year preparing for print his *German Evangelical Mass*, which, due to the technical complexity of the typesetting, did not see the light of day until August (although it was considerably shorter than his Church Office, running only to eighty-six pages). This work had as uncompromising a title as the earlier liturgy: 'The German Evangelical Mass, which has hitherto been in Latin and used as a sacrifice by the popish priests, to the great detriment of the Christian faith, but is now in these dangerous times reformed to expose the abominable idolatry perpetrated for so long in the abuse of the Mass.'[33]

Müntzer's introduction to his Mass was more hard-hitting than that to his previous liturgy; by now, he had experienced the opposition to his reforms: 'Recently several Offices and songs of praise were published by me', he wrote, 'which have enraged some academics and made them jealous and they have sweated to suppress them.'[34] He condemns 'priests who laze about all week like Junkers and only on Sundays give a sermon', and he makes several thinly concealed attacks on Ernst of Mansfeld and other 'raging tyrants' who tried to prevent the education of the people. And then, evidently in response to the critics of a Wittenberg persuasion, he writes:

> They accuse me of wishing to resurrect and perpetuate the old Popish gestures, masses, matins and vespers, which has never been my wish or intention; but rather I did it to help the poor, miserable, blind consciences of men and to show them in a short version what was once sung and read in Latin in church and cloister by deceitful false priests, monks and nuns.

Luther would set out his position on the Mass clearly a year later, in his long and merciless anti-Karlstadt pamphlet *Against the Heavenly Prophets*.[35] There, Luther stated that he wanted the liturgies to be completely overhauled, in both form and content. But Müntzer argued that the old forms were neither irrelevant nor ill-suited; on the contrary, they were absolutely vital:

> As the evangelical preachers themselves admit that the weak are to be spared . . . so there is no better or more suitable way to be found than by treating the same songs of praise in German, so that people's poor weak consciences are not dragged off on some dizzy spree or satisfied with loose, worthless ditties, but are rather allowed to travel at their own pace, with psalms and hymns changed from the Latin into German, towards the word of God and a correct understanding of the scriptures.

This is an amusing reversal of roles: in early 1522, Luther had forbidden the Wittenberg reform of the Mass for the very reason that the 'weak' were to be spared the pain of rapid change; in 1524 the arch-Satan of Allstedt himself was using precisely the same argument, while Luther was all for change.

By the start of 1524, then, Müntzer had made great advances in the education of the people of Allstedt, and had laid the basis for their further education with his new liturgies, his three pamphlets on doctrine, and a practical and successful reorganisation of public worship. On top of this, he had built up a fruitful relationship with the town council and with the local electoral official. He had even got married. And, for now at least, he had faced down the local rulers. All this, in a hectic twelve months. Truly, for the first time in his life as a reformer, Müntzer must have felt profound satisfaction.

From this position of strength, both external and internal, he progressed to the next stage of his reformation: to directly challenge the social order.

7

His Face Was as Yellow as a Corpse's

Rebellion in Allstedt (1524)

Yes, he stood there before the Princes and Councillors as if struck dumb . . . his face was as yellow as a corpse's and he was in deep despair.

Johann Agricola (1525)

In March 1524, Sophie von Schaffstedt, abbess of the nunnery at Naundorf, was not amused. First of all, the ungrateful people of Allstedt had refused to stump up the annual tithe to which the nunnery had been entitled for centuries. When at length they were forced to pay, they did so with very bad grace, which soured relations even further. And finally, in a truly scandalous act, they turned up one night and burned down a chapel belonging to the nunnery.

How could things have come to this?

At the start of 1524, Müntzer had been settling into a busy life as pastor of Allstedt. He had family, responsibilities and visitors, and at the end of March Ottilie gave birth to their son. Unfortunately, the baby's name and everything else about him is, of course, now unknown. He does not appear in any subsequent records.

A stream of interested visitors arrived throughout the year to see for themselves how the reformed church services at Allstedt were conducted. One such was Martin Seligmann, a curate from Heilbronn, situated some considerable distance to the west. He had evidently been to see Thomas in the early May: 'Only a few days have elapsed since I saw you', he wrote to Müntzer, addressing him as 'a man of admirable and remarkable learning'; Seligmann was concerned that Müntzer and Luther were falling out with each other, and wanted to know how Müntzer had fared in Weimar – this was based on misinformation, however, since although Müntzer had been summoned to Weimar to explain himself before the Saxon authorities, he never actually went.[1] Earlier in the year, another visitor was most likely Georg Amandus (also known as 'the limping preacher'), a dedicated reformer who was later to throw in his lot with rebellious miners in the town of Schneeberg, near Zwickau. Müntzer wrote to 'Jeori' (the familiar version of 'Georg') in March, apologising for not being more attentive during his recent visit:

> After you came to me looking for instruction, I failed to give you any. And that is no wonder, since caring for so many souls keeps me very busy. Do you know, on the very same day as you were here, I had other visitors who occupied my time and I was already quite tired because I had to conduct a church service on the same day.[2]

The pastor had little time for himself; rather wearily, he describes the daily grind to his visitor with an analogy most likely drawn from his new domestic circumstances: 'It is such a labour to deal with people these days, like the work a mother has in cleaning her children after they dirty themselves.' But one thing Müntzer did give his visitor from Schneeberg was instruction on how to conduct the new divine services – Amandus had most probably gone off home with a copy of the *German Church Office* in his bag. 'You must conduct the service every day', Müntzer wrote, 'and read out the laws of the prophets and evangelists, so that the common man becomes as familiar with the texts as the preacher.' Sure enough, by September 1524 Amandus was reported to be campaigning for a reformed German church service in Schneeberg.[3] Throughout that summer, Amandus was mentioned several times in the letters and reports which crossed Duke Georg's desk, and was just as frequently summoned for interview. Perhaps most annoyingly for the duke, the preacher was recommending that 'the people should govern their town council, and a country should govern its prince'.[4] All of which led to enthusiastic demonstrations by the local miners. It was only in July 1525 that Amandus was finally rooted out from his pulpit at Schneeberg.

Hard work and not much pay – that was the lot of a priest in a sixteenth-century church. Hence arose – without wishing to make excuses – some of the inventive ways in which church officials generated extra income from the special Masses and other little services which so upset the reformers; the 'Mass priests' were not the same as the pastoral priests – the latter were slightly better paid, leaving the former to scratch a living as best they could. Perhaps, then, it comes as no surprise that another surviving letter, dated July of that year, was from a bookseller based in Halle, who was hounding Müntzer (ever so politely) for the payment of one florin for a book he had purchased some time before. 'I thought you would have sent me the money by now', he wrote. 'So now I ask you again . . . That is my friendly request.'[5]

On the one hand, the exacting life of a reforming preacher; on the other, the quite extraordinary life of a man battling against the combined might of Church and State. Barely a week before Ottilie's son was born, an event took place just outside Allstedt which was to cause ripples for months to come. This was the affair of the Mallerbach chapel.

The sermons which Müntzer preached during his reformed services included attacks upon the existing Church institutions. Both he and his fellow preacher Haferitz condemned the Cistercian Order which possessed several properties in the area. Already in 1523 the citizens of the town had refused to pay the customary tithe owed to the nearby Cistercian nunnery at Naundorf. This obviously did not go down well with the abbess. She made strong and repeated representations to Duke Johann and Prince Friedrich, and in the end Friedrich ordered the tithe to be paid. And this did not go down well in the town. Such was the spirit of anti-monasticism at the time that swift revenge was taken on the abbess and her nunnery. During the night of 24 March 1524,

the Mallerbach chapel, just outside Allstedt, and a place of pilgrimage in the care of the nunnery, was ransacked and set alight.
There is naturally some confusion about the events – those who
took part could not be expected to give a faithful account. But
contemporary reports tell of a band of men arriving after dark
and advising the elderly watchman to take to his heels. The men
then burned the chapel to the ground.

The abbess immediately complained, and Hans Zeiss as the
duke's local representative was obliged to investigate. A somewhat summary inquiry followed, with Zeiss and the town
officials returning the evasive verdict that 'persons unknown'
had committed the criminal act. The initial report even suggested
rather boldly that it had been agents of the abbess herself who
had torched the place; this was later toned down to the less provocative suggestion that the culprits were probably not citizens
of Allstedt. To add insult to injury, the abbess was accused of
'bringing out sweet words that concealed in them bitter gall,
as every Christian believes'[6] – that is, of bringing a false suit
against Allstedt in order to damage the reform movement.
Relations between the nunnery and the town of Allstedt did
not improve with time. In May 1525, when the peasant unrest
around Naundorf was at its peak, the abbess complained bitterly
that her requests for protection were effectively met with a shrug
of the shoulders from Zeiss, who excused himself with the news
that most of the men of Allstedt were away supporting Müntzer.[7]

It is fairly certain that Müntzer was at least indirectly responsible for the Mallerbach affair. His confession in 1525 stated:
'He was at Mallerbach and saw how several citizens of Allstedt
removed pictures from the church and then burned it down;
and had preached that the chapel was a gin-shop and that an
idol made of wax was not favourable to God.'[8] What credence
can be given to this confession is debatable. It is not improbable
that the arsonists would have tried to save from the fire pictures
which they had probably paid for in the first place. Another
contemporary report suggests that the night-watchman had been
warned of the imminent attack and that the pictures had been
removed to safety beforehand by the Cistercians. Yet the question
of whether Müntzer was at the chapel on that dramatic night is,

Duke Johann of Saxony, painted by Lucas Cranach (1532).

in the wider context, not an urgent one; what mattered was that his sermons had encouraged such iconoclasm, and that he was nevertheless defended to the hilt by the Allstedt town council. If such an event had occurred in Zwickau, or Erfurt or Halle, Müntzer would have found himself, in short order, either outside the gates or delivered into the hands of the authorities.

The Mallerbach affair naturally attracted the attention of the authorities. Duke Johann, unconvinced by the desultory inquiry, summoned Zeiss and the councillors to Weimar on 9 May and instructed them to find the true culprits. Müntzer was also ordered to attend, but the town council seems to have thought it best to leave him at home. (This is the Weimar interview which Seligmann was worried about.) Johann's intervention resulted in a demand that someone be held to account, within fourteen days. Someone, anyone. Disappointingly for the duke, no such scapegoat was found. Spies were evidently sent to Allstedt to determine if more information could be winkled out; all that was reported back were statements alleged to have been made by Müntzer and Haferitz which were not at all complimentary: the former had stated that Friedrich, 'the old grey-beard, that prince, has as much wisdom in his head as I have in my arse'.[9] Perhaps no surprise, then, that shortly afterwards Friedrich was asking his brother Johann to relieve Müntzer of his post. (To be fair, at a later hearing in Weimar in July, Müntzer denied having said any such thing.)

On 14 June, a letter was sent by 'the council and whole parish of Allstedt' to Duke Johann giving their final judgement on the Mallerbach affair. While not in Müntzer's handwriting (it was in that of his secretary, Ambrosius Emmen), the letter was largely his work. The Cistercian nuns were condemned for laying false accusations at Allstedt's door, even after the citizens had faithfully paid them tithes and taxes. The reason for the nuns' infamy, the letter stated, was 'so that they could advance their godless and unchristian cause hatefully and jealously and present it to Your Grace as something good'.[10] The council had clearly not changed their minds about Müntzer; far from it – they now urged the duke to punish the 'criminals and the godless, for the honour and protection of the pious'.

Three days before the letter to Johann, Hans Zeiss and the Allstedt magistrate Nikolaus Rucker found themselves caught in divided loyalties between duke and town. Zeiss, as Johann's representative, realised that he had to do something, otherwise his own position would be in danger. The idea he and Rucker first hit upon was to arrest one of the town councillors, a man named Ciliax Knauth, and accuse him of being the Mallerbach arsonist. But widespread protest inevitably resulted, a highlight of which was the arrival in haste of a deputation of miners from the Mansfeld district – whom Müntzer himself had evidently called to arms – demanding to know whether he, Müntzer, was safe from prosecution.[11] On 14 June, Zeiss decided to try to calm things down. His strategy was not the best: it involved gathering people from the villages outside the town, taking possession of the town hall and forcing the council to arrest those implicated at Mallerbach. But the plan, to be carried out at night, failed dismally. It was leaked to the citizens, the alarm bells were rung, and supporters of both town council and Müntzer appeared on the streets, armed with whatever they could find. Müntzer himself called on women and girls to arm themselves with pitchforks and defend the reforms, and they did so with praiseworthy vigour, also helping to ring the alarm bells. In the excitement, it was proclaimed that one person could strangle a thousand, and two could do away with ten thousand.[12] After several hours of demonstration and negotiation between castle and town, the protest died down. A few days later, Zeiss wrote again to Weimar asking for permission to release the unfortunate Knauth, following it up with a rather lame letter to Friedrich explaining that there was really nothing else he could do, since everyone in Allstedt was still enraged by the conduct of the abbess of Naundorf, and any further action was liable to lead to more popular resentment.

And there the matter rested, for all of a month.

In the middle of July 1524, two things happened almost simultaneously. Firstly, Müntzer preached a sermon in Allstedt castle to Duke Johann and his son Johann Friedrich. The duke was inclined towards Church reform, although in a rather lukewarm fashion; his son was more enthusiastic and was in close contact with Luther. The second event was the harassment of Müntzer's supporters in Sangerhausen, a small town about twelve kilometres north-west of Allstedt, in the territory of the Catholic Duke Georg. This was an incident which was to have major repercussions.

In early July 1524, Duke Johann, his son Johann Friedrich, and an assortment of important courtiers set out on a journey to Halberstadt accompanied by a troop of 200 horsemen – the princes of Saxony liked to put on a good show. On their return south, their noble work done, the princes spent a night at the castle at Allstedt. The next morning, 13 July, before they set off on the next stage of their homeward journey, the group were lectured by the notorious reformer of Allstedt. It has been suggested that the princes invited Müntzer to appear before them, so that Johann could formalise the preacher's appointment to the pulpit of the Johanniskirche; this seems unlikely – both because it was a bit late for that and because Johann tended to let Allstedt get on with its own church administration. Plausibly, Müntzer himself had asked to speak to the princes, in the hope of converting them to his version of the Reformation. Equally likely, the princes simply wanted to see the man for themselves. Not only had there been much mischief afoot in Allstedt, but Müntzer had also set up a print shop in the town, 'hoping to print anything he pleases, notwithstanding that we do not know whether good or bad, and not supervised by any learned or professional person'.[13] Friedrich the Wise had proposed to Duke Johann on 9 July that 'whatever Thomas Müntzer intends to write or print should previously be sent to Your Lordship or myself for examination'. Either way, both sides had much to gain from the occasion.

What Müntzer preached to two of the most powerful men of the region that morning would become one of his most famous texts, the 'Sermon to the Princes' – a work which, with its uncompromising tone, has been rightly celebrated across the centuries. Once delivered orally, it took only a few days for Müntzer to have all twenty-five pages of the text printed on his own press, which was now in Allstedt itself. With the act of printing, the sermon, delivered in private to the 'great and dear dukes and rulers', was shared with the general public. This was entirely in keeping with Müntzer's oft-stated intention of having debates out in the open for everyone to hear. The printed version was probably longer than the spoken one: its 7,500 words would have taken at least an hour to read aloud – would the princes have sat politely for that long?

Its published title was the *Interpretation of the Second Chapter of Daniel, preached at Allstedt Castle before the great and revered dukes and rulers of Saxony*. Müntzer chose as his text the second chapter of the Book of Daniel, the story of that prophet's interpretation of the dream of Nebuchadnezzar. First of all, the chapter was read out in German to the princes, and then the sermon commenced. It is tempting to quote large sections of this sermon to illustrate Müntzer's vigorous and colourful use of vocabulary and the power of his prose; but because of its length we shall restrict ourselves to examining several aspects of the text over and above the now familiar argument for the 'living experience of faith'.[14] These are: firstly, a vision of history and expectation of the millennium; secondly, arguments in favour of dreams and visions as means of communication with God; thirdly, a warning to the worldly authorities that their time as 'tyrants' was coming to an end; and fourthly, a call to action in defence of such reforms as would usher in the millennium, with Müntzer himself willing to accept the unconditional help of the princes.

The dream of Nebuchadnezzar – in which a huge and fearful image appeared, only to be shattered into pieces by a stone from a mountain – is seen by Müntzer to represent the various ages of the history of Man:

> The first is depicted by that great golden bonce on top, that was the empire of Babel; the second is the silver breastplate and arms, that was the kingdom of the Medes and Persians. The third was the empire of the Greeks, which dazzled by its cleverness, depicted by bronze; the fourth, the Roman Empire which was won by the sword and was an empire of oppression. But the fifth is what we now have before us which is also of iron and would like to oppress, but it is also made of muck, as we see, stuck together by that plain hypocrisy which creeps and crawls over the whole earth.

The history of mankind, here, is one of degenerating stages, with the present Holy Roman Empire as the most debased of all, held together by 'the eels and the snakes [which] couple together in one writhing mass. The priests and all evil clerics are snakes . . . the secular lords and rulers are eels.' So far, so uncompromising. But this view of history reveals some interesting aspects of Müntzer's belief. Many intellectuals who had an expectation of the imminent Apocalypse had founded their view of history on that of the twelfth-century Italian theologian Joachim de Fiore. Fiore posited that human history was divided into three ages: the age of the Father – up to the birth of Jesus; that of the Son – up until the Middle Ages; and that of the Holy Spirit – the Golden Age yet to come. But Müntzer's conception completely sidesteps the Joachimite theory. His ages are delineated by actual human history, not by some divine pattern; the birth of Jesus fell smack in the middle of the Roman age, and had no bearing on its course.

In fact, for Müntzer there were but two epochs in history: the first was the slow and steady fall of the human race up until 1524, characterised by woeful ignorance on the part of clerics and the common people: the 'scribes . . . threw away the pure knowledge of God and in its place they have installed a pretty, fine, gilded god . . . [which] is nothing other than a simple idol made of wood. Aye, a wooden idolatrous priest and a coarse, stupid and boorish people incapable of having the slightest recognition of God.' The second epoch would be the millennium, when the 'stone' in the dream shatters the great statue:

> Oh, dear sirs, how splendidly will the Lord shatter the old pots with an iron bar . . . For the stone from the mountain has grown large. The poor laymen and peasants see it much clearer than you . . . Aye, the stone is grown large and is what the foolish world long feared. It overwhelmed the world when it was young; so what shall it now do that it is so great and mighty? So, my dear rulers of Saxony, stand firmly on the corner-stone.

As we shall see, this 'shattering' of the old world was to be assisted by the conscious activity of both the Elect and those whom they could persuade to fight for God. This is no passive expectation of Apocalypse, but a joint venture between the Elect and God.

The 'Sermon to the Princes' also contained Müntzer's most explicit argument in favour of revelation and the power of dreams and visions. One of the more startling features of Daniel's interpretation of Nebuchadnezzar's dream was the fact that the king did not even recount the dream – Daniel shared it in a vision, and then went on to explain it. The role of dreams and visions in the radical reform movement has been indicated earlier; in Müntzer's theology such revelations represent the actual moment of direct and living communication with God, that alternative source of faith which is counterposed to the 'fraudulent faith' of academics and priests. By allocating a major role for such communications, the way is cleared for the equality of all believers before God.

Müntzer, perhaps developing the ideas about revelation he had shared with Storch in Zwickau, now proceeds to adduce all kinds of examples of revelation from the Bible, and on that basis to argue against Luther and for the acceptance of spiritual revelation in the reform movement. (His names for the Lutherans are not complimentary.)

> It is in the true apostolic, patriarchal and prophetic spirit that one waits for visions and overcomes them with painful sorrow. Therefore we should not be astonished that Brother Fattened Pig and Brother Soft Life [i.e. Luther] rejects them. For when a man has not learned the clear word of God in his soul, then he needs visions . . . From this I now conclude that whoever ignorantly wishes to be an enemy to visions, out of worldly understanding, and rejects or accepts them all without difference, claiming that false dreamers have done great harm to the world by ambition or pleasure-seeking – he will come to a bad end and stumble over the Holy Spirit . . . our sons and daughters will prophesy and will have dreams and visions, etc.

Müntzer made a careful distinction between dreams and revelations from the Devil and those from God, explaining that dreams had to be tested in spiritual torment or held up to the Bible for comparison. It scarcely matters to us now that such subjective things as dreams were to be tested by such subjective things as spiritual torment or the interpretation of the scriptures; what is important is that the individual was authorised to follow her or his own judgement in spiritual affairs. The usual checks and balances of restrictive religious convention did not get a look-in.

Müntzer's offer to place himself at the princes' disposal as some kind of official soothsayer seems now a little forlorn, but it must be viewed in conjunction with the alternative which he foresaw for the princes themselves:

> The stone torn from the mountain is now grown large . . . Aye, God be praised, it has become so large that if other lords or neighbours tried to persecute you for the sake of the gospel, then they would be driven out by their own subjects. This I know for certain.

Müntzer gives the nobility fair warning of their likely fate should they continue to defend the Papal Church or the reforms of Luther; far greater forces stand waiting to act. The 'lords or neighbours' referred to Duke Georg, Count Ernst of Mansfeld and the abbess of Naundorf. The only hope for the princes was to throw in their lot with the Elect and the poor:

> If you now wish to be righteous rulers, then you must grasp government by the root, and act as Christ has commanded. Drive his enemies away from the Elect, for you are the instrument for that. My dears, do not give us any cheap tricks and say that the strength of God should manage without recourse to your swords, or else they will rust in your scabbards . . . God is your shelter and will teach you to fight against His enemies.
>
> So the sword is also necessary for the destruction of the Godless, Romans 13. But in order for this to happen properly and effectively, our dear fathers the princes, who confess Christ with us, must use the sword. If they do not act thus, then the sword will be taken away from them, Daniel 7 . . . But the angels who sharpen your sickles for the harvest are the serious servants of God who refine the zealousness of God's wisdom.

An alliance was being proposed: the princes of Saxony had to dissociate themselves utterly from the old ways of the Church and from Wittenberg. They had to join in league with the common people to defend the changes being effected in Allstedt. The alternative was their overthrow by the combined force of God, the Elect and the people of Saxony. In return for this alliance, Müntzer and other members of the Elect would guide them towards correct spirituality and ensure that they remained unharmed in the Apocalyptic upheaval. Müntzer concluded his sermon with a rather startling demand to be appointed as their sole religious adviser:

> Therefore a new Daniel must arise and explain to you your revelations, and he must march in the forefront. He must reconcile the wrath of the princes and of the enraged people . . . If the truth is to be brought to the light of day, then you rulers must (God willing,

Allstedt castle, as it is today.

whether you want to or not) conduct yourselves according to the conclusion of this chapter, where Nebuchadnezzar appointed Daniel to an office where he might judge fairly and well, as the Holy Spirit dictated.

Müntzer was reaching out boldly into the realm of politics in order to resolve the burning questions of spiritual salvation. A crisis in government and religion demanded human intervention, prior to the imminent punishment of humanity by God. That Müntzer should turn to the princes of Saxony – even those inclined towards reform – seems fanciful to us now: the mismatch between his aspirations and reality reflects the huge gap between the aims of the German radical reform movement and the actual social and political conditions in which these aims were nurtured. There was, of course, no way that the princes of Saxony would ever form an alliance with Müntzer.

The sermon over, the princes continued on their procession back to Weimar. Barely had the lengthy column of horsemen disappeared round the corner of the road than there came disturbing news of events in the countryside south of Allstedt and in nearby Sangerhausen to the north. Both of these areas were firmly within Catholic territory. To the south, the local lord, Friedrich von Witzleben, had drawn the same conclusions from the Nürnberg mandate of the previous year as had Count Ernst of Mansfeld, and with much the same outcome. He set his troops to attack any of his peasants who were on their way up to Allstedt to attend Müntzer's sermons; he also cracked down ferociously on any likely 'sympathisers' among his own local vassals in the village of Schönewerda, some ten kilometres south of Allstedt. Meanwhile in Sangerhausen, encouraged by Witzleben's actions, Duke Georg's local administrator decided that the time was ripe to take steps against their very own 'Müntzerite' pastor, Tilmann 'Tilo' Banse.

Since February, Duke Georg had been expressing concern at the reforming spirit in Sangerhausen. 'We have heard reliably that several of your people have gone to Allstedt to hear preaching', he wrote. 'But the preacher there has supported many misleading demands against the order and tradition of the holy Christian church, and stirred up the simple folk to revolt.'[15] Georg was used to keeping a tight rein on Sangerhausen, to the extent of rescinding the democratic election of councillors; earlier that summer he had joined in the noble sport of preventing people from the town and surrounding villages from going to Allstedt to hear Müntzer. In July, he accused Müntzer of fomenting riot in Sangerhausen itself – 'he wishes to arouse disobedience, war, bloodshed by the subject against his lord, all in the name of the holy gospel'.[16] The duke decided that the time had come to break up this movement, and ordered the civil authorities in Sanger-hausen to arrest Banse. (Tilo Banse, described as 'a large portly priest', continued to suffer from persecution; some years later, in Lutheran Magdeburg, he was reported 'being placed on a donkey and stoned to death by a rabble with dung and stones'.)[17] On 15 July, Banse's supporters began to flee the town. Many of them headed straight for Allstedt, where they felt certain of asylum. Shamefully, like so many modern refugees, they found asylum to be not what they had hoped.

As we would expect, Müntzer was not slow to react to this provocation against his fellow reformer, and he fired off several letters in quick succession. The first, dated 15 July, was addressed to 'all the god-fearing people of Sangerhausen', advising them not to lose heart.

> The beginning of the wisdom of God is the fear of God . . . If you
> do not have this self-same pure fear of God, then you will not be
> able to survive any trial. But if you do possess it, then you will

achieve victory over all the tyrants, and they will be dreadfully humiliated beyond description.[18]

On the same day, he also wrote to the authorities in Sanger-hausen, likewise wishing them 'the pure fear of God', but with one unmistakable difference: he warned them of punishment to come should they persist in their slanders and harassment. 'I tell you now, as a promise, that if you do not improve your behaviour, then I will not hold back any longer those people who wish to deal with you.'[19] Continuing on this theme, and in words very reminiscent of his letter to Count Ernst of Mansfeld a year previously, Müntzer threatens:

> If you do any harm to Master Tilo Banse, then I will write against you, and sing and read aloud, and do to you the worst things which I can think of, just as David did to his godless persecutors . . . You will fall under my feet, be you ever so mighty bigwigs . . . I know that there is no one in this country more idolatrous than you.[20]

A few days later, Müntzer wrote once more to Banse's fol-lowers, his 'dearest brothers in Christ in the tyrannical prison of Sangerhausen'. This time he advised them to let the authorities do what they like with goods and possessions, but resist firmly when it came to faith:

> If your prince or one of his people orders you not to go to this place or that to hear the word of God . . . then you should not obey them, for then the fear of Man is being put in place of the fear of God . . . The dangerous time is upon us, a time when a bloodbath will be unleashed upon this poor obstinate world because of its lack of faith.[21]

He had much more to say on the necessity of fearing God alone, and paying no heed to the threats of the secular authorities. The letter was marked 'from Allstedt, in haste'. If dashed off in haste, it was a truly impressive piece of writing – it runs to some 2,000 well-chosen words.

The refugees who had managed to flee Sangerhausen were initially given a warm welcome in Allstedt. But the influx only piled more pressure on Hans Zeiss. This came not just from how he thought Duke Johann might react, but also from the authorities in Sangerhausen itself, the representatives of Duke Georg now insisting that the refugees be sent back. Within a week, Zeiss was preparing to accede to these demands. Müntzer, in one of his several letters to Zeiss on the matter, tells it this way:

> The affair with the poor people went like this: when Hans Reichart [one of the mayors] came back down from you in the castle, he gave the appearance of being extremely saddened; he gave them a report of the warning which had been issued; and they could only understand that as meaning that they would be handed over, so they came to me and asked if it was our gospel that people should be sacrificed on the butcher's block. Of course I was astonished and tried to think where this was all coming from . . . Shortly after that I met Hans Reichart coming out of the print shop. So I said to him: 'What kind of game is this you're playing, trying to expel people?' Then he said that you [i.e. Zeiss] had ordered him to do this.[22]

For some reason, Müntzer still felt disposed to think that – or act as if – Zeiss was very much on his side. There are no words of real complaint in this letter; quite the opposite: 'I have no wish at all that pious administrators should face the wrath of the common people', he wrote. 'I have always preached that there are still pious servants of God in the courts of their lordships.'

Müntzer took a positive view of events, and urged Zeiss – and, evidently in no doubt that Zeiss would alert his superiors, thereby warned the authorities – to take steps to curb the oppression:

> The fugitives are going to turn up here every day: should we let the cries of those poor people make us the friends of the tyrants? That does not agree with the gospel, etc. I tell you that a dreadful time of discord will arrive . . . For it is as clear as day that they have absolutely no respect for the Christian faith. Their power

will come to an end, and it will very shortly be handed over to the common people.

Instead of capitulating to the demands of Sangerhausen and Duke Georg, Müntzer decided that it was time to resist. On 25 July, in another letter to Zeiss, he described the establishment of a defence organisation:

> There must be organised a simple league, so that the common man may unite with pious administrators only for the sake of the gospel . . . [It] should only be a warning to the godless that they should cease their raging so that the Elect may learn the knowledge and wisdom of God with all proofs.[23]

This league was for self-defence, a deterrent against further provocations; at the same time, however, it was to be a link between the pious (preachers and administrators), as the vanguard pursuing God's will, and the people as the main body of troops. It should be noted here that Müntzer did not yet see this league as some kind of revolutionary organisation; he was at pains to ensure that social demands were kept at bay: 'And where feudal dues are concerned, it must be made quite clear to the members of this league that they should not think that they are thereby permitted to give nothing to the tyrants.' Although he was suggesting that the league had yet to be formed, in fact it had already been established on the previous day, after Müntzer had preached one of his usual fiery sermons to an audience of townspeople, refugees and a sizeable contingent of miners.

This was not the first time Müntzer had come up with the idea of a league. In late June or early July, he had proposed the idea of an alliance of radical preachers and their congregations across central Germany. The letters he sent out to prospective comrades have not survived, but he received two replies – one from Andreas Karlstadt and another from his congregation in Orlamünde. Both letters betrayed signs of panic. Karlstadt (who by then had returned to Wittenberg in a futile attempt to regain favour with Luther) started his reply by hoping that Müntzer would not think badly of him, but, he said, 'your letters

were scarcely very pleasant to me'. He sincerely wished that
the people in Allstedt would not engage in writing provocative
letters and forming leagues, for 'our people fear that this would
lead to acts which we would not forgive in thieves and rebels'.[24]
His congregation, for their part, in a letter written at much the
same time, stated quite unequivocally that 'if we join in a league
with you, then we would no longer be free Christians, but we
would be bound to men ... and the tyrants would celebrate,
saying: see, they proclaim a single God, but now they are joining
together in a league, because their God is not strong enough
to fight for them'.[25] Orlamünde, we gather, was not in favour;
the people of Allstedt would have to go it alone. Both of these
letters were printed as a leaflet in Wittenberg, probably just
after they were written, at the instigation of Karlstadt himself –
who clearly did not wish to take any risks of contamination.
At a later date, he claimed to have reacted to Müntzer's letter
as follows: 'My blood froze as I read it, and I shuddered fright-
fully', as 'those who saw the colour of my face and the hastiness
of my speech and my complaint against Müntzer's letter' would
testify; so appalled was he that he ripped up the letter – only
to have to stick it together again in order to write the reply.[26]
Notwithstanding this cool reception in July 1524, Karlstadt's
loyal congregation at Orlamünde did not baulk at giving Luther
a distinctly colder one when he turned up there a month later.
Luther had been encouraged to conduct an inspection tour of
Saxon parishes by Prince Johann Friedrich, with the purpose of
identifying and rooting out the radical elements. On stopping off
at Orlamünde, Luther's clumsy attempts to denigrate Karlstadt
and dazzle his flock with theology were robustly countered by
the articulate arguments of the parishioners; Luther was obliged
to make a quick getaway.[27]

There is also a suggestion of an earlier organisation in Allstedt, which may have been established without any prompting
by Müntzer. One of its members, Hans Reichart, confessed in
1525 that, at its first assembly, thirty men swore 'to stand by
the gospel, to give no tithes to the monks or nuns, and to help
destroy and expel them'.[28] The facts about this small organisation are, at best, vague. That such a body of men existed is not at

all unlikely. But from that brief statement of its aims, it sounds as if it was set up around the time of the Mallerbach affair.

And finally, there is the claim – rather far-fetched – by Müntzer himself, in the first of his letters to Sangerhausen, that 'more than 30 pacts and leagues of the Elect have been formed. In every country the game is ready for playing.'[29] Maybe what Müntzer meant by this is that he had sympathetic contacts in thirty towns across Germany – as evidenced by the visits from people like Amandus and Seligmann. And, of course, Tilo Banse himself was a member of Müntzer's 'Allstedt League'. A bit of exaggeration in a tight situation is understandable: it raised morale.

The Allstedt League was founded on Sunday 24 July. Some 500 people immediately signed up as members, 300 of whom were from outside the town – refugees from Sangerhausen, who had nothing left to lose, and copper miners from the Mansfeld district. Miners had been zealous attendees at the reformed church services and sermons in Allstedt for several months, and a determined deputation of miners had turned up in June when Zeiss was attempting to pin the Mallerbach arson on Ciliax Knauth. The remaining 200 members of the new league comprised a fair proportion of the people of Allstedt as well as the entire town council – who put their names down on the understanding that the league would not promote the withholding of taxes. In the event, the league did not have to undertake any self-defensive actions. Karlstadt would have been mightily relieved. But when events reached a crisis point barely two weeks later, it acted neither as a deterrent nor in self-defence. (Despite its ineffectiveness, the establishment of a league was a momentous step: it must be remembered that swearing an oath and joining any kind of organisation was illegal, as it meant breaking feudal or civic oaths of loyalty.)

In those tense July days, Müntzer encouraged Zeiss to approach the princes of Saxony and – in effect – ask them to join the league. He had already made this request himself – if not in so many words – during his sermon up at the castle: 'But what are you supposed to do with the sword?' he had asked the princes.

What you must do is this: clear out the evil men who obstruct the gospel, cast them down, if you wish to be the servants of God and not devils yourselves . . . If you wish to be righteous rulers, then you must grasp the order of things by the root, and act as Christ has commanded. Drive his enemies away from the Elect, for you are the instrument for that.[30]

In his letter of 25 July, Müntzer advised Zeiss to tell the princes that they must defend the reforms, 'for otherwise there will be much trouble and labour, and Germany will be made worse than a slaughterhouse'. This letter was later passed on by Zeiss to his superiors as 'a lesson on how to avoid future riot in a godly manner'.[31] It did little good.

Hans Zeiss is something of an enigma. Since 1513, he had held the job of empowered local representative of Duke Johann in the town of Allstedt. His duties brought him into regular contact with dukes and princes, as well as town councillors and preachers, and he lived and worked in the castle. Yet he was evidently greatly inspired by the popular reforms which were being developed by Müntzer. It was probably Zeiss who introduced Müntzer to his cousin Christoph Meinhard, the rich owner of an iron works in Eisleben; Müntzer and Meinhard thereafter conducted an instructive correspondence on matters of faith. For a short period, perhaps, there was no great conflict of interest between these two important parts of Zeiss's life. But the swift succession of events in Allstedt soon thrust him into a very uncomfortable dilemma, having to choose between his daily bread and his conscience. It could not have been easy. He reacted as best he could. Instead of locating and arresting the most likely Mallerbach arsonists, he chose to prevaricate and then arrest just one man; being thwarted in this modest design, he then argued with the duke for the whole affair to be swept under the carpet. Where possible he tried to downplay events in reports to his noble employer. In his dealings with Müntzer, he managed to obscure his own role in some of the counter-strikes against the people of Allstedt and Sangerhausen. As insurance, he also kept Spalatin, Friedrich's secretary, fully informed on

Müntzer's activities; almost certainly, Spalatin would have passed some of this intelligence on to Luther. But at no time did Zeiss ever appear to condemn Müntzer himself, or have him arrested – which he would have been fully authorised to do, and for which he would most likely have received plaudits from his employers and from Wittenberg. He repeatedly supported Müntzer's refusal to be interrogated 'behind closed doors', promoting instead the idea of a public disputation. In August 1524, Friedrich the Wise wrote Zeiss a cautionary letter, remarking that his continual defence of Müntzer had been noted.[32] Even in May 1525, when Müntzer was active in the very heart of a rebel army confronting the Saxon princes, Zeiss was at pains to suggest that Müntzer was not their leader, merely a preacher. Adopting such a stance in 1525 was brave, but ill-advised: in the fallout from the defeat of the Thuringian peasantry, Zeiss was sacked from his post at Allstedt.[33]

What is quite clear from the several letters written by Müntzer to the electoral official is that Müntzer held him in high esteem. All his letters to Zeiss were signed 'your brother'. Strangely, no letters from Zeiss to Müntzer have been preserved; perhaps much of their communication was verbal; or perhaps Müntzer or Zeiss, when their friendship had cooled later, got rid of them. The relationship between the two men is that intriguing one in which they hold similar views on what they consider to be personally important, but occupy stations in life whose essential interests are diametrically opposed. In short, an unusual – but not unique – friendship. After Müntzer left Allstedt, he wrote at least one more letter to Zeiss, in late August or September 1524; frustratingly, it has not been preserved. Thereafter, the only other time Zeiss is mentioned by Müntzer is in a letter he wrote to Meinhard, from Nürnberg, in December. He tells Meinhard that he does not know whether Zeiss is hostile or loyal to the cause. Evidently, there had been no communication between the two in recent weeks, and Müntzer must by then have had suspicions that Zeiss had chosen his career over his faith.[34]

Zeiss himself came to an unhappy end: during the Schmal-kaldic War of 1545/6, waged between Lutheran and Catholic princes of the Empire, he was captured by a Count of Stolberg, tortured and put to death.[35] (Zeiss's predecessors in the post at Allstedt had also come to sticky ends – Wolf von Selmenitz had been stabbed to death by an employee of Cardinal Albrecht of Brandenburg, and Selmenitz's precursor had been shot dead by his colleague in Sangerhausen. Not a job for the faint-hearted.)

The summer of 1524 was filled with relentless excitement, civil unrest and inspiring rhetoric. Into all of this, with some inevitability, barged Martin Luther. Already on 18 June, he wrote a private letter to Prince Johann Friedrich, warning him of the 'Satan of Allstedt', and demanding that Müntzer be forced to come to Wittenberg to debate.[36] In the middle of July, he expanded on the letter and had it printed as an eighteen-page *Letter to the Princes of Saxony, Concerning the Rebellious Spirit*[37] – no prizes for guessing that the rebellious spirit in question here was Müntzer. It is difficult to pinpoint exactly what prompted Luther to publish this pamphlet. From its length and likely date of publication, it seems improbable that he was reacting to the ill-concealed personal attacks made by Müntzer in his 'Sermon to the Princes'. Improbable, but not impossible: the leading figures in the German Reformation excelled at putting pen to paper at short notice, and if news of the sermon had got back to Wittenberg within a day or two, Luther could well have dusted down his earlier letter to the princes in double-quick time. Perhaps the trigger was the news that Müntzer was proposing some kind of nationwide league of alternative reformers. That, and the entirely unwelcome news that Müntzer was making some kind of approach to his – Luther's – very own Saxon princes.

The object of Luther's letter was to slander Müntzer as much as possible, to provide incriminating 'evidence' of past behaviour, and to have him expelled from Allstedt. He cited the destruction of the Mallerbach chapel and Müntzer's doctrine of 'spirit' as prime examples of disruption; and he accused Müntzer of being afraid to dispute with him – this, despite Müntzer's repeated insistence that he would be happy to discuss issues, but only in a public setting. (Luther, it should be noted, never did hold a debate with Müntzer, nor did he ever make a detailed written critique of Müntzer's ideas.) Luther had no doubt experienced an unpleasant sense of déjà vu about events in Allstedt, a feeling that the events of Wittenberg from late 1521 were being re-enacted:

> Now when the Satan had been expelled [from Zwickau], he wandered around in the desert places for one year or three, and sought a resting-place, but did not find one, until he settled down in Your Princely Graces' principality and made himself a nest there, from where he thought to attack us, under our shelter and protection . . . But he also cried out horribly and complained that he had to suffer greatly, so that no one up until then dared touch him with fist or words or quill-pens, and he invented a great cross on which he suffered. Satan, however carelessly and causelessly he might lie, just cannot hide himself.

Luther was pleased to remind the princes that the Wittenberg movement had not behaved like this. He attempted a very brief and dismissive analysis of Müntzer's theology:

> You must (they say) hear God's voice yourself, and suffer God's work within you, and feel how heavy your burden is. The Scripture means nothing, yes, Bible Babel Bubble, etc. If we were to talk about them with such words, then their cross and their suffering would (I believe) become even more cherished than Christ's suffering, and they would value it even higher – that is how much the poor spirit boasts about his suffering and his cross.

Having placed at Their Graces' disposal all the necessary theological arguments required to condemn Müntzer, Luther then suggested that preaching from the scriptures was perfectly acceptable, 'but if they want to fight with more than just words, if they want to destroy and use their fists, then Your Graces should step in: it is either us or them'. After a dozen pages of condemnation, Luther felt that his duty was done. He left it to his noble sponsors and protectors to decide what to do; it was their call entirely – just as long as they silenced his radical opponent, and in doing so ensured that 'the cause of uproar – to which Mr. Everyman is more than inclined – [can be] set aside'.

This was not the first time Luther had expressed his fear that the struggle for religious reform would spill over into social revolt and bloodshed. During his appearance at Worms, he had voiced concern about the boisterous support of the German people for his stand. In his interventions in Wittenberg in early 1522 he had instructed his followers to be quiet and polite and to take things slowly. And ever since early 1522, he had been tirelessly on the lookout for 'false prophets'. Müntzer represented a new and dangerous variant of this spirit of riot.

Although uncompromising on the matter of Müntzer's theology and alleged rabble-rousing, Luther's letter seemed fairly relaxed; he evidently had every confidence that the Saxon authorities would carry out their duty in respect of their Reformation. Had he had sight of the 'Sermon to the Princes', and the insulting way Müntzer had treated him there, his tone might have been a little different. Aside from any immediate effect on its recipients, his letter has an historical importance beyond July 1524, for it was the foundation stone on which was built the perception of Müntzer in history, which persisted completely unchallenged for three centuries and more.

At the start of August, matters came to a head. Taking stock of the events of July, the princes decided that further investigation was required. Accordingly, the various suspect parties in Allstedt were summoned to appear before a panel at Weimar. Perhaps Luther's warning contributed to this summons, perhaps not. Weimar lies some sixty kilometres south of Allstedt; it would probably have taken the town delegates a couple of days to reach. They arrived there on the last day of July – Zeiss, Müntzer, Rucker the magistrate, and the two mayors Reichart and Hans Bosse. They were interrogated separately over two days by persons unknown. It seems, from the decisions subsequently reached, that Rucker and Reichart readily capitulated before the authorities and resolutely pointed the finger of blame at Müntzer alone. No decisions were announced at Weimar, and the party returned home.

While everyone of importance was safely away in Weimar, back in Allstedt Simon Haferitz, the preacher at St Wigberti's Church, was busy delivering a sermon against those 'knaves',

the princes, counts and other nobility.[38] Sometimes there is just
no stopping insubordination. In May of that year, Haferitz had
preached that:

> Our lords founded the cloisters – that is, the whore-houses and
> murder-pits – and they still protect them; those who are born
> princes cannot do good, they need to be removed and we must
> elect new ones; they grind and scrape you; when you address them,
> you should not say, 'By the grace of God, Dukes of Saxony' –
> rather you should say, 'By the disfavour of God', and not our
> lords.[39]

After returning to Allstedt on the third day of August, Müntzer
was summoned to the castle where Zeiss had the unenviable task
of delivering the verdict from Weimar. It was not good news:
Müntzer was to close down his print shop and dismiss his printer
(perhaps Widemar, although we cannot be sure); on the basis
that no one was currently preventing attendance at sermons and
services in Allstedt, the league was to be disbanded; Müntzer
himself was effectively given a gagging order and told not to stir
up trouble; and – last but not least – culprits had to be found for
the burning of the Mallerbach chapel. The decision on the print
shop was not particularly good news for the town council either.
They had previously been persuaded by Müntzer to invest the
tidy sum of 100 guilders in the printing of his *German Evangelical Mass*, a job which was then nearing completion, and they
begged Duke Johann to be allowed to complete the printing.
Miraculously, this request was granted: it seemed easier for a
liturgical work to get past the censors than a simple pamphlet
or book. The final printed product shows some signs of being a
rushed job, but at least it was finished. (Johann took a pragmatic
view of censorship: in a letter to Friedrich at around this time,
he declared himself quite happy for Müntzer to print whatever
he liked – just as long as it was undertaken beyond the borders
of Saxony.[40])

But now Müntzer had very few options left. His league for self-
defence proved to be toothless in the face of the Weimar decision;
both Müntzer and the league had lost the all-important support

of the town council. And, although Müntzer was not aware of it, both Count Ernst of Mansfeld and Friedrich von Witzleben had decided to take full advantage of the setback. Ernst demanded apologies from everyone in Allstedt, while Witzleben escalated his campaign of discouraging wayfaring worshippers – this time his soldiers were ordered to shoot arrows to stop anyone attempting to reach Allstedt.[41] With the print shop closing down, and the threat of further intervention should he continue preaching against secular authority, it seemed unlikely that Müntzer could reasonably keep or expand his audience. In one last throw of the dice, he wrote a letter to Friedrich the Wise,[42] deliberately bypassing Duke Johann, Friedrich's brother, and going straight to the man whom he considered more sympathetic to his reforms. He complained to Friedrich about 'that lying man Luther and the shameful letter which he sent to the dukes of Saxony'; he asked Friedrich for permission to continue his preaching and writing so that he could answer Luther in an appropriate manner; and he stated, once more, that he wanted to be judged in a public arena rather than in some secluded study. Müntzer then pointed out that, in accordance with a request from Duke Johann, he had already submitted his next pamphlet, entitled *The Testimony of the First Chapter of Luke* (later to be expanded and printed as *An Explicit Exposure of False Faith*), via Zeiss, for examination: examination not so much in terms of censorship, but more – both Müntzer and Zeiss thought – as a guide to the duke on 'how to deal with any future rebellion in a godly manner'. He ends his pitch to Friedrich with this ill-disguised threat:

> if you wish to be my gracious lord and prince, then I will spread my aforesaid Christian faith in the bright light of day to the whole world, both orally and in writing, and I will expound it with complete honesty. But if such an offer does not meet with your benevolent wish, then you must reflect that the common people will feel dread and hopelessness towards you and others like you. For the people have a great expectation in you, and God has given you, before all other lords and princes, a great deal of understanding. But if you misuse this respect, then it will be said of you: see,

there goes the man who did not want God as his shield, but relied instead on worldly ostentation.

The letter, as we might expect, raised noble eyebrows, but went unanswered.

Müntzer could wait no longer. In the night of 7/8 August, he climbed the walls of Allstedt in the company of one Martin Rüdiger, a goldsmith from Nordhausen, and abandoned the town. It was a rather hurried departure: left behind were his wife Ottilie and their son, as well as his secretary Ambrosius Emmen. Shortly afterwards, Thomas turned up in Mühlhausen, some seventy-five kilometres to the south-west. And here his development towards becoming a full-blooded revolutionary took another significant step forward.

8

Using God's Name, He Spoke and Acted for the Devil

Müntzer's Theology

God damned the rebellious spirits and insurgents and it was his will to punish them with wrath. For here you see how this murderous spirit boasted that God spoke and acted through them . . . And before he could turn round, he lay in the mud with several thousand others. Since Thomas Müntzer failed, it is quite clear that, using God's name, he spoke and acted for the Devil.

Martin Luther (1525)

With Müntzer's moonlight flit from Allstedt, where he left behind his friends and enemies, he also left behind any idea that the Saxon princes could be guided by the radical theologians. Abandoned too, several months before, was any hope that Wittenberg would tolerate his reforms. In both theological and political terms, Müntzer and his immediate supporters were on their own. He now had two options: either give up his aspirations for radical religious reform, find a quiet spot to settle down and make a living by promoting the 'Martinian' Reformation, or continue to work for the overthrow of the godless tyrants and their apologists. He chose the second road.

The quotation from Luther at the head of this chapter relates to the outcome of the battle at Frankenhausen in May 1525. Its message is clear and simple: Müntzer lost the battle, therefore he was the Devil's man. It was a reasonable conclusion to draw in the sixteenth century. And, in a nutshell, this was the argument that characterised the vast bulk of Müntzer historiography over the next 350 years. Alongside this clear message lay another, explicitly stated elsewhere: that Müntzer's theological teachings were largely to blame for the uprising of 1525. It is not our business here to claim moral legitimacy for one or other theological view; nor do we intend to argue whether Müntzer was 'right' or 'wrong' to engage in revolutionary activity under the historical circumstances in which he found himself. What is important here is the relationship between historical events and Müntzer's ideas, and the routes by which they interconnected. Müntzer's contemporaries were convinced that such connections existed, but took the view that it was all one-way traffic: that Müntzer's ideas gave birth to the social upheavals. The Catholic critics of the sixteenth century went one step further and concluded that Luther's ideas spawned Müntzer, and that Luther was therefore ultimately responsible for the uprisings and riots. The reality was far more complex than either of these simplistic judgements.

Müntzer's trajectory towards participation in the Peasants' War was determined by what he believed about God, about the Apocalypse and about the role to be played therein by his fellow men and women. It seems to us a rather oblique trajectory, but it could not be otherwise: no one reaches revolutionary ideas by a straight path. By August 1524, all the elements of his belief were in place and plainly visible, and although certain shifts of emphasis took place in the last few months of Müntzer's life, the basis of his theology had by now been firmly established.

The exile's journey from Allstedt to the town of Mühlhausen lasted several days. So let us grab the opportunity to sit down by the side of the road and consider his beliefs at that time. Doing so will give us a clear understanding of his revolutionary activity over the following nine months.

The Apocalypse

Like many of his contemporaries, Müntzer was convinced that 'the end of time' was imminent. For at least a century, Apocalyptic pronouncements had been common; all over Europe, small bands of believers would either hole themselves up in some secure place to await the unleashing of God's wrath upon a sinful world, or – occasionally – launch out in acts of defiance and violence to expedite the matter. The favoured year was 1500, but when that came and went, more subtle and refined calculations came into play; 1524 soon began to be touted as a year in which there would be great floods and other signs of the end of the world. Luther, Melanchthon and other Wittenberg reformers all believed initially in some imminent great disaster. No dates were set – a wise move – but expectations were high.

Such, too, was Müntzer's belief. In his 'Prague Manifesto' of 1521 he wrote,

> In this time of ours, God will pour his insurmountable anger over such proud, wooden men, who are impervious to all good . . . All villainy must urgently be brought to light. Oho! how ripe are the rotten apples! Oho! how ripe are the Elect! The time of the harvest is here! For this, God has sent me to his harvest.[1]

Similar thoughts were expressed in his letters written between 1521 and 1524, and especially in his 'Sermon to the Princes':

> Oh, dear sirs, how splendidly the Lord will shatter the old pots with an iron bar . . . For the stone from the mountain has grown large. The poor laymen and peasants see it much clearer than you . . . Aye, the stone is grown large and is what the foolish world long feared. It overwhelmed the world when it was young; so what shall it now do that it is so great and mighty? What, when it is so powerful that it strikes unstoppably against the great statue and shatters it right down to its clay pots?[2]

But the role of true believers in these 'end times' was not, according to Müntzer, simply to sit back and wait. Their role was to be proactive. Men and women who, through suffering, had received the divine word into their spirit should work tirelessly to ensure that the godless preachers and rulers did not have their way. Indeed, the God-fearing people should take the initiative and try to overthrow such preachers and rulers, and thus clear the way for the arrival of a new age. There is here, however, a slight difficulty. Müntzer nowhere states just how the Apocalypse was to unfold. There is no vision of a great flood, or plague and pestilence, or the falling of the heavens, or – for the sake of argument – an invasion by the Turkish armies; and definitely no indication of a likely date. While it is clear that Müntzer believed that, at some imminent but indeterminate point, God would build on what his chosen people had begun, it is by no means apparent just how much preparatory work had to be done, and for how long.

The Elect and the Godless

What was crystal clear, however, was who was to undertake that work. This would be the 'Elect', the chosen ones, whose communication with God was direct and unmediated. And against them would be ranged 'the godless', whose ranks encompassed the officials and supporters of the Papal Church, alongside Luther and his group, and the feudal lords and their representatives.

Müntzer considered the dynamic tension in history to be the separation of people from God, and that the main purpose of God's messengers on earth, the Elect, was to overcome this separation – first individually and then by spreading the word and acting against God's enemies. Müntzer always described his calling as preacher as a task set by God: 'It is not my work, but God's' was his maxim in 1521; and in 1525 he advised the peasant rebels (with a subtle but mighty change of person) that 'It is not your fight, but the Lord's.'[3] He regarded the cosmic division not as that between God and Satan, which was the traditional medieval and Lutheran view, but as that between humankind and God.

A study of Müntzer's vocabulary yields some interesting statistics on the use of the words 'God', 'godless' and 'Devil' in his printed works of 1523/4, and on the use of epithets for the opponents of God.[4] Not surprisingly, the word 'God' is used 480 times, but the words 'Devil' or 'Satan' appear far less (sixty-one times – and of these, half are in fact quotations from the Bible or by Lutherans), and are outnumbered by 'godless' (sixty-seven times); other positive terms ('Elect', 'Christian', 'God-fearing' and so on) turn up regularly (132 times); while other derogatory terms with a human quality (academic, villain, monk, priest, doctor, tyrant, damned, etc.) appear more than 100 times. Even superficially, then, the concept of a God-vs-Devil dichotomy recedes far into the background, and the responsibility for salvation or damnation is placed firmly on the shoulders of men and women. And since the responsibility lay with the mortal world, the unavoidable conclusion was that the solution to social evil must be found in social activity. Which is not to say that the Devil did not exist for Müntzer – merely that such a being was well down the pecking order of blame.

Opposed to God, then, were the human reprobates in one guise or another. It is instructive to observe how Müntzer gradually brought more and more social groups into this classification – from the Papists and monks, through the academics and modern Philistines, to tyrants and Lutherans – as his activity steadily brought him into conflict with these people. In Jüterbog, there was mention of 'tyrants', referring to the bishops of the Papal Church. In Zwickau, the 'hypocrites' were largely the Franciscan monks, and later the Humanists around Egranus. In Prague, the vocabulary is extended to describe monks, priests, academics and students as 'damned', 'accursed' or 'heretical', and this terminology was also deployed in Erfurt and Nordhausen. It was only in Allstedt that the 'damned' came to include the Lutherans, and even then not immediately: if we look at Müntzer's major writings and letters up to September 1523, those who impeded God's word were solely the Papal authorities and Catholic priests. It is perhaps worth noting that the expression 'godless' did not appear in his letters or writings until the early summer of 1523; something clicked in Müntzer's mind in that year. In his letter of October to the elector Friedrich, the term 'godless' is applied to that 'heretical scoundrel' Ernst of Mansfeld, the Papists and possibly to the Lutherans 'who have chased me from one town to another for no real reason'.[5] By December 1523, Müntzer had clarified in his mind the role of the Lutherans, and was quite happy to describe both Catholics and Lutherans as 'academics', 'damned' and 'godless'. After the felonious burning of Maller-bach and the resultant half-hearted inquiry, the term 'godless' is used specifically against Catholics, Lutherans and secular author-ity. By the summer of 1524, the term had almost entirely replaced the use of the word 'damned', and was applied quite openly to all of Müntzer's opponents: in one of his letters to his supporters in Sangerhausen, he wrote: 'The godless will cast you out of the community . . . We are in those dangerous times of which St Paul spoke: everyone who wishes to act righteously and to be guided by the gospel will be considered by the godless as a heretic, a rogue and a knave.'[6] From that summer onwards, there were only the Elect and the godless, Müntzer's followers and the rest of the world.

The one unifying characteristic of the godless was that they hindered God's work by opposing the Elect. The Elect were men and women of all backgrounds, in all historical periods and in all countries, who communicated directly with God and performed God's work on earth. Müntzer cited many examples: Moses, Elijah, Daniel, Jesus, the Apostles – and himself. There was no absolute need for the Elect to be baptised Christians or to be familiar with the Bible, as he explicitly stated in several places:

> If someone has never heard or seen the Bible in his whole life, then
> he could still have an honest Christian belief for himself, by means
> of the correct teaching of the Spirit, just like all those who wrote
> the Bible without any books at all.[7]

The argument was quite simple: if the people described in Old and New Testaments had managed to communicate with and act for God without the aid of Bible, Canon Law, decrees from Rome or sermons from Wittenberg, without formal education or any other human device, then why would similar people not exist in any period under any conditions? In his letter to Friedrich the Wise, in August 1524, Müntzer made the following declaration:

I preach such a Christian belief as does not agree with that of Luther, but which is present in all the hearts of the Elect, the same across the whole world. And even if someone was born a Turk, still he will have the beginning of this same belief, which is the movement of the holy spirit.[8]

The Elect, then – those who open their hearts and minds to the direct word of God, regardless of their social status, culture, religion, ethnicity or education – stand against the godless – just about everyone else, with the notable exception of the common people, who had been kept in ignorance by the traditional preachers and secular lords. Note, incidentally, Müntzer's startling view that 'a Turk' – a Muslim – could unknowingly be one of the Elect. And this is no isolated instance: he had earlier proposed to expose Count Ernst of Mansfeld before 'the Turks, the Heathens and the Jews',[9] and in earlier writings had suggested that these other religious groups were on the same level as 'Christian' unbelievers. At a time when the Turks and Jews were generally considered beyond salvation by the Christians of western Europe, this is an astonishing position.

Suffering and Pain

To become one of the Elect, a person had to experience inner torment and suffer disbelief, going through a bitter and painful refining process that would effectively burn away any old faith and leave them wide open to the new faith. No kind of formal baptism could constitute a correct entry into the true faith. Suffering and pain, and an understanding of that suffering and pain, were essential. It might be suffering that was deliberately sought out, or it could simply be suffering arising from a loss of faith or confidence. Müntzer's insistence on the necessity for suffering was by no means new in theology, nor was it alien to the reform movement initiated by Luther. The individual torment involved in the mystical 'imitation of Christ' was a long-established tradition within the Christian religion, with an excellent pedigree. In Germany it had been expounded by such men as Eckhart, Tauler and Suso, and the author of the *Theologia Deutsch*. Luther himself, an editor of the last-named work, had had his own spiritual experiences and torments, and his reaction to Storch's visit to Wittenberg shows his unquestioning acceptance of the idea of spiritual suffering before belief. Indeed, his most funda-mental tenet – 'justification through faith' – was inseparable from the continual testing of the believer in daily life. Müntzer spent some considerable time studying the mystics at a period in his life when the basis of his faith was being challenged – between 1517 and 1520. The message of the mystics was so radically different from the customary high-road to faith that Müntzer, Luther and many others embraced it enthusiastically. But for Müntzer more than any of his contemporaries, the idea that individual suffering and doubt must precede true belief ran very deep indeed, cover-ing all aspects of faith: it was not enough to reach belief and then expand on this by learning from books; suffering and individual experience continued to have primary importance even after the acquisition of faith. Müntzer's pamphlet *On Fraudulent Faith* begins thus:

> For just as the furrow in the field cannot bring forth a great harvest without the action of the ploughshare, so a person cannot say he is a Christian if he has not first suffered the cross which allows him to receive the work and word of God. In such tribulation the elect friend of God suffers the word; the fraudulent listener cannot be one of these, only the eager pupil of his master.[10]

He then goes on to talk at length about suffering, misery, pain and desolation. This was no easy faith.

In similar manner, Müntzer advised Christoph Meinhard just how a true faith was to be attained:

> Your eyes must first be opened by suffering the work of God, as the law explains . . . Those who have not suffered the long night will not come to the knowledge of God, for the night unto the night reveals knowledge, and only after it will the true word emerge into the light of day . . . They must use every moment to mortify the flesh, and in particular our name must stink terribly

to the godless, for only then can someone who has been tested preach God's name.[11]

One question arises from this emphasis on mental – and sometimes also physical – suffering: did Müntzer himself experience episodes of such pain? It would be rash to suppose that he did not. His repeated banishments and his enforced peripatetic existence triggered in him neither defeatism nor passive acceptance. Instead he regarded these setbacks simply as proof that he was on the right track. From this flowed also his unshakeable belief that he was one of God's Elect – more, even: that he was the messenger of God, a 'Gideon'. To arrive at such a self-assessment required some powerful motivation. Müntzer was a prolific writer of letters and tracts, but the one thing he rarely gave to posterity was any inkling of his personal life. From the simple things – where he was born, where he was educated – through to the important things – illness, love, sorrow, despair: of these we have almost nothing. Did he experience, like Luther, a 'road to Damascus' moment when, in spiritual suffering and mental turmoil, he saw the path he had to follow? Luther had at least one such moment, when caught in a violent thunderstorm, and he liked to tell everyone about it for years afterwards. The Harz area is noted for spectacular storms – deafening thunder, terrifying lightning, and flash floods surging down its rivers. Perhaps Müntzer had a near-death experience in one of those? Or perhaps it was something less dramatic, but no less devastating – an existential crisis while at university, such as is not uncommon among young people far from home. We can only guess at the origins of his personal beliefs.

Dreams and Visions

Also key to Müntzer's theology was his attitude to dreams and visions. Clearly, he was convinced that some dreams might be messages from God. This was not at all uncommon in the period; the causes of dreams were not understood – they were just as likely to be messages from a supernatural world as anything else. But, like many others, Müntzer was not blind to the equally valid explanation that dreams and visions could come from the Devil (or one's stomach or other physical stimulation). That he took dreams seriously is evident from two documents which were preserved in his precious collection of letters, containing reports of (to the modern mind entirely banal) dreams or visions experienced by a couple of his followers.[12]

By 1524, the Allstedt reformer had elevated dream and prophetic vision to an important role in his theology, all the while acknowledging that every such vision had to be further attested by the living spirit of God, evidenced by prior torment and suffering. A person had to

> take great care that such figures in the visions or dreams are witnessed in all their circumstances by the Holy Bible, so that the devil does not rush in and ruin the ointment of the Holy Spirit with his sweetness ... And the elect person must take care that the vision does not burst out after human excitation, but rather flows simply out of God's irrevocable will.[13]

(It is noteworthy that this acknowledgement accords exactly with Luther's admonition to Melanchthon in 1522 concerning the Zwickau prophets, that 'The spirits are to be tested ... Inquire whether they have experienced spiritual distress and the divine birth, death and hell. If you should hear that all their experiences are pleasant, quiet, devout ... then do not approve of them.'[14]

Müntzer believed that dreams could be a form of communication with God, or at least could be revelatory. This was also clear from the amount of time and effort he spent on his 'Sermon to the Princes', which was, after all, the description of a prophet – one of the Elect in the past – analysing a dream and drawing conclusions which had crucial importance for the understanding of divine and mortal history. While a true prophet opens his mind to the potential of dreams and visions, the Wittenberg academics do the opposite:

They stick mired in their inexperienced ways, Ecclesiastes 34, and poke fun at those who have experienced the revelation of God, as the godless did in Jeremiah 20. Hey, has God spoken to you lately? Or have you had a chat with him recently? Have you got the spirit of Christ, eh? They do this with great derision and mockery.[15]

Education and Participation

Through suffering, spiritual torment, dreams or visions, any individual – without any training in theology, without even being literate – could claim an authority from God that surpassed the authority of his or her social or intellectual superiors. This, in turn, implied that anyone with a grievance could challenge the rule of civil law, or present their own interpretation of any situation and expect it to be taken seriously.

At around this time, the peasantry of south and central Germany were beginning to stand up for their rights, citing scriptural authority as justification for their demands. It was one of the last great popular explosions in Europe for which the added accelerant was religious doctrine. Müntzer proposed to take that one step further: authority was to come not merely from the Bible, but also the 'living word of God'. His shift from scripture to spirit meant that there was no requirement to be literate or educated; therefore the lowest and meanest classes could participate in the political life of the German nation. Müntzer was well aware of the educational problems faced by the peasantry; in his pamphlet of late 1524, *An Explicit Exposure of False Faith*, he wrote that the 'poor man cannot learn to read because he is troubled for nourishment, and they preach unashamedly that the poor man should let himself be skinned and scraped by the tyrants. So how can he learn to read the scriptures?'[16] The only alternative option available to the illiterate and the needy was a 'living' witness; and Müntzer provided the theoretical justification for such a witness.

With their election by God, the agents of God's work on earth were obliged to repair the damage done to the faith by Papists and Lutherans, to open the eyes of the people and bring them back to communion with God. This task – not unusual in itself, since that was precisely the vocation of most priests and preachers – was to be rooted in education. In Prague, Müntzer had lamented the miserable ignorance of the people and the wilful lack of education provided by the Church: 'I do not doubt in the people. Oh, you just, poor and pitiful little band, how you thirst for the word of God!'[17] In his major pamphlets, and in most of his important letters, the question of educating the people is repeatedly addressed. Müntzer's major achievement in Allstedt was to begin this education, through his reformed church services and preaching. When Ernst of Mansfeld sent out his militia, Müntzer's explanation of his reforms to Prince Friedrich ran as follows:

> I have often thought how I should like to cast down the iron walls before the poor in spirit, and I have seen that Christianity cannot be rescued from the jaws of the raging lion unless one promotes the pure clear word of God and removes the bushel or lid that conceals it, and one deals with the Biblical truth before the whole world . . . to sing and preach it unhidden and tirelessly.[18]

A commitment to education also determined his insistence that theological discussion was to be conducted not 'in camera', in the studies of academics or in the private chambers of a castle, but rather before the people; this became important in 1524, when both Luther and his princes were attempting to muzzle Müntzer.

Another way of promoting God's word among the people was the setting up of defence leagues, organisations whose main function was to provide the material strength to defend the spiritual word. It was through these leagues that the popular rebellion would contribute to Müntzer's higher aims; it is notable that, in his letter to the people of Allstedt shortly before the battle at Frankenhausen in May 1525, Müntzer applied to them the maxim he had previously reserved for the Elect: 'It is not your fight, but the Lord's.'[19] By 1525, the popular uprising had convinced Müntzer that his goal coincided with that of the peasants, and that the struggle against the tyrants was a process by which the people would come to God.

The Fear of God

In parallel with his advocacy of the individual and living experience of faith against book-learning and the authority of the Church, Müntzer developed his doctrine of fear. This doctrine described two opposites: the fear of Man and the fear of God. When Müntzer was impelled to overt revolutionary activity by the stance of the authorities in Allstedt, his doctrine of fear began to assume greater importance in his letters and tracts, and became a yardstick by which revolutionary activity could be measured. In essence, the doctrine stated this: as long as people feared the secular authorities or tyrants more than they feared the will of God, then so long did they perpetuate the rule of the godless; and as long as they feared God more than they feared Man, then so long would God stand by them and guarantee final victory to the Elect. 'The fear of God . . . must be pure, with no fear of man or any creature . . . Oh, the fear is most necessary for us. For, just as no man can honestly serve two masters, Matthew 6, so no man can honestly fear both God and the world.'[20] In the autumn of 1524, in his pamphlet *An Explicit Exposure of False Faith*, Müntzer accorded crucial importance to the two-masters antithesis. Confronted with the provocations and hostility of first Catholic and then Lutheran government, he considered that the only way forward for his cause was to ignore utterly the demands of the 'bigwigs'. As a theologian, he expressed his essentially political idea of civil disobedience in biblical language – the phrase 'fear of God' is drawn from various places in the Bible, for example Psalm 19 ('The fear of the Lord is pure and abides forever') and Psalm 111 ('The fear of the Lord is the beginning of wisdom'). Other theologians also cited these passages, but it is Müntzer's interpretation of the phrase which is crucial. His doctrine of fear can be traced right back to his earliest writings, to his condemnation of the mingling of worldly reasoning with divine knowledge in the works of Thomas Aquinas and the Scholastics. In Zwickau, he spoke of the necessity of having 'the fear of God' in the face of the attacks of the opposition. In the 'Prague Manifesto', he wrote:

Where the seed falls on good ground, that is in the heart which is full of the fear of God, that is then the paper and parchment upon which God writes the real spiritual word . . . Students and priests and monks . . . do not experience the suffering of faith in the spirit of the fear of God . . . They do not wish to be frightened by the spirit of the fear of God, and so they eternally mock the temptations of faith.[21]

When the Count of Mansfeld had the temerity to apply the terms of the Imperial mandate to the weekly pilgrimage to Allstedt, the core of Müntzer's polemic was this:

You should know that I do not fear even the whole world in such mighty and just matters. For the key to the knowledge of God is that one should govern the people so that they learn to fear God alone, Romans 13, for the beginning of true Christian wisdom is the fear of the Lord. And now you wish to be feared more than God.[22]

In this one short passage Müntzer argues that a Christian is not required to bow to the secular might of the nobility, that the nobility should not block the progress of reform, and that true knowledge or faith is identical to the undiluted 'fear of God'. In the complementary letter to Prince Friedrich, Müntzer had stated:

The princes do not frighten pious men. And if they turn against us, then the sword shall be taken from them and given to the zealous people for the overthrow of the godless, Daniel 7, and the noble jewel of peace shall be taken from the earth, Revelations 6.[23]

Although the 'princes' here probably designated the Catholic ones, there was a veiled warning to Friedrich himself.

A year later, when the hazy picture of the revolutionary era was coming into sharper focus, the principle of fear became outspokenly social. In July 1524, Müntzer urged the unfortunate 'God-fearing people of Sangerhausen' not to bow to their persecutors, but to 'Fear the Lord God alone; then the fear will be pure, Psalm 19. Then your faith will be tested like gold in the fire.'[24] Notice the conflation of 'fear of God' and the confirmation of faith under conditions of suffering. When his supporters were imprisoned or banished by the Sangerhausen authorities, this advice was repeated:

> Do not fear those who kill your body, for then they can do no more; but I will show you whom you should fear: fear him who has the power, after he has killed the body, to cast the soul into the fires of Hell; him, him should you fear . . . If you fear life, then consider the example of the holy martyrs, how little they valued their lives and mocked the tyrants to their faces . . . In short, you must fear no one beside God . . . If your prince or his official commands you not to go here or there to listen to the word of God, or makes you swear to go there no longer, then you should swear nothing, for then the fear of Man would be set up in place of the fear of God and set up as an idol.[25]

The counterposing of obedience to God to obedience to mortals is drawn scripturally from Romans 13. But Müntzer's interpretation of the advice given in that chapter is diametrically opposed to Luther's: Luther took this passage at face value, arguing that the authorities were instituted by God and therefore had the right to act as they wished; Müntzer read it in such a way that the authorities had no right to interfere in matters of faith; if they did so, then they were to be swept aside.

The message to the princes in Müntzer's sermon at Allstedt castle in July 1524 was much the same:

> If you wish to be righteous rulers, then you must grasp government by its roots as Christ has decreed. Chase out the enemies of the Elect . . . God is your shield and he will teach you to fight against your enemy. He will make your hands skilful for the battle and will succour you. But you will have to bear a great cross and suffering for this, until the fear of God is completely clear to your eyes.[26]

Remember: this piece of advice was given not to the oppressed, but to the potential oppressors themselves. Müntzer offered them one last opportunity to change their ways and become 'righteous', to obey the same – democratic? – divine law as every other man or woman. That Müntzer was now intent on levelling social differences in the interests of God's work is also clear from his greeting to Prince Friedrich in a letter of August 1524: 'The pure righteous fear of God with the invincible spirit of divine wisdom be with you instead of my greeting.'[27] This address contrasts starkly with the usual humble self-abasement which the subjects of a prince were expected to display, and even with Müntzer's address to the same prince just a year earlier: 'Most shining high-born prince and lord, may Your electoral Prince's Grace receive the righteous fear of God.'[28]

By the time of the peasant uprising in Thuringia in April 1525, almost all of Müntzer's advice and encouragement to supporters or insurgents was being rooted in the idea that 'Man' was not to be feared. In a letter to the peasants gathered in rebellion at Eisenach, he wrote: 'Have the best courage and sing with us: "I will not be afraid of one hundred thousand, even though they surround me." May God give you the spirit of strength.'[29] And in his famous address to the people of Allstedt, he called:

> On, on, while the fire is hot! Do not let your sword grow cold, do not let it hang loose in your hands. Smite cling-clang on the anvil of Nimrod; cast down their towers! As long as they live, it is not possible to be emptied of the fear of Man. One can say nothing of God as long as they rule over you . . . God will strengthen you in the true belief without the fear of Man.[30]

The idea that an exclusive fear of God and an absolute reliance on the commands of inner experience were essential for true faith thus developed beyond its subordinate role within Müntzer's theology. Between 1519 and 1525, it assumed a more prominent position in his doctrines, leading to the defiance of the 'godless tyrants' and becoming a rallying call for the insurgents of 1525. What drove this doctrine forward was quite simply the reaction of the Saxon authorities to religious reform in general and to Müntzer's reforms in particular. And their reaction was in turn conditioned by a reasonable dread that too many steps along the road of Church reform would turn the people against secular authority as well. By the time the German peasantry was beginning to stir, in late 1524, Müntzer's doctrine already constituted a platform for civil disobedience.

These, then, were the categories by which Müntzer interpreted his world and attempted to change it. Obviously, his ideas developed over a period of five or six years, and he expressed himself in different ways in the period leading up to 1525. What we have outlined above delineates his position in the months of the peasant uprising. The important thing with these categories is not their theological correctness – or otherwise – but the historical effect which Müntzer hoped they would produce. His perception of sixteenth-century social conditions produced a somewhat distorted image of the world, one in which there were Elect and damned, godless and poor-in-spirit – a universe where mortals struggled with mortals on God's behalf. This image reflected real social conditions and real struggles, but it was distorted because it was premised on a tradition of thought which could not see beyond divine machinations. It could not have been otherwise. The solution proposed by Müntzer was constructed on a series of opposed categories which were sometimes loosely defined: God and Man; past witness and present revelation; scripture and spirit; the individual believer and the combined authority of Church and State. But as the revolutionary crisis of 1524–5 unfolded, this construct offered to the oppressed the divine authority to rise up against the oppressor. Müntzer's God spoke and lived within the individual; his godless spoke and lived within Church and State authority. To fight for God was to flout authority; to oppose the godless was to advance the needs and aims of the oppressed. It is clear that even had individual princes or counts or their local representatives been tempted to join Müntzer for spiritual reasons, they would have undermined the very structure that gave them privilege and power. Müntzer's demands reflect the very similar social demands of the lower-class participants in the Peasants' War, when the feudal lords were effectively told to submit to the democratic voice of the common people.

Müntzer's reasons for developing these doctrines should not be construed as 'political' in the modern sense: he was no proto-Leninist or early proletarian revolutionary, or suchlike fabulous beast. In his ideas and practice, the more modern hand of political revolution lay in the glove of late-medieval mystical theology. Or, in the well-known words of Karl Marx:

> Men make their own history, but they do not make it as they please; they do not make it under self-selected circumstances, but under circumstances existing already, given and transmitted from the past. The tradition of all dead generations weighs like a nightmare on the brains of the living. And just as they seem to be occupied with revolutionizing themselves and things, creating something that did not exist before, precisely in such epochs of revolutionary crisis they anxiously conjure up the spirits of the past to their service, borrowing from them names, battle slogans, and costumes in order to present this new scene in world history in time-honoured disguise and borrowed language.[31]

(Marx went on to cite Luther adopting the mask of St Paul; he could equally well have cited Müntzer wielding the sword of Gideon.) Widespread physical suffering and intellectual doubts regarding the Church were reflected in the 'bitter' renewal of faith, while lower-class revolution was foreshadowed in Müntzer's uncompromising rejection of state power. The objective logic of his religion was aimed at overcoming the social, economic and political chasm that divided the rulers from the oppressed. Although Müntzer's theology dictated his political strategy, it was his political stance that largely determined which elements of mysticism were emphasised. His call to revolution was based on a human interest in the poor and oppressed, and a rejection of the material separation between rulers and ruled, since both were, ultimately, mortals before God. This was expressed in the language which he and all his contemporaries knew intimately: the language of prophecy, mysticism and religion.

And so it was that the next ten months of Müntzer's life were spent in synthesising religious belief and political revolution.

9

The Devil Never
Let Him Rest

Mühlhausen and Nürnberg (1524)

*So Duke Friedrich banished him from his lands. Thomas forgot
all about his great spirit and ran off and hid for half a year; after
this, he poked his nose out again, for the Devil never let him rest,
and moved to Nürnberg. But the Nürnberg council chased him in
good time from their town.*

Philipp Melanchthon (1525)

Having left Allstedt on the night of 7 August, Müntzer
would have arrived in Mühlhausen two or three days
later. That he travelled frustrated and deeply resentful
is understandable. He had had to leave behind a secure job, his
wife and child, and a promising ministry, forced out by people he
had once trusted. Prior to leaving, he penned a short letter to the
town council of Allstedt explaining his sudden departure. It was
almost apologetic: 'My affairs have obliged me to move across
country', he wrote 'so I must ask you quite amicably not to be
angry with me or be astonished by my behaviour.'[1] No sooner
had he reached Mühlhausen, however, than he gave vent to his
true feelings. He wrote three drafts of another letter to Allstedt.
The first, which was probably intended for the town council,
began unpromisingly: 'Instead of a greeting, I, Thomas Müntzer,
wish the aberrant people amongst you an aberrant God and I
wish the innocent a compassionate and innocent fear of God.'
The tone of this draft rather went downhill after that – 'Stir it all

up, dear sirs, let the shit stink nicely. I hope you will brew a heady beer from it, since you like drinking such filth.'[2] The second draft, written after taking a few deep breaths, was less insulting – it was possibly composed for his late parishioners – but still betrayed a deep hurt: 'Now you are so fearful that you deny the covenant with God . . . just like the people of Orlamünde – well, now there is nothing more I can do.'[3]

Having got the rage out of his system, Müntzer sat down on 15 August to write a third draft; this was the one which was actually sent back to Allstedt. In it, he explained to the people of the town what he had been trying to do – which was to 'scold in the bitterest tones those who tyrannise over Christian belief', and to convince people that 'a Christian should not sacrifice another Christian on the butcher's block, and that if the bigwigs did not prevent that from happening, then the reins of government should be taken from them'.[4] 'Perhaps', he continued,

> I should have kept quiet like some dumb dog? But why then should I make a living from preaching? . . . Perhaps I should have just let it all crash down on me and suffer death, so that the godless could do what they wanted with me and afterwards boast that they had strangled Satan? No, certainly not! The fear of God in me will not yield to the insolence of another.

One reason this letter was less immoderate than the previous drafts was that Müntzer still needed some assistance from Allstedt. He asked them to extend some charity – 'just as much as you can spare' – to his wife (his son is not mentioned) so that she would have something to live off in the interim. He also asked them to send on 'the Mass-books and Vesper-books' to Mühlhausen, 'for the people here are keen to use them'. (And they did indeed get some use: there is a report of a 'German mass' being celebrated in two churches in Mühlhausen on 16 March 1525.)

Also left behind in the hasty departure was his servant-cum-secretary Ambrosius Emmen, to whom he wrote a letter at the start of September. Emmen had been tasked with bringing to Mühlhausen the remnants of the household. These included 'the little pig' and someone named 'father'. His wife Ottilie was not mentioned, so one assumes by this point she had already joined Müntzer. The pig is self-explanatory; the 'father' was probably an elderly man named Herold von Liedersdorf, who had been in Müntzer's retinue in Allstedt, kept specifically, it seems, to report his dreams. The arrangements for the final house clearance had not gone well: a carter was supposed to have picked up Emmen and the various household goods a week previously, but, in the time-honoured manner of carters everywhere, had failed to turn up. Müntzer evidently needed his secretary more than he needed the furniture – 'just leave them with Peter Warmut and then join me'. (Warmut was a member of the Allstedt League, and was later killed at the battle of Frankenhausen.) Müntzer also reported that 'the people of Mühlhausen are slow, and as ignorant as folk are everywhere', but that this was not necessarily bad, since 'where cleverness resides so also does deviousness'. In a postscript to this letter, Müntzer said that he had written both to Zeiss and to the town council, 'but I will never write another word to that Judas Iscariot' – though the traitor was unnamed, this probably referred to the magistrate Nikolaus Rucker, who was deeply implicated in Müntzer's expulsion from Allstedt.[5]

The career of his colleague Simon Haferitz continued in Allstedt for only a short time. In late August, Zeiss advised Friedrich that Haferitz had distanced himself from Müntzer.[6] Whether this statement had any truth in it at all is debatable, but it at least served to ease the pressure on Zeiss. Haferitz disappeared for a while before turning up in Magdeburg in 1531, where his reputation caught up with him and he quickly became involved in controversy with the Catholic Church. Rather oddly, he was rescued from this predicament by Luther – who even accommodated Haferitz and his 'great army of children' in his own house in Wittenberg. Müntzer's reforming replacement in Allstedt was one Jodokus Kern, sent there specifically by Luther to undo any damage which Müntzer had done.

Ambrosius Emmen was required in Mühlhausen because Müntzer was busy writing. He was completing a lengthy broadside he had begun in Allstedt, and had made a start on another.

Rather unexpectedly for such a large town, Mühlhausen had no print shop of its own, so both documents had to be printed in Nürnberg towards the end of the year.

The first of these was entitled *An Explicit Exposure of False Faith, Presented to the Faithless World,* in which the author's name appeared as 'Thomas Müntzer with the Hammer'.[7] This was a reworking of the essay on the first chapter of the Gospel of St Luke which he had submitted to the Saxon censor in early August – nothing more was ever heard from the censor; the document disappeared into the chancellery and did not emerge again for 300 years. Perhaps a third longer than that submitted version (the printed edition ran to thirty-four pages), the *Explicit Exposure* – while also a very good summation of Müntzer's beliefs – is an open attack on all of his opponents, both secular and religious, demonstrating that there was no further hope of compromise. The initial address itself set out the agenda:

> Dear fellows, it is now our turn to make the hole in the wall wider, so that the whole world might understand who these great bigwigs are who have thus blasphemously turned God into a painted figure, Jeremiah 23. Thomas Müntzer with the Hammer . . . Jeremiah 1: 'I have set up an iron wall against the kings, princes and priests, and against the people. Try as they might to fight against you, a wonderful victory is prepared for the downfall of the strong and godless tyrants.'[8]

The pamphlet begins with a 'Preface to Poor, Confused Christianity', repeating the proposition that only true teaching by the Elect could save faith from academic 'lettered belief'. This preamble – and indeed the pamphlet in its entirety – was a direct and energetic reply to the accusations contained in Luther's letter to the princes of Saxony. But there was also something new: a direct appeal to the common man to break away from the Lutherans:

> Our scholars really want to lock away the testimony of the spirit of Jesus in the university. They will fail miserably in this, for they have not become learned just so that the common man might become their equals; rather they wish to judge belief only with

their stolen scripture . . . Therefore, you, the common people, must become learned yourselves, so that you are no longer led astray.[9]

The knowledge required by the common people was then laid out by Müntzer in the eight sections of his pamphlet dealing with the degenerate secular authority and the necessary regeneration of the spiritual realm. His main attack was on the Lutherans and their 'counterfeit' belief, their reliance on books rather than on subjective and direct revelation. Only the Elect could experience true revelation, and one of Müntzer's models here was Gideon:

> Gideon had such a firm, strong belief that he overwhelmed a large and countless world with only three hundred men . . . The fear of God creates the holy spirit, so that the Elect may be shaded by that thing which the world fears in its stupidity.[10]

This was a lucid restatement of Müntzer's theories on election, suffering and the acquisition of wisdom, but also contained a new idea – that the Elect could form a material force capable of overthrowing the existing political order.

Müntzer went on to explain just why the existing order of things should be overthrown. Firstly, there was the path to knowledge propounded by the Lutherans, and their intolerance of the idea of a living and perpetual source of faith:

> They come along with such an insipid and stale hypocrisy and say quite barefacedly: See, I believe the scripture! And then they get all jealous and annoyed, so that they grunt from behind their beards, saying: Oho, this one here denies the scripture! And then they want to stop up the mouths of everyone with their slanders, far worse than that oaf the Pope and his butter-boys.[11]

(The 'butter-boys' were those involved in selling Papal dispensations which allowed the purchaser to eat butter during Lent, without peril to the soul. There was indeed good money to be made in religion.) Müntzer explicitly draws the line between his view of the Bible and that of the Lutherans: 'The Son of God said: the scriptures give witness. The academics say: they give belief.'[12]

It was precisely their reliance solely on scripture that marked the academics as godless people in league with the tyrants when the practical issue of education arose:

> All these words and works mean that the poor man cannot learn to read because he is troubled for nourishment, and they preach unashamedly that the poor man should let himself be skinned and scraped by the tyrants. So how can he learn to read the scriptures? 'Yes, dear Thomas, you are raving: the scholars should read beautiful books, and the peasant should just listen, for faith comes through listening.' Ah yes, they've found a nice trick there, which would put much worse scoundrels than ever before, since the world began, in the place of the priests and monks.[13]

Here we approach the essence of Müntzer's revolutionary ideas, in passages positively blazing with anger: the existing political, economic and social structures constituted a wall between the common people and their God. This wall was shored up by the doctrines of both Papists and Lutherans. The only solution was for this entire structure to be overthrown, so that the true belief might be passed on to the illiterate and the poor. There are passages in this pamphlet addressed directly to 'you, the common people'; passages, too, where we glimpse how Müntzer's theology meets social revolution:

> In short, there is no other way to do it: a person must smash their stolen, fraudulent Christian belief to pieces, by mighty great suffering of the heart and by painful tribulation and by the unavoidable amazement which follows. Then that person becomes very small and quite despicable in their own eyes; in order that the godless may puff themselves up and swagger about, the Elect must sink to the very bottom. Then they can be lifted up by God and made great again and can, after heartfelt sadness, rejoice with all their heart in God the saviour. Then the great must yield to the small and become shameful before them. Oh, if the poor, abandoned peasants only knew that, it would be of much use to them.

Müntzer had few good things to say about the secular authority – and especially the Lutheran princes:

> Those who should stand at the forefront of Christianity, who are therefore called princes, show their supreme lack of faith in everything they do, fearing to do the right thing because of their brother-princes . . . And they like to be called 'most Christian' but tie themselves in knots to defend their godless fellow-princes, and say quite barefacedly that they would not lift a finger if their own subjects were persecuted by their neighbour on account of the gospel.[14]

Because Luther's teaching supported this tyrannical social order, Müntzer now proceeded to engage in a lengthy denunciation of the Wittenberger and his methods, apostrophising him as 'Brother Easy-Life and Father Tread-Softly',[15] and linking Luther's erroneous beliefs with his interpretation of the role of the secular authority. The Papists, the easy-living Lutherans and the tyrannical feudal lords prevented the common man from glimpsing the truth either as witnessed in the Bible or as taught by the Elect. But things were going to change: 'The weeds must now be winnowed from the wheat. For the time of the harvest is now here. Dear brothers, the weeds now shriek from every corner, that it is not harvest-time. Oh, the traitor betrays himself!'[16]

From start to finish, the pamphlet was a rousing and passionate condemnation of the present state of the world and its religious practices. The solution to all these problems lay in the common people preparing themselves for God's Apocalypse by overthrowing the godless tyrants.

Scarcely had Müntzer arrived in Mühlhausen than Luther was informed. He wasted no time in writing from Weimar 'An Epistle to the Honourable and Wise Lord Mayor, Town Council and Entire Parish of Mühlhausen'. The object of this letter of 21 August was quite simple: now that the Saxon authorities had at last chosen to move against Müntzer, Luther could re-establish his own leadership in the region. For this to succeed, Müntzer had to be prevented from settling again. In his letter, Luther

MVLHVSIVM.

11. Waldsch thor.
12. S. Kilian.
13. Newe pforte.
14. S. Martin.
15. Erfurtisch thor.

Part of a panoramic depiction of Mühlhausen (Mattheus Merian c. 1650). There were fifteen churches in the town. The one marked (4) is the Marienkirche, where Müntzer was installed as preacher in 1525.

warned the authorities in Mühlhausen about the teaching of this 'false spirit and prophet who goes about in sheep's clothing but underneath is a ravening wolf'.[17] He informed them of Müntzer's past in Zwickau and Allstedt, where he had proved 'what kind of tree he is, for he bears no other fruit than murder and riot, and provokes bloodshed'. And he advised the council to probe Müntzer's theology with the greatest care.

However, the council was in no position to pursue such a praiseworthy task. For the previous nineteen months, the town had been subject to almost permanent unrest and riot, and the town council itself rocked to and fro in the storm.

Mühlhausen was a fairly rich trading town with a population of around 7,500. It was the second-largest town in Thuringia after Erfurt, and in its heyday it had stood on one of the main medieval trading routes to and from the south-east. By the start of the sixteenth century these days were long gone – the trade which used to go through to Erfurt now went to Leipzig instead, and the route completely by-passed Mühlhausen. Nonetheless, past glories lingered on. The town contained fifteen churches and three cloisters, a palpable reminder of the wealth and worldliness of religious institutions. It was also a 'Free Imperial Town', which had for decades enjoyed the privileges of being self-administered, having representation at the Imperial Diets and being – in theory at least – answerable only to the Holy Roman Emperor. But with the downswing in its prosperity, it had been obliged to strike sundry military and political deals with the surrounding territorial princes: the usual suspects – the Archbishop of Mainz, and the electors and the dukes of Saxony.

There was tension between the patricians who controlled the municipal authority through the town council and the middle classes and poorer burghers. The latter were in the great majority – 65 per cent of the citizens in the suburbs were in a low taxation bracket, possessing less than eighty florins (taxation was not based on income, but on the valuation of property and possessions); only around 17 per cent of all citizens had possessions valued at between 800 and 60,000 florins.[18] The urban revolts throughout Germany in the second and third decades of the sixteenth century therefore soon found an echo here. The rich burghers in the town were able to invest their capital not only in the labour of the poorer sections of urban society, but also in the land and work of the local peasantry. It was not uncommon in Germany for farms and villages to pay rent to richer residents in the nearest town, and there were distinct advantages for a town in having the surrounding agricultural economy in its dependency. Indeed, throughout the period of unrest, the role of the townspeople was usually ambivalent – anxious to have their own liberties, but unwilling to side wholeheartedly with the peasants. Some eighteen villages were scattered within a radius of ten kilometres around Mühlhausen; these came under the governance of the town council and contained a further 2,400 people. But although the town council and individual town burghers owned much of the land surrounding Mühlhausen, it was the Church which made by far the highest profits: in possession of just over half of the land rented to the peasantry, it raked in rents which were on average some 50 per cent higher than those charged by either the burghers or the lay nobility.[19] Small wonder then that the Church was easily hounded out of Mühlhausen during 1524. But the great majority of townspeople, including burghers of the middle estates, were denied a role in political life: in early 1523,

Mühlhausen boasted a town council which was scarcely fit for purpose. Each year, an electoral college of 120 rich patricians and leading members of the more respectable guilds would elect, from among themselves, thirty councillors to hold office for a year; a different thirty would be chosen in each of the three succeeding years, after which the honour would return to the first thirty; and so on in endless rotation. This council had full civic powers in fiscal and criminal affairs, but a small inner core of 'senators' took the more important decisions. With many more than 120 citizens being of the opinion that political liberty came with economic liberty, a healthy democratic movement grew in the town.

In Mühlhausen, then, several contradictions interlocked: political, economic and social tensions which often found expression in religious controversy. With the arrival of the reform movement in 1522, and with bad harvests in both 1523 and 1524, the scene was set for riot.

Onto the stage stepped Heinrich Pfeiffer. Born with the family name of 'Schwertfeger', Pfeiffer perhaps adopted his new name, meaning 'piper', in recognition of the leader of the 1476 peasant revolt in Niklashausen, who had various nicknames including 'der Pfeiffer'. Our Pfeiffer was a native of Mühlhausen who had once been a monk in the Cistercian monastery at Reifenstein, not far away, where the abbot – doubtless with the benefit of hindsight – considered him to have been 'the worst monk of all'. In 1522, along with hundreds of his colleagues throughout Germany, Pfeiffer left the cloisters and established himself as a wandering preacher (and part-time cook) before settling in Mühlhausen in February 1523. On his arrival, the nascent reform movement in the town was galvanised. On 8 February, Pfeiffer gave his first sermon, using the opportunity afforded by the admirable German habit of buying the week's supply of beer immediately after attending church:

> When a cross was carried about the church . . . and the beer-seller stood on a stone beside the presbytery door . . . and called out his wines and beers to those in the churchyard, this monk in secular clothes got up on the same stone and said: 'Listen to me, I will call

another beer to you!' And he began to discuss the text for that Sunday, and to insult priests, nuns and monks.[20]

This was the very first 'reformed' sermon ever preached in the town. The response from Pfeiffer's audience to this dramatic intervention was enthusiastic, so he promised to preach again on the following day. The patrician council summoned the offending ex-monk, and he duly appeared before them after his promised second sermon, accompanied by a rowdy crowd, 'so that the council was relieved that the people could be dispersed with good words'.

On 1 April, similar scenes occurred; once again the council was unable to deal effectively with Pfeiffer's popular support. More importantly, however, the clumsy attempts to silence him triggered a new action by his supporters: the election of a body of sixteen men, collectively known as *Achtmänner* (district men). Their numbers included three tailors, three weavers, two cobblers, two tanners, a smith, a butcher and a carter. They were later to play an important role in the organisation of the democratic movement in Mühlhausen.[21] It was they, and their successors, who maintained the drive towards democracy in the periods of Pfeiffer's absence, and they who formed the embryo of a new town council. Also at about this time, several other lapsed monks arrived in town, including Matthäus Hisolidus, who 'insulted bishops, priests, monks and nuns', and one Master Hildebrant, who 'asked to preach, and attracted a great mob . . . He climbed into Caspar Ferber's house and preached from the gable window, mocked divine grace, compared it with a scabby sow, and many people willingly listened.'[22] Hisolidus had studied at Wittenberg, and was an eager follower of Karlstadt; indeed, there are good reasons for supposing that Karlstadt's teachings strongly influenced Pfeiffer and the early reforms in Mühlhausen. There is also some evidence that contact was made with the movement in Allstedt, which might explain why Müntzer moved here. But what is important to note is that, some sixteen months before Müntzer's arrival, Mühlhausen already boasted three radical reforming preachers.

Throughout 1523 there were riots and demonstrations against

the Catholic Church, its servants and its supporters. On the night of 18 June, adopting the modern fashion set by other towns, a mob chased several priests out of town. On 7 July, the tocsin was sounded while the town council was in session; on the initiative of Pfeiffer and Hisolidus, 'the people and several men from the Eichsfeld [i.e. the surrounding countryside] . . . ran up before the town-house with their weapons and wanted to execute their masters, and several shots were fired'.²³ These demonstrations continued for four hours until the *Achtmänner* began negotiations with the council; in the meantime, several presbyteries and cloisters were ransacked and acts of iconoclasm took place.

Accompanying these unruly escapades was a more constructive initiative. On 1 May, fifty-six representatives had been elected by the townspeople, and two weeks later they presented a list of fifty-five demands to the councillors – it was the latter's delaying tactics which had led to the July riots. Only two demands – significantly the only two dealing with purely religious matters and insisting on reformed preachers – were conceded immediately. The more political and social demands – relating to a more representative council, taxes, civic laws, public health and so forth – were not forced through until July. All the demands constituted a statement of early bourgeois democracy, attracting wide support from most of the townspeople. And after a new council was elected, open season was declared on the Church and its possessions.

And then, on 24 August, Pfeiffer and Hisolidus were expelled from the town. This suggests that the citizens, having achieved their primary goal of a form of civic democracy, wanted a respite from unrest – not an uncommon reaction after an exhausting period of tumultuous change. The Imperial mandate of March 1523 – the same one which had empowered Ernst of Mansfeld against Müntzer in Allstedt – was invoked to justify the expulsion of the two preachers. Of course, the mandate could have been ignored – it was easy enough to do in that period, even in a Free Imperial City – but the balance of power in the town still remained with the wealthier inhabitants, who were by now tired of upheaval and apprehensive about where things might lead once the religious changes were complete. Hisolidus, after fruitless attempts to regain entry, moved to a small town near Eisenach to carry on the good work. But by Christmas, Pfeiffer had returned, and the winter months saw further dramatic events. (Surprisingly, Pfeiffer had petitioned Duke Johann to intercede on his behalf – even more surprisingly, the duke duly did so.) On 27 December, a crowd of women chased a priest through the town and ransacked his home, after he had criticised Pfeiffer; in March 1524, a riot was sparked off after a monk had declared somewhat undiplomatically that 'the citizens were pilfering murderers'. It was reported that they almost killed him.[24] All through the spring and summer of that year, Pfeiffer was at the forefront of continued attacks on the 'old' Church; preaching from the pulpit at the Nikolaikirche, he instigated iconoclasms in the several religious institutions of the town, and actively sought to gain the support of the outlying villages for the Church reforms.

Thus, when Müntzer arrived in August 1524, perhaps on an open invitation from those who knew his work in Allstedt, the town council was really in no fit state to act as Luther would have wished. Müntzer was conceivably the least of their worries. In any case, he was then, and for the initial eight-week period during which he lived there, a refugee without any formal standing in the community. He had no parish, no pulpit, no house to call his own. Despite his low profile, however, he was active. Apart from his labours on his two new pamphlets, he had also teamed up with Pfeiffer in an effort to drive forward the necessary reforms in religious and political affairs. He had arrived, after all, with the doctrinal weapons to destroy the godless opposition. He came ready to educate and to organise the people, free from the immediate gaze of any feudal authority. There was to be no further attempt to hold a dialogue with such tyrants, no rapprochement with Wittenberg.

In 1524, Mühlhausen effectively became the centre for the radical Reformation in central Germany. An impressive collection of young and energetic reforming preachers had assembled. Here was Pfeiffer, Hisolidus, Simon Hildebrant and Johann Laue – who later confessed that he had 'preached that princes and lords were geese, blockheads, dissolutes, slave-drivers; and so no one should obey them. And he did that because he saw that the people approved of it.'[25] And now here was Müntzer as well, one among several dangerous equals. Under the leadership of these men, the unrest continued unabated well into September. On the 18th of that month, Pfeiffer and Müntzer, with a red cross and a naked sword held aloft, led a procession of around 200 people, including the *Achtmänner*, to a wayside chapel at a place named Eiche, a little way out of town. Here they camped for one night and then returned to town the following day. Quite what the purpose of this excursion was is anyone's guess. It may simply have been a public demonstration of strength, or a bonding exercise of some sort; at all events, the chapel was left undamaged. There is speculation that this was when a group known as the 'Eternal League of God' (*Ewiger Bund Gottes*) – later to become significant in Mühlhausen's short history of revolution – was formed. The scanty evidence available suggests that it was formed either then or in the spring of 1525. We shall return to this league later.

In reacting to these interesting events, the old town authorities mis-stepped. On 19 September, over-indulgence at a wedding led a sexton, a known iconoclast, to drunkenly insult one of the mayors. The insult clearly touched a nerve, for the mayor had the sexton thrown into the prison in the town-hall basement.[26] The *Achtmänner* demanded the release of the unfortunate man – among the agreements reached in the previous summer was one which forbade imprisoning anyone who should simply be fined – and then convoked a council meeting for that same night. But the two mayors and ten other members of the town council fled under darkness to Salza (around sixteen kilometres to the south-east, now named Bad Langensalza), taking with them all the town insignia – flag, seals, keys – not to mention the municipal horse. This act was a grave violation of civic law (the seals were a necessary piece of equipment for legal government) and an insult to the citizens. So the people turned their attention to more plundering of churches and abuse of religious relics. The days that followed were full of confusion, since no one could reach agreement on how to resolve the situation. Messengers were sent off to Salza to demand the return of the insignia – which the council-in-exile refused point blank to do. Neither seals nor horse were coming back any time soon.

On 22 September, Müntzer wrote a letter to the 'parish of Mühlhausen' in which he condemned the 'fear of men' as a hindrance to any satisfactory resolution of the problems, and encouraged his and Pfeiffer's followers to publicise the godlessness of the town's authorities:

> If all this is printed and placed before the whole world, then you will have the consideration of all Christendom, and it will be said: 'See, the pious people have been far too patient. They have obeyed the law of God'; and Christendom will speak of you as of a chosen race, Deuteronomy 4: 'See, this is a wise people, it is an understanding people, this will become a great people. These are those who dare to fight alongside God. They wish to act justly and do not fear the devil with all his attacks, spite and pomp.'[27]

Müntzer called for the resignation of the town council because of its refusal to help the reform movement, and 'in order to avoid future evil. For the common man (God be praised) has now accepted the truth in almost every place.'

To coincide with Müntzer's letter, he and Pfeiffer drew up a set of demands to present to the council – the so-called 'Eleven Articles'.[28] These were prefaced by a statement that several parishes of the town had agreed upon them, adding – as was usual for such articles – the qualification that 'if these conclusions go against God's word, then they should be altered and improved'. The first demand set the tone: 'A completely new council [should] be appointed. Why? To ensure that actions are taken in the fear of God; that old hatreds do not linger on; that arbitrariness ceases.' In any event, the departure of the ten councillors meant that the old council now failed to constitute a quorum, so a new council was essential. In the following ten articles, few concrete economic or social demands were set out, the single exception being a demand for the establishment of a poor fund to help the needy. Instead, the main thrust of the list was purely political, arguing for an advanced form of democracy, with the immediate dismissal of any councillor found hindering 'the fulfilment of God's commandment', and threatening the present council with massive bad publicity if it did not agree to the demands. Also in there, almost by necessity, was the requirement for a new seal to be used on future official documents – the old seal being in Salza with the horse. The list closed with a restatement of the principle of the fear of God, indisputably marking this document as one heavily influenced by Müntzer:

> we would much prefer to have God as our friend and the people our enemy than to have God as our enemy and the people as our friends; for it is a grievous thing to fall into the hands of God . . . You should fear him who has the power to cast body and soul into the fires of hell.

These demands met with widespread approval among the town's inhabitants, and were greeted with especial enthusiasm by the guild of weavers, one of the poorest groups of the town. But it was still impossible to progress – many of the better-off citizens were already beginning to wonder whether things had really gone too far. An immediate setback was provided by the peasants who lived around the town, since none of the Eleven Articles addressed issues which might benefit rural inhabitants. On 24 September, a preacher named Johann Behme arrived in town. He may have been sent there by Luther, who was watching nervously from afar; disappointingly for him, however, Behme immediately joined Pfeiffer and Müntzer in supporting iconoclasm. On the same day, an assembly of the peasants formally complained that the town's 'unchristian action was insufferable' and threatened to seek new landlords – a matter of some concern for those in town who derived a good income from rural leaseholds. In reprisal, urban persons unknown sent a threat to one of the more prosperous villages – Bollstedt – that it would be set on fire. Sure enough, on the following day, Bollstedt was ablaze, and the attempts of the town council to send firemen were thwarted.[29]

On 26 September, the discredited remnants of the council attempted to regain the initiative by summoning 200 armed peasants to one of the town gates. Their hope of taking back control faltered, however, when a good number of the peasants decided they would prefer to join the common people of the town; the council hurriedly sent most of them back home. In the meantime, Pfeiffer took the slightly counter-intuitive step of leaving Mühl-hausen along with a group of his supporters. The town council instantly closed the town gate behind them, forcing the party to spend the night out of doors. They were permitted re-entry the following day, just in time to witness a gathering of the citizenry outside the town hall, where – by popular vote – it was decided that Müntzer and Pfeiffer should be run out of town. These were indeed confusing times.

The two men did not leave immediately.[30] They remained in town for about a week and then headed south. Müntzer's wife Ottilie, in a repeat of what had happened in Allstedt, was left behind. (Pfeiffer would return to Mühlhausen just before Christmas, and Müntzer in late February – both with entirely undiminished energy. The town council had won a battle, but not the war.)

We know where Müntzer ended up next; we just do not know precisely how or when, because once again he slips off the radar – although this time he disappears more by necessity than by the sport of the daemon of archives. In early November, both he and his two new manuscripts turned up in the Imperial city of Nürnberg, some 250 kilometres south of Mühlhausen. Not quite halfway between the two is the small village of Bibra, close to the town of Meiningen; in Bibra lived a bookseller named Hans Hut, sometime teacher, and a future leader of the German Anabaptists.

We can only speculate where and when Müntzer and Hut had become acquainted: it is possible that Müntzer's printer Widemar of Eilenburg was a mutual acquaintance; or that Hut passed through Allstedt on business during Müntzer's ministry there; or perhaps Hut was in Mühlhausen in September 1524. As a book-seller, it was Hut's business to travel around central Germany, visiting suppliers and customers, so it is likely the paths of the two men would have crossed at some point. The record of Hut's own confession, made in 1527, stated that 'Müntzer, when he was expelled, spent one night and one day in his house at Bibra,

Portrait of Hans Hut, by Christoffel van Sichem, 1608.

but he [Hut] had nothing to do with him, except that Müntzer gave him a pamphlet to print, the first chapter of Luke.'[31]

He had nothing to do with Müntzer except arrange for the printing of a subversive pamphlet? It seemed rather a lame excuse. This pamphlet was the *Explicit Exposure*, the manuscript of which was probably handed over to Hut after Müntzer's expulsion from Mühlhausen (he was not 'expelled' from Allstedt). This would also suggest that the two men had known each other in Allstedt: Müntzer would scarcely have entrusted such an important document to someone he had only just met. With the manuscript safely in his keeping, Hut left for Nürnberg; it is possible that he was accompanied by Pfeiffer, since they both arrived in the city at much the same time. As for Müntzer – here we are obliged to repeat an old refrain: we do not know what Müntzer did for the rest of October. On the plus side, we are fairly sure of what Hut and Pfeiffer did.

❧

Before our narrative turns to Müntzer's activity in Nürnberg, let us look at his other pamphlet, which was to be his last. He had spent much of his time in Mühlhausen preparing this virulent and richly worded attack on Martin Luther. The title says it all: *A Highly Provoked Vindication and a Reply to the Spiritless Easy-Living Flesh in Wittenberg who has Sullied Wretched Christianity with his Falsification and Theft of the Holy Scriptures.*[32] The name of the author was given as 'Thomas Müntzer, of Allstedt'. This manuscript he had not entrusted to Hut; indeed, it is likely that it was still in draft form, and not completed until November. A contract was agreed in Nürnberg with the Lutheran printer Hieronymus Höltzel. But the manuscript may have been handed over to the printer by someone other than Müntzer: Höltzel identified the man who gave it to him as an unnamed pedlar or traveller. Circumstantial evidence suggests that this could have been Martin Reinhart, himself a radical preacher associated with Karlstadt, and lately expelled from the town of Jena; but it is not out of the question that behind this disguise was Müntzer himself. Or perhaps Höltzel simply misled the authorities with some vague tale of a pedlar who had long since gone elsewhere. Typesetting duly began for the thirty-two-page pamphlet. But then – by pure chance – in mid-December a raid on Höltzel's workshop in search of a pamphlet on the Eucharist by Karlstadt (by now exiled from Saxony, at Luther's behest) also uncovered Müntzer's work, which was promptly confiscated. Several copies survive, so some had already been distributed. Höltzel was imprisoned, refusing resolutely to identify his client; meanwhile the authorities took a closer look at the text.

For the Lutherans, it was a shocking document. The Wittenberg movement had made good progress in Nürnberg since 1522, under the able guidance of the theologian Andreas Osiander, and had attracted the best of the intellectuals and craftsmen to the cause, as well as the flourishing middle and entrepreneurial classes – among those supporting Lutheran reform were the painter Albrecht Dürer and the poet Hans Sachs. In 1524, official recognition was given in Nürnberg to the reforms. But the course of the movement was as bumpy here as anywhere. In the summer of 1524, peasant disturbances around its northern neighbour

Bamberg threatened to inspire a ready echo in Nürnberg; there were numerous radicals, largely supporters of Karlstadt, in the city. The city council therefore had to tread carefully and nip in the bud any signs of democratic radicalism. And now up popped Müntzer with an explosive condemnation of Luther. The reaction was foreseeable.

The tract was dedicated and addressed to Jesus Christ in a manner obviously intended to satirise Luther's recent letter to the 'high-born' princes of Saxony. Compare the two addresses:

Luther	Müntzer
To the most shining, high-born princes and lords, Lord Friedrich, Elector of the Roman Empire, and Johann, Duke of Saxony, Landgrave of Thuringia, and Margrave of Meissen, my dear lords . . .	To the most illustrious first-born prince and almighty lord, Jesus Christ, the gentle king of kings, the bold duke of all believers, my most merciful lord and faithful protector . . .

And in case the point was missed, Müntzer gave 'all praise, name, honour and worthiness, all homage and splendour to you alone, you eternal son of God'.[33] Müntzer immediately launched into a bitter attack on the godless academics and their false belief. His writing is passionate, frequently earthy, sometimes gross; halfway through he suddenly switches from referencing Luther in the third person to directly addressing him in the second person. He makes continual comparisons between himself and Jesus. But most of all he attacks Luther and all that he stands for. A hundred and one names both folkloristic and eschatological are applied to him: 'the most ambitious Doctor Liar', 'the sycophantic scoundrel of Wittenberg', 'the easy-living opinionist', 'Doctor Ludibrius' (ridiculous), 'the godless Wittenberg flesh', 'the spiteful black raven', 'Father Tread-Softly', 'the proud, inflated, spiteful dragon', 'Esau' – or quite simply, but no less abusively, 'monk'. And many more. One could see in this an over-egged response to Luther's refusal to mention Müntzer by name in his letter to the princes. But there is a further purpose to the name-calling, which is to place Luther firmly in the same camp as the monks and Papists, princes and tyrants. The arguments adduced to back up these insults are those we already know – the opposition of living revelation to dead letter, of worldly doctrine to experienced belief, of faith to suffering, and so on.

> Anyone can see with their own eyes that the present-day scholars do nothing different from the Pharisees of yesteryear, priding themselves in their use of the holy scripture, writing and scribbling whole books full and chattering more and more loudly: believe, believe! But they deny the very foundation of faith, they scoff at the spirit of God and quite simply believe in nothing.[34]

To these arguments is now added the accusation that the Lutherans prefer the good and comfortable life of salaried priests, with an eye for money and rich widows. Luther himself was the worst, a man who had manifestly become a creature of the princes:

> We could quite easily fall asleep listening to your boasting and nonsensical foolishness. The fact that you were able to stand before the Empire at Worms is all thanks to the German nobility, whose mouth you have smeared well with honey, because they fully expected that you would make them some gifts of the Bohemian kind with your preaching – that is, hand over monasteries and religious foundations to them – as you are now promising the princes.[35]

'Bohemian gifts' refers to one practical outcome of the Hussite reforms in Bohemia, which transferred wealth and land from Church estates into the hands of the nobility. The Reformation across Europe led to similar results, and Müntzer clearly saw the same outcome being the practical effect of Lutheranism in Saxony. He reminded Luther of the promising beginnings the latter had made with his pamphlet on 'Commerce and Usury' in 1524, in which he had condemned the princes as thieves and robbers; but Luther had failed to draw the conclusion that robbery was inherent to feudalism. Now he stood accused of condoning the social tyrants, not simply of acting as some unconscious tool; the ruling class steal everything for themselves – fish, birds, plants – and yet they hang any poor man who commits the least crime. 'And to this Doctor Liar says: Amen . . . And if saying this makes me a rabble-rouser – then so be it!'[36]

This was one of Müntzer's most outspoken social criticisms, a clear reflection of the complaints of the peasantry whose conditions were being eroded precisely by the nobility's urge to accumulate land and wealth. His final phrase – 'then so be it!' – echoes Luther's famous (but probably apocryphal) 'Here I stand, I can do no other, so help me God' at Worms; Müntzer is just as rousing. He accused Luther of abandoning the movement at Worms, of crossing over to the camp of the tyrants and leaving true reform to others: 'Saul also started something good, but it was David, after wandering around for a long time, who had to complete it.'[37]

Müntzer also took the opportunity here to explain his sermon before the princes. What he regarded as the most important message there, 'which I clearly put to the princes', was

> that a whole community should have the power of the sword, just as they should have the key to forgiveness; I taught them that the princes were not lords over the sword, but rather its servants, and that they should not act however they want: they should bring justice. And that is why it is traditional for the people to be present whenever someone is brought for judgement before the law.[38]

This willingness to conduct a very public discussion on reform is contrasted with Luther's approach, which was based on secrecy, machinations and disputation behind closed doors. Müntzer cited as evidence Luther's role in the altercation with Ernst of Mansfeld and in the attempts to suppress the new liturgical practice at Allstedt, his letters to the princes, and even the problems which Müntzer had had in Nordhausen. What Luther's actions amounted to was a major campaign to keep the common people from an education in true religion and to maintain the tyrants in power.

In short and in conclusion:

> O Doctor Liar, you wily fox, with your lies you have saddened the hearts of the righteous, whom God did not sadden, you have

increased the power of the godless villains so that they have stayed in their old ways. And for this you will end like a captured fox. The people will be free from your tyranny and God alone will be lord over them.[39]

When Müntzer arrived in Nürnberg – probably at the start of November – he deliberately kept a low profile. In a letter to Zeiss's cousin, Christoph Meinhard, written at about this time, he reported:

I could easily have played a fine game with the people of N[ürnberg], if I had wanted to stir up trouble in the way that the lying world accuses me of. But I want to turn my accusers into cowards by my words alone, such that they will not be able to deny it. Many of the folk in N. advised me to preach, but I told them that that was not why I had come, but only to state my case in print. When the city authorities heard that, their ears fairly sang, because they like having good days. The sweat of the working people tastes sweet to them, so sweet, but it will turn into bitter gall. And then no debates or mock-battles will help them – the truth will out . . . The people are hungry, they must eat and they will eat.[40]

More and more now, Müntzer's writing references the common people and their spiritual and physical suffering. This is a reflection, as we shall see, of the growing storm of the Peasants' War.

It seems unlikely, in truth, that the authorities were aware of Müntzer's presence, since he remained in the city after his two companions had already been expelled for their misdemeanours. But his tactics are worthy of note: he considered it imperative that he should reach a wider public through his writings at this stage – so keeping well hidden was the best option. Even so, it is astonishing that he avoided coming under scrutiny during the weeks in which he was in town.

Hans Hut had been commissioned to organise the publication of the *Explicit Exposure*, and for this purpose he assumed the name 'Heinrich von Mellerstadt' to avoid detection – Mellrichstadt being a town not far from Hut's home at Bibra. By the start of October, he had succeeded in finding a printing establishment willing to take on the risky business, an enterprise owned by Johann Hergot and his wife. Hergot had already nailed his colours firmly to the mast of reform by printing works by Karlstadt and other radicals, as well as pirated works by Luther (in 1527, he would be executed by the authorities for his Utopian pamphlet, *On the New Change of a Christian Life*). Whether Hergot actually knew that his press was printing Müntzer's work is another question; he may have been away on business, leaving his four assistants to conduct day-to-day affairs. As a further precaution against discovery, the title page of the pamphlet carefully named Mühlhausen as the place of publication. But Hut's luck ran out: the city fathers somehow got to hear of this unlicensed project, raided the print shop on 29 October and confiscated 400 copies of the *Explicit Exposure*. One hundred copies, fortunately, had already been despatched to Augsburg, and there distributed. One recipient was Augustin Bader, a radical tailor and future Anabaptist leader, of whom more later. Hut and Hergot's assistants were arrested – then immediately released; Hut was even compensated for any financial inconvenience.

Heinrich Pfeiffer fared worse. Using his original name 'Schwertfeger' as cover, he adopted the opposite approach to Müntzer. On 26 October, the city authorities noted that Pfeiffer 'ventured to attract a large following through disputation'; they felt constrained to investigate: 'it should be established whether a disciple of the false prophet Müntzer is here . . . and what his deeds and teachings are'.[41] It is not unreasonable to suppose that Pfeiffer's activities alerted the city fathers to Hut's venture. Three days later, the authorities had in their hands copies of two leaflets attributed to Pfeiffer and the evidence thus obtained encouraged them to expel the man straight away. In order that the people of Nürnberg might be improved and protected, the Lutheran Andreas Osiander was invited to pass judgement on the leaflets.

The originals are no longer traceable, but Osiander's report on them was not positive: 'I have read them', he wrote, 'and, in short, I have found nothing good anywhere in them'.[42] The author of the tracts was judged to have ideas very similar to Müntzer's:

He would like to bring back the law according to which false prophets are beaten to death . . . But he means here . . . all preachers who do not move about in his spirit . . . The scripture is nothing more than a witness . . . God himself must speak to us with the living voice.

Osiander's evaluation of the politics of the pamphlets was entirely consistent with Luther's views: Pfeiffer allegedly wished

to introduce murder, riot, overthrowing of authority, and to make a worldly kingdom from the spiritual kingdom of Christ, which would not be governed by God's word, but by the sword and by violence – which would be unchristian and utterly devilish.

Before he could be arrested, the author of these tracts left Nürnberg in a hurry on the second-to-last day of November, and by mid-December he was back in Mühlhausen.

Another contact of Hut, Pfeiffer and Müntzer in Nürnberg was Hans Denck, a man destined to become – with Hut – one of the leaders of German Anabaptism. Denck had come to the city from Basel in 1523 to take up a teaching post, and within a year had emerged as a major figure in Humanist, radical-Lutheran and mystical circles. His mentor in Basel had been the Swiss Humanist and reformer Johann Oekolampad, and Denck's doctrines contained something of the Humanist ideal. In September and October, Denck extended hospitality to Hut, perhaps also to Pfeiffer, and he may have met Müntzer. In January 1525 he was cited in the trial of the 'three godless painters' – whose religious beliefs were very much of the radical sort and who stood accused of distributing Karlstadt's and Müntzer's tracts. (The three painters – the brothers Sebald and Barthel Beham and Georg Pencz, who may have worked in Albrecht Dürer's studio – were expelled from Nürnberg after their trial; they returned not long afterwards, only to be accused of creating pornographic images, and were expelled once more. It is a seductive thought that any one of these three could have made a portrait of Müntzer when he was in Nürnberg – the original portrait from which van Sichem worked decades later.) Hans Denck, in his statement to the city council at the trial, reportedly suggested that he wished 'neither to know nor hear the scriptures except as a testimony alone'.[43] This admission accelerated his own banishment from the city at the end of January. Fortunately, either Hut or Pfeiffer had made him an open offer to go and teach in Mühlhausen, and this he did in the early part of 1525.

Exactly when Müntzer arrived in Nürnberg, where he lived and whom he met there are all unknown. One thing we do know, however, is rather a curiosity. This was Müntzer's dealings with a man named Christoph Furer. Furer was no ordinary person. He was in fact one of the wealthiest mining magnates resident in Nürnberg, an educated, powerful man, and an important member of the patrician city council. But in common with a number of Müntzer's 'establishment' contacts – Hans Zeiss, Christoph Meinhard, Michael Ganssau – he showed a serious desire to question and understand the reformed religion; it was partly to Müntzer that these men all turned for advice. In that era, people from different classes could be seriously moved by religious ideas, even the most radical ones. Meinhard, for example, was concerned about purgatory and the afterlife, after Luther had, in 1523, abolished special Masses or celebrations for the dead; his brief correspondence with Müntzer centred on such basic questions of faith. These men were figures for whom Müntzer seemed to have respect. This sits rather ill with the common perception of Müntzer as a revolutionary red in tooth and claw – and, indeed, in his *Explicit Exposure*, he had expressly condemned those who sought to serve both God and Mammon: such people 'must remain eternally empty of God'. His relationship with these men is thus difficult to understand: on the one side a well-educated, intelligent, but very radical preacher who called openly for the overthrow of both the Papal Church and secular authority; on the other, men around whom the finances and administration of late feudalism and early capitalism tightly revolved. Why would either side maintain contact with the other? To which the answer must be: that is what it was like in the German Reformation up until 1525 – rebellion had not yet flipped over into revolution, so the red lines between debate and condemnation had not yet been laid down.

In Furer's case, it is clear that he was of an enquiring mind. He was certainly not a Lutheran – he is better described as a 'liberal Catholic', sceptical both of the Roman religion and of several elements of Luther's reforms. Over the years, he accumulated a small collection of Müntzeriana in his library, including copies of letters from Müntzer to the Counts of Mansfeld, and a copy of his later 'confession'. But there was also a short document in which Furer had posed to Müntzer five questions relating to faith – very specifically, to Luther's doctrine of 'justification by faith alone' – and on this same piece of paper Müntzer had scribbled his answers. It is a document whose physical appearance – an unaddressed letter – suggests that the two men were living not far from each other in Nürnberg.[44] To his credit, Furer did not alert the authorities to Müntzer's presence.

In the space of four months, Müntzer had prepared three major works which succinctly summarised his own radical anti-authoritarian philosophy and firmly positioned him as Luther's most vehement critic. These works were to be his final publications, for he now found himself facing an entirely new situation, one which required new tactics in the battle for the salvation of the world. Although Nürnberg was one of the few places which Müntzer did not find himself obliged to leave in a hurry (Melanchthon, quoted at the head of this chapter, was misinformed), his visit ultimately failed. He was unaware of the full extent of his failure, since he had left the city before Höltzel's print shop was raided. In early December, he was already heading into south-west Germany; to get there, he journeyed some 400 kilometres on foot in early winter.

For it was there in the south-west that the peasantry was mustering for its great revolution, the German Peasants' War.

10

His Poisonous Seed

In South-West Germany at the Time of the Peasant Uprising (1524–1525)

When he was driven from Allstedt, he next went . . . into Upper Germany, and then journeyed through Basel, to Griessen in Klett-gau . . . and in the peasant uproar which shortly followed, he planted his poisonous seed in the restless rebellious hearts of the peasants. At that time he also spread the doctrine of Anabaptism.

Heinrich Bullinger (1560)

In June 1524, Clementia, Countess of Lupfen, was a lady in dire straits. Sitting in the family castle at Stühlingen, she realised she had run out of snail shells, as well as juniper berries and barberries for making jam. The barberries may have been simply a whim, but the shells were absolutely vital sewing accessories, needed by her maids to spool their threads. What was a countess to do? She summoned her husband's serfs and told them to drop everything until they had collected a sufficiency of shells. She ignored their protest that it was the middle of the harvest and no one could be spared. In her defence, it should be noted that her husband, Sigismund II, had very recently ordered some of his serfs to traipse 100 kilometres over to his other estate in the Alsace, to deliver some game and bring back a cartload of wine (at their own expense, of course) from his vineyards, a journey which would have taken them more than a week. And if the count's wine was needed, then no way could berries and shells be refused to the countess. Lamentably, one thing led to another, and the irritated, ungrateful peasantry of Stühlingen took it into their heads to band together and be done with feudalism once and for all. So began the German Peasants' War of 1524 to 1525.[1]

That is one theory at least. And not an unattractive one either, even if it sounds a little too much like Marie Antoinette and her cakes. History frequently demonstrates that a minor event can prove to be the final straw. But this event was not the only trigger for an uprising that spread over most of south and central Germany within weeks, involved tens of thousands of peasants and townspeople, and, over the course of almost a year, threatened the governance of huge swathes of territory. Perhaps the point about the Clementia story is that – even if it seems extraordinary to us – it was perfectly plausible. Feudal lords and ladies, both secular and religious, did indeed have the right to stop a harvest dead in its tracks and oblige the peasantry to undertake any other form of labour. And, quite understandably, the peasants of Stühlingen were not amused.

The first rumblings of rebellion occurred in the Black Forest as early as May 1524, and throughout that summer other minor disturbances took place.[2] Then came Lupfen. By late summer, the peasants around Stühlingen, in the Klettgau district west of Lake Constance, had massed 1,200-strong under the ex-soldier Hans Müller of Bulgenbach. They marched on Klettgau's administrative capital, the town of Waldshut, to unite with its citizens for the defence of civic and religious reforms against their Austrian Habsburg overlords (Waldshut lay in a large exclave of Austria). At the start, it resembled more of a strike, a downing of tools in order to make a point. But this local event was the signal for a general insurrection by groups of peasants in the entire southwest corner of Germany, who slowly but surely banded together in ever larger armies over the following six months.

We have already noted the social conditions for this turn of events; for over 200 years, groups of disaffected peasants and town-dwellers had formed occasional leagues to defend themselves against the changes taking place in the economy and society. Protest against feudal excess abounded and anti-clericalism was

Peasant carrying a 'Freedom' banner. Depicted by Thomas Murner in his book *Von dem grossen Lutherischen Narren* (1522).

rife. Between 1300 and 1600, Germany witnessed far more urban and rural revolts than any other region in Europe.[3] The southwest of Germany, in particular, had a long history of rebellions, under the banners of the 'Poor Conrad' or 'Peasant Shoe' (*Bundschuh*); these demanded the cancellation of debts, the abolition of tithes and interest rates, changes in the legal system and major reforms to bring the Church institutions under some control. There were rebellions in 1493, 1502 and every year between 1513 and 1517, in Alsace, Swabia and the Black Forest. After 1517, the number of local disturbances increased and spread across the whole of south Germany, encouraged by Luther's and Zwingli's new ideas. All of this laid down a rich seam of experience for the peasants who, in 1524, now took up the struggle in the national arena.

Quite why this uprising was qualitatively different from all the previous revolts is a matter of considerable debate. But the contributing factors can be loosely categorised as follows: firstly, a decline in the rural economy, caused in part by an increase in feudal dues and duties and higher taxes – the 'death tax' was especially harsh, frequently dispossessing entire families on the death of the breadwinner; secondly, a growing gap in the living standards between rich landowners and the mass of poorer peasants, sometimes made all the worse by regular crop failures – severe weather destroyed large areas of standing crops in the summer of 1524 (tellingly, the Catholic authorities were quick to blame the 'unchristian Lutheran' reformers for the weather; the Lutherans retaliated by explaining that God had sent the storms as a punishment against those who refused to reform!);[4] thirdly, an improvement in the political awareness of the peasantry, who had been dipping their toes in the waters of rebellion for several decades, and who were also exercising some degree of self-government as villages grew in size; and fourthly, in the second decade of the new century, a widespread feeling that 'God's Law' was not being observed by the representatives of the Church or its wealthy supporters in the nobility. The peasants' demands, then, ranged from localised and specific grievances against some petty tyrant right up to much more widespread and generalised complaints about serfdom, restrictive tenancies, access to common ground, water and woods, and the payment of tithes.

The Swiss and German movements for religious reform served to propel many of the local demands into the national arena while adding greater justification for all the demands relating to the Church. The reform movement under Huldrych Zwingli in Zürich had as much – arguably, a greater – effect on the consciousness of the common people of the Black Forest and Swabia as did the German reform movement centred in Wittenberg; the south-west Germans had for years been looking jealously at the democratic freedoms in the Swiss confederation just over the border. Not only did the reform movement give voice to the concerns of the peasantry and their leaders, but reciprocally it also influenced and encouraged them. This new religious dimension provided the peasantry with a regional framework that allowed them to pass beyond merely local uprisings, to link up with other peasant groups and with the lower classes in the towns, and so turn the rebellion of 1524–5 into something that looked very like a revolution. The driving force was the simple idea that 'God's Law' could be cited to challenge established legal and socio-economic structures: such a law had the beauty of being practically what anyone wanted it to be, just as long as it could be justified with reference to the Bible. Which was never a very difficult task.

The summer of 1524 saw the beginning of the great peasant rebellion. And it was no coincidence that this was also the year that the territorial princes finally began to pay serious attention to the radicalisation of religious reforms in Saxony, Thuringia and elsewhere – Karlstadt was expelled from Saxony, Müntzer was forced to leave Allstedt, the radicals in Nürnberg were summoned before the city fathers, and Balthasar Hubmaier came under attack from the Habsburgs for his reforms of Church and civic authority in Waldshut. Although these attacks were intended to forestall any challenge to authority, in either religious or secular realms, they in fact precipitated events that led to an even graver threat to the social order.

When the Stühlingen peasantry finally made its move in August 1524, the Swabian authorities were caught off guard. The armed forces and mercenaries on which Habsburgs and other nobles usually relied were largely already committed to two major arenas of war in the Empire: against the Turks of the Ottoman Empire, who by then were deep into Hungary and threatening Austria; and in Italy, where any self-respecting European monarch or nobleman was embroiled in the campaign to parcel up that unhappy country. It was not until after the Imperial victory at the battle of Pavia on 24 February 1525 that their mercenaries (*Landsknechte*) could be recalled to deal with the threat at home. Even then, problems arose with the financing of the armies thus reassembled in Germany: on occasion, Swiss mercenaries went home in disgust after non-payment of wages; and the Swabian and Habsburg nobility was heavily reliant on agreeing credit-lines with the Fugger bankers to see them to victory. Adding to the problems, many German soldiers were of peasant stock and had no desire to kill their own. The nobility of south Germany was therefore obliged to negotiate with the rebels and discuss their grievances in the courts of law or in hastily convened parliaments. The authorities dragged out these negotiations through the winter in order to gain time to regroup their armies and meet the rebellion with force in the spring. The lengthy discussions, however, also enabled the peasantry to spread their cause to other areas. The rebel leader Hans Müller toured the entire region with his own troops, and a deliberate effort was made to include lower-class townspeople in the uprising, with many territorial towns welcoming the rebels with open arms. In March 1525, an army under Müller marched on Stuttgart, while other armed groups gathered near Ulm in the Allgäu, around Lake Constance and in Alsace in the west. (Some temporary assistance to this campaign was provided by the wily Duke Ulrich of Württemberg, banished in 1519 after falling out with other branches of the nobility. He now used the troubles to pursue his personal case for restitution, announcing himself as a fully paid-up Lutheran and presenting himself to the peasant army as – rather incredibly – 'Ulrich the Peasant'. Unfortunately, he rapidly ran out of cash, his mercenary army deserted him, and he fled once more over the border, leaving his fellow peasants to their fate.)

By April, the area affected by the uprising covered several hundred square kilometres, stretching north-eastwards into Franconia and from there into Thuringia and Saxony. The north of Germany was left relatively untouched. So, too, was Bavaria (then considerably smaller than the present-day region); this had a lot to do with Bavaria's relatively advanced centralisation of government and consequent lack of an ill-disciplined lesser nobility. But the rebellion did spread south-eastwards into Tirol where, under the very able leadership of Michael Gaismair (an almost exact contemporary of Müntzer), a revolt of the Austrian peasants and plebeians lasted from May 1525 well into 1526.

This popular uprising was, by any measure, quite extraordinary. But it was not a coordinated one. At best, local or regional groups of peasants would see what their brothers in neighbouring states were up to and decide that now was the time to do the same. By April, huge – but separate – armies of between 12,000 and 40,000 peasants were massed and moving around the countryside. Ultimately these local armies were unable to unite in any significant way across wider areas. Georg of Waldburg, the skilled commander of the nobles' 'Swabian League' army, simply moved around the country, picking off peasant bands one by one, either by treachery and brute terror, or by superior military skill. Indeed, treachery and broken truces had as much influence on the final outcome of the uprising as did the uncertainty of the peasants; the Swabian League also had a military and technical advantage, as well as mercenaries who provided the territorial nobility with an irresistible force.

In the early months of this regional uprising, the peasants produced lists of demands – almost every small county had its own set to present to its feudal lord. Most complained about the tithes, the restriction on movement and the many other grossly oppressive measures discussed above. The demands of the urban communities ran more towards religious reforms, democracy, the regulation of trade, and some rudimentary social care policies. Rather naively, the peasantry believed that their lists of grievances quite naturally and legally demanded justice, and that matters could be resolved through negotiation – perhaps with some assistance from God. Some of these demands reveal the quite astonishing small-mindedness of the feudal authorities: the rebels of Stühlingen, for example, complained that whenever a criminal was burned at the stake, the peasants had to supply the wood for the pyre. Other minor details paint a picture of communal reckoning. In the town of Schleusingen in central Germany, in among twenty-two complaints and demands was one urging the sacking of the church organist and the selling-off of the organ – we can only suppose he was not a very proficient musician.[5] But the most famous and representative of these lists was the 'Twelve Articles' of March 1525, drawn up in the southern town of Memmingen and printed and adopted all over Germany within weeks. This became the default list of demands across the nation.

The Memmingen Articles were drafted by two leaders of the Swabian peasants, Christoph Schappeler (a trained preacher) and Sebastian Lotzer (a journeyman furrier). The assembly at the Imperial Free City of Memmingen was in effect a peasant parliament, at which all kinds of proposals were discussed in an attempt to unify the rebels. One result of this meeting was to radicalise the uprising even further, while introducing some basic democratic procedures into the process of decision-making. The Twelve Articles which came out of this parliament were a summary of the demands of all the groups represented at Memmingen. In the printed editions of the Articles, the margins are cluttered with references to chapters of the Bible, each reference providing scriptural justification for their 'humble plea and request'. It was only in the early months of 1525 that formal religion began to play a major role in underpinning the demands of the lower classes; significantly, the justification by biblical reference marched in lockstep with the adoption of standardised demands – here was the Reformation in synthesis with revolution.

Included in the demands made by the peasants were: the election of reformed preachers by the parishes; the abolition of all feudal duties and tithes; free access to wood, water and game; proper contracts for leasing or owning land; the care of the poor from a communal poor chest; the re-communisation of pasture; and the principle of equality before the law. The list ended as follows:

> Twelfth, it is our conclusion and final opinion that, if one or more of the Articles presented here be not in accordance with the Word of God (which we would doubt) . . . then we will abandon them, when it is explained to us on the basis of the Scripture.[6]

Here were calls for economic reform, a primitive democracy and a religious structure in keeping with that democracy, all justified by reference to the Bible. But even these modest changes were in themselves revolutionary. They could not be conceded, since to do so would immediately and irrevocably shake the pillars of established government over town and country. (In 1526, at the Diet of Speyer, an aristocratic committee was set up to address all these issues; unexpectedly, the committee agreed that the complaints were mostly justified, but then the Diet decided that nothing should be done. Some things never change.)

Issued at almost the same time as the Twelve Articles, and most likely written by the same authors, was another document, the 'Federal Ordinance' (*Bundesordnung*): this was a set of procedural guidelines on how the rebels should conduct themselves towards neighbours, allies, priests, fellow rebels and potential

enemies. Like the Twelve Articles, it was printed in several editions across south Germany.[7]

During the main period of the armed uprising, between March
and May 1525, the peasants' demands were almost always
backed by assaults on castles and monasteries, along with plundering in revenge for centuries of exploitation. In Franconia, for
example, it is estimated that well over 200 castles were destroyed.
Rarely, however, were members of the nobility put to death.
Indeed, practically the only time the peasant armies resorted to
killing their feudal lords away from the battlefield was at the
castle of Weinsberg, near Heilbronn, when twenty-four noblemen, forced to run the gauntlet, were killed by the peasantry.[8]
(The most important of those killed was Count Ludwig von
Helfenstein, whose wife was a daughter of Maximilian I, the
late Holy Roman Emperor. Fortunately, she was but an illegiti-
mate daughter – one of an impressive thirteen – so perhaps no
personal offence was taken by the new Emperor, Maximilian's
grandson. The social offence was another matter.) This act of
retribution by the rebels stands almost alone in the history of
the war; it turned out to be a brutally effective act, focusing the
minds of nobles and peasants alike; but it was at the time fiercely
condemned by the leaders of the German peasant armies. By
contrast, the Swabian League and other armies of the nobility
thought nothing of massacring hundreds, if not thousands, of
peasants during and after every single encounter. In the town of
Saverne in Alsace, it is estimated that 8,000 peasants were killed
in cold blood after they had agreed to put down their weapons
and return home. At Frankenhausen in Thuringia, an estimated
6,000 rebels were slaughtered in a couple of hours.

The man who had unwittingly provided the religious justification
for this rebellion, Martin Luther, had by 1525 moved in quite
a different direction from the peasantry. In various letters and
pamphlets, he chastised the commoners for abusing the Bible in
a worldly way. In April he wrote:

> The peasants themselves . . . are so disloyal, false, disobedient
> and wanton, and plunder, rob and remove what they can, like

barefaced highwaymen and murderers . . . And worst of all, they carry on such wild raging and horrible sins in the name of Christianity and under cover of the Gospel.[9]

This, we should note, was his considered opinion on a treaty, signed at Weingarten, between the Swabian League and the peasant army of Lake Constance, under the terms of which the peasants agreed to disband and go home. Luther was never a man to forgive and forget.

In his commentary on the Memmingen Articles, also written in April, Luther struck what he undoubtedly thought was a neutral pose, wagging a finger at both the peasants and their oppressors in equal measure, and encouraging the two sides to reach agreement. Nevertheless, he insisted that the peasants had no right – legal or moral – to rebel. 'He who takes up the sword', he wrote, 'shall die by it.'[10] Let us be perfectly clear: this warning was directed at the peasants, not the nobility, whose life largely revolved around taking up the sword. Melanchthon delivered much the same message in his own commentary on the Articles. He had plenty to say, but it boiled down to this: 'the Gospel demands that we obey our masters'.[11] The very next month, in a shameful tract entitled *Against the Robbing and Murdering Hordes of Peasants*, Luther described the Memmingen Articles as 'the Devil's work' – more specifically, the work of Müntzer; he considered the activities of the peasant hordes to be a mortal sin. He accused them of murder and bloodshed, and of bringing disaster upon their families. He called on the 'Christian' nobility to take punitive measures: 'So, dear lords, redeem us, save us, help us, take pity on the poor people, stab, smite, strangle, every one of you! And if you die in so doing, then it is good, for there is no holier death to be had.'[12]

To call this open letter a strategic mistake by Luther is something of an understatement. His stance on the uprising proved damaging to the popularity of the Wittenberg reform movement, and many people, even some of his closest colleagues, became openly hostile to him over this.[13] Yet it should not have come as a surprise to anyone: Luther's doctrine on secular authority never did condone challenge from below. It was an incredibly ill-timed letter; in April and May, the 'Christian nobility' were already engaged in 'stabbing, smiting and strangling' – routing the rebels, executing their leaders, burning whole villages and exacting tribute in blood and money from the surviving peasantry and townspeople. Although accurate figures are hard to come by, a death toll of 100,000 across Germany is often quoted. Such a figure is impossible to prove or disprove, as sixteenth-century chroniclers tended to exaggerate numbers wildly. But it was assuredly a very large number indeed, and the figure gives some idea of the repression conducted by the nobles' armies. At that time, Germany had a population estimated at between 8 and 10 million; if we take only the regions affected by the uprising, the total figure drops to perhaps half of that.[14] A death toll in the many thousands, primarily of family breadwinners and young men, was both indefensible and catastrophic.

What had changed Luther's mind so drastically between April and May? Simply this, in his own words:

> But scarcely had I turned round [from advising the peasants] than they set off on the road and, forgetting all their promises, took violent action, robbing and raging and behaving like mad dogs. And now we can all see what they had concealed from us and that everything which they proposed in their 'Twelve Articles' was a pure lie made up in the name of the Gospel.

He referred implicitly to the killing of the noblemen at Weinsberg castle: mad dogs they were, 'carrying out the Devil's work, most especially the work of the arch-devil who ruled in Mühlhausen and stirred up nothing except robbery, murder and bloodshed'.[15]

But at least Wittenberg was pretty much in the clear when it came to stirring up things in Swabia. For reasons as much geographical as anything else, the religious leadership of the insurgents in the south-west tended to orientate towards the Swiss under Zwingli rather than towards Luther. In the south-western town of Waldshut, for example, the reform movement led by Balthasar Hubmaier was initially of a distinct Zwinglian hue (although Hubmaier later fell out with Zwingli), and when the town came under siege from the Habsburgs, the people of

Armed peasants, as depicted on the frontispiece to the 'Federal Ordinance' which accompanied the Twelve Articles, 1525.

Zwinglian Zürich, a day's march away, despatched a militia to assist the besieged. Zwingli's reforming ideas found support along the valley of the Rhine, as far north as Strassburg, where the reform movement showed itself quite disinclined to follow the lead of Wittenberg.

What, then, of the arch-devil of Mühlhausen himself? With his journey into south-west Germany, Müntzer again entered that familiar area where hard evidence is totally absent. We simply do not know for sure what he did here – although his contemporaries thought they knew. This is most inconvenient for the historian and biographer. But what is certain is that the experience was transformative for Müntzer: on his return to Mühlhausen in early 1525, he immediately began to organise the Thuringian people for 'the downfall of the strong and godless tyrants'.

News of the promising beginnings of the uprising would have reached Müntzer in Nürnberg at the latest by November, and he would have regarded the development as a vindication of all his theories. Pausing only to dash off a letter to Christoph Meinhard, in which he asked for 'some funds for the journey, whatever you can spare',[16] he headed south-west, stopping in Basel to visit Denck's mentor Johann Oekolampad (a Humanist with Zwinglian sympathies; his real surname of Hausschein – 'house lamp' – was rendered into Greek in the rather trendy Humanist manner). He arrived in Basel around mid-December, where he hooked up initially with Ulrich Hugwald, a young reformer swithering somewhere between Zwingli, Humanism and Luther (he eventually, and briefly, became a leading Anabaptist). A year later, Oekolampad, fearing for his reputation and anxious to make it quite clear he had no association whatsoever with that man Müntzer, wrote:

> Listen how it was concerning Müntzer! An exile came here and visited me; I did not know him by sight, and could scarcely catch his name, which he did not give on the first occasion . . . Being an exile myself, I invited him to eat; he agreed and appeared with Hugwald. Only then did he give his name and the reason for his journey. What was I to do? I encouraged the man . . . and we talked a great deal on the theme of the Cross, and the man laid so much emphasis on it that I gained a good impression of him.[17]

Frustratingly, Oekolampad does not say what 'reason' Müntzer gave for his journey. From this very silence, it is likely that it had something to do with intervening in the uprising on behalf of the radical Reformation. In 1527, two years after the Peasants' War had ended, Oekolampad was more forthcoming about the visit. Müntzer had turned up, he said, in the company of an 'elderly peasant' (no longer the controversial young Hugwald, then). A lengthy conversation ensued, during which Oekolampad lamented the split between Luther and Müntzer; Müntzer, for his part, complained bitterly about Luther. When the debate turned to baptism and secular authority, Oekolampad rather put the dampeners on matters by suggesting that 'what is not against God is for the people to obey. [Müntzer] did not subscribe to this at all.'[18] Müntzer had then left the house and Oekolampad never saw him again.

These conversations, then, were not exactly fruitful. But the stopover in Basel may well have provided the traveller with some useful contacts for his journey to the tiny market town of Griessen in the Klettgau district. Also active in this corner of Europe were Conrad Grebel and his colleagues, who formed the earliest known group in what later became the Anabaptist movement. They had long been tracking and sympathising with Luther, Karlstadt and – to some degree – Zwingli. But during the course of 1524, the group found itself looking for more answers; they had observed how Luther had dealt with Karlstadt and Müntzer, and their sympathies were not with Luther. So, in the late summer of 1524, Grebel tried to contact both Karlstadt and Müntzer. He received a reply from the former, but not from the latter. The letter to Müntzer was a lengthy piece of writing, with a postscript signed by a number of his colleagues – among them Hans Huiuff, who had been a comrade of Müntzer in Halle – proclaiming themselves to be 'thy brethren and seven new young Müntzers against Luther'.[19] But Müntzer never received this letter, dated 5 September 1524, since it was addressed to Allstedt, and he had left there in early August. The letter seems to have been carried to Allstedt by Huiuff, and even by the time he got there, Müntzer had left Mühlhausen as well; so Huiuff had to carry it all the way back to Grebel in Zürich. And there is no evidence that Müntzer met up with Grebel on his journey to the south-west.

Despite the jaunty signature of the 'new young Müntzers', the contents of the letter were scarcely in tune with Müntzer's view of life. Grebel's group claimed to have studied Müntzer's pamphlets *On Fraudulent Faith* and the *Protestation or Proposition* and to have been greatly instructed by them. Huiuff's cousin, who was apparently resident in Allstedt, had informed them about the 'Sermon to the Princes'. But the group then proceeded to disagree with Müntzer on almost every major position: on the use of liturgy ('this cannot be right, for we find no teaching about singing in the New Testament, no precedents'); on the sacraments; on the use of violence to defend the faith ('One should not protect the gospel and its adherents with the sword'); on baptism ('You and Karlstadt do not write sufficiently against the baptism of children'). The only two points of agreement concerned Luther – 'the negligent Biblical scholars and doctors in Wittenberg' – and the necessity for spiritual suffering to attain faith. But even this necessary torment was described in terms of 'love and hope', which were very far removed from Müntzer's painful theology of inner crucifixion.

What, then, did Müntzer really do in Griessen, where – allegedly – he stayed for eight weeks? Mighty deeds have been ascribed to him: initiating the entire uprising; drawing up the 'Twelve Articles' and the so-called 'Article Letter' which accompanied them; introducing Anabaptism into Switzerland and south Germany; plundering and, of course, murdering. The Swiss reformer Heinrich Bullinger was the source of many of these reports, but his chronicling of Müntzer's activities tells us more about Bullinger than about his subject. Bullinger's bête noire was Anabaptism, and his main concern was to prove that such a doctrine could not possibly have emerged out of Zwinglianism or any respectable Swiss theology, but was rather the fruit of some foreign gospel.

The idea that Müntzer had a hand in the twelve Memmingen Articles is the most persistent in this historiography. In rather vague terms, both geographical and temporal, Müntzer himself confessed in May 1525 that: 'In Klettgau and Hegau near Basel, he had made several Articles on how one should rule according to the gospels, and then other Articles.'[20] But the language used in the Memmingen Articles betrays no sign of Müntzer; the theological arguments adduced are filled with the spirit of 'brotherly love' rather than the suffering of the faithful or preparation for the Apocalypse; and the legal arguments used had no place in any of Müntzer's doctrines. The very address of the preamble to the Articles is enough to rule out any involvement by Müntzer: 'Peace and the Grace of God through Christ to the Christian reader'; not much further on, there is the statement that 'the Gospel . . . speaks of Christ, the promised Messiah whose word and life taught nothing other than love, peace, patience and concord, so that all who believe in this Christ are loving, peaceful, patient and of one mind'.[21] This has so little in common with Müntzer's theology as to be almost a parody of all that he shunned. Certainly, the preamble seeks to justify the rebellion and the demands set forth, but this cannot be confused with any justification provided by Müntzer. And, should any doubts remain, the Articles were not composed until February or March 1525, by which time Müntzer was safely back in Mühlhausen.

The 'Article Letter' (*Artikelbrief*) which was intended to accompany the Articles was more radical in tone, designed to nurture solidarity among the various groups of peasants. It was a political document, but concerned with the conduct of the uprising, not with future government. It was specifically addressed to the recalcitrant residents of the town of Villingen to encourage them to join the rebellion. The encouragement was strengthened by a threat to boycott the community; members of the 'Christian League', the Letter stated, should have no dealings with those who refuse to join – 'to wit, by eating, drinking, bathing, milling, baking, ploughing, reaping, or by supplying or letting others supply them with food, grain, drink, wood, meat, salt, etc., or by buying from or selling to them'.[22]

Radical and far-reaching though this is, there is no flavour of Müntzer here: his view of non-members or backsliders would surely have been expressed in more Apocalyptic terms. At the end of the Article Letter is a paragraph known as the 'Castle Article', in which lords, monks and bishops were asked to voluntarily leave their castles, palaces and monasteries and live in 'common houses'. Although the message is radical, the wording is a little too tame to be a Müntzer production – and indeed seems to have been taken verbatim from a general 'standing orders' document circulating among the peasant armies. (And, once again, the Article Letter almost certainly post-dates Müntzer's return to Thuringia.)

There is, however, a further document that may be connected with Müntzer – the so-called 'Draft Constitution' (*Verfassungsentwurf*).[23] This is known to us only partially and only through the kind offices of a hostile third party: it was found in the possession of the Anabaptist Hubmaier in 1528, when he was arrested and subsequently executed for heresy by the Catholic-Imperial authorities in Austria. One of his captors helpfully summarised the document for the benefit of Duke Georg of Saxony. The text which survives contains only four pages out of a likely total of thirty. But even in that brief extract, there are a couple of phrases which remind us of Müntzer; for example: 'The time has already come when God will no longer suffer the secular lords' flaying, fleecing, fettering, shackling, grinding, binding, and other tyranny. They deal with the poor folk as Herod with the innocent children.' There is also talk of the 'bloodthirsty tyrants'. We are forcefully reminded of a passage in *An Explicit Exposure of False Faith*:

> Thus, when the grace of God was announced in the birth of John and the conception of Christ, Herod was the ruler, he with that pious blood which leaks from the dribbling sack of all the nobility of this world ... Aye, some are now beginning to chain and shackle their own people, to skin and flay them and so threaten all of Christianity, and with the utmost severity they torture and ignominiously kill both their own people and others.[24]

There is a seductive similarity of language and biblical reference between the two passages. And yet the remainder of this truncated 'Draft Constitution' does not wholly bear out this promise. There is mention of 'the Word of God' being used to justify approaches to the nobility, but nothing of 'the fear of God'. On the other hand, there is talk of giving the nobles three chances to repent of their ways, which is something Müntzer could conceivably still have considered in late 1524. So the document may have been drafted by Müntzer – that is all we can definitely say.

Nevertheless, there is no doubt that Müntzer did do something in Griessen and the Klettgau district. But we still do not know what. There exist unverifiable reports of him preaching in a variety of places across the south-west, and Müntzer would of course have used each and every opportunity to preach. But it has to be remembered that, for the peasants of south-west Germany, a man from Thuringia was effectively a 'foreigner', with a very non-local accent; so Müntzer may well have been treated with some reserve. He may also have offered his skills as writer to further the cause of the peasantry, and he may have made contact with Hubmaier in Waldshut. To Zwingli's great disappointment, Hubmaier had begun to evince Anabaptist tendencies in February 1525; on his next visit to Zürich after that, Zwingli had him arrested and forced him to recant his offensive doctrines on baptism and worldly authority. But his recantation was of short duration: Hubmaier later went on to become an important Anabaptist leader in Germany and Bohemia until he was burned to death in 1528 by the Austrian authorities. Interestingly, all three of the peasants' documents discussed above were originally ascribed to Hubmaier on the occasion of his execution. It was quite convenient to do so. Could it perhaps have been Müntzer's influence in January and February which pushed Hubmaier towards Anabaptism? On balance probably not: Hubmaier's theological doctrines bore little resemblance to any of Müntzer's, particularly in relation to the question of the use of force against tyrants.

One thing Müntzer did not do in south-west Germany was experience any of the significant military campaigns of the peasantry. The first battle of the war took place on 14 December at Donaueschingen, just north of Klettgau. This led to the swift defeat of an inexperienced peasant troop, and brought a halt to all campaigning for the season. Winter activity took place only in law courts and parliaments, as one side strove to take advantage of the ongoing absence of Swabian League mercenaries, while the other procrastinated for the same reason. Müntzer may have contributed to these discussions and negotiations, and may have joined embassies into towns, seeking alliances. During late December and January, the peasants in their various troops were preparing themselves for the main uprising of the spring, and were either encamped in scattered locations across south-west Germany or had temporarily disbanded. Also in those two months, the peasant leaders sought the support of the Zwinglian Swiss, which was given rather grudgingly. Meanwhile, radical religious reforms and social protests were combining, and by the end of January the populace stood in open revolt. But the real action did not begin until well after Müntzer had returned home to Thuringia.

Perhaps the right question has not so far been asked. It is not so much 'what did Müntzer give to the uprising in the south-west?' as 'what did the uprising in the south-west give to Müntzer?' Living among the rebels for a few weeks, he would have acquired valuable insights into the mind and motivations of the common man. This was a completely new period in his life, and a totally new experience: he was well outside of his comfort zone, which had until then been largely defined by church services, preaching and study in an urban environment; he was now immersed in large gatherings of country people with little or no learning, who were engaged in a tangible struggle for social and economic justice. It was very raw, very immediate, and largely hopeful and inspiring. There would have been days of great enthusiasm and hope, but also – inevitably – days of despair and disenchantment. That this experience must have profoundly affected him is clear from the next few months of his life: he wrote no more pamphlets, and by and large he ignored Luther and Wittenberg. Instead, he concentrated on rousing ordinary people – peasants and poor townspeople – to action, on attacking the secular authorities in letters and sermons, and on raising militias for the final overthrow of the godless state.

In his 'confession' of May 1525, Müntzer stated that he 'had talked to the peasants of Klettgau and Hegau near Basel, asking them if they would join him in Mühlhausen. They said that they would, just as long as they were paid.'[25] There was a strong tradition among the peasants of south Germany and Switzerland of joining up with random armies to fight anywhere in Europe as mercenaries, and so their response to Müntzer's invitation, while disappointing, rings true. When the Thuringian rebels took up arms in April 1525, Müntzer held up the rebels of Klettgau as models – but with a cautionary note attached:

> The whole German, French and Italian lands are up in arms, the master will have his game, the evil-doers will have to take care . . . the peasants of Klettgau and Hegau in the Black Forest have risen, three times one thousand strong, and the army is growing ever greater. My only worry is that the foolish people will accept

some false peace-treaty, because they cannot recognise the harm that could be done.[26]

(In this context, the claim about 'French and Italian lands' – 'französisch und welsch land' – is probably a result of wishful thinking. The uprising had spilled over into Alsace, now in France, but in the sixteenth century a German territory.) As he experienced the preparations of the south German peasantry over the winter, it became obvious to Müntzer that the rebellion had to be extended to other parts of Germany – principally Saxony and Thuringia. And so, in late January or early February, he returned on his own to Thuringia, to rouse the common people for the final battles. En route, he was reported to have been in Schweinfurt, and then to have passed through the town of Fulda, which on 5 February had seen riots by the plebeians; as a result, strangers passing through the town were eyed with the greatest suspicion. Müntzer was apparently locked up for a couple of days by the civic authorities. But evidently they had no idea who he was, so he was allowed to proceed on his way. In Allstedt, Zeiss got to hear of this fortuitous oversight, writing that 'Thomas Müntzer was in Fulda, and was thrown into the dungeon there, and the abbot said that if he had known that it was Müntzer, then he would not have set him free.'[27]

It is not unlikely that Müntzer used his journey back to Mühlhausen – some eighty kilometres to the north-east of Fulda – to visit like-minded preachers and give them news of events in Klettgau. Two radical preachers operated on or near the road home, Melchior Rinck and Hans Sippel. Rinck later joined Müntzer at the battle of Frankenhausen; Sippel would doubtless have done so as well, had he not been executed shortly beforehand, for leading the peasant army of the Werra valley.

Around the middle of February, Müntzer re-entered Mühlhausen. Here he met up again with Pfeiffer and other colleagues from the previous autumn. The Imperial Free City was once more in the hands of the radicals.

11

The Time Was Come

The Thuringian Uprising (1525)

In the year 1525, when the peasantry of Swabia and Franconia rose up . . . then Thomas thought his hour had come; the Princes were terrified, the nobles were chased away, and the peasants would be masters; and he wished to be part of this game and begin his reformation, and preached that the time was come.

Philipp Melanchthon (1525)

Heinrich Pfeiffer had returned from Nürnberg and arrived at the gates of Mühlhausen in mid-December 1524. He had been invited back by the congregation of the Nikolaikirche, a church which stood just outside the town walls, and on the morning of 15 December, he was there in the pulpit, preaching. To be safe, the town council promptly shut the town gates and guarded them with light artillery to prevent the congregation from coming back within the walls. However, the stand-off did not last long, and overwhelming popular support ensured that an agreement was reached to let 'evangelical' preachers such as Pfeiffer continue – just as long as they did not incite anyone to 'outrage and uproar'. The reform movement was in such a dominant position that, at the end of December, a commission was appointed to review the town's procedures for fines and punishments and ensure that they conformed to the teachings of the Gospels. The members of this commission? Among others, the radical preachers Pfeiffer, Laue and Behme.

Thus, within days of Pfeiffer's return, the Church reform movement in Mühlhausen had taken on a new lease of life. During

January, altarpieces were removed from the churches and convents, and the two small friaries belonging to the Dominicans and Franciscans were looted and the inmates chased away. In an action comparable to a controlled burn to stop a wildfire, the council prevented a nunnery from being attacked in the same way, by removing the valuables to the town hall and then prohibiting the nuns from celebrating old-style Catholic rites. As if that wasn't enough, a group of women from Mühlhausen took it upon themselves to interrupt the evening prayers of a small convent close to Salza; one of them was Müntzer's wife, Ottilie. Duke Georg of Saxony was incensed at this, demanding that the women be interrogated and fined; in particular, he demanded that a close eye be kept on Ottilie, and if possible that she should be arrested and imprisoned. It is uncertain whether the authorities in Salza were able to follow any of the duke's orders, and Ottilie seems to have escaped punishment.[1] (Women were only rarely found involved in direct actions like this, but Müntzer and Pfeiffer often relied on their fierce dedication to support their actions. Ottilie evidently shared wholeheartedly her husband's beliefs, independently advancing the radical cause in his absence.)[2]

Between them, the *Achtmänner* along with Pfeiffer and his supporters effectively took over the municipal reins, while the deposed authorities kept a low profile. Zeiss reported to Spalatin, rather deprecatingly, that 'Mr Everyman has removed the rule of the council, who may now do nothing without permission, neither punish, nor rule, nor write, nor act.'[3] Pfeiffer seized this unparalleled opportunity to tour the surrounding countryside, mustering support for a programme of Church expropriation. Monks and clerics complained bitterly to the appropriate authorities, but nothing was done, except that the princes of Saxony began to discuss punishing the rebels. Duke Georg wrote on 20 January that his peasantry was to be ordered to have nothing to do with Mühlhausen, and that armed patrols should stop all traffic to and from the town and if possible arrest the rebel leaders. But the princes were themselves still unsure: the Catholic Georg wished to stamp out revolt and reform together; the Lutheran Duke Johann would have none of his cousin's meddling with Church reform; while Friedrich the Wise tried to suggest a compromise. In a series of meetings in Naumburg in January and February, also attended by the Mühlhausen dignitaries who had been chased away the previous September, little more than vague plans were adopted by the territorial princes.

Müntzer arrived back in the town at some point in the second half of February 1525. But well before this, the Reformation in Mühlhausen was effectively complete. On his return, Müntzer was immediately appointed as preacher to the pulpit in the Marienkirche, giving his first sermon on the 28th. Nominally, the appointment was in the gift of the Order of Teutonic Knights, but since the knights were now nowhere to be seen, three of Mühlhausen's poorer districts stepped forward and voted for Müntzer's installation. As part of the deal, the council paid him eleven groschen every Sunday; much more impressively, he and his family moved into the spacious premises vacated by the Teutonic Knights. He now proceeded with the theological re-education of the poor. It was reported that Müntzer had already 'translated into German the Mass and other hymns', and when 'he was asked a question in the street, and he had his book with him, he would sit down and teach in public, so that very many people ran after him everywhere'.[4] The book, doubtless, was the

The house of the Order of the Teutonic Knights in Mühlhausen. After the knights had been evicted by the townspeople, Müntzer lived here briefly in 1525.

Photo by Michael Sander (CC BY-SA 3.0)

Bible. This form of street education suited Müntzer well. He was back in his element, in an urban setting, with a pulpit and with people who wanted his advice. These were strange times for his audience: the civil authority had been replaced, the representatives of the old religion had been chased away; it was natural for there to be hopes and doubts in the minds of the common people. They seemed to be making history and they needed reassurances that what they were doing was right. They were quite capable of undertaking reforming or revolutionary actions on their own; but they could not do it consistently without some form of theoretical underpinning. Müntzer provided that support.

It goes without saying that Müntzer and Pfeiffer got together at the earliest opportunity to discuss tactics and strategy. They were both radical reformers; as far as can be determined from the records, they saw eye-to-eye on many of the basic questions of faith and politics. They both had broad popular support on the streets and in their respective churches; and they had the backing of the *Achtmänner*. But it is worth stressing again that in Mühlhausen it was Pfeiffer, not Müntzer, who had been the instigator of many of the Church reforms until then; he had also been a prime mover of the democratic reforms. The events of the following weeks suggest quite strongly that whatever Pfeiffer proposed, the rebels of Mühlhausen undertook. When iconoclastic events took place, Pfeiffer was deeply implicated, not Müntzer. This much is evident from the contemporary reports. Whatever Luther might have thought, Müntzer was not the ruling arch-Satan of Mühlhausen; Pfeiffer, on the other hand, was. But this slightly unequal relationship does not appear to have either harmed the rebellion or upset Müntzer. And so, in a shared spirit of optimism, they advanced to the next stage in their reforms.

It was not a great triumph.

On 9 March, a general muster of the people of Mühlhausen was called. All men capable of bearing arms were to gather in a field just outside the town walls in order to be reviewed and inspected. It is unlikely that this was at the initiative of anyone other than the town council, but Müntzer intended to take full advantage of the occasion, to encourage the people to sign up for a more radical Reformation. Two thousand infantry and 130 men on horse duly assembled – this figure included men from the surrounding villages as well as from the town. The town's arsenal of firearms and small cannon was polished to a shine and hauled out to the parade ground.

The exercise was instructive in an unexpected way: 'they had to load their muskets with paper and similarly their field-guns. And the captain, on an order, ran into the firing, got one right on the nose and was somewhat stunned.'[5] After these exercises, which doubtless caused great amusement, Müntzer decided that the time was right to make a speech against those who compromised with the authorities. He mounted a horse belonging to one of the *Achtmänner* and called the assembled militia around him. Once again he foretold the fall of the princes. And then he called on those gathered to swear 'to stay with God's word, and to die by it . . . He who does not wish to do so should step out of this league.' Whereupon, foreshadowing future events and expressing the limited vision of the ordinary people of Mühlhausen, the captain – still rubbing his nose – stood up and replied:

> 'Dear citizens, I think there is no man here so ignorant as not to stand by God's word, and so it is unnecessary to take an oath.' Then the Allstedter [Müntzer] said that it was necessary and proper. The captain then said: 'Dear citizens, have you not sworn enough oaths, enough to fill a basket and hang it round your necks?' . . . So the crowd did not want to swear, and went back into the town complaining.[6]

Once back in town, the militia consumed several dozen barrels of beer; next, a festive band of rioters went off to trash that same nunnery which the town council had recently taken great pains to protect. The events of this day illustrated the inadequacy of the preparations for any kind of military uprising or defence, but they also demonstrated the parochial 'common sense' of the insurgents which prevented Müntzer from assuming overall leadership. The people of Mühlhausen were quite happy to destroy the buildings and icons of the old religion, and pleased to accept the new reformed religion; but they were not yet ready to take seriously Müntzer's Apocalyptic vision, or even the more mundane likelihood of armed retaliation from the ruling houses of Saxony.

Despite these setbacks, Müntzer and Pfeiffer continued to collaborate in the campaign for a new town council. After several days of fruitless negotiation between the council, the *Achtmänner* and the two preachers, an assembly was held in the Marienkirche on 16 March. There, Pfeiffer announced from the pulpit that the council had agreed to resign. The mayor protested that they had not agreed to this at all, but if the people wanted new elections, then they could have them. A vote was then taken in the assembly: 660 voted for a new council, 204 against. On the following day, the new 'Eternal Council' (*Ewiger Rat*) was installed, a group of sixteen citizens, elected and subject to recall at any time by the citizens of the town. The council was 'Eternal' only in so far as, according to the third of the Mühlhausen Articles of September 1524, it had no fixed term of office. Its members could hold office for life, unless they offended by corruption or disgrace. In composition, despite the events which brought it to power, it was not exactly a nest of revolutionaries, or some kind of early soviet: there were craftsmen, intellectuals and three of the richer *Achtmänner*; its richest member paid 351 marks in taxes, while the poorest paid only three. It was a committee of political compromise: while the less radical democrats were strongly represented, none of them dared publicly to advocate any policy which went against Müntzer or Pfeiffer. Indeed, the majority gave the pair open or tacit support. (An 'Eternal Council' was also established in the city of Erfurt after it had deposed its own town council in April 1525; disappointingly, the 'Eternal' membership was composed entirely of the councillors from the deposed council.[7])

The very act of electing a new council raised matters to a different political level. As the respectable magistrate of Mühlhausen put it, with unbecoming enthusiasm: '[God] has cast down the mighty from their thrones and raised up the mean; what a wonderful God this is!'[8] Following the appointment of the new council, a German Mass was held in the two churches under radical preachers. The task of the new council was to complete the redistribution of Church property and to reform municipal affairs along the lines of the September Articles. And it did so with admirable efficiency. The Catholic Church was financially closed down in Mühlhausen, and a sheep farm belonging to the Teutonic Order was expropriated to the advantage of the community. At around this time, an exasperated Duke Georg decided that he would no longer act as the 'protector' of the town – something the Saxon princes had been doing unofficially for several decades – and he tried to encourage the Lutheran princes of Saxony to do the same.[9]

The Eternal Council should not be confused with an organisation established by Müntzer himself, the 'Eternal League of God'. There is some debate as to whether this more revolutionary organisation was created in September 1524 or in March 1525. There are valid arguments for both dates. Either way, the formation of the League represented a conscious effort to take the Church reforms in a radical new direction. What we know of the organisation comes mostly from hearsay – no 'articles' or programme have survived, and only two items signal its existence. The first was a membership register of 219 names, with a complementary military structure – but the members are not matched up to the structure, so it is unclear who did what. The only name assigned to a post is that of Pfeiffer, as chaplain, and the list does not even include Müntzer's name. But that Müntzer was heavily involved in this body is clear from his action in the middle of April, when he arranged for the creation of a huge flag which was to be the League's banner. The Eternal Council had been persuaded to put up the funds to acquire the cloth, and one of the councillors who was a tailor sewed the flag together. He created a dramatic agitational prop: it was '30 ells' long – about thirteen metres – and made of white silk. On it was painted a huge rainbow, beneath which were the words *'verbum Domini maneat in eternum'* ('may the word of God endure forever') and 'a rhyme which said that this was the banner of the Eternal League of God, and all who wished to stand by the League, should gather beneath it'. (The membership register was also headed with the words 'For the Eternal League of God' and 'So that God's word endures forever'.) The banner was initially set up next to Müntzer's pulpit in the Marienkirche, as a permanent visual reminder to the people of Mühlhausen that, while changes had already taken place, higher aspirations had not been forgotten. It is not certain whether this impressive flag was taken on all of the subsequent sorties into the countryside, but it did accompany a contingent of men to Frankenhausen in the middle of May.

While all this was happening, Müntzer's correspondence with the outside world began to flow once more. Two letters in particular stand out during March. One came from a Humanist-cum-Lutheran pastor named Georg Witzel, based in a village down near Eisenach; the letter scolded Müntzer for stirring up the common man, and urged him to 'calm down'. Its pompous tone is reminiscent of some small-town clergyman from the Victorian era berating a schoolmaster who has shown liberal tendencies. 'Repent,' the pastor urged, 'submit so that you can be saved.'[10] There is no record of Müntzer ever bothering to reply to Witzel (who by the 1530s had returned to the fold of the Catholic Church). More pertinently, Müntzer wrote to his former parishioners in Allstedt, warning them against backsliding and advising them that any attempt to place their trust in the Lutherans was likely to do them no good whatsoever. It is not clear what provoked this letter, but it seems that Müntzer's successor in Allstedt – Luther's appointed preacher, Jodokus Kern – had been allowed to dismantle many of Müntzer's reforms. Kern is referred to by Müntzer as 'the messenger of the devil' and – in an ironical reference to Luther's hobby-horse – a representative of 'the false prophets'.[11] Müntzer might also have been tacitly chastising his friend Hans Zeiss who, in February, had recommended that the roads to Mühlhausen be barred to prevent all manner of rascals from heading in that direction.[12]

That Luther had not forgotten about Müntzer was evident from the arrival in Mühlhausen, on 24 April, of a 'peasant' – a man transparently sent from Wittenberg in the hope of unmasking Müntzer as a false prophet and usurper of the confidence of the common people. Müntzer and Pfeiffer agreed to a public disputation with this emissary on the question of whether the Elect were truly possessed by the Holy Spirit. The debate lasted some four hours, and involved heated controversy before a divided audience. It was reported that our Lutheran was in perpetual physical danger from Müntzer's exuberant supporters. The outcome of the disputation is not recorded, from which one supposes that the 'peasant' left Mühlhausen roundly rejected.

In south-west Germany, the main events of the Peasants' War kicked off in March. In central Germany, they began in earnest in the middle of April – possibly as a direct result of hearing the news from the south-west. On 18 April 1525, the peasants began to gather in the vicinity of Vacha, in the Werra valley. We have come across this place before as the home of Müntzer's colleague, the preacher Hans Sippel. Sippel was elected as leader of a rapidly growing army of peasants and local townspeople, which within days had swept across the countryside to the east and north of the Werra. They occupied and plundered monasteries, forced local nobles to submit to their authority, and adopted the 'Twelve Articles' of Memmingen. By 23 April, the rebels, by now around 8,000 strong, had captured the town of Salzungen; four days later they took the town of Schmalkalden – both sizeable and prosperous places. Heading southwards from there, the army took the town of Meiningen on 3 May, where later, during a democratic debate on what to do next (a fundamental characteristic of all the peasant armies of 1525), some advised heading back north to link up with the forces from Mühlhausen. But the majority voted to continue southwards to plunder and destroy more castles. A couple of days later, the Werra army split, with one group returning to their homes and the other deciding belatedly to move northwards to the town of Eisenach. Heading for Eisenach turned out to be a fatal mistake.

Taking their cue from the peasants of Werra, the people of Salza staged their own uprising on 25 April. This was undertaken in defence of a reformed preacher who, it was alleged, was about to be expelled by the town authorities – more specifically, by the local administrator for Duke Georg, a man named Hans Sittich von Berlepsch. Within hours of the threat, the townspeople had occupied the town hall and the town gates, blockaded Berlepsch in his residence, disarmed the town militia and begun to plunder the monasteries and nunneries, whose residents were, following the contemporary fashion, chased out of town. The next day, the insurgents forced twelve of their own men into an expanded membership of the town council and then presented the new council with a list of demands, which were duly accepted. There is strong evidence that the Salza people had consulted the Article Letter and the Twelve Articles of Memmingen for guidance – the latter having recently been printed in Erfurt.[13] Not content with all this, some of them took the precaution of writing to Mühlhausen, requesting support.

The community at Mühlhausen needed very little encouragement. No one had forgotten that their two ex-mayors, together with the town's insignia and horse, were still lying low in Salza. Here was an opportunity to right some historical wrongs. The letter from Salza arrived at around midnight on 26 April, and on the following morning a troop was sent southwards, many of whom were already kitted out for another muster of the militia, which had been scheduled for that day. Müntzer did not accompany them; Pfeiffer led around 300 Mühlhausen men, reinforced immediately by around 200 peasants, with the rainbow flag prominently displayed to the fore. (Significantly, the Eternal Council did its best to prevent the expedition.) However, by the time they arrived at Salza, things had settled down. Berlepsch was still besieged in his house, and the townspeople had firm control of the democratic processes and – more importantly – of the militia. Indeed, they had even found the time to write a follow-up letter to Mühlhausen, explaining that help was no longer needed.[14] When Pfeiffer and his troops turned up at the gates, the people thanked them kindly with two barrels of beer (containing a total of 800 litres, and probably purloined from the local monastery) to refresh them, and politely turned them away. The beer was consumed later that day during a picnic out in the fields. Meanwhile, the Salza councillors used the proximity of the Mühlhausen contingent to push through the last of their religious and civic reforms. It was a neat symbiosis.

Duke Georg's man, Hans Erich Sittich von Berlepsch, was not at all loved in Salza. Ever since the first rumblings of religious reform, he had kept an eagle eye on anti-Church dissenters, and was particularly observant of events in Allstedt. More recently, he had demanded that eight cartloads of local Lutherans be taken off to Dresden to face trial in Duke Georg's law courts.[15] But now he himself was held prisoner in Salza for several days. On the last day of April, a letter arrived from Müntzer, requesting that the townspeople put him to death: Müntzer took a stern view of anything resembling clemency in this case.[16] Berlepsch came from a regular clan of court officials; a cousin of his – also confusingly named Hans von Berlepsch – was a counsellor to Friedrich the Wise and, as castellan of the Wartburg, instrumental in hiding Luther there in 1521. (This other Berlepsch owned a rather beautiful country pile at Seebach – just outside Mühlhausen – which was ransacked on 30 April, either by his own feudal subjects or a foraging party from Pfeiffer's expeditionary force. In the course of this, a significant number of horses, cattle, pigs and sheep – not to mention large amounts of beer and wine – were liberated. Berlepsch was married to the sister of another local lord, Apel von Ebeleben, whose castle shared the same fate a couple of days later. Later, on 20 May, Berlepsch launched an ill-fated expedition to recover his livestock, raiding the fields around Mühlhausen – only to be caught in the act, arrested by the vigilant townspeople and imprisoned for three days.)[17]

Of the 500 men who marched to the relief of Salza, most now returned to Mühlhausen to get on with their lives or prepare for the next excitement. The remainder, perhaps a hundred in all, headed for the abbey at Volkenroda, just east of Mühlhausen, there to plunder its riches. In short order, the abbey's library was destroyed, furniture and icons burned, the granary looted, the fish-pond drained, 2,000 sheep expropriated and – most welcome of all – the wine and beer cellars emptied. The alcohol was consumed over the next couple of days, shared with reinforcements from their home town, who had arrived a little later with Müntzer.

For Müntzer had not been idle in these days. After a small delegation from the Werra army turned up in Mühlhausen, Müntzer decided that it was time to start rallying his supporters. On 26 or 27 April, he wrote once more to the people of Allstedt, urging them to raise their game and join the fight. The letter is one of his most famous pieces of writing.

May the pure fear of God be with you, dear brothers. How much longer will you sleep, how much longer will you resist God's will because you think He has forsaken you? . . . Stop flattering those perverted fantasists, those godless evil-doers, but rather begin now and fight the Lord's fight! It is high time . . .

The peasants of Klettgau and Hegau in the Black Forest have risen, three times one thousand strong and the army is growing ever greater . . . Even if there are only three of you who stand tranquil in God and seek only his name and honour, then you will not fear a hundred thousand. So: on, on, onwards! It is time, the evil-doers are running scared like dogs . . . On, on, onwards, for the fire is hot! Do not let your sword grow cold, do not let it hang loose in your hands! Smite cling clang on the anvil of Nimrod; cast down their towers! As long as they live, it is not possible to be emptied of the fear of Man. You can be told nothing about God as long as they rule over you. On, onwards, while you have daylight. God marches before you, so follow, follow! God . . . will strengthen you in the true belief without the fear of Man. Amen. Thomas Müntzer, a servant of God against the Godless.[18]

('Three times one thousand strong' grossly underestimates the size of the peasant armies. Luther's pamphlet *A Dreadful History and Judgement of God on Thomas Müntzer* of May 1525 reproduced this letter by Müntzer. This phrase about the number of peasants in arms was there multiplied – more accurately – to 'three times one hundred thousand', presumably to scare the living daylights out of his readership.)[19]

The message of Müntzer's letter was simple: that the insurrection was an act for God against the godless tyrants, and its driving force was the pure fear of God, to the exclusion of any other considerations. After the military victory, the Elect could spread God's word. Müntzer proclaimed the necessity of human intervention on behalf of God: the Apocalypse about to overwhelm the tyrants required the common people to make preparations.

Müntzer's letter to Allstedt is also commonly known as the 'Letter to the Miners', since he asked the people of Allstedt to 'get this letter out to the miners'. The metaphor of hammering on the anvil was probably deliberately chosen to appeal to the miners and ironworkers of Thuringia.

For Müntzer the miners constituted a most important material force to aid in the destruction of the godless. He remembered how they had flocked to see him in Allstedt and had been instrumental in defending his reforms; and now he hoped to bring them into his military plans. He could not contact them directly, so asked his supporters in Allstedt to pass on the message. It was not just the miners of Eisleben and the Mansfeld lands who were now threatening insurrection, but also those from Stolberg and the south Harz region. And the people of Allstedt appear to have responded positively: Zeiss had to advise Friedrich the Wise on 3 May that 'all of our citizens [i.e. arms-bearing men], except 10 or 12, have gone off to Mühlhausen to join Müntzer'.[20]

In this same letter to Allstedt, Müntzer also mentioned that 'my printer will arrive in the next few days'. Quite who this printer was, and what he was to do in Mühlhausen, is a bit of a mystery. Conceivably it was Widemar, who had done work for him during the Allstedt period. Whoever he was, he apparently took up residence, along with accompanying family and printing press, in Müntzer's house in Mühlhausen; and he managed to leave the town (abandoning his equipment) before it was captured by the princes in May. As far as we know, however, he never printed anything. Perhaps Müntzer had plans for more pamphlets once the immediate crisis was over; if so, the employment of a printer indicated that he was confident of success.[21]

In April, the south German uprising was well advanced. The whole of Swabia and the Black Forest was stirring. In Franconia, directly to the south of Thuringia, a peasant army of 19,000 men, standing partly under the leadership of two Imperial knights – the radical Florian Geyer and the mercenary Götz von Berlichingen – had based itself around Rothenburg and captured several towns in the Main and Tauber valleys. At the peak of its power, this army of insurgents chased the Bishop of Würzburg from his residence in early May, and three days later they were masters of the town. These tremendous events naturally found an echo in Thuringia and affected the tactics of the radical movement there. The towns of Fulda, Erfurt, Allstedt and Sangerhausen, and those around Eisenach and Halle further south, had already been scenes of sporadic unrest in 1524 and earlier. Now in April, the citizens of Erfurt were inspired to demand economic and democratic reforms, and those of Fulda had united with its dependent peasantry in a troop around 10,000 strong, under the leadership of the radical preacher Hans Dahlkopf. One advantage the central German rebels possessed was that the Twelve Articles of Memmingen had already been printed in hundreds of copies, and were circulating widely in the region: with such a template, they had no need to think too long and hard about their demands.

The Saxon authorities were naturally concerned to see that the wildfire did not leap over into their territory. But the Albertine Duke Georg and the Ernestine princes Friedrich and Johann could not come to an agreement on who was to have the privilege – and in alliance with whom – of putting down the unrest in Thuringia: the political and religious structures were so closely intertwined that neither princely party trusted the other with control of the repression. Friedrich the Wise, in particular, was nervous of permitting his Catholic cousin Georg to take any steps against the rebellious towns, lest that endangered the religious reforms which Friedrich himself had championed. For the Ernestines, the task was made doubly difficult by a momentary political paralysis: Friedrich (admittedly on his deathbed, when one imagines he was feeling low) wrote to Johann as late as 14 April that 'if God so commands, then so shall it be, that the common man shall rule', while Johann himself had stated that 'God made me a prince so that I can ride with many horses; if He does not wish to sustain me, then I will gladly ride with four, or even two; if He wishes to protect me, then no one can overpower me; if not, then I can as well be a commoner'.[22] As long as the princes were unsure of the outcome of the uprising, so long were they prepared to compromise; only in late April, when it became known that an army under Philipp of Hesse was on its way to crush the rebellion, did they shake off their lethargy.

There were several peculiar features of the situation in Thuringia. Firstly, Saxony and Thuringia were by far the richest areas of Germany, due to the criss-crossing trade routes and the advanced development of the silver and copper mines there; in addition the area had a fairly well-off peasantry and a considerable number of miners and other embryonic elements of a proletariat. Secondly, due in part to this advanced social make-up, the reform movement was largely urban and the subsequent insurrection was nurtured and led by the townspeople rather than the peasantry. Thirdly, since the Lutheran reform movement was developed initially in Saxony, the conflict between the opposing religious parties was here at its sharpest. Fourthly, Thuringia was still parcelled up into numerous small estates and counties, and the trend towards territorial centralisation under the great princes had not yet taken hold; thus, the region represented one of the most vulnerable political targets for the insurgents. The classic cycle of urban revolt, installation of reformed preachers and the overthrow of councils – exemplified by Mühlhausen – was played out in Fulda, Eisenach, Erfurt and elsewhere. The townspeople, and particularly the lower classes, played a major role in the Thuringian events. On 1 May 1525, Zeiss wrote that 'the people are all ready to rebel . . . Doctor Luther is in the Mansfeld lands, but he cannot prevent such rebellion and riot there . . . And they are gathering from Sangerhausen and from Duke Georg's lands. What will come of it, I do not know.'[23] Doctor Luther had indeed begun his tour of that area in mid-April, in the company of Melanchthon and Johann Agricola, ostensibly to oversee the establishment of a school sponsored by Count Albrecht of Mansfeld – but his interventions in towns like Eisleben and Nordhausen demonstrated that a second purpose was to quench the flames of rebellion. However, the rebellious populace left him in no doubt as to his unpopularity, demonstrating against him and interrupting his sermons until he retired in disarray to Weimar. As for the people of Allstedt, Duke Johann was forced to issue an order forbidding them to join the 'Eternal League' in Mühlhausen. And at last on 28 April, Duke Georg, sensing that the situation was getting out of hand, urged the entire nobility of Saxony and Thuringia to make themselves ready for conflict.[24]

৵

On that same day, the troops under Pfeiffer and another militia led by Müntzer convened at the village of Görmar, just a mile or so outside Mühlhausen. The spot was probably chosen because disparate groups of other rebels were flocking into Mühlhausen from every corner of Thuringia, and the town council was understandably anxious to keep such boisterous people outside the town walls. Görmar was a less alarming place for them to be. It was here that several plans were hatched to emulate the mighty deeds of the peasants of Franconia and Swabia. While discussions were in progress, one group set off eastwards to ransack a nunnery and castle at Schlotheim, before returning to the main encampment – provisions were thereby restocked. (The lord of the castle later submitted an extremely detailed claim for damages and loss, listing everything from roof tiles, windows and doors, through legal documents, fish and livestock, right down to the stockings and shirts of his manservant.)[25] On 29 April, a letter arrived from Frankenhausen, about fifty kilometres to the north-east, asking for 200 men to be sent immediately to support the town's own uprising. Müntzer replied – in the name of 'the Christian gathering in the field at Mühlhausen' – offering to send not just 200, but his entire force, everyone he could spare.[26] And with that, the assembled rebels set off for Ebeleben, which they reached that evening.[27]

Here they found time to ransack another couple of castles and press into service at least three minor knights, along with their weapons and military skills. This recruitment was done with some care; one of the knights was questioned as to how he had treated his vassals, and was not permitted to leave the gathering until it was established that no one had a grievance against him. All of the knights were made to swear that they would permit evangelical preaching, that they would lighten their peasants' load and would abandon their worldly titles. They all agreed readily to these conditions, though it would appear they did not have much choice.[28]

Just beyond Ebeleben the agreed plan was abruptly changed. Müntzer had it in mind to continue on to Frankenhausen and on the way besiege and neutralise the castle at Heldrungen. This was the castle owned by his long-time enemy, Count Ernst of Mansfeld; as it stood not far from Frankenhausen it was a stronghold from which the people of that town could be easily attacked; its capture would therefore be a sure way to pre-empt that possibility. By now, however, the Mühlhausen militia had gathered up more recruits – largely peasants from the Eichsfeld plain which lay to the north and west of Mühlhausen. Pfeiffer had been in close contact with these peasants over the years and was receptive to their pleas to settle accounts with the inhabitants of the castles and monasteries in the area. In addition, many of the rebels in the army would have felt more comfortable remaining close to home, rather than striking out into unknown territory. So it was decided 'in the ring' (the gathering established by the peasant and mercenary armies, in which speeches could be made and decisions taken) that, instead of continuing north-eastwards, the troop should cut north-westwards across the Eichsfeld in the direction of the town of Heiligenstadt. Doubts were still expressed among the troops, however, about their military capabilities. Would they be able to capture all the castles that lay in their path? Allegedly, Pfeiffer dismissed these concerns with a joke, stating that, with the exception of one impressive fortified castle just beyond Heiligenstadt, he could take all the others

'Varus III' (Wikicommons 2006)

Heldrungen castle as it is today; the tower on the left is allegedly the one in which Müntzer was held captive during his torture and interrogation in May 1525.

'by firing soft cheeses' at them; it sounded good, but what the more experienced soldiers in the troop thought of this military innovation is not recorded.[29]

The question may justifiably be asked: did this change of plan reflect significant differences in strategy between Pfeiffer and Müntzer? It is unrealistic to suppose that the two preachers were always of one mind. Pfeiffer was, if anything, more of a pragmatist than Müntzer; but he held similar views on the need to overturn the social order and defend the preaching of the reformed religion. He was a local man, and had close contacts both inside and outside Mühlhausen. Müntzer was a newly arrived preacher, albeit one who was demonstrably respected across all of central Germany. Without a doubt, they trusted each other and they seemed to operate in tandem. Even when the decision was made to head for Heiligenstadt rather than Heldrungen, Müntzer acquiesced – he could, after all, have continued north-eastwards with a small body of men. The question might be asked another way: what else could Pfeiffer and Müntzer actually have done differently? While their small army was impressive enough, they could not be certain that, some distance from their home patch, they would manage to link up with other small armies and face the territorial princes with their professional soldiers in pitched battle. And there is a subsidiary consideration: although the two men exercised political leadership, they did not necessarily exert military command. Indeed, Zeiss regarded Müntzer simply as the chaplain to the army.[30] This view needs to be taken with a pinch of salt, for he was self-evidently more than just a spiritual adviser, but Zeiss's opinion at least illuminates some of the issues facing Müntzer – and Pfeiffer – in trying to direct a body of armed, enthusiastic, but ill-disciplined men towards a strategic goal.

With or without the soft cheese, the Mühlhausen-Eichsfeld army made a decent job of their expedition through this landscape. They left Ebeleben on the first day of May, reaching the town of Heiligenstadt late on the following evening. En route they managed to plunder and burn a number of religious institutions and castles. They were also able – as Müntzer gleefully reported in a letter to Count Günther of Schwarzburg – to persuade a further four knights to join the League, permitting them 'their Christian freedom' provided they did not 'hinder the righteousness of God and did not persecute any preachers'.[31] (Günther himself had been forced to join the rebels at the end of April.) Neutralising these individuals forced other knights to think twice about taking up arms against such a host. The rebels' march across the Eichsfeld plain served therefore to distract the Saxon and Thuringian authorities. A close watch was being kept by the nobles' observers:

> The army from Mühlhausen last week marched into the Eichsfeld and plundered the castles and manors of noblemen . . . There are many crowds of peasants springing up in many places in Thuringia, and they have marched on the houses of many counts and noblemen, captured them, plundered them, taken the owners prisoner, even chased them away, attacked all the monasteries in Thuringia and laid them to waste.[32]

The archives tell a quite extraordinary story of the amount of damage done to buildings and the amount of plunder taken.[33] Individual buildings were literally taken apart, tile by tile, stone by stone; doors and windows vanished. What little remained was set on fire. Fish ponds were cleared, livestock removed. Beer and wine cellars were swiftly emptied, preserved meats and bacon captured, with all liquids and edibles either consumed on the spot or taken along as provisions. It is estimated that, over the course of this five-day expedition, some 30,000 litres of beer were consumed (which sounds a lot, but when spread across five days and perhaps 5,000 men, it is not so much; it also has to be remembered that beer was a basic foodstuff in those days – healthier than the water available in most places, and a good source of nourishment). Furniture was taken for firewood, and feather-beds found new homes. Most prized were church bells and organ pipes, which were soon melted down to provide ammunition or basic weaponry. Not all the damage was done by the army which had set out from Mühlhausen: there is evidence that a supporting role was played by local people, who, on hearing of the exploits of the peasant army, simply accepted their own responsibilities with praiseworthy zeal. All of this could be justified: how else did the nobles become rich, and store up so many possessions and provisions, if not by exploiting the labour of the peasantry? Taking back the wealth was the first step towards the settlement of old debts. Opportunities were also taken to rectify long-standing annoyances. The priest of one village was obliged to stand before Müntzer and Pfeiffer and be married to his housekeeper, with whom (we suppose) he had been living in a hypocritical relationship.

No one, in all of this, was killed. The residents of religious institutions seem to have had forewarning of the approaching army and fled the scene beforehand with whatever they could carry; the nobles and their families adopted much the same strategy. Even where such people were captured, their injuries amounted to nothing more than bruises, minor cuts and humiliation. The only death recorded was that of an unfortunate peasant who was caught in the flames when setting fire to a chapel.[34]

Having reached Heiligenstadt, the army stayed there for a couple of days. A local administrator described them, slightly nervously, as having 'around 6,000 men, but they are merely foot soldiers and completely unskilled [in war]; they have 3 light field guns, 2 demi-culverins and one gun for firing grapeshot'.[35] Although the troops were camped outside of town, both Müntzer and Pfeiffer preached in its churches, thereby triggering iconoclasm and the plundering of a local religious institution – these actions were not exactly encouraged by the town authorities, but neither were they discouraged. Here, as in Salza and other places during these dramatic days, the civic authorities were quite willing to let the common people indulge in iconoclasm, the sacking of Church institutions and the chasing away of priests. This fulfilled two desirables: firstly, it allowed the lower classes to let off steam and so divert their attention from other – more politically confrontational – concerns; secondly, the expropriation of Church possessions, buildings and lands, as well as the potential weakening of the power of the local nobility, improved the town's own budgetary position.

On leaving Heiligenstadt on 4 May, the plan was to capture the fortified castle at Rüsteberg – the one that could not be taken by cheese alone – where a number of the nobility had barricaded themselves in. However, second thoughts soon prevailed and the route was changed to include the small town of Duderstadt, before heading southwards back into the Eichsfeld plain to plunder a further selection of nunneries and small castles. On the Friday 5 May, a rest was called at a spot where the road split: one branch headed eastwards to Nordhausen and Frankenhausen, the other southwards to Mühlhausen. Müntzer preached here, and then – for reasons that remain unclear – the decision was made to break up the crusade and head for home. It may have been an issue of provisions – by now the army would have exhausted the ready supply of institutional larders which had not previously been ransacked on the journey north; equally pressing was the need for peasants to return to their villages and farms of the Eichsfeld, to attend to their crops and livestock. Müntzer, as will be seen shortly, still had plans to go to the aid of Frankenhausen, but he would only be able to do so effectively with an army that was rested and focused.

Whatever the reason, Pfeiffer and Müntzer and the men of Mühlhausen were back home on the following day.

If any of them imagined that reaching home was the start of a few days of rest, they were to be sorely disappointed. No sooner had they arrived than further letters from the surrounding region began to stream in. On 6 May, the rebels of Sangerhausen wrote (from neighbouring Frankenhausen) to 'our blessed father in God and our trustworthy master, Thomas Müntzer', reporting that, in both town and country, they had taken up arms against their lords and that the local nobility had responded by confiscating weapons and threatening the rebels, so that 'our poor wives and children have had to live and sleep in the fields and woods, out of great fear of the authorities'. They also reported that Count Albrecht of Mansfeld – a supporter of Luther's reforms – had attacked the village of Osterhausen, set it on fire and killed as many as twenty peasants (an act of state terrorism which immediately drew Luther's applause).[36] In short, the people of Sangerhausen were desperate for Müntzer's help.[37] On the very next day came a letter from Frankenhausen itself, saying much the same thing – that 'the tyrant at Heldrungen' (i.e. Count Ernst), Duke Georg and other nobles were now presenting a real and credible threat to the town. Could 'the Christian brothers gathered at Mühlhausen' please help 'with all the resources at your disposal'?[38] In a similar vein, a letter written by Müntzer to the people of Sondershausen – a town not far from Frankenhausen – also promised support, implying that his forces were on their way to attack 'the eagle's nest', referring to the fortress at Heldrungen. 'Do not spare them out of pity', he encouraged; 'this is necessary if Germany is not to turn into a sinful murder-pit'.[39] Finally, on 7 May, Müntzer wrote to the rebels in Schmalkalden – that is, the Werra troops under Sippel – in reply to yet another call for assistance; he promised that help would be sent just as soon as possible, and signed off with a biblical quotation: 'Keep up your courage and sing with us "I will not be afraid even of an hundred thousand, even if they surround me."'[40] Any reinforcements that Müntzer might have sent there, however, would have arrived too late. On 6 May, as mentioned earlier, the Werra army had split up, some heading for home, others for the town of Eisenach, hoping to gain support and buy weapons. The authorities in Eisenach invited Sippel and the other army leaders into town (along with their war-chest) – and then locked them up. Hearing of this treachery, Müntzer wrote to the 'community of Eisenach' on 9 May: he began by wishing the 'dear brothers' 'the pure unadulterated fear of God', before going on to demand the release of Sippel and the war-chest. It was a calm letter – the tone was serious and reproachful, but not Apocalyptic (although he did sign off suggestively as 'Thomas Müntzer, with the sword of Gideon'). He told the people of Eisenach that 'God has moved the whole world . . . to a recognition of the divine truth, and this is proved by the most zealous mood against the tyrants, as Daniel 7 says clearly: power should be given to the common people.' But then he reminded them that the insurrection had less to do with material gain than with fighting for God:

> How is it ever possible that the common people should be able to receive the pure word of God when they are troubled by temporal matters? . . . So you are advised that the poor are not to

be despised (as you do), for the Lord raises up the weak to cast the mighty from their thrones, and rouses the foolish people to humiliate the disloyal, treacherous academics.[41]

His letter did little good. Neither the men nor the money were released. On 11 May, the same day Philipp of Hesse and his huge army arrived before Eisenach, Sippel and his companions were beheaded.

During the month of May, then, the pressure mounted on both sides – on the authorities from the insurgent peasants and plebeians, and on the rebels from the threats and sporadic reprisals of the authorities. Despite a setback caused by the death of Friedrich the Wise on 5 May, the princes of Saxony had managed to wrench themselves out of their inertia. They were thus able to link up with the Lutheran Prince Philipp of Hesse, who was quite independently scoring victories in his inexorable march eastwards through his own territory. He was joined in this crusade by the Catholic Heinrich of Braunschweig – religious differences were largely set aside when it came to suppressing a peasant rebellion. On 3 May, Philipp defeated the uprising in the Fulda district (and took the opportunity to appropriate to himself the local abbey) and then marched on with 7,000 troops to Eisenach, Salza, and then on to Heldrungen – reached on 14 May – with the intention of putting down the rebellions in Frankenhausen and Mühlhausen. That Mühlhausen loomed large in the calculations of the nobility is amply demonstrated by Philipp's ambitious plan for attacking that town ('the font and origin of all these rebellions') with no fewer than 6,000 infantry, 6,000 cavalry and eight artillery pieces.[42]

A passionate reformer, Philipp of Hesse had nevertheless married one of the passionate Catholic Duke Georg's several daughters, Christine, in 1523. He managed to father ten children with her, but remained of the opinion that she was 'pious, but unfriendly, ugly, and smelled bad'. That he himself suffered from syphilis was neither here nor there. In 1540, having tired of his unfortunate wife, he bigamously married another one, twenty years younger than himself, and thereafter fathered another nine children with her (and, for good measure, three more children with Christine). Luther and Melanchthon (and Christine herself) agreed to this illegal second marriage. (As if to prove that some of the German nobility lasted for generations without visible improvement, a distant descendant of Philipp, also a Philipp of Hesse, was complicit in several Nazi atrocities in Germany, before eventually falling out of favour with Hitler.)

In a letter of 8 May to Mühlhausen's Eternal Council, Müntzer advised that he was about to face the crisis head-on at Frankenhausen. By now, a contingent of the arms-bearing men of Allstedt had also arrived. Müntzer wrote that 'before we move off, if it is possible, we would like to discuss our plan seriously with the whole community'.[43] The council duly met to decide on what assistance to give Müntzer's expedition; they voted to provide moral support, to write to the neighbouring towns to solicit material support, and to permit Müntzer to recruit volunteers as he wished. No 'official' contingent was to be sent to Frankenhausen. The burghers of Mühlhausen exercised a powerful influence over the town council; for the purposes of the insurrection, they had effectively said little more than those traditional hollow words: 'we stand with you'. Müntzer remained in town for a further two days, gathering his troops and equipment, and perhaps also hoping for reinforcements from the south. Time was running short: on the day that Müntzer finally left for Frankenhausen, Philipp of Hesse took Eisenach. Two days later, Duke Georg moved out of Leipzig with his contingent of 1,800 men.

The scene was set for a final reckoning.

12

Thomas Would Catch All the Bullets in His Sleeves

The Battle of Frankenhausen (May 1525)

Many of them took comfort in Thomas's great promise that God in heaven would help them and that Thomas himself would catch all the bullets in his sleeves.

Philipp Melanchthon (1525)

After returning from the campaign in the Eichsfeld – perhaps even during it – Müntzer would have been acutely aware that the situation had reached a crisis point. To the north and south, the peasantry and the urban lower classes were up in arms, attacking castles and religious institutions, and driving through religious and social reforms with an energy of which Luther could scarcely have approved. Letters had come pouring into Mühlhausen, asking for Müntzer's advice, and for troops to reinforce local uprisings. Communication between non-military groups was rarely swift, so by the time Müntzer received each piece of news, good or bad, it was usually long out of date. And now Philipp of Hesse was marching through Franconia and entering Thuringia from the south. By 11 May the Werra army was crushed. The rebels up in Frankenhausen and Sangerhausen were begging for more troops to be sent from Mühlhausen. So were towns and villages to the south. Müntzer had previously promised troops for Schmalkalden (sixty kilometres to the south) at the end of April; now he was being asked – again – to send troops to Frankenhausen (fifty kilometres to the north-east). But he had none available. All he had was a relatively small militia of doubtful commitment in Mühlhausen, backed up by a group from Allstedt and the peasants of the Eichsfeld, who were by now growing weary of campaigning. Müntzer was no fool: he knew exactly the character of his fellow citizens. In his letter to the people of Schmalkalden, he asked them to 'be patient a little longer with our brothers, because we have had a great deal of trouble getting them into shape: they are far coarser than anyone could have thought possible'.[1] He was now in an impossible position. He could not step back; he had to go forward. History (and Müntzer's God) demanded it.

The campaign across the Eichsfeld itself, although modestly successful, had not been what Müntzer originally intended. True, it had hamstrung a number of the lesser nobility, thereby preventing any immediate danger. But it had been a relatively easy – even rather festive – campaign, during which no resistance was encountered. It raised morale, but had not done much to establish a region-wide army capable of countering the combined might of the Saxon princes, not to mention the troops under Hesse. The step from localised acts of plunder to a pitched battle was monumental. From a military perspective, the one place that had required neutralising was Ernst of Mansfeld's moated castle at Heldrungen, one of the strongest fortresses in central Germany. It was here that the forces from across Saxony would gather before marching on both Frankenhausen and Mühl-hausen. Müntzer was by no stretch of the imagination a trained soldier, but he clearly understood the danger presented by the alliance of Count Ernst with Duke Georg. For the Eichsfeld expedition, despite its temporary gains, had permitted the princes and nobles to catch their breath, regroup and plan their campaign. Now, Müntzer was desperate to break out of Mühlhausen, link up with the other insurgents and face the armies of the princes.

Müntzer's attempt to stir up the people of Mühlhausen on receipt of the latest plea from Frankenhausen did not fall entirely on deaf ears. The rebels in Frankenhausen were in grave danger; they warned that forces were gathering at Heldrungen, and that unless Müntzer fulfilled his earlier promises, 'blood will be shed in great quantities'.[2] When he put this to the Eternal Council, the town's advocate was tasked with writing out a notice asking for volunteers from both the town and the villages. The summons pointed out, entirely realistically, that if the rebels at Frankenhausen were defeated, then 'we too will be lost'.[3] But the council's efforts were limited to this announcement. It was down to Müntzer to actually undertake the unenviable task of persuading men to volunteer. At least one 'battle wagon' was required (for transporting provisions and weapons), and a contingent of men from each and every village. From those who volunteered, the most experienced and suitable would be selected. Service, it was optimistically promised in an open letter from Müntzer, would last no longer than three or four days. (The peasant armies frequently operated on rotation, allowing troops to return home every few days to tend to crops and livestock; while a sensible agronomic idea, this was an inherent weakness when it came to facing up to the mercenary armies.) However, volunteers were asked to bring along their own provisions, or money, since the availability of food along the way had been severely limited by the previous plundering expeditions.[4] Perhaps because of this, the response was slow. After two days had passed, fewer than 1,000 men had come forward – disappointing given that more than twice that number had assembled for training back in March. From this muster, 300 men were selected to go to Frankenhausen, along with eight pieces of light artillery, with a further 300 placed under the command of Pfeiffer and left behind in town as a defence force. The remainder were sent back to their villages. That Pfeiffer was to remain in Mühlhausen need not, again, be seen as a sign of disagreement between the two radical preachers. It made sense for someone to stay behind and protect the reforms from attack – either from outside the town or from within: the Eternal Council had not proved to be the most reliable or proactive supporter in recent days.

Even as these preparations for a final Apocalyptic showdown with the godless took place, Müntzer was still being consulted on matters far less grave. The parishioners of a tiny place named Grossenehrich, about thirty kilometres east of Mühlhausen, were sending him letters reporting on – among other things – the division of spoils from their plundering of local churches and monasteries, progress on liturgical reforms, disputes with neighbouring peasants on the matter of timber, and ongoing conflicts with local landlords. It is clear that Müntzer was, at least in some quarters, regarded as an arbiter on all manner of 'reform' issues.[5] But the time for him to occupy himself with minor complaints and disagreements was long past.

Late on 10 May, Müntzer and his small contingent set off. By late afternoon the following day they had arrived in Frankenhausen.

Frankenhausen was a small town of around 1,800 inhabitants. One of its main industries was salt-panning; ninety salt-panners were registered there, and their 117 panning huts, complete with a maze of basins, canals and fires, not to mention the day-labourers who did all the hard work, were spread out rather untidily inside and outside the town walls. The rebellion had begun here late in April when the town's craftsmen, salt workers and other plebeians presented the council with a set of fourteen articles which included demands for a more democratic council, the introduction of reformed religion, the dispossession of the

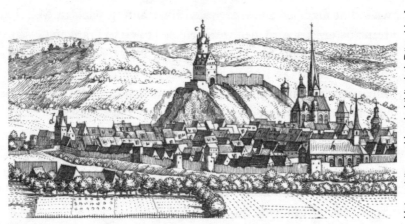

A segment from a panoramic view of Frankenhausen (Mattheus Merian, 1650). The hill on which the battle of 1525 took place is to the left of the watchtower marked (c). The top of the hill was levelled in the 1980s for the construction of the Panorama Museum, which is dedicated to the Peasants' War. The town gate (d) on the left is near where Müntzer was captured.

old Church institutions, revised taxes and free access to forest and meadow. When the councillors did not immediately react, the town hall was stormed, the council overthrown and – it almost goes without saying – the local castle and nunnery plundered. This attracted the attention not only of the territorial authorities, but also of the peasants and townspeople from the surrounding area. Peasants and miners streamed in from Nordhausen, Sondershausen, Sangerhausen and Stolberg, to name just a few, and even from Allstedt. On 4 May, around 4,000 troops presented themselves for a muster in Frankenhausen; chaplains were appointed and a committee of twelve elected to provide some command structure. Also in the army were several minor noblemen, those from Stolberg and Schwarzburg and other small places, persuaded that their only hope of survival lay in acceding, if only temporarily, to the rebels' demands (which included abandoning their hereditary titles, the destruction of all their castles except one per knight, and granting freedom of access for fishing, hunting, wood-cutting and so on). Hans Zeiss, who was still in Allstedt, reported that decisions were being made in several rebel camps that knights would be obliged to march on foot, and that 'a prince could only keep 8 horses, a count only 4 horses, and any other nobleman only two'.[6] It was around this time that Zeiss began to have second thoughts about where his loyalties lay; one of his reports describes Müntzer's adherents as 'less reasonable and more bloodthirsty' than the rest of the peasantry.[7] Mysteriously, a man claiming to be Zeiss's brother, and bearing a message from him, turned up in Frankenhausen on 6 May, politely asking the assembled rebels not to attack reformed communities or the possessions of reformed princes. The Frankenhausen leadership retired to consider this request, and then just as politely agreed, with the strict proviso that the reformed princes did not threaten the rebels.[8] (Despite these late attempts at proving his loyal credentials, Zeiss was dismissed before the end of the month; his successor was already, in the first week of June, assiduously imprisoning and interrogating Allstedt citizens suspected of being rebels – and complaining bitterly that the local prison was not fit for purpose.[9])

Those of the nobility who had managed to escape the close attentions of their subjects headed straight for Heldrungen, where Count Ernst was by now gathering an impressive pack of his colleagues. While Ernst was encouraging Duke Georg to raise an army and come to his assistance, his brother – the Luther-leaning Albrecht – thought it best to try to negotiate with the rebels. To that end, he wrote to the people of Frankenhausen on 10 May, pointing out that they were being disobedient (citing Luther's teachings on the matter of civil authority) and asking them to avoid bloodshed. He offered to act as a mediator, and listen to their complaints. This was the same Count Albrecht who, five days earlier, had sent his troops to attack a mixed band of 'his' miners and peasants at the small village named Oster-hausen. They had been on their way to join the growing band at Frankenhausen; according to contemporary accounts, twenty of the miners and peasants were killed on the spot.[10] Despite this being common knowledge, the 'Christian Gathering at Frank-enhausen' agreed to send delegates to a meeting on 12 May. In what was plainly a delaying tactic, Albrecht wrote back saying that the 12th was rather inconvenient, so could they make it the 14th instead?

While Albrecht was exercising his skills in delay and decep-tion, his brother Ernst was more open about his intentions. On 4 May his troops burned down a village close to Frankenhausen and made off with a flock of sheep; the rebels in the town then marched out and burned down several castles, managing to capture three of Ernst's representatives. (In connection with these events, it is worth pointing out that German armies commonly employed someone in the post of 'fire-master' – tasked not with putting out fires but, quite the opposite, with burning down buildings or villages if the inhabitants did not yield up provi-sions, men or quarters on demand. In 1525, both sides employed fire-masters. It was all very efficient.) Ernst then wrote to the rebels at Frankenhausen, demanding that they abandon their plans for attacking him, and that they release the three prisoners. The reply from Frankenhausen was less than polite, remind-ing him that the theft of the sheep a few days earlier had been 'against God, honour and law', and that his earlier execution of a 'pious Christian' because of his reformed beliefs now forced them to 'deal with all faithless tyrants . . . with the help of God'.[11] The words 'faithless tyrants' must have seemed disturbingly familiar to Ernst, a reminder of his attempts to muzzle Müntzer back in the summer of 1523. In the meantime, he complained to Duke Georg that the numbers of troops he could raise had been severely limited by the defection of the minor nobles and knights of the area. So widespread had these defections become that Georg could now only rely on the various Counts of Mansfeld (there were five altogether) – everyone else was in no fit state. On 13 May, Ernst begged Georg to send at least 200 cavalry and assorted infantrymen, to face up to 'the army of Müntzer' which had just arrived in Frankenhausen.[12]

But Duke Georg himself was not having much luck; his attempts to persuade his cousin, Friedrich the Wise, to raise a united Saxon army against the rebels had not been greeted with much warmth. The Lutheran Friedrich was dithering. His great fear was that Georg would gain military victory over the rebel armies and then use this as an opportunity to reverse the progress made by the reformed religion in towns across Saxony. As events proved, this is precisely what Georg later attempted to do. But in any event, Friedrich did not live to see it – he died on 5 May, and his brother Duke Johann became Elector in his place. Johann, to Georg's disappointment, had equally little appetite for open

Mercenary soldiers, *Landsknechte*, of the early sixteenth century, commonly employed by the territorial princes. Drawing by Daniel Hopfer, c. 1520–36.

conflict. Georg did his best to raise mercenaries in a region as yet untouched by the uprising – in his lands around Meissen, some 150 kilometres to the east of the main theatre of conflict; but even there his recruiting officers told him there would be delays in sending the reinforcements.

If the Saxon and Thuringian authorities were having difficulties in maintaining order, this was not the case with the territorial princes to the west. Philipp of Hesse, barely twenty years old but making a name for himself as an able military commander, was cutting a swathe through the uprisings to the south and west; by 11 May, he was fast approaching Frankenhausen. He had linked up with Duke Heinrich of Braunschweig, and jointly they commanded 1,700 cavalry and 3,000 infantry. Philipp was an enthusiastic supporter of Luther, which must have been a considerable embarrassment to his father-in-law, Duke Georg. His concern, however, was not for the religious reforms. There were far more important things than that: the uprisings in Fulda, Werra, Frankenhausen and the Eichsfeld were right on the eastern border of his extensive lands and, as such, had to be stopped before he found himself in an awkward situation with his own subjects. Duke Heinrich – a staunch Catholic – had similar issues to Philipp: his territory bordered Frankenhausen and the Eichsfeld from the north.

Meanwhile in Frankenhausen, the assembled rebels had elected their commander-in-chief, a peasant going by the rather exotic name of Bonaventura Kürschner. Almost nothing is known of this man, other than that he seemed to have a decent grasp of military strategy, suggesting a lengthy service as a mercenary.

It was Kürschner, not Müntzer, who commanded the troops, up to and including the battle at Frankenhausen. Nor did Müntzer have a monopoly on the religious leadership; there were other preachers within the army, chaplains for their own local contingents. But the political leadership – if we can designate it thus, in a slightly anachronistic manner – lay very decidedly with Müntzer. The Mühlhausen contingent had arrived in Frankenhausen late on 11 May; the following day Müntzer was already writing letters to the two Counts of Mansfeld in an attempt to persuade them to step back. In the case of Albrecht, there would have been the additional motive of ensuring that the Frankenhausen rebels did not fall for his offer to negotiate, postponed to the 14th.

The letter to Albrecht began promisingly: 'Fear and trembling be upon everyone who does evil.' It continued by directly targeting Albrecht's professed Lutheran ideas:

> Do you think that the Lord God cannot stir up the uncomprehending people so that they will overthrow the tyrants in his wrath? Have you not been able to spoon up from your Lutheran gruel, your Wittenberg soup, that which Ezekiel prophesied? And have you not been able to taste in your Martin's peasant gruel what the same prophet further said, that God would command all the birds of the air to feast on the flesh of the princes and command the unthinking beasts to lap up the blood of the bigwigs? Do you really think that God has less interest in his people than in you tyrants? ... If you will admit that God has given power to the common people, and if you will appear before us and give an account of your faith, then we will be glad to allow this and to accept you as a common brother. But if you refuse, then we will not pay any attention to your lame, insipid mug: we will fight against you as against an arch-enemy of the Christian faith: you know what to expect now.[13]

The letter was signed 'Thomas Müntzer, with the sword of Gideon.' Müntzer was clearly attempting to neutralise the second-last of the local noblemen who had not yet submitted to the rebels; he offered the hope of forgiveness – but solely on the rebels' terms.

His letter to Count Ernst was similarly uncompromising. Addressing him as 'Brother Ernst' (an interesting contrast with that earlier letter of September 1523, which was politely addressed 'To the noble and well-born Count, Lord Ernst of Mansfeld and Heldrungen'), and introducing himself as 'one-time pastor in Allstedt' (just in case Ernst had somehow forgotten), Müntzer accused the count of tyrannising and oppressing Christians:

Now tell us, you miserable, wretched sack of maggots – who made you into a prince over the people whom God redeemed with his own precious blood? . . . I give you my honest word that you will have a genuine safe-conduct to allow you to publicly confirm your faith: our whole community, standing in a ring, has promised you this . . . But if you stay away, then you will be hunted down and rooted out, for every man will be far keener to gain an indulgence at your expense than any indulgence that the Pope ever offered . . . In short, you will be destroyed by God's mighty power . . .

We want to have your answer by this evening, or else we will hunt you down in the name of the God of hosts. So you know what to expect. We will not hesitate to carry out what God has commanded us to do. So do your best, too. I am coming for you.[14]

It is unlikely that Müntzer expected either brother to do what was demanded, but perhaps he hoped to provoke one or the other into an ill-timed or premature assault, when the rebel army might stand a chance of picking them off singly. (That we still have both of these letters five centuries later is all down to Luther. They were evidently forwarded to Wittenberg on receipt or a few days later. Just after 15 May, Luther was busy preparing his gloating obituary of Müntzer, entitled *A Dreadful History and Judgement of God on Thomas Müntzer*. He included these two letters in his text, and the whole thing was printed and distributed on 21 or 22 May. Had it not been for Luther, we might never have been able to read the letters. God bless Martin Luther!)

As well as composing ultimatums to the enemy, Müntzer made some last-gasp attempts to bring in more reinforcements. His letter of 13 May to the city of Erfurt (some forty-five kilometres to the south) echoed the one to Albrecht. Müntzer hoped that the Erfurters had not succumbed to a pair of 'Lutheran soup-slurpers with their greasy mercifulness' and that they would 'give no credence to those plate-lickers' (the slurping twosome was in fact Luther and Melanchthon, who had been invited to visit Erfurt imminently); he urged Erfurt to send men and cannon just as soon as they could. 'Come and join us in the dance,' he exhorted them, 'so that we can settle the score with the blasphemers of

God'.[15] Müntzer's letter was accompanied by one from a radical preacher named Simon Hoffmann who, two years earlier, had fallen foul of the Erfurt authorities, but had probably maintained links to the more radical sections of the populace. Both letters were carried by hand to Erfurt by two Frankenhausen men.[16] By this time, unfortunately, the peasant army which had occupied Erfurt and helped drive through reforms just a week before had once more withdrawn; the city authorities, whose sense of responsibility for the people in the surrounding countryside was minimal (their commercial interests lay in the wider national and international arena, not the parochial one), steadfastly refused to take delivery of Müntzer's letter and spurned the invitation to come to the ball.

On that same day, the rebel army at Frankenhausen took the decision to execute the three emissaries in Ernst's service who had been captured at the start of May. On 13 May, they were brought inside a 'ring' in the midst of the army; the overwhelming majority of the troops voted for the prisoners' execution, which was immediately carried out. Müntzer gave the decision his backing. The executions may have represented a further attempt to provoke the Mansfeld counts into premature action, or it may just have been an expression of frustration by the rebels at the continued inactivity. But it was an act which would be taken up gleefully by Lutherans and Catholics alike as evidence of Müntzer's – and the peasants' – fiendish bloodthirstiness. Curiously, in his confession under torture three days later, Müntzer stated that 'he had given the judgement on Matern of Gehofen and the other servants of Count Ernst as a judgement of the community and had himself agreed and done it for fear'.[17] Lutheran editors of this confession added the words 'for fear of Count Ernst and the community' for good measure here. But what did Müntzer confess himself afraid of? Of the rebel army? Of the consequences of leaving the three prisoners alive in the camp? Of God Himself? Or was this 'fear' simply an invention by his captors? Another document reports the captive Müntzer's conversation with Duke Georg, in which he justified his action thus: 'I did not do that, I acted only according to the law of God.'[18]

With these executions, events hurtled towards an almost inevitable tragic conclusion.

On Sunday 14 May, Frankenhausen was overflowing with an 8,000-strong army of rebellious peasants, miners, artisans and plebeians. Approaching the town from the west were the combined troops of Philipp of Hesse and Heinrich of Braunschweig. Still some distance off in the east, and not to arrive until the following day, was the army raised so laboriously by Georg of Saxony. Together these troops amounted to around 2,800 cavalry and 4,000 infantry, possibly more.[19] Early that Sunday morning, a scouting patrol sent out from the main Hesse/Braunschweig army encountered peasant troops just outside the walls of Frankenhausen, at the foot of the hill which would later become the battlefield. Possibly in a declivity known as the 'Barren Chalk Gully' (*Wüstes Kalktal*), which runs down the hill towards the west side of the town, the scouts were surprised by rebel guards; they were shot at, one soldier was hit and wounded, and the horses suffered some damage, but an orderly retreat saw them return safely to the main body of the army, which was slowly arriving at an encampment near the village of Rottleben (about five kilometres west of Frankenhausen). Late in the evening, the rebels began to move their own forces out of the town and up the hill which lay immediately to the north – the Hausberg, now known as the Schlachtberg, or Battle Hill. It was a hill with a relatively flat top. (It has an even flatter top today – in the 1970s, the East German authorities blasted the top off and levelled it in preparation for building a museum to commemorate the Peasants' War, thereby destroying any hope of an archaeological analysis of the battleground.)

By the morning of Monday the 15th, the rebels had fully occupied the hill overlooking the town. Most of the troops had been moved there, with a small detachment left behind to defend the town. Near the top, a 'wagon-fort' was established – a traditional circle of battle-wagons and other carts set out in a circle and chained together. Protected by this rather restrictive arrangement, the troops could fire their guns at anyone coming towards them. It is possible that the site was chosen because it offered a number

of escape routes should things go badly wrong – either northwards into the Kyffhäuser forest; or southwards down two gullies
which gave on to the north-west corner of Frankenhausen. From
here, too, they would have had a good view of what the opposing
armies were up to. Georg's troops finally arrived that morning,
and set up camp on a small hill immediately to the south of the
town. The leaders of the three noble armies gathered to lay their
plans for the attack; evidently they had been taken by surprise at
the rebels' relocation. From their vantage point to the north, the
rebels tried to pepper the convention of princes with artillery fire,
but did not have the range. Throughout the morning, the princes'
armies moved towards the town. The Saxon contingent settled
in a semi-circle around the southern part of the town, while the
remaining troops advanced up the eastern and western slopes
of the hill in a pincer movement to surround the wagon-fort.
Although the overall numbers of troops on both sides were – on
paper – more or less equal, the princes had the very significant
advantage of more artillery: Georg was reported to have brought
along two heavy siege-guns, two 'culverins' and three light field
pieces; Ernst chipped in with more cannon from Heldrungen,
while Philipp had five cannon and siege guns, three field artillery
pieces, as well as 200 hundredweight of gunpowder, and 200
cannonballs. In contrast, the few artillery pieces which the rebels
possessed were lightweight models.[20]

At some point in the morning, the rebels sent a brief message
to the princes' armies: 'We recognise Jesus Christ. We are not
here to hurt anyone, John 2, but to maintain God's righteousness.
Neither are we here to shed blood. If you wish to do likewise,
then we do not wish to harm you.'[21] It was a short message and
to the point; and it revealed what must have been obvious to
anyone – that the rebels were hopelessly out-classed in military
terms and badly needed a ceasefire. The princes' reply was longer
and seems to have been sent late morning. It accused the rebels
of murder, arson and sacrilege and threatened them with punishment as 'slanderers of God' unless 'you hand over to us, alive, the
false prophet Müntzer with his henchmen, and render yourselves
up to our mercy and punishment'.[22] It was a deliberately ambigu-
ous offer: in return for handing over Müntzer and his immediate

circle, the princes only promised to 'deal with you so that you can receive our mercy, according to circumstances' – not exactly an unequivocal offer of leniency. This written ultimatum was accompanied by a three-hour deadline.

What happened next, and in what order, is a little unclear. As luck would have it, though, Philipp Melanchthon – some 150 kilometres away in Wittenberg – was able to craft a good story. It is a complete fabrication; manifestly so, since it supposes that, after Müntzer had made a speech to his troops, Philipp of Hesse, having heard every word, answered Müntzer point for point. Despite this, the story is still accepted as good coin by some historians. According to Melanchthon, Müntzer reiterated the main points of his doctrines – 'the princes are nothing but tyrants who flay the people; they fritter away our blood and sweat on their pomp and whoring and knavery' – before promising that 'you need not fear their guns, for you will see that I will catch in my sleeves all the bullets that they fire at us'; finally he pointed to a rainbow that had appeared and announced 'this means that God will help us, for we carry the rainbow on our banner, and he will truly judge the murdering princes and punish them'.[23] Some of the words are not implausible, though the promise to catch bullets in his sleeves is somewhat far-fetched. A correspondent of Luther quoted two miners from the rebel army who testified that Müntzer had simply said 'No shots will harm you.'[24]

Hans Hut, who, unlike Melanchthon, had been present at the battle, gave what was probably a more accurate account of Müntzer's speech, reporting that he had said:

> God the Almighty now wished to cleanse the world and had today taken the power from the princes and given it to the common man. Then they would be weak . . . and they, the authorities, would beg, but no one should believe them, for they would hold to no pact, and God was with them [the peasants], for the peasants had painted a rainbow on every banner. Müntzer said that that was the covenant of God. And when Müntzer had preached to the peasants in this way for three days in succession, there appeared a rainbow in the sky around the sun. Müntzer pointed out this rainbow to the peasants and comforted them and said that they

could now see the rainbow, the covenant and the sign that God wished to be with them. They should now fight with heart and be of courage.[25]

It goes without saying that Müntzer would have made some kind of rousing speech to the army; indeed he had to, since the princes had sent their final warning to the peasants and there was a real danger of capitulation. It also seems very likely that a 'rainbow' did appear in the sky – a sun-halo, not uncommon in central Germany – and its appearance, echoing Müntzer's banner which had accompanied the Mühlhausen troop, would have been certain proof to the rebels that God was on their side. (In a gratifying coincidence, Luther had reported that, when Friedrich the Wise died on 5 May, a rainbow appeared 'as a sign'. Luther also mentioned that the death was marked by a baby being born without a head and another with inverted feet. Make of signs what you will.)[26]

At around noon, the rebels convened in a ring within the wagon-fort to consider the ultimatum – and decisively reject it. They were probably paying little attention to the enemy movements. Philipp of Hesse seized the opportunity to launch an artillery barrage into the wagon-fort, causing immediate damage and panic. Only fifteen minutes had elapsed since the notification of the deadline. While Müntzer rode around desperately trying to persuade the troops to stand firm and fight back – and it was later reported by two captured miners that the men of Mühlhausen and Nordhausen did indeed stand their ground – the Hesse and Braunschweig infantry and cavalry streamed across the undulating ground at the top of the hill to attack the Frankenhausen rebels.[27] Melanchthon depicted the peasant army standing singing a hymn 'as if they were all mad', and making no attempt either to flee or to fire their weapons; whereupon the army of the princes charged. But even Melanchthon had to concede that the attack came without warning, that no mercy was shown, and that 'five thousand men lay dead' – a number also proposed by one of the noblemen who joined in the slaughter.[28]

Within a matter of minutes, the 'battle' was over, the fate of the Thuringian revolution of 1525 was decided, and with it the radical Reformation of Thomas Müntzer. Faced by a well-armed and well-trained cavalry, infantry and gun battery, the rebels were massacred. Out of 8,000 men, around 3,000 were cut down on the hilltop. The rest turned and fled for their lives, some towards the forest to the north, but most towards the town. As they fled, they were pursued and scythed down. They ran down the Barren Chalk Gully or an adjacent one now named – for obvious reasons – the 'Bloody Gully' (*Blutrinne*). Some managed to put up a fight in the gullies and inflict injuries on their pursuers, but it was hopeless. Those who reached the foot of the hill alive encountered Georg's troops, who finished them off, chasing them across fields, into town or across the salt-panning works, cutting them down as they ran. A small number gave themselves up and were fortunate to be taken as prisoners.

It is estimated that between 5,000 and 7,000 rebels died that day – the figure is understandably approximate, but surprisingly consistent over several reports[29] – with a further 600 taken prisoner. Half of the adult male population of Frankenhausen was put to the sword. A history written in 1747, based on Frankenhausen's archives before they were destroyed in a fire, suggested a total of 7,323 victims – a very precise number, but not thereby trustworthy. It is suggested that the opposing army suffered only six fatalities – a figure that is without doubt an underestimate, but not necessarily a gross one, since the rebels had barely had time to use their own weapons.[30] For the nobles and their troops, the affair was treated almost as a sport: two minor aristocrats sent to the campaign by Prince Joachim von Brandenburg had been commissioned by their sponsor to bring home the ear of a peasant; in a letter, they regretted that this had proved impractical.[31]

Müntzer was not one of those killed. Neither, remarkably, were a fair number of his immediate circle – several of them, having escaped into the forest, turned up over the next few years as leaders of the Anabaptist movement. Müntzer managed to get down from the Hausberg unharmed, and entered Frankenhausen by the north-west gate in the town walls. In an inn near the gate, he took refuge in a bedroom in the upper storey. But his escape was short-lived. A mercenary seeking accommodation for his employer discovered Müntzer and demanded to know what he was doing there. Müntzer's reply failed to convince, so he was searched and then identified by the satchel full of letters which he carried around with him at all times. The letters were the most recent he had sent and received, twenty-two of the many from which we have quoted throughout this book. They tell us about Müntzer's thoughts and life; ironically, they contributed directly to his capture and death. His identity revealed, he was taken off to the princes' headquarters. His captor was rewarded with 100 guilders.

13

How God Punishes Disobedience

The Aftermath of Defeat at Frankenhausen

We should give careful consideration to the fate of Thomas Müntzer, and all learn from it that we should not believe those who boast of divine revelation . . . And we should also learn how severely God punishes disobedience against the authorities, for God commands us to honour the authorities and to obey them.
Philipp Melanchthon (1525)

It was a curious sight: a preacher – bruised, shaken, but not broken – standing before three of the most powerful noble-men of central Germany. Duke Georg wanted to know why Müntzer had executed the three hostages. Müntzer, addressing the duke as 'brother', explained that it had been a communal decision, founded on godly justice. Outraged, Heinrich of Braun-schweig berated Müntzer for his disrespect for the duke, and wanted to know if he thought he was now a prince himself. Philipp of Hesse, for his part, engaged Müntzer in a brief the-ological debate on the matter of secular authority: Müntzer resolutely cited the Old Testament on the matter, Philipp prefer-ring to stick to the Lutheran interpretation of Romans 13 in the New Testament ('The powers that be are ordained by God').[1]

After this quite extraordinary conversation between the four men, Müntzer was tied up and sent in a cart to Heldrungen as a trophy owed to Count Ernst. Georg headed that way as well, while Philipp and Heinrich busied themselves with finishing off the Thuringian revolt. Their immediate activities included interrogations and executions at Frankenhausen, although it is perhaps indicative of their priorities that most of the town's salt-panners, who generated a tidy tax income for their feudal lords, were spared. Miners also were more commonly sent home than killed. Sometimes economic considerations took precedence over injustice.

On arrival at Heldrungen, Müntzer was locked up in a secure tower in the fortress; on the following day, 16 May, his interrogation began. Müntzer was fully aware that he would shortly die. He had tried, and failed, to lead the rebellion in Frankenhausen and Mühlhausen to a successful conclusion, and even with his firm belief that God would somehow intervene in the process, he knew that this would not save his life. What mattered instead was to save his supporters – and his family – from the worst acts of retribution by the godless tyrants. But he had very little opportunity to do so.

Much to Luther's annoyance, the interrogation ran along political lines, not religious ones. That it was so is to be expected: the flames of rebellion might have been extinguished, but the glowing embers still lay scattered across Thuringia and Saxony; in the minds of the rulers of Germany, theology was at that moment of minor importance. Attending Müntzer's interrogation were probably Duke Georg, along with Ernst, a couple of Ernst's noble neighbours, a scribe to write everything down – and the torturer. The interrogation, which was effectively his trial, took place in two sessions, as was common in those days: a first session in which Müntzer 'freely' confessed to a number of things; and a second session in which he confessed 'painfully' – i.e. under torture, most probably with the application of thumbscrews. Luther justifiably raged about the proceedings: it really did seem shambolic. A random series of questions was asked and answered. Although several copies were made of Müntzer's 'confession' and at least six versions were printed as a pamphlet in the weeks that followed, there appears to have been no editorial attempt to put things into any order.

Philipp of Hesse had earlier and very efficiently drawn up a standard set of questions to be posed to any prisoner captured during the campaign:

> The prisoner should be asked where he comes from, what his trade and employment are, why he had got involved in this rebellion against our dear lord etc. Philip [of Hesse], who was his captain, who had started the rebellion and had spread it among the people, and to state their intentions and what they would have done if things had gone their way.[2]

That this kind of basic intelligence does not appear to have been gathered from Müntzer suggests that everyone was already very familiar with their prisoner's past life. What were of more immediate interest to his captors were the names of his co-conspirators and a list of all his misdemeanours, especially those against the Catholic Church and local knights going back months and years.[3] We have mentioned some of Müntzer's answers in previous chapters – assuming the 'confession' has any value at all, many of his own statements on events in his life only reached the light of day here. Thus, for example, his denial that he had somehow started the uprising in south-west Germany; his confirmation that he had supported the proposal that nobles should have a limited number of horses; that he had on several occasions fallen out with Luther; that he had been at the burning of the Mallerbach chapel; and so on. His bitter argument with Ernst of Mansfeld in the summer of 1523 was – obviously – mentioned, as was the plundering of the castle of Apel of Ebeleben, during the Eichsfeld expedition; this otherwise arbitrary mention of one criminal act out of several dozen strongly suggests that the wronged gentleman of Ebeleben was in attendance at the interrogation. Müntzer also stated that 'The Mühlhausen town council did not voluntarily support the [Eternal] League, but permitted the common man to do so', thereby providing the council with something of a mitigation. Also mentioned in this 'voluntary' section of the confession was another preacher – 'Master Gangolf, the chaplain in the hospital, [who] had taken charge of one detachment, in which the people of Heringen and

Graussen served'. Further details on this man are not known. We only know that Gangolf too had been delivered in captivity to Heldrungen; in all likelihood, he was one of the five preachers who were promptly executed in the fortress, much to the horror of some Lutheran commentators.[4] A further two local preachers were handed over to women in Frankenhausen who, in exchange for their own husbands' lives, beat them to death with cudgels. (To all of which, Luther's rather placid comment was: 'Yes, it is to be regretted. But what else could one do? It is essential that the people be frightened and cowed . . . else Satan will do far worse things . . . Who takes up the sword, shall die by the sword.'[5])

Fifteen items were confessed by Müntzer 'freely'; a further twelve were confessed under torture. In the latter, far more names were mentioned – those of co-conspirators in Allstedt, Mühlhausen, even in Halle and Zwickau. Of immediate concern to his hosts was a confession that 'if he had taken the castle at Heldrungen, as he and his supporters intended, then he would have taken off Count Ernst's head, as he had often said', which was further elaborated on: 'He had stirred up the rebellion in order that Christianity should make all men equal and that the princes and noblemen who did not wish to support the Gospel should be driven out and put to death.' In a similar tone, Müntzer supposedly said that 'he would take control of all the land for 10 miles around Mühlhausen, and the land [belonging to] Hesse, and deal with the princes and noblemen as indicated above'. The 'miles' referred to are the medieval German miles, ten of which equate to around seventy-four kilometres. And then there was one further confession that was just what his captors wanted to hear, concerning Müntzer's supporters in Allstedt:

The Articles which they proposed and were putting into effect were: 'omnia sunt communia' [all things are to be held in common], and goods should be shared out amongst everyone according to their need, as occasion demanded. Any prince, count or nobleman who did not want to do that, having been once reminded of it, should have his head chopped off or be hanged.

There needs to be some caution here. Müntzer's confession and his later 'Recantation' were both written down and publicised by those who now had full control of events. Furthermore, as we know, any confession made under torture or the threat of it is utterly meaningless, serving most likely only to confirm the prejudices of the interrogators. With the probable exception of confessions which mention specific names, there is no guarantee that any words attributed to Müntzer are actually his own. This is particularly the case with the phrase 'omnia sunt communia', so often quoted by radicals and conservatives alike in the centuries since. There is absolutely nothing in any of the Thuringian or Mühlhausen articles, or in anything Müntzer wrote, even in the very last hours of his defiance at Frankenhausen, which marks this aspiration as one of his. While he railed against usury and the oppression of the peasantry, nowhere did he hint at some form of early communism. It simply did not feature in his view of the future – indeed, he never wrote about the future at all. Cutting off heads – yes; making everyone equal in rank – decidedly; common ownership of all property – probably, but it was never specifically mentioned. The principle of common ownership was not new, and it was one that had been advanced by many earlier movements, from the early Christians (see Acts 2:44), right through to the Humanists, and even to Zwingli, who approvingly wrote of communal possession in a pamphlet dated 1522. But it was the fact that the insurgents had very recently been in a position to put the principle into practice that was most disturbing for the interrogators. They gave Müntzer no opportunity to clarify his own interpretation of this; their goal was simply to confirm their worst suspicions.

The twenty-seven recorded items of the confession constitute a bizarre amalgam of irrelevancies, falsities and half-truths, alongside accurate thumbnail depictions of Müntzer's doctrine and practice. It is difficult to know quite how to classify the document, which is ample reason for being very circumspect about it. Any temptation to build grand theories on it out of context should be avoided.

The same – a hundred times over – must be said of Müntzer's 'Recantation',[6] dated the following day, 17 May. The original aim of this document must have been to show the world that Müntzer was wrong and that he now realised he was wrong – and that therefore all of the rebels were wrong:

> The statements which follow were made by Thomas Müntzer, willingly and after due contemplation of his own conscience . . . and he asked [those present] to remind him of these in case he forgot, so that he could repeat them in front of everyone before he died and affirm them with his own lips.
>
> Firstly, in respect of the nobility, to whom one should always be obedient and give due service, he had preached quite the opposite in immoderate language, and his audience and the lords' subjects listened immoderately, and he had then involved himself with them in shocking and wanton sedition and rebellion and disobe-dience . . .
>
> Secondly, he had preached many kinds of beliefs, madness and errors about the most revered sacrament of the holy and divine body of Christ, and also had preached rebelliously and seditiously against the order of the common Christian Church, he now wants . . . to yield peaceably to everything and . . . to meet death as one who is wholly and truly confirmed in it.

This 'Recantation' remains a rather mean-spirited curiosity. To even suggest that Müntzer, a man of proven single-mindedness, now certain of his impending martyrdom, should suddenly cave in to the tyrants and to the Church he had despised for most of his career, and abandon all of his theology, the mainspring of his own personal relationship with God, shortly before meeting his God, is unthinkable.

One further document emerged from Müntzer's captivity – a letter addressed to the 'dear brothers' in Mühlhausen, written on the same day as the 'Recantation'. It was signed in the name of Müntzer, but the letter itself explains that it had been written down by Christoph Laue, Count Ernst's secretary. After the thumbscrews, Müntzer's hands were by now incapable of holding a pen.[7] The main purpose of the letter was to dissuade anyone in Mühlhausen from engaging in any hopeless adventure against the victorious armies of the princes. (That this might prove necessary was demonstrated by events in Allstedt in mid-June, when three 'hot-heads' were reported to be stirring up rebellion again. These proved to be three preachers from surrounding villages who were perpetuating Müntzer's doctrine, 'especially among the women'.[8] It was clear, even towards the end of that month, that certain people in Allstedt were not cowed by the catastrophic defeat of the peasantry.[9])

Müntzer begins his letter by urging the people of Mühlhausen not to be downhearted by his imminent death; he then continues:

> Dear brothers, it is most necessary that you should not receive such a beating as the men of Frankenhausen . . . Present yourselves before the clear, constant, divine justice, so that nothing similar may befall you . . . In order that you innocent people should not get into the same difficulties as the people of Frankenhausen, you should now avoid any gatherings and rebellions, and should ask mercy from the princes . . . so that no more innocent blood may be spilled.

Müntzer must have envisaged Pfeiffer or others attempting a last stand against Philipp or Georg and thereby prolonging the agony of defeat. As such, the letter made very good sense; and – yes – also served the interests of the princes, who wished to subjugate Mühlhausen as quickly as possible. But there is another layer of meaning here: Müntzer suggests that the cause of the disaster lay in the fact that the people of Mühlhausen and Frankenhausen

> did not understand me correctly and only considered their own profit and thus destroyed God's truth . . . [Those of Frankenhausen] sought more their own profit than delivering justice to Christian people . . . Do not enrage the authorities any more, as many have done for their own profit.

This is a fascinating letter for a number of reasons. Firstly, it has nothing in common with the so-called 'Recantation' which, allegedly, he had just provided. There is nothing in here that denies any of his beliefs about 'the fear of God' or spiritual suffering.

On the contrary, the tone of the letter confirms those beliefs. Secondly, he states that the rebellion failed because the people of Mühlhausen and Frankenhausen did not go far enough: they aimed for some form of democracy, for equality before the law, for all the material things listed in the various 'Articles', but they had not aimed higher. While the rebels regarded the uprising as the means by which socio-economic reforms could be attained and some form of democracy introduced to Thuringia, Müntzer regarded it as only the first step in the necessary cleansing of the world to prepare for the kingdom of God. So to halt the revolution at the point where material or political advantage had apparently been gained was in fact to knock down one barrier to true faith only to erect another. If this letter was an accurate reflection of Müntzer's thoughts on the defeat, then he interpreted the result of the battle in an entirely logical fashion. But in any case, the letter did not justify the victory of the princes. After the trauma of the massacre, it would have been astonishing to find Müntzer viewing the potential for revolt in the same light as before. What we do find is a conviction that had always been expressed in his arguments – that God also punished the common people when they put material gains before spiritual goals. In his open letter to 'the brothers in Stolberg', of July 1523, Müntzer had advised against over-hasty actions and the erroneous belief that spiritual suffering could somehow be avoided – 'for the pay and the reward of the lazy Elect is just the same as that of the damned, Luke 12'.[10] Two years on, it is the same message. Finally, the letter demonstrates Müntzer's leadership: the rebellion was over, so every effort should be made – by the princes as much as the ordinary people – to avoid any further bloodshed.

There is, however, considerable doubt whether the letter was ever delivered to Mühlhausen; none of the town archives mention it. Events, perhaps, overtook it.

The course of Müntzer's interrogation was reported back to Wittenberg by Johann Rühel, the counsellor of Albrecht of Mansfeld (and a distant relative of Luther). Luther and Melanchthon were concerned that the Catholics had unrestricted access to Müntzer; Melanchthon grumbled that they did not ask 'about his revelations, or what had moved him to start such troubles.

It was also unwise, since he took pride in his divine revelation, that they did not ask whether he had invented it or whether the Devil had seduced him with visions. Such things would have been useful to know.'[11] Melanchthon's slightly naive worries reveal an entirely different approach to the Müntzer problem from that of Duke Georg. Luther had already said quite enough about riotous disobedience; but now the Lutherans wanted to establish the connection between Müntzer's doctrines and his disobedience. None of the documents emerging from Heldrungen proved at all helpful in this.

Count Ernst of Mansfeld received Müntzer as booty from the battle, while Duke Georg had the more useful reward of the huge financial penalty he imposed on Frankenhausen, estimated at 300,000 guilders – a tidy sum, and more than enough to pay his mercenaries for their services over the campaign. The princes now headed for Mühlhausen, where the final embers of revolt had still to be stamped out. They left Frankenhausen on 19 May and halted at the village of Schlotheim, where they picked up Müntzer, who had arrived under close guard from Heldrungen; Duke Georg wished to have his principal rebel close at hand. Along the road, the army razed and pillaged whatever was available to raze and pillage. (And they did not necessarily target only defenceless farms and villages: the unfortunate Apel von Ebeleben wrote to Duke Georg on 19 May, griping that a senior officer from Philipp's army had – in an amusing rerun of the depredations of the rebel army in early April – 'today opened the vault in [my] church and removed silver to the value of 3,000 guilders ... and taken away with him some monstrances, the big crucifix, also chalices and other jewellery'; and, to add insult to injury, the army's 'plunder officer' (Beutemeister – an analogous post to the 'fire-master') had refused to compensate Apel and his neighbour and fellow victim, Hans von Berlepsch, for any damages.[12] It was on the following day that Berlepsch decided to take matters into his own hands, and undertook a night raid to retrieve his stolen livestock, as described above. Such is the comedy and tragedy of war.) After resting for a couple of days at Schlotheim, the army moved on to camp just outside Mühlhausen, at Görmar where, just three weeks earlier, the Mühlhausen rebels had themselves gathered in hopeful mood. Here Georg and Philipp were joined by the new Saxon elector, Johann; their combined armies comprised around 4,000 cavalry and 8,000 infantry. It was clear they meant business.

But before Mühlhausen could be taken and punished, there was a minor legal technicality to be negotiated. Mühlhausen was an Imperial Free City, responsible only to the Emperor. Taking it by armed force would be impolite. Luckily, such legal niceties did not feature high on the nobles' agenda – and, in any case, the new Imperial elector, Johann of Saxony, was on the spot to give the go-ahead. The Eternal Council of the town had already realised they were in a very tricky situation; they had written letters to other towns and cities, asking them to intercede with the princes and dukes for some mercy to be shown. Nürnberg obliged, but Erfurt – repeating its stonewalling with Müntzer's letter from earlier in the month – professed that the Eternal Council had no authority, and refused to do anything of the sort. But, in any case, it would all have been too late. Once the nobles' armies had arrived, a list of demands was sent into the town; the town council had no choice but to agree to them.

In the interim, Heinrich Pfeiffer had also seen the direction in which things were moving. During the night of 22/23 May, he and a large number of the rebel troops who had been left behind in Mühlhausen escaped southwards. Their intention was probably to join up with the remnants of the Franconian peasant army, which remained in action around Würzburg against the troops of the Swabian League, until their defeat in the middle of June. In his confession, Pfeiffer stated,

> He wished to go to Basel with the schoolmaster. If, on the way, he had been able to join the army of peasants in Franconia, then he would have done so . . . Asked what his own and Müntzer's intentions had been, [he said that] after the destruction of all authority he wanted to make a Christian Reformation.[13]

This 'schoolmaster' was Hans Denck, who had been teaching in Mühlhausen at Müntzer and Pfeiffer's invitation. But Pfeiffer did not get far: he was captured in Eisenach along with between fifty and one hundred men and taken back to Mühlhausen. When the princes' troops entered the town on 25 May, fifty rebels were executed – most likely the men who had been captured along with Pfeiffer.

(As an illustration of the business side of punishment, the archives contain an invoice raised by the authorities in Eisenach, in which the costs of housing, feeding and watering these prisoners were set out. These included: 12 groschen for two sets of chains to secure Pfeiffer and his men after their capture; 2 groschen for lights used when suspects were tortured; 21 groschen for ropes for tying up prisoners; 20 groschen for beer; 1 groschen for three wooden jugs from which the prisoners drank water; and 1 groschen for wine given to one prisoner when he was executed.[14] Slightly more gruesome was the invoice from the official executioner of the Margrave of Brandenburg, during the suppression of the rebellion in Franconia: he claimed a florin for every beheading, and half a florin for such minor matters

Bayerische Staatsgemäldesammlungen (CC BY-SA 4.0)

Duke Georg of Saxony, painted by Lucas Cranach, c. 1534.

as putting out eyes and chopping off fingers. His invoice total amounted to 118½ florins.[15])

On 25 May, the town council of Mühlhausen surrendered. The keys to the town were handed over. All conditions imposed by Georg and Philipp were agreed to: the town walls were to be demolished and all weapons handed in; a penalty of 80,000 guilders was imposed – an eighth of which was to be paid immediately; the entire population had to formally beg for mercy and swear an oath of obedience; anyone suspected of rebellion, but who avoided execution, was banished from the town, along with their families; the old town council was restored, headed up by the two mayors who had fled to Salza back in September 1524; and all decisions made by the Eternal Council were to be revoked.[16] Everyone who had suffered losses from the uprising – primarily the nobility and the Church – was to be compensated in full. Such people needed little encouragement: for months and years thereafter, claims were sent in by everyone from the lowest impoverished nobleman to the highest Church archbishop.[17] The Saxon princes levied fines on virtually every town, village and hamlet in their territories, at a fixed rate of around 5 guilders per household. Duke Georg was, in this respect, more insistent and rapacious than his Lutheran cousins; some of the lesser nobility not unreasonably saw the likely financial ruin of their peasantry, and the consequent loss of their own income. They found themselves begging the princes for leniency.[18] Finally, the princes of Saxony and Hesse drew up formal agreements, taking it in turns to 'protect' Mühlhausen (at a cost to the town of 300 guilders annually, 'in perpetuity'), and adopted other measures aimed at streamlining the noble response to any future rebellion.[19]

And, on 28 May, in a final symbolic act of retribution, the Latin Mass was reinstated in the churches.

On 27 May, the leaders of the rebellion met their end. Müntzer could have been executed at Heldrungen, but that would not have been enough; Duke Georg demanded that Müntzer and Pfeiffer be put to death in front of those they had led astray. Just outside the east gate of Mühlhausen, in an open area named the 'Rieseninger Berg', both men were beheaded with the sword.

It is reported that Müntzer used his final words not to make a full confession, as was traditional, but to warn the princes not to punish the poor any further and to take heed of the biblical Book of Kings, in which it was explained how pious rulers should act. This final speech sounds quite plausible: although it was only reported by Melanchthon, which would normally caution us, he would have had no reason to put this particular spin on the facts.[20]

A further twenty-six rebels were executed at the same time. The heads of both Pfeiffer and Müntzer were impaled on stakes and set up in prominent positions around the town, while their bodies were put on display to discourage passers-by from acts of disobedience. Several weeks later, the town executioner was paid 6 groschen to stand Müntzer's body upright again, for better viewing.[21] This particular act of petty vengeance rather backfired. It seems that the spots where the heads and bodies were exposed became places of popular – if clandestine – pilgrimage. In 1531, Luther complained that a footpath had been trampled out by people coming to pay their respects to Müntzer 'as if to a saint'.[22]

Duke Georg used the opportunity presented by the submission of Mühlhausen to search the house in which Müntzer had lived with Ottilie and his family. In his confession, Müntzer had mentioned that a sack full of letters to him was kept there. Georg wanted to see these. All the documents found in the house were seized and, together with those taken from Müntzer at Frankenhausen, sent back either to Dresden or to Philipp's residence in Marburg.

Ottilie was still at home; and she was pregnant. Müntzer, in his final letter to the town council, had specifically asked that she be given all of his possessions (books and clothes) and that she should not be punished. He also asked that she should be 'given good advice'; but if she was given any – and it seems unlikely she was ever at the top of anyone's list of priorities – it did her no good.[23] She appeared before Georg at the Swan Inn, where he was staying, and asked permission to collect her possessions. Georg agreed in principle; but for good measure also ordered the town council to make sure Ottilie did not leave town. However, she did not receive her possessions. Then, despite Georg's injunction, Ottilie managed to make her way to Nordhausen, where she stayed until early July. A captain in the ducal forces, apparently a relative of Ottilie's, made representations to the Mühlhausen council on her behalf. They agreed to let her come back and retrieve what was hers. She returned once more; and once more, she was prevented from collecting anything. Next, to the town council's bewilderment, she went off to Erfurt to stay with friends, before returning again to Mühlhausen. In despair, on 19 August, she wrote a letter to Georg, begging for access to her possessions, since she was 'in terrible misery and poverty' and had entirely run out of money.[24] She did not write the letter herself – it is in the hand of the court clerk of Mühlhausen, who probably gave her expert advice on how to address the duke – but her wretchedness comes through clearly in every word. The only reaction from the very Christian duke, in early September, was an instruction that a close eye be kept on her, repeating that she should not be allowed to leave Mühlhausen, and that he should be told when Ottilie gave birth.[25]

Luther had something to add to these reports of Ottilie's desperate situation, suggesting that 'the poor wife of Thomas Müntzer, now a widow and pregnant', had been propositioned in Mühlhausen by one of the officers of the occupying army. To his credit, Luther was outraged by this 'bestial' act, and condemned it in the strongest terms, going on to state that it was the kind of thing he expected the triumphant nobility to do – a curiously tangled position to find himself in. The report is by no means implausible, but cannot be verified.[26]

No more is heard of Ottilie after this. It is almost certain that she was never permitted to retrieve any of her possessions. She noted in her letter to Georg that he had advised her to return to a nunnery (this turned out to be the only advice she ever received); she said she would be content to do that, if it could be arranged. Perhaps she did. Nowhere in this depressing saga was there any mention of her son, who would by then have been a year old. It is possible he had died in the meantime. And nowhere is there any mention of the birth of the second child. Like so many women in history, Ottilie and her children drift away like smoke.

14

Rebellious Violent Preachers

The Early Anabaptists

In villages and towns there are many rebellious violent preachers,
who are said to incite the common people to riot, disloyalty and
give bad guidance and mislead them, and some wicked people
who had been at Frankenhausen and other places in the last revolt
and who had escaped are now said to have set themselves down
in the villages.

Philipp of Hesse (1525)

In December 1527, the radical preacher Hans Römer had a
plan. He would collect a small band of followers and together
they would enter the town of Erfurt at the New Year. There
Römer would preach publicly, and 'four of his brothers would set
fire to four presbyteries on the Petersberg, and then two others
would prevent the town gates from being closed'. A riot against
the priests would ensue and 'people who had gathered outside
the town would rush in and strike dead anyone from the town
who did not share their faith, and so they would take possession
of the town'.[1] In the event, only two comrades assembled for
the annihilation of Erfurt. Shrewdly, Römer had also laid plans
for escape – the conspirators were told to 'bring a good pair of
shoes and half a guilder in a purse . . . in case the conquest of the
town did not succeed and they had to leave the area'.[2] It was a
plan which stood little chance of success: in mid-December, the
authorities had already reported in considerable detail to Duke

Georg that Römer was in town: 'he has curly hair and a circular scar above his right eye, and he wears a grey coat'; one of his companions was suspected of being from Mühlhausen.[3]

In the same month, some two and a half years after the death of Thomas Müntzer, a group of Anabaptists were arrested in Salza. During their interrogation they expressed the view that 'Müntzer and Pfeiffer were true teachers, and were unjustly slain. And all those who had received the sign of baptism again should wait in the hills, for it would rain locusts and the world would not last longer than eleven months.'[4] Ten years later, in 1537, a Thuringian Anabaptist, Jakob Storger, confessed that 'Müntzer's teaching was correct, and he followed him in so far as the inner word was concerned', while his comrade Hans Hentrock 'valued Müntzer's teaching highly and considered it correct, although he disapproved of the uprising'.[5] A woman of the same group, when asked how long she had been an Anabaptist, replied: 'since Müntzer and Pfeiffer had been preaching'.[6]

Thomas Müntzer may have been dead, but it is clear from the archives that his name and his spirit lived on in central Germany. The cases mentioned above are of people described as 'Anabaptists', and in each case a direct or indirect connection was indicated between them and Müntzer. Broadly speaking, Anabaptists rejected the idea that infants should be baptised at the font, and that godparents could somehow act as guarantors. Instead, the faithful should receive baptism only when they were old enough to understand what it meant. But not all of those tagged as 'Anabaptists' were greatly concerned about the sacrament of baptism, nor was there unanimity of doctrine among those who were. A more widespread feature common to all these people was their determined opposition to the religions of Rome, Wittenberg and Zürich. Wishing to reform the ways of the world and to permit the spirit of God to govern material life, they rejected Rome; finding that Luther and Zwingli made concessions to worldly authority and promoted an academic solution to biblical problems, they turned to the 'inner spirit' and took a more independent approach to social issues. In doing so they earned the undying hatred of the mainstream reformers, who had – it must be said – no particular interest in differentiating between the various doctrinal trends within the opposition, describing them interchangeably as 'Enthusiasts' (*Schwärmer*) or 'Baptists' (*Täufer*). There were peaceful Anabaptists and others who were more ready for violence – including small groups in the 1530s who specialised in arson.[7] Very many were simply trying to come to terms with the trauma of the Peasants' War and its effect on their spiritual and material lives. Another significant feature common to all flavours of Anabaptism was the 'closed community' – a congregation of believers, often comprising just family and close friends, existing outside of the institutional churches. Predominantly – though not exclusively – they came from the lower classes.

The Anabaptists' rejection of infant baptism constituted illegal action of a serious nature. Baptism denoted the entry of believers into the faith and their lifelong acceptance of the authority of the established churches; any rejection of this authority was necessarily a rejection of the highest authority imaginable. This was why the Anabaptists were so mercilessly persecuted. In the eyes of Zwinglians, Lutherans and Catholics, as well as the secular authorities, they were criminals. In 1541, Luther commented on Melanchthon's recommendation that leading or unrepentant Anabaptists should be punished (not always by death, although frequently so): 'This pleases me', wrote Luther, 'although it may seem cruel to punish with the sword, it is even crueller that [the Anabaptists] damn the ministry of the scripture and do not teach certain things, and suppress true doctrine, and on top of that want to destroy secular government.'[8] Infant baptism was not some matter of arcane religious debate; it was a matter of the utmost socio-political significance.

Due to the conditions in which Anabaptism came into the world, the movement was necessarily disorganised and disunited. After the defeats of the peasants and urban radicals in 1525, dissent was driven underground, and the authorities in reformed areas resolutely applied Luther's doctrine of civil obedience:

> Christian freedom does not consist in the removal of rents, interest, dues, tithes, taxes, services, or other similar external burdens, but is only an inward and spiritual thing . . . All subjects are

obliged to obey their authorities in such temporal business, affairs, and commands . . . Every true Christian must endure injustice, but should not do injustice.[9]

These were the wise and considered words of the Lutheran Margrave of Brandenburg – Georg 'the Pious' – whose executioner, as we noted in a previous chapter, had been busily beheading and maiming those self-same 'true Christians'.

Anabaptists were frequently arrested, tortured and put to death in a number of cruel ways. It is estimated that, over the course of the century, some 5,000 radicals of central Europe were executed for their Anabaptist faith.[10] The printing of Anabaptist texts was fraught with danger, and few have survived. Congresses and discussions between various like-thinking groups did take place – most notably in the Moravian town of Nikolsburg (present-day Mikolov, south of Brno), under the protection of a tolerant (and reportedly re-baptised) local nobility – but such exchanges of ideas were few and far between. These oppressive conditions did not nurture any uniformity of doctrine. But it was precisely this lack of formalisation which helped the radical movement to survive, since it had to organise itself into small, trusted communities, each with its subjective and individual interpretations of the Bible or current events.

In the ten years after 1524, Anabaptism spread across the German-speaking territories. From two sources – Switzerland and Saxony – the movement expanded firstly into Franconia and Bavaria, then into Austria and Tirol, and thence into Moravia and Hungary. With a slight time-lag, Anabaptists began to appear in Hesse and down the valley of the Rhine. Reaching the Netherlands, the movement met with great success, not least because of contemporary rural and urban rebellions and the growing nationalist resentment at Burgundian and Spanish rule. From there, the movement spread back into northern Germany to culminate in the extraordinary 'Kingdom of Münster' of 1534–5, when that city was transformed into a commune and maintained as such for almost eighteen months.

While it is very difficult to estimate the number of individuals involved in the Anabaptist movement, it has been suggested that, between 1525 and 1550, some 8,500 people in 1,600 locations were converted to the radical faith in south and central Germany, as well as in Austria and Switzerland. In central Germany, radical Anabaptists were still turning up well into the 1580s. In the immediate period after 1525, many Anabaptists fled to Moravia to join other exiles from central Europe who had found a safe haven there. By around 1550, the Moravian Anabaptists are reckoned to have numbered some 25,000.[11] In each geographical area, there were people of more moderate or more radical persuasion: those who defended the use of 'the sword', and those who rejected it; those who permitted believers to hold high office in the world, and those who condemned such laxity.

But the struggle between the Anabaptists and the Lutherans and Catholics was not simply a religious disagreement. As it had been in the years prior to 1525, the underlying driving force was a broad desire to regain lost rights, to establish social justice and to alleviate the effects of a steadily increasing gap between wages and prices.[12] After the defeats of 1525, the desire for these changes did not disappear, but the immediate means to attain them did; social militancy was therefore mostly sublimated into religious dissent, which found considerable support among the lower classes. An analysis of the social status of Anabaptists in these first few years shows that the lower classes predominated, even among the leadership – carpenters, stonemasons, tailors, smiths, peasants, shepherds, labourers, millers and so on far outnumbering intellectuals, teachers or professional preachers. In the years after 1525, the records of arrest and interrogation of radicals show a mix of urban craftsmen and rural workers; millers feature heavily.[13] A similar situation was found in Moravia, to which many of the Anabaptists were drawn; craftsmen predominated, and only rarely do we come across an ex-priest or a clerk; least of all do we find many merchants, since trading for personal profit was deemed 'a sinful business'.[14]

The polemicists in Wittenberg and Zürich, and prosecutors across Germany, Austria and Switzerland, did not go to great pains to differentiate between the doctrines of the radicals. Just as Luther was quite happy to create a composite devil from Müntzer, Karlstadt and Storch, so he and his colleagues were pleased to tar all radical opponents after 1525 with the same brush – and this methodology also passed over into the judicial processes conducted against the radicals. It is sometimes very difficult indeed to verify what those arrested really believed and thought. Arrests often came in waves; all those arrested were assumed to be members of some great plot against the local authorities, all entertaining the same fiendish ideas; interrogations therefore followed the same patterns, and questions were posed in expectation of a specific answer. While some of these confessions reveal a startling defiance and independence of thought, words were frequently put into the prisoners' mouths; but the fact that the interrogators were doing so is strong evidence of prevailing fears among the ruling class. Thus, as was the case with Müntzer's confession, some care must be taken when examining the confessions of the Anabaptists; their few publications are more reliable pointers to their beliefs.

If the year 1522 marked the beginning of the Lutheran, 'Thermidorean' reaction to the secular reform movement, then the peasant defeats of 1525 marked a nadir for the popularity of the reformed Church among the lower classes of south and central Germany. Many who had previously sympathised with Luther now regarded him with extreme distrust. In Leipzig it was common opinion that his pronouncements on the uprising had been made in an attempt to curry favour with Duke Georg after the death of his cousin, Friedrich the Wise. Others lamented Luther's betrayal of the 'ignorant' people: 'Martin has not done well in Zwickau and in the countryside and towns', wrote the mayor of Zwickau; 'he has written the truth in condemning rebellion, but the poor have been greatly forgotten.'[15] Ultimately, however, Luther's teaching on the moral necessity of obeying the princes stood him in good stead. While the reformers who had opposed secular authority in south and central Germany were being neutralised, Wittenberg's relative importance grew by leaps and bounds. In those regions under the protection of Lutheran nobility, the reforms developed slowly but surely, and as they developed so the Lutherans condemned the more radical aspirations which Wittenberg had promoted between 1517 and

1522. Thus, although some social and political reforms were conceded in the aftermath of the uprising, the ability of the common man to find religious expression for democratic ideals was severely constrained. Catholicism was often reintroduced, even in places where the new reforms had taken a firm hold, as in Mühlhausen. Everywhere else, radical reform was uprooted and cast out, and the more reliable plant of Lutheranism allowed to flourish.

Books were heavily censored in an attempt to control the minds of a rebellious populace. Those who dared to print radical documents were harshly punished. An Austrian edict of July 1528 was typical of the attitude all across the Empire: 'Book-printers and book-sellers who deal in sectarian forbidden books . . . should be treated as arch-seducers and arch-poisoners of all lands, and should be mercilessly punished in water with their lives and their forbidden wares burned in fire.'[16] Men such as Philipp Ulhart of Augsburg managed to print the works of Hans Hut and Hans Denck from 1526 onwards. Some printers avoided detection by moving their operations underground. It took great courage to spread radical ideas. But there seems to have been no lack of men and women willing to do just that, particularly in Thuringia and Franconia. In December 1525, it was reported that

> in villages and towns there are many rebellious violent preachers who are said to incite the common people to riot, disloyalty and give bad guidance and mislead them, and some wicked people who had been at Frankenhausen and other places in the last revolt and who had escaped are now said to have set themselves down in the villages around Erfurt.[17]

Throughout the next half-decade, reports flooded in of people following in Müntzer's footsteps, calling for the overthrow of godless tyrants.

How, then, did Müntzer influence this radical movement? There is no room here to give a proper overview of early German, Swiss and Austrian Anabaptism.[18] For our purpose, we shall undertake that most dangerous of things – a potted history.

It is generally accepted that Anabaptism first emerged in Switzerland in 1524, under the guidance of Conrad Grebel and a small group of supporters. In Zürich, Grebel split from Zwingli in 1523, and was soon reaching out to Karlstadt and Müntzer in Germany, looking for fellow thinkers. At much the same time, the German preacher Balthasar Hubmaier had also been attracted to Zürich, but, like Grebel, he soon fell out with Zwingli. By early 1525 Hubmaier had become a rip-roaring radical: he had abandoned infant baptism, was beginning to reform the sacrament, had removed the altars from his church and had reportedly flung the baptismal font into the River Rhine. There were reports that he had preached against 'all authorities' and that 'no one was bound to perform any [feudal] service any more, and only the Lord God was to be honoured'.[19] In 1525, he was heavily involved in the uprising of the south-west German peasantry, and in April of that year he was himself re-baptised. In December

BALTHASAR HVBMOR DOCTOR VON FRIDBERG.

Portrait of Balthasar Hubmaier made by Christoffel van Sichem in 1608. Behind him on the right, Hubmaier is being burned to death, and on the left, his wife drowns in the Danube.

1525, Grebel and Hubmaier were arrested in Zürich by the Zwinglians; Grebel eventually managed to escape, but Hubmaier was forced to recant his baptismal doctrine – only to un-recant it immediately, be rearrested and recant again. In April 1526 he left for Moravia, where he brokered a safe haven for Anabaptists and converted large numbers to the new faith – for this, in 1528, he was arrested and burned to death by the Habsburgs in Austria. (A few days after his execution, his wife was thrown into the Danube with a heavy stone tied round her neck. Thus were heretics efficiently dealt with.)

Both Grebel and Hubmaier had fundamental doctrinal differences with Müntzer, partly on the importance of baptism (Müntzer was largely unconcerned about the whole issue – there were more momentous things to trouble him); we have already noted the extent of Grebel's disagreements with Müntzer, in his letter of September 1524. More importantly, they differed on the question of whether the faithful were justified in rising up against their secular lords.

Hubmaier, for his part, stressed time and again the importance of a visible, formal baptism, had a very laid-back attitude towards the millennium, and promoted a rather Lutheran policy on the use of 'the sword' by secular rulers. Both Grebel and Hubmaier, in any case, had reached their own form of Anabaptism well before Müntzer visited their part of the world. Both also, contrary to Müntzer, tended to stress the more passive teachings of the New Testament, rather than the active histories of the Old. Thus, although the Lutherans and Zwinglians were keen to identify an affinity between the leading Swiss Anabaptists and Müntzer, it is clear that Grebel and Hubmaier were not influenced by him at all. We shall therefore pass on to other radicals who most certainly were.

Another tradition of Anabaptism emerged in central Germany in 1525. The leading light here was the bookbinder and bookseller Hans Hut. As we saw earlier, Hut had done business with Müntzer and was present in Mühlhausen in early 1525 and later at the battle at Frankenhausen, from which he managed to escape. (In his final interrogation he stated – slightly implausibly – that he had seen the gathering at Frankenhausen as an opportunity to sell books; that the rebels captured him and confiscated his books, until Müntzer vouched for him; and that, after getting caught up in the battle, he was captured by Hessian troops and then was somehow set free.)[20] Returning to his home in Bibra – where he had already made enemies by his refusal to have his child baptised – he reportedly preached the destruction of all princes, before proceeding to Nürnberg. In the summer of 1525, Hut teamed up with Hans Denck and the pair began to organise like-minded radicals in south Germany, particularly in Augsburg, a city which soon rose to prominence as a seething nest of Anabaptism. Later that year Hut travelled to Nikolsburg in Moravia for the congress of Anabaptists, and there came into sharp conflict with Hubmaier. Constantly harassed and occasionally imprisoned, he baptised converts throughout Moravia and Lower Austria, until he ended up in a dungeon in Augsburg where, by accident or design, he perished in a fire in late 1527. (The authorities, frustrated in their intention of burning him to death as a live Anabaptist, tied his corpse to a chair and burned that instead. Thus, again, were heretics efficiently dealt with.)

Hut's pamphlets, and the reports of his sermons, contain much that is very credibly derived from Müntzer. His pamphlet *On the Mystery of Baptism* began 'I wish the pure fear of God as the beginning of godly wisdom',[21] words which clearly echo Müntzer's common address. Hut then goes on to use vocabulary and ideas almost identical to Müntzer's: he talks of the 'invented belief' purveyed by the 'academics', and of the necessity for spiritual torment. There are several other major points of similarity between the two preachers; Hut, for example, defended the primacy of the spirit over the scripture. He was as uncompromising as Müntzer on this question, and it formed the basis for his attack on the Lutherans:

> Our new evangelists, the tender academics, have cast the pope, monks and priests from their thrones. Now that they have succeeded, they whore anew with the Babylonian woman . . . Christ never directed the poor man towards books, as our academics now do in their ignorance, but rather he taught and gave examples

from their work, the peasant tilling the fields, sowing, removing
weeds and thorns and rocks . . . As the peasant tills his field before
sowing the seed there, so God does with us before He places His
word in us.

Hut even used the same derogatory term Müntzer had applied
to Luther: 'Brother Soft-Life'. He also shared with Müntzer the
idea that true knowledge is achieved through suffering and
'bitterness', and sometimes through dreams and visions. Hut's
rendition of Müntzer's doctrine of 'spirit' can be seen in his
concept of baptism. One of Hut's followers told how he had
received adult baptism: 'Hans, who baptised him, said that he
must also be baptised in fear, in necessity and in suffering.'[22]
This was therefore a twofold baptism: first inwardly, in spiritual
suffering, and then outwardly as a sign of community. Religious
and sociological significance attached to the received baptism;
but for Hut and his followers, there was something more – an
eschatological dimension: the sign of the cross which Hut drew
with water on the forehead of his adherents marked them clearly
as 'Elect', to be passed over when God visited vengeance upon
the godless world.

So there is strong evidence of Hut's debt to Müntzer, without
in the least detracting from the former's independent theological
ideas. Hut saw his epoch as the 'last and most dangerous time
of the world', and in 1527 it was reported of his followers in
Elbersdorf (in eastern Saxony) that they 'consider that Christ will
come again to earth in a short time and will set up a temporal
kingdom and will give them the sword to kill all authorities'.[23]
Hut himself was reported as making a rather fantastical statement about where true Christians should secure themselves
during the Apocalypse. 'These people are to be taught and baptised in all countries', he wrote:

when it came to judgement, then they were to flee to both the
towns of Mühlhausen, the one in Thuringia, the other in Switzerland [Mulhouse]; they were to stay in these same Mühlhausens
until the Turks invaded, and whomsoever the Turks left alive, they,
the small band, were to kill.[24]

This End-time in which the godless would be destroyed by some agent of God harked back to the Taborite expectations in Bohemia in the previous century, but it was now synthesised with the memory of Müntzer and the blessed town of Mühlhausen. Indeed, both Mühlhausen and Frankenhausen often crop up in the annals of Anabaptism over the course of the sixteenth century.[25] Hut's expectation of the Apocalypse was based on an interpretation of the Book of Revelation, particularly Chapter 11, in which the reign of the Beast is calculated at forty-two months; in 1527 Hut stated that, three and a half years after the end of the peasant uprising of 1525, 'the Lord would gather His own people in all countries and in each country these people would punish the authorities and all sinners'.[26]

(Hubmaier, by contrast, considered that each day of the prophesied forty-two months represented a full mortal year – so the faithful would have to wait a while: 1,278 years, give or take. The two men argued over this very point at Nikolsburg, and the disagreement neatly reveals the gulf that lay between them. But it is notable that many other central German radicals predicted the Apocalypse for forty-two months after the end of the Peasants' War in Thuringia.)

An Augsburg Humanist reported that Hut 'and his Anabaptists judge themselves righteous and wish to administer punishment'.[27] Hut frequently intimated that outside help might be required: the Ottoman Turks – not so very far away geographically in that period, and threatening to invade Hungary across the southeastern borders of Europe – loomed large in Hut's vision. After the threat of the Turks had receded in 1532, some of the expectations changed subtly; no longer was it the Turks who would act as the unsuspecting agents of God, but more desperate characters altogether. In 1533, there was an Anabaptist prediction that 'Nürnberg would be destroyed in future years by a dragon which had been aroused outside the town. And at the same time God would awaken a prophet, whom they would deprive of life, but could not harm.'[28]

Where Müntzer latterly intended to stride out side by side with God to destroy the godless, Hut and his associates were content to await some Apocalyptic event and then dart out to finish off any godless sinner left alive. The difference between the two is rooted in the defeat of 1525: Müntzer called on a potentially mighty social force which had not yet been defeated; Hut called on isolated social groups which existed in conditions of defeat.

The problem of how to deal with the enemies of God also brings up the question of secular authority. Hut found himself embroiled in serious controversy with, on the one hand, pacifists who rejected violent methods and, on the other, those who permitted fellow believers to take civil office and carry a sword. In Moravia, the discussion among the assembled Anabaptists turned to secular authority:

> Hans Hut also came to Nikolsburg, and came to the castle to discuss the use of the sword, whether it should be used or carried or not, and whether one should give taxes for war, and other matters; in these matters, however, they could reach no agreement ... But because Hans Hut could not and would not agree with Herr Leonhart von Lichtenstein [lord of Nikolsburg] on carrying the sword, he was imprisoned against his will in the castle.[29]

Several of the delegates protested against this, and, with the help of one of them (and the creative deployment of a net used to trap hares), Hut managed to escape from the dungeons during the night; but this episode gives some flavour of the bitterness of a dispute which split the Anabaptist ranks right from the very start. Against people such as Hubmaier, Hut was not prepared to contemplate fellow believers holding positions of worldly authority, since this tied them to the forces of the godless. But he was prepared to envisage wielding the sword at the appropriate time. In Hut, Müntzer's political doctrine had found an inheritor, albeit one who operated within a new reality.

Hut's teachings guided some of the early Austrian Anabaptists, but most particularly the radicals in and around the German city of Augsburg – the Anabaptist movement here flourished after bad harvests in 1526 and 1527, and a collection of Anabaptist hymns, including some written by Hut and Müntzer, was printed there in the late 1520s. After his arrest and death in 1527, Hut's followers split into factions. Some eventually abandoned baptism as a sacrament and instead took up strongly the doctrines of dream and vision – these were the so-called 'Dreamers'.

The case of another preacher operating in the same region as Hut provides us with some idea of the mood and inclinations of the radicals in the years after 1525. Augustin Bader was a tailor from Augsburg who was baptised in 1526 along with his wife, and for this was exiled from the city.[30] His travels thereafter took him to Moravia, Nürnberg, Strassburg and Switzerland, before he settled in a miller's barn near Ulm in October 1529. Here he founded a commune with his family and the families of his supporters, and began to prophesy the Apocalypse for Whitsun 1530. Opportunely, one of his companions then experienced a vision of Bader and his family surrounded by the regalia of royalty, a dream which was interpreted as signifying that Bader's newborn son was the Messiah who had returned to save the faithful during the Apocalypse. In preparation for the event, the commune pooled its financial resources, amounting to around 380 florins, of which 111 were spent in the purchase of a gilded sword, dagger, sceptre, chains, clothes and a crown – much to the surprise and delight of the local goldsmith.[31] Bader assumed the role of regent, and began to canvass other Anabaptists as well as the local Jewish community – who had their own expectations of an imminent Apocalypse – for support. Unfortunately the Bader group came to the attention of the authorities, and its members were incarcerated and tortured. Bader was interrogated closely, tortured with burning irons, then drawn and quartered in Stuttgart in March 1530, before the Apocalypse could begin. (Bader's widow Sabine managed to flee to Strassburg, where the leading 'mainstream' reformer Wolfgang Capito came close to marrying her, and thereby – as one historian has remarked – becoming stepfather to the Messiah.[32]) In Bader's confession, there are indications that his belief in the Apocalypse resembled Hut's: after the cataclysmic event, there would be no more baptism, other than 'sadness', which indicates the true baptism in God; there would be no 'altar' other than the congregation of God – the bricks and mortar of the institutional Churches would no longer be required.

Bader's extraordinary story reflects in exaggerated form some of the features of the early Anabaptism fostered by Hut and others. The followers of Hut lived in perpetual expectation of the Apocalypse; until Hut's death, this was perhaps tempered by his insistence on inner preparation. After 1527, the movement effectively had both no leaders and many leaders, as each group went its own way, some towards vision, dream and acts of fantasy, others to 'quiet belief', tucked out of sight in hidden communities.

The influence of Müntzer stretched further. We have already mentioned Hans Denck, another recognised leader of the German Anabaptist movement after 1525, who promoted many ideas similar to those of Müntzer. Like most of his comrades, Denck rejected Luther's reliance on the scriptures, and he did so in terms which resemble Müntzer's: 'Whosoever honours the scripture, but is cold in divine love should take care that he does not make an idol of scripture, as all the academics do who are not educated for the kingdom of God.'[33] As early as January 1525, when he was obliged to appear before the city council of Nürnberg to give evidence on the 'three godless painters', he stated: 'It is not in my nature to believe the scripture. But what is in me, which drives me without any effort or will, drives me to read the scripture for the sake of a witness.' Compare this with Müntzer's words: 'The son of God said: the scriptures give a witness. The scholars say: they give belief.'[34] In a statement made two years later, Denck wrote that he valued 'the holy scriptures above all human treasures, but not so high as the word of God which is living, powerful and eternal'.

The Bible was therefore only one witness to the living word of God, the spiritual truth. It could only be understood correctly after the implanting of the living faith. As with Müntzer and Hut, Denck's attitude to the scriptures formed the basis of his condemnation of the Lutherans:

> Christ tells the academics in John 5: 'You study the scriptures, and you suppose you find life, for they give witness to me; but you do not wish to come to me for that life.' . . . So along come

the academics and false prophets and say without any consideration or differentiation: 'Peace, peace, just believe and you will be
accepted, and everything will be all right!' But it cannot be otherwise: you must also taste the bitter cup of divine wrath.

It is impossible to ignore the similarity of this passage to one
in Müntzer's *Protestation or Proposition*, where the academics
advise suffering believers that 'You should not be concerning
yourself with such lofty matters. Just have simple faith, then
you'll forget your worries.'[35]

Denck was driven as much by Humanist ideals as by the
urgent mysticism of Müntzer. His ideas undoubtedly influenced
people such as Hut and others, although he disagreed fiercely
with them on the expectation of the Apocalypse. It has also been
suggested that his theology influenced Melchior Hoffman, the
man who was unwitting godfather to the Anabaptist 'Kingdom
of Münster'.[36]

A more direct heir of Müntzer was Melchior Rinck, who had
studied in Leipzig, where he became an enthusiastic Humanist
(earning the nickname 'the Greek' as a result of his proficiency in
the Classics), before becoming a reforming preacher near Fulda
in 1523. Expelled the following year, he was appointed to a pulpit
in a small town near Eisenach in Thuringia, and there reportedly
began to spread 'Müntzerish' ideas among the people. Later,
he was recorded as saying that the Lutheran reformers 'taught
nothing but a simple, lazy and dead belief, which had no more
use than shouting out your own name. But Thomas Müntzer, he
was a real hero with his sermons . . . and taught more in one year
than a thousand Luthers could in all their lives.'[37]

In May 1525, after participating in the peasant insurgents'
campaign in the Werra valley, he joined Müntzer, and fought at
the battle at Frankenhausen. Like Hut, he managed to escape
from the massacre, and was next heard of in Worms – at the same
time as Denck – in 1527, and in various locations across Hesse
and Thuringia. Official reports accused him of being 'a special
ringleader and troop-leader in the late peasant uproar, along
with Müntzer and Pfeiffer'.[38] Over the next couple of decades,

he spent a great deal of time languishing in prison cells, or being expelled from towns in western Germany, and was last heard of, in 1551, in 'perpetual imprisonment' in Hesse.

In his opposition to Luther and Lutheranism, Rinck fitted the standard mould of Anabaptists. Much of his teaching was devoted to attacks on the sacraments, and he promoted communities held together by a conscious baptism. This was, of course, a dangerous thing which, the authorities feared, would lead to revolution. An official of Philipp of Hesse had this to say:

> The doctrine and life of the Anabaptists, and especially this Melchior Rinck, are that they invent the greatest public blasphemy for the following reasons. Firstly, Rinck teaches that no man should have any magistrates; at first he made authority despicable in the hearts of men and then, if he could arrange it, the common man would stand up against their magistrates and clear them away, and finally end up simply overthrowing the whole structure, and in its place arouse a Müntzerish army without magistrates.[39]

MELCHIOR RINCK.

Rijksmuseum, Amsterdam (CC0 1.0 Universal)

A persuasive-looking Melchior Rinck, in a portrait made by Christoffel van Sichem in 1608.

The horror of this picture was perhaps laid on thick by the eager official, anxious to draw political conclusions which Rinck may never have intended. But a manuscript by Rinck which attacked infant baptism does contain a section entitled 'Advice and warning to all members of the magistracy', in which he called on the princes to act for the good of the community; failing this, God would surely punish the 'godless tyrants', and institute the only moral government – 'obedience to God alone'.[40]

In March 1532, a group of forty followers of Rinck were involved in an extraordinary siege at a mill in the Fulda district, where they barricaded themselves in with enough food to last six months, in certain expectation of the Apocalypse. (Flour mills seemed to attract those awaiting the end of the world; conspirators frequently met in mills,[41] and a significant number of radicals, before and after 1525, were millers by profession.) The local authorities despatched soldiers to clear the building; they were met by a hail of bullets, and then, as standard ammunition ran out, cheeses and meats. One of the soldiers suffered three broken toes as a result of the bombardment, while six of the Anabaptists were killed or fatally injured. On being interrogated, the prisoners, echoing the adherents of Bader, said they expected God to sweep the godless from the earth at Whitsun. Even while imprisoned, the survivors engaged in bizarre behaviour as they experienced visions and dreams – bleating like sheep and barking like dogs. Just to be safe, the authorities opted to execute a further six of them.

While Rinck may have toned down some of the more confrontational aspects of Müntzer's doctrines, his contact with the Thuringian leader in 1524 and 1525 had left its mark. It is perhaps incredible that Rinck was not actually deprived of life, rather than freedom; but this may be explained by the sporadic leniency which Philipp of Hesse showed towards Anabaptists in his lands.

A good deal of scattered evidence indicates that Müntzer, though dead, was greatly admired among the lesser-known figures of early Anabaptism. Even the distant Austrian Anabaptists had this to say:

Thomas Müntzer from Allstedt in Thuringia was a highly gifted, well-spoken man, and drew up many excellent articles from the holy scriptures against the Roman and the Lutheran churches. He taught of God and also of His word which gives life and of His heavenly voice against all those who revere the written word.[42]

But Müntzer's inheritance was taken up primarily in Thuringia. In 1526 and 1527, the Anabaptists of Eisleben described the 144,000 Elect (the number comes from the Book of Revelation, identifying the descendants of the tribes of Israel), who, having been chosen by God, had no need of the sacrament of baptism: 'And these baptists said that there were many thousands of them, scattered across the world, even here and there in Turkey' – a conception which harmonises with Müntzer's stated belief that the Elect were to be found even among Muslims and Jews.[43]

The town of Mühlhausen itself was of symbolic importance for some of the Anabaptists. In February 1526, the authorities uncovered a radical plot to attack the town by night, with 800 men. After his arrest, the lead plotter Caspar Federwisch confessed:

> When they had captured Mühlhausen, they wished to cut off the heads of the town councillors, and take their wives in marriage and so occupy the town . . . He said that they would then be reinforced by mercenaries and advance on Duke Georg of Saxony, and then damage everything round about, so that taxes, interest payments and treasuries would be abolished and all the waters would be for common use, and a troop would be raised like the one defeated at Frankenhausen.[44]

This very ambitious plan was thwarted before the leading citizens of Mühlhausen were placed in any danger. But between the lines of this fantasy can be read the passions and ambitions which had been inflamed by the events of the early summer of 1525.

Müntzer's name also featured large in the plans of the Erfurt plotter Hans Römer. A Thuringian by birth, and a furrier by trade, Römer had been with Müntzer in April and May 1525, and was at Frankenhausen; after his escape in the aftermath of the battle, he was active as a radical preacher in Franconia, and was probably guided in his further career by Hans Hut. In December 1527, followers of Römer in Sangerhausen confessed that one of their number 'had taken Thomas Müntzer's books in her hands and prayed from them'.[45] (The group who listened to her included a laundrywoman, a mason, a clog-maker and a cooper.) The preservation of 'Müntzer's books' among poorly educated people was in itself something of a miracle. By late 1527, when he was laying out his plans for the utter destruction of Erfurt, Römer had gathered a dedicated following.

Anabaptism flourished in Thuringia and Franconia in the decade after 1525. It was an extraordinary period in radical history, and richly rewards closer examination. The ruling princes, and the Emperor himself, were terrified that the continuing radical movement would spawn another uprising. Duke Georg of Saxony in particular saw Anabaptists under every bed, and expressed the view that 'an uproar such as we had previously, if not greater', was being plotted.[46] The radical movement also brought numerous women into the public eye, and into the historical record. In 1528, the Imperial Diet proposed that 'each and every Anabaptist, man or woman, should be killed by fire, sword or similar'.[47] Many records of arrests and confessions survive, and they bear witness to a large number of individuals unrepentant even before the certainty of death. This was not just some religious squabble: in the radical groups the ruling class perceived a very real risk of lower-class rebellion. By organising themselves into small groups, in which membership was initiated by a special baptismal ceremony, the Anabaptists were taking a hugely illegal step. With the new faith went a complete rejection of authority, both religious and secular. Klaus Hofmann, a tailor involved in Römer's Erfurt escapade, 'wanted to kill all lords from his own hatred of them'.[48] Another exemplary advocate of the contempt in which the radicals held their social betters was Jakob Storger. On his arrest in 1537 – just after settling in Mühlhausen – he was asked what he thought of infant baptism; his pithy reply was that he considered it 'a dog's bath and a pig's bath'. His interrogators found him no more respectful towards the sacrament of the Eucharist: 'Our Lord God does not allow Himself to be bitten.'[49] Storger's companions gave voice to similar thoughts, firmly rejecting the fundamentals of an orderly and blameless life: the Mass, confession, worldly authority and obedience. Their hatred for established doctrine extended, not unnaturally, to the Lutherans: Storger thought 'less of Luther than of the Pope, for at least the latter had a little deceptive compassion'.[50] He expressly referred to Pfeiffer and Müntzer as inspirations: 'he said that Müntzer's teaching was correct and he approved of him, since . . . he wielded the outer sword according to the inner word'. Among this group, some specifically mentioned the year 1525 as the watershed in their spiritual life – they had not received the sacrament since the events of that year. For such crimes, Storger and members of his group were sentenced to death by drowning.

But Müntzer's importance for the Anabaptist movement did not reside solely in revolutionary aspirations. Social conditions after the summer of 1525 could not support the same kind of seditious activity as before, despite isolated after-shocks of rebellion in Germany and Austria; it was impossible that an insurrection by the lower classes could now overthrow the worldly authorities. Any actions necessarily took on a terrorist character – as evidenced by Römer and Federwisch. For the majority of those whose secret hopes were focused on social justice and democratic government, the Anabaptist communities offered an asylum in which some of these ideals could at least be played out in microcosm. Here, the ideas of Müntzer, as laid out in his theological writings, gave comfort, hope and confidence. For this closed community, the outward sign of baptism became important – it was a ceremony of initiation into a new society and a sign that they should be spared by God during the annihilation of the godless world.

That the memory of Müntzer lived on in the early years of the Anabaptist movement is beyond question. A remarkable number of the early leaders had been, or confessed to having been, at the ill-fated battle of Frankenhausen, and were influenced by Müntzer's ideas. The ensuing years of repression did not diminish the admiration many radicals felt for Müntzer. But in those years, Müntzer's doctrines, and even those of men like Hut and Römer, underwent a transformation. The movement was riven into factions. Some sought to prepare actively for the coming Apocalypse; many others took the line of least resistance against the powers of the State and the Church (whether Catholic, Lutheran or Zwinglian). Sporadic acts of violence, or plans for violence, are documented in the archives; so also are the tragic fates of men and women who wished only to adhere to their own non-violent religious beliefs. But one event which stood out in the decade after Müntzer's death was the north German 'Kingdom of Münster'.[51]

The establishment in Münster in 1534–5 of 'a citadel of the Elect' was greeted enthusiastically in the Netherlands and north Germany. It was only with considerable difficulty that the authorities prevented hundreds of ordinary people from joining the revolutionary community at Münster, having abandoned hearth and home in expectation of a safe haven at the end of time. How did this happen? What path led here from the Anabaptism of the previous ten years?

Melchior Hoffman, a furrier who had been promoting Anabaptism in various parts of north and western Germany, was to be found in the Netherlands in the early 1530s, preaching and baptising significant numbers. Hoffman had a firm belief in the coming Apocalypse, predicting that the wrath of God would sweep aside the godless temporal and religious powers, ushering in God's kingdom on earth. But he did not advocate active military preparation for the event, and displayed no signs of being a follower of Müntzer (or Hut or Römer), despite having penned a pamphlet with the effortlessly Müntzer-like title *A True and Godly Lesson on the Pure Fear of God*.[52] In both his millennial expectations and his pacifistic leanings, he was representative of the majority of German Anabaptists at that time. But the spectacular growth of Anabaptism in the Netherlands owes much to Hoffman. Among those he baptised was Jan Matthijs, a baker from Haarlem who went on to establish the 'Kingdom of Münster' during a period when Anabaptism unexpectedly became, once more, militant and assertive.

Under Matthijs and his successor, a Dutch tailor named Bockelson (aka Jan van Leiden), radical forms of government were introduced to Münster, along with the community of goods. At a late stage, Bockelson attempted to adapt to changing domestic situations by introducing polygamy – for a variety of reasons, women outnumbered men by three to one. This measure proved unpopular in the town (and deeply shocking to the outside world), and Bockelson further alienated many of his followers by proclaiming himself 'King of New Zion' and launching a merciless campaign of terror against anyone who criticised him. Despite support from Anabaptists in the Netherlands, the community collapsed, defeated by internal discord, starvation and, ultimately, the besieging army of the Catholic Bishop of Münster and his allies, both Lutheran and Catholic, whose capture of the town in June 1535 resulted in the deaths of 650 townspeople. But this short-lived experiment triggered a measure of panic among the ruling classes of Germany and the

Rijksmuseum, Amsterdam (CC0 1.0 Universal)

Portrait of the Dutch Anabaptist Jan Matthijs, made by Christoffel van Sichem in 1608. Behind him, the siege of Münster is being brutally ended.

Netherlands, fearful that it would be repeated in other places.[53] This was entirely understandable: in May 1535, around thirty Anabaptists had attempted to take control of Amsterdam and set up their own 'Münster' there. (Three months earlier, the authorities had been given due warning of radical unrest when a group of 'naked runners' – *naaktlooper* – had burned their clothes and run through Amsterdam announcing the imminent Apocalypse. For their pains, they, like their comrades later in the year, were executed.)

Although it is tempting to trace a direct link between Müntzer and Münster, or even an indirect one through the medium of early German Anabaptists such as Denck (and both scenarios were assiduously promoted by Lutheran and Catholic rulers and historians), the establishment of the Münster commune was fuelled by a wide variety of influences, not least the social upheavals in the neighbouring Netherlands, where attempts were being made to cast off Spanish rule. It was under these conditions that Hoffman's relatively passive form of Apocalyptic expectation was abruptly transformed into something more active, more akin to the open rebellion of 1525: in Münster, Anabaptism suddenly appeared as a revolutionary movement. As had happened ten years earlier in the Peasants' War, the radicals of the Netherlands and north-west Germany combined heretical religious beliefs with the very real political demands and hopes of ordinary people to establish – albeit briefly and in a tragically flawed manner – an early communist society. What was different, of course, was the strategy of retreating to a citadel; this had formed no part of Müntzer's plans, nor those of the peasantry and plebeians of 1524/5. It was the strategy which had underpinned, for example, the Taborite movement in Bohemia a century earlier, and which re-emerged almost immediately after the defeat of the peasant uprising, as typified by Römer's plot in Erfurt. But the connection between Müntzer and the rebels of Münster lies in the willingness of both to step fearlessly onto the stage of history, at a time of widespread social upheaval, attempting to turn their ideals into reality.

Before we leave Anabaptism, let us consider one small historical spiral: many Dutch Anabaptists, escaping persecution in their homeland, fled to England in the 1530s. Here they fared little better: Henry VIII was not at all keen on radicals, even – or especially – those who upheld 'reformation'. But they survived, in part because in England there were still significant pockets (as measured by the numbers arrested and executed) of Lollards and other religious radicals. One of the principal influences on the Hussite reforms in Bohemia had been John Wycliffe's 'Lollardy' movement. So there is a trail which leads from fourteenth-century England to Hussite Bohemia, from the radical Hussites of Bohemia to the radical reformers of Saxony, from the radicals of Saxony to the Anabaptists of the Netherlands, and thence to sixteenth-century England, and, without stretching a point too far, to the dissenting radicals of the seventeenth-century English Revolution.[54] The revolution is indeed global and permanent.

From this necessarily short review of some of the strands of German radicalism over a lengthy period after 1525, it is clear that Müntzer's views on the acquisition and responsibilities of faith were given new life after his death, albeit in different guises. Self-evidently, the term 'Anabaptism' was a somewhat inaccurate and lazy branding of the 'opposition', grouping under one generic designation men and women with widely differing beliefs: some were totally unconcerned with the question of adult baptism; some traced their heritage back to Grebel or Hubmaier; but some also explicitly stated that Müntzer had been one of their forefathers, and the ideas they expressed demonstrate very clear similarities to those of Müntzer. The basic principles of spiritual primacy, suffering and election had been espoused by other forebears of Anabaptism, in sporadic movements largely rooted in the lower classes of town and country. But it was Müntzer who had brought all these aspects together in one body of doctrine which in due course nourished a determined anti-authoritarian stance among so many leaders of the early Anabaptist movement.

15

The Devil in Person

Historiography

Lucky the man who has seen Müntzer with his own eyes, for he can boast that he has seen the Devil in person.

Martin Luther (1525)

Thomas Müntzer was dead. His head was stuck on a pole for everyone to see. But Wittenberg was not finished with him yet. His reputation had to be utterly destroyed. More importantly, the men of Wittenberg had to ensure that no blame for the peasant uprising was pinned on them. Even before the final massacres of the peasants of Germany were completed, accusations were being levelled at Luther and Wittenberg: if Luther had not stirred up the hornets' nest back in 1517, would there ever have been rebellion across much of Germany? The Papal Church and the Emperor saw a very clear connection. But Luther, alive to the dangers of being a co-accused, had been busy ever since early 1522 distancing himself from anyone who looked remotely like a rebel. Müntzer and Karlstadt were the principal targets of his several tracts against 'false prophets'. In 1525, following their leader's signals, the talented writers of Wittenberg began to weave the myth of Thomas Müntzer. Anxious not to be left behind, Catholic and Zwinglian commentators joined in.

First into the fray, naturally, was Luther himself. His two open letters of 1524 against Müntzer – *To the Princes of Saxony, Concerning the Rebellious Spirit* and *To the Town of Mühlhausen*[1] –

have already been analysed. In these, Luther quite unblushingly conflated Müntzer with Nikolaus Storch – a neat demonstration of his method of dealing with opponents. The 'spirit' that worked in radical opposition to Luther was not in fact a single person; it was the physical manifestation of the Devil. In early 1525, he also composed a lengthy pamphlet directed against Karlstadt, *Against the Heavenly Prophets*,[2] which followed the same methodology. There was talk here of 'murderous and rebellious spirits', of Satan working against Luther. Luther did not merely berate Karlstadt for his iconoclasm, but argued that the logical next step from iconoclasm was murder and rebellion against authority – something which Karlstadt had never imagined in his worst nightmares. Luther viewed his enemies from a moral point of view, in which personalities could change but the basic evil nature remained; from here, anyone could be accused of anything. It was a highly convenient approach.

Luther's *Dreadful History and Judgement of God on Thomas Müntzer* was published on 22 May 1525.[3] The judgement of God was simply the fact that Müntzer had been defeated at Frankenhausen a week earlier; the 'dreadful history' refers to all his heinous activities leading up to that battle. Based around four letters written by Müntzer in April and May 1525, this short tract ran to no fewer than eight editions in the summer of 1525. In writing it, Luther unwittingly rendered a great service to later generations, since two of the letters – those addressed to the brothers Ernst and Albrecht of Mansfeld on 12 May – only survive today because they appeared in Luther's edition. Also reproduced here were Müntzer's call to action addressed to Allstedt on 26 April, and his letter from Frankenhausen to Heldrungen, dated 11 May. Luther introduces his pamphlet with the words:

> I have arranged for this dreadful history to be published concerning the teaching and writing and plotting of that murderous and bloodthirsty prophet Thomas Müntzer . . . For here you can read how this murderous spirit boasted that God spoke and acted through him . . . And yet before he can turn round, he lies there with several thousand others in the mud.

These words sound a little incongruous coming from the pen of a man who, barely a week earlier, had called for the merciless massacre of all rebellious peasants.

In his critical comments concerning the letters, Luther lays all the blame for the tragedy of Frankenhausen at the feet of the 'rebellious spirits'. Then, in a series of rhetorical questions, he introduces two myths which immediately passed into the main body of Müntzer historiography:

> Oh dear God, you miserable rebellious spirits, where now are your words with which you excited and stirred up the poor people? When you said you were the people of God, and that God fought for you, and one would slay a hundred, yes, with a single felt cap they could strike five men dead? And the bullets would turn back when they were fired and hit the enemy? Where are Müntzer's sleeves now, in which he claimed he would catch all the bullets which were fired against his people? Where is the God now who shouted such promises through the mouth of Müntzer for almost a whole year?

Luther introduces something rather picturesque: the amazing power of felt caps and the catching of bullets in sleeves seem to be based on popular legends of magicians current in the later Middle Ages. Müntzer had certainly scoffed at bullets, and his sleeves may or may not have appeared in some garbled report of his speeches to the army at Frankenhausen, but claims for their magical powers were a figment of someone's imagination. Luther had evidently learned some such story, one he embroidered, again, with features from other sources to lend greater weight and colour to his polemic.

Over the following twenty years, Luther returned frequently to the subject of Müntzer, in the process weaving a few more threads into the historical image. In one of his 'table-talks' of 1531, he had managed to get hold of this tale:

> On the subject of Müntzer there is a certain true story about a girl who confessed this on her death-bed. When Müntzer was in Zwickau, he came to this virgin and said that he was sent by a

divine voice to ravish her: and if she did not agree to this, then he himself would not be able to teach the word of God. This story has come from Hätzer.[4]

Based on very suspect evidence (Ludwig Hätzer was an Anabaptist tortured and executed in 1529), in Luther's eyes Müntzer had now become a libertine, a useful characteristic to add to the list of: a Satan, a bloodthirsty murderer, a revolutionary and the cause of the tragedy of the peasantry. Luther had to depict Müntzer as something more than an individual: he became the composite representative of an entire group of 'rebellious spirits', to whom the collective doctrines and supposed feats of all could be ascribed. Correct biographical details were as welcome as Banquo's ghost at the feast, while the chronology was, at best, vague.

A much more detailed account of Müntzer's last days was dished up by Philipp Melanchthon, in his *History of Thomas Müntzer, the Fomenter of the Thuringian Tumult; A Most Useful Lesson*, written in early June 1525 and rushed into print shortly afterwards.[5] This pamphlet focused on the events at Frankenhausen, although the Allstedt period was also covered. Just like Luther, Melanchthon proceeded from the idea that Müntzer was the Devil incarnate, and that all his doctrines were satanic, particularly those concerned with revelation and dream. Differently from Luther, however, Melanchthon tried to establish certain stages in Müntzer's development by analysing the radical's theological arguments. Some of these were of Melanchthon's own invention, or were simple misunderstandings. In Müntzer's early career, for example, he is supposed to have preached that:

At first one must abandon manifest sins such as adultery, murder, blasphemy and suchlike, and thereby one must learn to chastise and martyr the body, through fasting, poor clothing, silence, gloomy looks, not cutting off one's beard. He called this and similar childish discipline 'mortification of the flesh, and a cross, as is written in the gospel'.

Being gloomy and wearing a beard? It is hard even to imagine where Melanchthon found this stipulation (it might have been based on Leviticus 19:27, although a follower of Luther, Eberlin von Günzburg, had recommended lengthy beards in his 1521 vision of a Lutheran Utopia, *Wolfaria*). Regardless of provenance, the habit of beard-growing thereafter clearly identified radical fanatics in Wittenberg historiography. Melanchthon then related that Müntzer recommended retiral to a quiet spot to await God – and if God did not arrive, to shout at him for not speaking to his Elect. More precisely, 'he said openly, which is shocking to hear, that he wished to shit on God if He did not speak with him as He did with Abraham'. Shocking stuff, indeed; but again drawn directly from Melanchthon's own fertile imagination.

In 1525 a sudden transformation had taken place: Müntzer moved to Mühlhausen and into the cloister of the Teutonic Knights, where (it is implied) he also took over their income. From this secure position of ease

Metropolitan Museum, New York (Open Access Public Domain)

Portrait of Philipp Melanchthon, by Albrecht Dürer in 1526.

> he taught that all possessions should be held in common . . . and
> the mob did not want to work any more, but if they wanted some
> corn or cloth, they went to a rich man . . . If the rich man did not
> want to hand it over, then they took it by force.

Farewell, then, the earlier bodily mortification and poverty;
welcome, laziness, greed and theft. The actions of the common
people were now attributed to the doctrines of Müntzer. But then
a surprise: 'He did this for almost a whole year, until the year
1525, when the peasantry in Swabia and Franconia rose up, for
Thomas was not so bold that he could have started this uproar
by himself.' So Müntzer had not the courage to incite the insurrection; this is quite a refreshing change from the view that he
did it all himself, but it was simply a prelude to the accusation
that Müntzer was a coward. When Pfeiffer had suggested the
expedition into the Eichsfeld, 'Thomas, from fear, did not want
to allow this or join it.'

Not the slightest attempt is made at consistency: shortly afterwards, Müntzer is to be found standing up before his army at
Frankenhausen, promising to catch bullets in his sleeves and
advising everyone not to fear the tyrants. In a dramatic passage,
Melanchthon described Müntzer's speech, which was then countered by one from the brave young Prince Philipp. And then the
battle – or rather slaughter – commenced. Melanchthon, despite
his many faults as a chronicler, was appalled by the barbarity of
the princes' troops. By his reckoning, two or three cavalrymen
were killed, as against 5,000 rebels. After the battle, Thomas
supposedly reverted to his cowardly ways, trembling in a garret
in Frankenhausen until discovered. On the day of his execution,

> he was faint-hearted in his last moments, and so confused that he
> could not even say his prayers, so Duke Heinrich of Braunschweig
> said them for him. He also confessed publicly that he had acted
> wrongly, but still warned the princes not to be severe on the poor
> people . . . and said they should read the Book of Kings.

The important element in this early historiography was not
consistency of time, place or character, but rather consistency of

iniquity. If the slandering of Müntzer by unfounded anecdote and mangled summaries of his theology served the dual purpose of distancing him from Wittenberg and discouraging his surviving followers, then that slander could – and must – pass as 'history'.

Luther had set the agenda for the character assassination, and Melanchthon had contributed his share of the labour by filling in some biographical details. The major task of countering Müntzer's doctrines, however, fell to Johannes Agricola, in his pamphlet *An Explanation of the 19th Psalm . . . by Thomas Müntzer.*[6] This appeared in late May 1525, possibly even before Müntzer's execution, and was based on a detailed examination of a letter written by Müntzer to Christoph Meinhard twelve months earlier.[7] Agricola had visited Meinhard in April 1525, as part of the ongoing campaign against 'Heavenly Prophets'; Meinhard must have handed the letter over to Agricola at that time. Agricola's work should at least get marks for effort (and, as with Luther, our thanks for the preservation in print of another of Müntzer's letters).

Agricola adopts an unmistakably Lutheran stance from the beginning: Müntzer's teachings are compared to the fiery out-pourings from the mouth of Behemoth; his work is that of the awakened Satan, progenitor of sects and heresies. After some commonplaces about 'murderous spirits', and a diversion into some of the more abstruse elements of academic theology, Agricola then explains that the real consequence of Müntzer's doctrine on mortification was quite simple: 'All his so-called studying, amazement and emptiness are designed to permit him to strangle and strike dead.' As evidence of this, here again are the stories about killing the enemy with a felt hat and wishing to trample the godless underfoot. In Agricola's view, 'mortification' inexorably leads to bloodthirstiness. The killer argument is this:

> They have three texts from which they study the judgement of God: the five books of Moses [the Pentateuch]; those of Joshua and Judges; the books of Samuel and Job; in these books there is mention of murders – such as those of Abraham, Joshua, etc. – so that they can claim to be Moses, Joshua, Abraham, etc. And

anyone who does not wear a beard or opposes them must be godless, and they have the right to kill and murder them.

Here is a fine picture: several seedy-looking Müntzerites gathered ghoulishly around the Old Testament, gloating over the goriest passages, all the while cultivating their beards. If this picture has any close relative, it must surely be in the antisemitic medieval depictions of the Jews and their designs upon Christian babies.

Agricola has a new story for us, one we have not heard before: 'At Allstedt, the Epistles were read during Mass, then immediately afterwards he led the congregation in singing the devil's rhyme: "The princes should be struck dead, and their houses burned down."' Agricola's piece was, on the one hand, a serious attempt to demonstrate the perceived inadequacies of Müntzer's theology – something Luther never bothered to undertake – and, on the other, a continuation of the character assassination begun by Luther. For lack of hard evidence, unfounded allegations were introduced to support the theological framework.

Uncharacteristically, Agricola made little of Müntzer's leadership of the rebellion. But this gap was filled by another of his pamphlets, which appeared in June 1525, promisingly entitled *A Useful Dialogue or Description of a Conversation between a Müntzerish Enthusiast and an Evangelical Pious Peasant, Concerning the Punishment of the Rebellious Enthusiasts at Frankenhausen.*[8] This heavy-handed fictional representation of a meeting between a refugee from the battle at Frankenhausen and a Lutheran peasant delivers no surprises; by the end, the Enthusiast has seen the error of his ways; he departs, thanking the well-informed peasant for his many insights. (During this period of the Reformation, the German peasant, long depicted as a boorish, drunken, farting simpleton, briefly appeared in the character of an intelligent, sober and rational citizen; this rather abrupt change is a reflection of the Lutherans' wooing of the common people away from rebellion.)

The main thrust of the pious peasant's argument is that tyranny should not be countered by the sword, for it could only be destroyed by God. Agricola brings his previous observations up to date, making specific reference to the events around the battle at Frankenhausen. In the course of their conversation, both the peasant and the Enthusiast present some quite entertaining 'facts' about Müntzer – facts known to Agricola at least, if not to anyone else. Apart from a lengthy discussion about Müntzer's supposed instructions on the growing of beards ('like the patriarchs of old'), three specific points emerge about our preacher: that he recanted his faith shortly before death, that he was a coward and that he sought material comforts. In the face of all this evidence, the poor Enthusiast begins to waver, and even volunteers the names of Müntzer's associates in Allstedt (beard-growers to a man). As the talk proceeds relentlessly to cover the campaign on the Eichsfeld, he reveals even more: Müntzer's drinking habits were not the worst of his faults. During the plundering of churches and castles in May 1525, the Enthusiast had seen 'eleven thousand guilders in money and silver' and 'eight hundred sheep' being redistributed among Müntzer and his followers. (The factual basis for this accusation lies in the distribution of plunder on the Eichsfeld – which was equitably distributed, after campaign provisions had been reserved, among all participants.) The peasant asks about the chasubles which were stolen; the Enthusiast replies: 'He had his wife make a jacket and cape out of them.' And then there is even more damning evidence of Müntzer accepting presents of fine foods and bags of big coins from 'rich fellows'.

Müntzer, the friend of the poor, is now exposed as a self-seeking glutton, in the pay of the rich. This proves to be the knock-out blow for the unfortunate Enthusiast, who begs the Lutheran peasant to show him the true faith. The solution is simple: 'Oh, my dear chap, let the worldly rulers govern worldly goods, and be content in Christ your Lord, who provided, through faith, all the eternal, immortal goods.' Finally, the peasant suggests that 'you can heal yourself by visiting the barber'. The reformed Enthusiast departs and heads straight to a barber's shop, clutching a guilder that the peasant has loaned to him to obtain a very Christian shave.

Between them, Luther, Melanchthon and Agricola had, by the end of June 1525, completed an all-embracing character assassination of Thomas Müntzer, the purpose of which was to turn his surviving followers away from his doctrines. Since his followers were deemed to include those of any other radical opponent of Luther, this historiography also fulfilled a wider need. The Lutherans never went so far as to accuse Müntzer of committing all the Seven Deadly Sins, but if they had, the only one they would have failed to pin on him was Sloth – for which omission the rebellious peasantry amply compensated by refusing to undertake feudal duties.

But there were other views of the events of 1525, of which the most significant was the Catholic one. Its tone was set by a pamphlet written by Johannes Cochläus against Luther's anti-peasant tracts.[9] He presents a detailed critique of Luther's vicious diatribes, then argues vigorously that Luther himself – and no one else – was to blame for the uprising.

Luther had good cause to feel nervous. It was not just the Catholic commentators who judged him the root cause of the uprising. Jakob Fugger, the richest man in Germany, wrote to Duke Georg expressing the view that, 'in truth, Luther is the root and very source of this uproar, rage and blood-letting in the German nation';[10] and Georg himself was not to be appeased – in early 1526, he rejected Luther's attempt at détente with the words 'we consider his words to be threatening, rather than humble'.[11]

When Cochläus deals with Luther's attacks on Müntzer, he is quite clear that the latter was small fry compared with the reformer from Wittenberg:

Luther is much more to blame than Müntzer, for you [Luther] have stirred up a thousand times more damage and seduction and riot among the people than Müntzer. And how? As follows: Müntzer only agitated in Thuringia, but you stirred up trouble all over the land of the German nation.

Despite pursuing a slightly different angle, the Catholics were just as adept at making up 'history' as their Wittenberg counterparts. An anonymous Catholic tract, *A Believable and True Lesson on How the Thuringian Peasants Were Punished before*

Frankenhausen for Their Misdeeds,[12] described how the expedition on the Eichsfeld involved 'murder, arson, robbery and pillage, which they pursued to such an extent that they spared neither pregnant women nor nursing mothers, nor the innocent little children in their cradles'. If Müntzer's actions and thoughts were misrepresented and twisted by the Lutherans and Catholics, it must be said that the peasants and urban rebels of 1525 suffered much the same fate.

There was one other early contributor to the Müntzer mythology: Heinrich Bullinger, a Zwinglian who wrote a lengthy work against the Anabaptists to demonstrate that Swiss Anabaptism had absolutely nothing to do with Zwinglianism – or, indeed, with the respectable Swiss. His *Origin, Development, Sects etc. of the Anabaptists* of 1560 traced the evils of Anabaptism back to Müntzer and to Storch.[13] He delivered a rough-and-ready critique of Müntzer's doctrines, and then described how Müntzer spread them among the Swiss radicals:

> When he was driven from Allstedt, he next went to Nürnberg and then into Upper Germany, and then journeyed through Basel, to Griessen in Klettgau . . . and in the peasant uproar which shortly followed, he planted his poisonous seed in the restless rebellious hearts of the peasants. At that time he also spread the doctrine of Anabaptism.

According to Bullinger, Müntzer had learned his heresy in the company of Storch, before founding a 'School' of spiritualists and Anabaptists in Saxony in 1521. Müntzer's main disciples had been Pfeiffer, Rinck and 'many others', while the town council of Mühlhausen was described as 'new Anabaptist or Müntzerish'. Bullinger remains a little vague as to whether Anabaptism arose in 1521, 1524 or 1525, but he is adamant that the sect was of Saxon and Müntzerish origin. Müntzer was responsible not only for the peasant uprising in the Black Forest, but also for all the radical religious movements which followed. Both of these legends slipped easily into the main body of Müntzer historiography. Bullinger shared Luther's ability to conflate separate movements in order the more economically to condemn them all.

To commemorate the first centenary of the 1525 uprising, a writer by the name of Rinckhardt penned a play entitled *Monetarius Seditiosus, or: the Müntzerish Peasants' War*, in which Müntzer was in cahoots with Satan, an agent of the Pope, bloodthirsty, greedy, smooth-talking, cowardly; Karlstadt also puts in an appearance as co-conspirator. Rinckhardt must have felt a little aggrieved when, after all his effort, the authorities banned his play: they said it conjured up 'uninvited memories'. The banning order took a different approach to the historiography, but with the same aim.

Many of the original myths of 500 years ago are still accepted uncritically today. In general histories in particular, where Müntzer merits only a paragraph or passing mention, it is not unusual still to find a random selection of the slanders from sixteenth-century historiography. It was only well into the nineteenth century that any serious questions were raised about Müntzer's portrayal in histories. By then, of course, the era of bourgeois revolutions had begun, starting with the British in the seventeenth century, and continuing through the American War of Independence and the French Revolution. In the following decades, revolutions took place with welcome regularity across South America, in the Caribbean, and in practically every country of Europe during 1848. These upheavals had a profound effect on intellectual life across the western world, not least on historiography. Seeing the present and the future changing before their very eyes, liberals and academics started to question the past with more energy than they had done before. Accepted 'history' – the history that had been authorised by the very class of people now being challenged or overthrown – was questioned; historians turned to the sources; archives were explored; and the German Peasants' War and Müntzer were considered in a different light.

But if the French Revolution inspired bourgeois democrats, the subsequent Terror horrified them. This duality is reflected in Strobel's *Life, Writings and Teachings of Thomas Müntzer*, which appeared in 1795.[14] Its first part deals critically with Müntzer's doctrines, in so far as they could be established from the letters and writings then available. In this section, Strobel is relatively even-handed. But when he moves on to deal with events in All-stedt and Mühlhausen, he is reminded of the Terror, shrinks back from any further objectivity, and all of Luther's slanders come into play. Four years later, another German historian, by the name of Köhler, published his *Gallery of New Prophets*,[15] which took a mildly critical view of the Lutheran myth, and spoke of Müntzer as 'more a deceived enthusiast, rather than a deceiver' – it is a fine distinction, but we must take what is offered. In 1842 the historian Seidemann published his *Thomas Müntzer – a Biography*, in which his overall judgement rested uneasily on the twin horns of liberalism and the fear of uncontrollable revolution.[16] Full of pity for the peasantry, Seidemann manages to justify the bloody repression of 1525; viewing Müntzer as a worthy and tenacious opponent of Luther, he repeats the suggestions of half-crazed fanaticism; while doubting the idea that Müntzer was a dissipated wretch, he accepts uncritically the beard-growing and the accusations of cowardice.

At much the same time, the Hegelian and liberal historian Wilhelm Zimmermann produced a pleasingly hefty three-volume *History of the Great German Peasants' War*.[17] These volumes differed radically from any other histories of the time: they were totally sympathetic, often lyrically so, to the peasants' rebellion and its leaders. The pre-1848 (*Vormärz*) period, in its search for a national revolutionary tradition, had found an episode – and in Müntzer a personality – to emulate. Müntzer was seen as a 'critical spirit', 'one of the boldest spirits', a man firmly rooted in his era, a dreamer in an immature political situation, a precursor of progressiveness. Zimmermann also gave equal importance to Pfeiffer in relation to events in Mühlhausen.

Although based on Zimmermann's sometimes faulty or incomplete information, Friedrich Engels's 1850 study, *The Peasant War in Germany*, still today manages to inspire and instruct, without at the same time leading the reader too far astray.[18] Even allowing for its inaccuracies and over-enthusiasm, Engels's book, as the first Marxist study of the period, was an extremely important foundation for the historiography undertaken by left-wing historians after 1918 and again after 1945. Engels's view of Müntzer's position, as an example of 'a leader of an extreme party', has largely stood the test of time:

> He is bound to the doctrines and demands hitherto propounded which . . . do not proceed from the class relations of the moment . . . but from his more or less penetrating insight into the general result of the social and political movement. Thus, he necessarily finds himself in an unsolvable dilemma. What he *can* do contradicts all his previous actions and principles, and the immediate interests of his party, and what he *ought* to do cannot be done.

Engels's book was followed up by similar Marxist/socialist histories of these events written by Bebel (1876), Kautsky (1895), Bax (1899) and Mehring (1910).[19]

After the unification of the German states in 1871 – which this time was clearly not a revolution, rather the opposite – a new feeling of patriotic pride swept over Imperial Germany, triggering a massive surge in interest in the new nation's many archives. In an eruption of research, local history societies sprouted like mushrooms, libraries of every shape and size were ransacked, and documents emerged that clarified hundreds of episodes from German local history. This feeding frenzy lasted up to, and beyond, the First World War. One of its many fruits was the discovery and publication of documents relating to the Peasants' War and to Thomas Müntzer and his colleagues. The opening of the archives quite simply brought out the facts – something which had been sadly lacking for several centuries. Among the resulting publications was a valuable two-volume set of documents relating to Duke Georg's Church policies.[20] The first decade of the twentieth century in particular saw the publication of great swathes of documents, mercifully devoid of critical commentary, which shed new light on the people and events of the early Reformation. Particular attention was given by researchers to Zwickau, Allstedt and Mühlhausen. But, while the basic materials for historiography were being laid down as a solid foundation for research, the period from 1848 through to 1918 was also notable for the fact that there were very few studies of Müntzer's theology, or analyses of his writings.

The revolutionary tide which swept across Germany in 1918/19 also produced an upsurge of interest in the revolutionaries of 1525. There began a tussle for the ownership of Müntzer – between the socialists and philosophers on the one hand, and the theologians and bourgeois historians on the other. It was a battle which continued uninterrupted until 1933. One of the most significant studies of this period was Ernst Bloch's *Thomas Münzer: Theologian of the Revolution* (1921).[21] Although greatly revered in its time – and it has the merit of being one of the first attempts to get to grips with Müntzer's theology – it is an annoying book; written in an opaque and lyrical style, with a great number of expressionistic-adjectival-and-compound-nouns, going on at great length, without much reference to the facts, on the sociology of radicalism ('the autochthonic sect-type of Müntzer's secret league'), not to mention asides on Oriental history and a general essay on the 'compromises between Christianity and the Secular World', it concludes with a purple passage predicting a time when 'heretics' such as Joachim de Fiore, Müntzer – yes, even Tolstoy – would unite with Liebknecht and Lenin in a grand revolt against 'History'. It was all very breathless and well meaning; inspiring, too. But not entirely helpful.

More useful, perhaps, was the continuing work of the archivists, which culminated in a two-volume collection of more than 2,000 enlightening *Documents of the History of the Peasants' War in Central Germany* (1934 and 1942).[22] This was preceded by the very first 'collected edition' of Müntzer's letters and writings in 1931.[23] Müntzer's correspondence had been available for some time – before 1842, some fifty-two letters had been published rather randomly; over the next seventy years, a further twenty-six were added; the new edition of 1931 brought them all together and added a further twelve to bring the total to ninety. Given that today only 102 letters to and from Müntzer have been discovered, that is a pretty solid early result. In this same volume were published for the first time other pieces of biographical documentation, including all four versions of the 'Prague Manifesto'.

Historiography is conditioned by contemporary history. In 1933, the NSDAP (Nazi Party) took state power in Germany. Research into Müntzer by no means stopped, but it took on a completely new character. A German academic, writing in 1937, proclaimed that Müntzer was 'first and foremost a theologian, a preacher and a liturgist, not a politician; a man of the Church, but not a demagogue'.[24] As another historian had explained in 1933, in the introduction to his history of the Peasants' War: 'Today, at the conclusion of the first victorious German revolution, the peasant has finally found in the Third Reich the position in life for which he strove in 1525.'[25] The word 'revolution' evidently has many meanings. This historian was Günther Franz, who went on to become a member of the SA, rise through the ranks of the SS, and until 1945 take a leading role in establishing anti-Jewish, anti-communist guidelines for academic research (a small matter which he optimistically tried to conceal in a long academic career after the war). And yet, despite his political views, Franz managed to produce many valuable archival results, and was for several decades the leading western scholar of the Peasants' War.[26]

Many things changed again in 1945. Not the least of these was the carving up of Germany by the Allies, and the establishment shortly afterwards of the German Democratic Republic (GDR). For three decades thereafter, research into the Peasants' War and the radicals was largely superintended by the Soviet and GDR states. This was quite different from what had gone before: where Müntzer had been seen as very specifically not a politician, now he was regarded as very specifically a political leader of the oppressed. The first major work to appear in the post-war years was by the Soviet historian M. M. Smirin, whose full-scale study was entitled *The People's Reformation of Thomas Münzer*.[27] The book first appeared in Russian in 1947 and in German five years later. The clue was in the title: this was a Peasants' War which was planned and led by Müntzer and his comrades, a peasant-and-proletarian uprising led by a revolutionary party. The 'Elect' were identified as 'the People' – perhaps not a great surprise, since it fitted very neatly with the Stalinist conception that the Party equalled the People. Little in this book was factually new – it was effectively a reworking of Engels's book – but Smirin did begin to investigate the relationship between Müntzer's theology, medieval mysticism and Hussite Taboritism.

The new approach was encouraged by the ruling Socialist Unity Party (SED) of East Germany. Here was a new and hopeful young country, and what a new and hopeful young country always needs are its own heroes and history. The GDR researchers responded admirably: through careful filtering of the archives, they gradually moved away from Smirin's idea of Müntzer as an early proletarian revolutionary leading a national uprising, towards a more nuanced picture. (Although, in a telling echo of the 1933 assessment of the role of the peasants in the 'national revolution', one leading GDR historian wrote: 'In the GDR, Müntzer's inheritance is now a living entity, and his most important thoughts, his sympathetic striving for a higher meaning, have now become reality.'[28]) Particularly after 1956, as the dead hand of Stalin was being lifted away by the new Soviet leaders, the East German historians developed the thesis that the uprising of 1525 was an 'early bourgeois revolution', with Müntzer as its theoretician.[29] They usually took the time to study the sources and fit them into the agreed general framework. (Since much of their work was based on archive material, the researchers were not greatly helped by the decision of the SED government of Saxony – despite despairing protests from the Dresden archivist – to send Stalin a seventieth-birthday present in December 1949: the gift comprised the originals of almost every single letter from Müntzer's own collection, up until late 1524, and a few more documents thrown in for good measure. They were photographed prior to being bound, and then furnished with a dedication to 'the Friend of the German People and the Wise Leader of the Soviet People'. Stalin eagerly tore the wrappings and ribbons from his present and placed it on the shelves of his private library; after his death, the collection was transferred to the Russian State Library in Moscow – and there it remains to this day.[30])

If the GDR set the pace in Müntzer studies, the west was not far behind. Much of the effort there was put into research into the Anabaptists, or into Müntzer's theology.[31] By and large, western historians took the view that, if the 'communists' were pro-Müntzer, then it was perhaps safest to be sceptical about Müntzer's influence over the rebels. Perhaps the single most important publication in the west was an edition of the *Complete Works of Müntzer* (1968), produced largely – but not solely – by the West German scholar Franz (mentioned above). The heavy volume contained all the known letters, all the printed works, the full liturgies, and other assorted documents relating to Müntzer's life. The edition had been planned in 1933, and was put together in 1942 – but then the manuscript was lost during the war. It took some time to put it all together again, in part because much of the relevant material was by then in GDR archives, and some of it inconveniently in Moscow. As a critical edition, it had its faults; but, until a revised 'complete works' edition was produced almost four decades later, it was the most anyone could hope for. (The latest, and best, complete edition is in three volumes, which appeared in slightly idiosyncratic order – Volume 3 first, Volume 1 last – between 2004 and 2017.)

If we take all the studies or editions of Müntzer from 1525 through to 2012, an intriguing pattern emerges from the statistics (see table in endnote).[32] What we see is a steady growth in interest that increases up until 1945. Immediately after the Second World War, there is a slight spike, which grows increasingly large towards 1974. But in the period 1975 to 1989 there is a huge upsurge. This was due to three events: firstly, the 450th anniversary of the Peasants' War, which was lavishly celebrated in the GDR in 1975; then the 500th anniversary of the birth of Luther in 1983; and finally Müntzer's 500th anniversary in 1989. The first was to be anticipated – indeed, alongside a truly Stakhanovite output of monographs, popular histories and detailed studies, GDR postage stamps and banknotes were printed bearing the image of Thomas Müntzer. After a lengthy gestation, the Peasants' War Panorama Museum, commissioned in 1974, was finally opened in 1989 on the battle hill above

Frankenhausen, containing a massive and rather beautiful depiction of the events of May 1525, painted by the artist Werner Tübke. But the celebrations in 1983 were rather more unexpected: like West Germany, the government of the GDR threw itself wholeheartedly into commemorating the life and works of Martin Luther. Was not Luther, after all, born in an area that now lay within the GDR? And Wittenberg was self-evidently the People's property as well. GDR historians took a while to adapt to the SED's complete reversal of its previous stance on Luther, but it seems to have had long-term benefits. However, it did lead to a slight quandary facing Müntzer historians in 1989, when it was time to celebrate Müntzer's birth: how was one supposed to reconcile the pro-Luther circle with the pro-Müntzer square? Luckily, fine distinctions like this did not worry the SED, who were quite happy to celebrate any national hero they could justifiably lay hands on. And in any event, in 1989, the East German government had things other than the Müntzer-Luther dialectic to worry about.

While the summary above is largely based on German-language histories and editions, this is not to say that the west (principally the UK and USA) had been idly twiddling its thumbs.[33] A respectable number of English-language contributions emerged after 1975 – around 180 in total between 1975 and 2022. The overriding concerns of most of these were theology and Anabaptism. Which is good: Müntzer was a theologian as much as a revolutionary. Without the labour of western researchers before 1990, this little fact might almost have been overlooked.

If 1933 and 1945 were major turning points in the German historiography of Müntzer and the Peasants' War, then the collapse of the Soviet Union and the GDR in 1989, followed swiftly by the reunification of Germany, gave it a whole new impetus. The historiography of Müntzer in this more recent period has been characterised largely by a sense of caution and scrupulous investigation, combined with an ambition to understand how and why Müntzer's theology related to his political actions. A group of historians and theologians, from both the old 'West' and 'East', has in recent years produced some remarkable new insights into Müntzer and his times.[34] Particular mention should be made here of the work of Günter Vogler and Siegfried Bräuer who, over five decades, produced an extraordinary amount of insightful and thought-provoking books and essays which synthesised the approaches of West and East.

But this is not to say that all of the old hoary myths have gone away. Very recently, at the time of the 2017 anniversary of the German Reformation, the German Evangelical Church chose to celebrate only Luther, and – despite intensive lobbying – chose not to mention Müntzer or Karlstadt if at all possible; and when Müntzer was inadvertently mentioned, some representatives of that Church took it upon themselves to compare him to the leaders of the Islamic terror groups ISIS and al-Qaeda.[35] Even by those who should know better, excitable and absurdly inaccurate biographical statements continue to be made.[36] Martin Luther would be content with such dreadful histories.

Conclusion

There's a Müntzer behind All This

The prophecy of Count Albrecht of Mansfeld is true, when he wrote to me: 'There's a Müntzer behind all this.' For whoever repudiates the teaching of the Law will tear down government and authority. And if the Law is thrown out of the Church, then there will be no more recognition of sin in the world.

Martin Luther (1537)

The history of Thomas Müntzer is a short one. It spans just thirty-five years, and most of them are for us a complete blank. It is challenging enough to uncover traces of his life and thought, but even more difficult to prise the truth from under the detritus laid down by centuries of hostile commentary, and almost impossible to find the man. If we compare what we now have of Müntzer with what we possess of his foremost opponent, Martin Luther, the difference is astonishing. Where there are just enough of Müntzer's letters and printed works to occupy two well-padded volumes, of Luther we have more than seventy volumes; compared with Müntzer's surviving 100-odd pieces of correspondence (and barely fifty of those were written by him), we have over 3,330 of Luther's; against eight printed works from Müntzer, there are sufficient to fill a good fifty volumes with Luther. And Luther's 'table-talks' of later years occupy another six volumes. Müntzer never had the luxury of sitting down to lengthy suppers with acolytes who jotted down his every word; instead, his remains slowly rotted away in a field outside Mühlhausen. It is almost incredible that we have anything of Müntzer at all. His printed works – when they were not confiscated at the print shop – never reached a wide audience, and anyone who did lay hands on them would not have been eager to advertise the fact. His letters were passed down almost by accident. It was only due to the hoarding of documents in castle archives that we still have any of these materials. That they survived five centuries of turbulent German history – religious wars, bourgeois and proletarian revolutions, Allied bombing, Stalin's birthday – is something of a miracle.

We now refer back to our first question: who was this Thomas Müntzer? If he was not a Devil, a Satan and a Ravening Wolf, then what was he and why should we remember him?

Thomas Müntzer did not talk of his own life, or of his own emotions. Lacking this personal touch, the only impression left is of someone highly intelligent and extremely well read, but perhaps a little opinionated and lofty, incensed by the injustices of his times, supportive of – and probably frustrated by – the uneducated people with whom he had daily dealings. In some of his letters, it is clear he was no different from any other decent person: he worried about his household and his family; he was enraged by fools; and he took care to dissuade his followers from pointless acts of resistance.

The evidence also indicates that he was a man well respected by those who came into contact with him. He was evidently a good listener, established relationships with people very quickly, and inspired loyalty. He had a wide network of correspondents spread out across Germany – fellow preachers for the most part, perhaps people he had met at one or more universities, but also people who were inspired by his ideas and methods. In the letters which have been preserved, he had contact with over fifty individuals. Some of his correspondents are quite unexpected – mining magnates, for example, and merchants, and the ducal representative in Allstedt; none of those had, even before the calamity of 1525, any particular reason to encourage or correspond with a man who so unashamedly stood against the existing social order. What attracted them was Müntzer's intellectual rigour and the persuasiveness of his answers, and perhaps the excitement of playing with fire in an era of theological arson. Over the years, however, it was not the great and the rich who featured large in Müntzer's correspondence; it was similarly inclined preachers, or worried town-dwellers, or enthusiastic lower-class radicals. These people, right up to the fateful days at Frankenhausen, turned to him for advice and guidance. (What is missing from the recovered correspondence are any letters from the leading lights of the south-west German Reformation and rebellion – for example, Hubmaier, Oekolampad or Hugwald; in his 'confession', Müntzer indicated that his wife had an additional sack full of letters, and specifically mentions letters from the latter two, but none such have come to light.[1])

And then, of course, there was Martin Luther – 'Doctor Liar, you poisonous little worm with your stinking humility'. Just as it is hard to understand Müntzer without his nemesis, so it would be ill-advised to try to understand Luther without his 'Devil of Allstedt'. Luther came back to the subject of Müntzer again and again, right up to his death in 1546. To be sure, he frequently bracketed Müntzer together with Karlstadt, Zwingli, Oekolampad and all other perceived 'spiritualists and baptists'. But it was Müntzer for whom he reserved his bitterest criticisms, and Müntzer for whom he established a veritable cottage industry of falsification. Luther saw in him nothing less than the real-life manifestation of Satan. Müntzer was the man who preached bloodshed and murder. Müntzer was the man who had stirred up the peasantry of 1525, and sown dissent and disobedience among the people of towns and villages. And yes, it is true that Müntzer preached bloodshed against the godless, and especially against godless rulers. But Luther carefully chose to ignore the fact that Müntzer killed no one and that his fellow rebels killed only very few – and that mostly in self-defence. And would you believe it? Luther, too, preached bloodshed and death: his tirades against the peasants of 1525 endorsed and justified the slaughter of many thousands of men and the utter destitution of families. Luther felt acutely uncomfortable that a fellow reformer – one who had shared his ideas in the early stages of the Reformation, one who was clearly a close associate in 1518/19 – was now embroiled in a massive social uprising against the established order. Luther's reforms were hitched firmly to the wagon of his Saxon princes. The fundamental difference between the two men was this: in May 1525, Müntzer stood with the lowest members of society, Luther with the highest. For Luther, the vital task from around 1522 onwards was to place as much distance between himself and the radicals as he could. If that task could be achieved by slander and simple name-calling, then so be it.

Müntzer was an intellectual. His surviving pamphlets and letters demonstrate a deep familiarity with the Bible, as well as the major theological works of the Middle Ages. Unlike Luther and many other mainstream and radical reformers, Müntzer had never been a monk; but over the years, and in many different places, he acquired a solid grounding in biblical knowledge and religious history. Müntzer developed a canon of ideas, a mixture of Old Testament faith and individual mysticism, which removed all the proxies and surrogates between a person and their God.

True faith came through suffering – assumed to be spiritual, but not exclusively so – and true faith gave authority to the individual; in other words, it allowed the burdened peasant and the disaffected town-dweller to find in themselves the justification for their social, economic and political acts of rebellion. To some extent, the religious justification of social demands had already been outlined by rebels in the previous century, and then encouraged by Luther in his early works – just consider the biblical citations which embroidered many of the rebels' lists of demands during the Peasants' War. But Müntzer went one step further: for him, the Bible was not the sole source of justification; it was just another 'witness' to faith, one among many past and present witnesses.

Müntzer was an intellectual, but he hated with a very deep loathing the 'academics', those who cloistered themselves away in religious institutions and universities, arguing about theology in a rarefied atmosphere and paying little or no attention to the needs of the common people, or – worse – supporting with their ideas the continued existence of a godless class of rulers. He had sympathy for the 'poor people' who had neither learning nor the time for learning. True, he would occasionally voice his frustration at the slowness with which his ideas were being picked up; if he had not been frustrated, he would not have been human. But for him, the task of the 'Reformation' was to educate the poor, by providing them with lessons in their own everyday language, so that they could really understand the underpinnings of faith, so that they could free themselves. His written works demonstrate a skilful use of the German language. His texts are generally perfectly clear; he uses simple analogy as well as Old Testament references, and a fecund and earthy vocabulary of insult that would have been familiar to all. His renderings of the Psalms were more than mere translations: they were guides to action. His language, as one commentator has observed, is complex, rich and brilliant, like that of Rosa Luxemburg, 'necessarily edgy, broken, pointing beyond itself'.[2]

When he was permitted the luxury of time, Müntzer worked tirelessly to reform religious practice. Central to this effort were his liturgical works: by means of these German liturgies and the participation of all parishioners in the ceremonies, another barrier between the people and their God was broken down. (And Müntzer achieved this several years before Luther did, much to the latter's annoyance.) As we have argued, the educational value of his reformed liturgies cannot be overlooked or overstated. The reported popularity of his sermons in Allstedt, attracting hundreds of people from miles around, suggests that his oratorical skills matched his writing abilities.

Even after his death, his religious reforms and doctrines lived on – either in the almost improbable survival of his liturgies and pamphlets in Thuringia, or in the lives and works of the more radical among the German Anabaptists. Admittedly, the doctrines did not last very long in a recognisable form. This was to be expected, given the zeal with which his memory was attacked by the Lutherans, the Catholics and the ruling nobility. But it has to be said here that Lutheranism, too, came within a whisker of fading out. Soon after Luther's death in 1546, a short, sharp war between the 'Schmalkaldic League' of Lutheran princes against the might of the Catholic Holy Roman Empire led to the imposition of severe constraints on the growth of Lutheranism in Germany.

If we strip Müntzer's doctrine of its religious shell, what remains? Nothing less than an absolute authority for rebellion. Sixteenth-century theology cannot be judged from the perspective of twenty-first-century hindsight. Is it still possible to be a religious reformer and – at the same time – a social revolutionary? Possibly not, although exceptions exist. But in the Europe of 500 years ago, you could not be a revolutionary without being a religious reformer. Virtually all forms of intellectual expression were circumscribed by the framework of the Christian religion. It was the common language of all, from the highest prince down to the simplest peasant, for the craftsman as much as the Humanist, for the capitalist as much as the wife and mother, for the miner as much as the ploughman. To change ways of thinking, you had no option but to take on the guise and adopt the language of the icons who had dominated thinking for centuries. You had to bend the only tools available, those of the Bible, to new uses. And you had to do it for 'God'. Müntzer spoke in words which seem strange – even uncomfortable – to us today; but his commitment to total societal change still resounds, crying out for a new era of social justice.

Religious doctrine can be argued over until, from exhaustion, everyone simply agrees to disagree. Do dreams and visions come from God or the Devil? Are the bread and wine in the Christian Mass actually flesh and blood, or merely representations thereof? Does the New Testament supersede the Old? The minutiae of all these arguments exercised intellectuals for decades; men and women were killed for holding the wrong opinion on obscure doctrinal matters. But what was important, as much with Luther as with Müntzer, was the practical result and outcome of religious doctrines: put simply, which social and economic structures did a religious doctrine benefit or challenge? Luther's early teaching cleared the way for more focused demands for social change: how else can we explain that huge upsurge after 1517 in the agitation for political, economic and legal reform in town and country, justified explicitly by referencing the Bible? For Luther, of course, such demands were unintended consequences, and he spent the rest of his life trying to distance himself from the events of 1525. He stated time and again that secular authority had to be obeyed. On the other hand, by the summer of 1524, Müntzer had rejected secular authority; his teaching was intended to clear the way for something even greater than reform – the Millennium. It was a vague concept, to be sure, and Müntzer never outlined the shape of the new society; but it was surely one which promised justice, knowledge and well-being – in short, a society which looked after all of its members. Without actually sketching out a Utopia, Müntzer looked beyond the rebellion to a time of new relationships between people and a new relationship between humanity and God; he provided his followers with the tools of thought that would lead to, and govern, this new era.

When those most affected are given responsibility for, or are closely involved in, a great project, they will take ownership; both they and the project will be the better for it. This is a simple fact which Müntzer recognised. It is what drove him to reform the liturgies, to explain faith in the simplest terms, to reach out to the common people and bring them into the ranks of the Elect who would become the revolutionary foot soldiers of the new age.

Revolutions are not simple things. They are great heaving masses of contradictions, twisting now one way, now another, now both ways at once. They inspire and give hope to millions. They overwhelm and crush the lives of thousands. Frequently they crash and burn, due to betrayal or hesitancy by the leaders, or the relative strength of the ruling order. Sometimes they break through to a new reality, a new status quo upon which further progress can – but need not – be made.

So was the German Peasants' War a 'revolution'? Certainly it was a rapid and widespread insurgency against the social and economic order, involving huge numbers of people across a vast swathe of territory in Germany and Austria. It was as coordinated as it could have been within the limitations imposed by the lack of swift long-distance communication. Ideas and tactics were shared and nourished by the pre-existing common knowledge of biblical teachings. But there was no 'central committee' armed with a single strategy. Instead, there were local leaders, people of enormous courage and conviction, struggling – sometimes with the barest minimum of insight – to achieve a great goal. Tragically, they could not hope to defeat a ruling class which perhaps no longer had God behind it, but which still had the next best thing: wealth and mercenaries.

Was Müntzer a 'revolutionary'? We have seen that, since Prague, and increasingly in 1524/5, Müntzer championed the 'poor' and the 'common people' against the triple oppression exercised by the Church, the State and the relations of production. His concerns were initially spiritual ones, but gradually began to cover very specifically the social and political aspects of life. From his earliest writings, we see that he espoused the cause of the spiritually and economically oppressed. In 1525, it fell to Müntzer to take on a leader's role in the peasant uprising in central Germany. He was not alone, however; it is clear that Heinrich Pfeiffer instigated the upheavals in Mühlhausen, and most of the official reports of the time talked of the leaders working in tandem – 'Müntzer and Pfeiffer' formed a two-headed monster in the annals of the Lutheran and Catholic authorities. And, of course, others had honourable and significant roles to play across Saxony and Thuringia. But in Zwickau and Allstedt and several places in between, Müntzer had laid the groundwork for the insurrection with his reforms, sermons, letters and pamphlets. He operated throughout his life in a very small, but significant, region: for the most part, it covered an area of about sixty-five by fifty kilometres. But, unlike many of his contemporaries who agitated for reform, he grasped the importance of the bigger picture: he took a very deliberate decision to travel in the winter of 1524 to the crucible of the uprising in south-west Germany. In the last months of his life, all the available evidence demonstrates that he was regarded by peasants, plebeians and nobles alike as the key player in the central German uprising. And at Frankenhausen, as the political leader of an army of the dispossessed facing overwhelming odds, he did not shirk his revolutionary responsibilities.

Relatively few revolutionaries succeed: think of the Scottish internationalist John Maclean, think of Karl Liebknecht and Rosa Luxemburg, of Trotsky and of Louis Blanqui and of the many others who rose to the challenges of their time – and were defeated. Thomas Müntzer, with his intellectual strength and courage, has a place in that honourable company. Arguably one of the most important theologians of the early Reformation period, he stood at the crossroads between medieval thought and modern political philosophy, at a time when early capitalism was beginning to construct the political framework in which it would flourish.

What makes Müntzer a figure worthy of our attention in the modern era? Simply this: that his understanding of the relationship between established religion, secular authority and social injustice obliged him to stand up and fight for the overthrow of all three, despite the massive forces which were stacked against him. He had that enormous courage required to fight for a seemingly impossible future. Against those who merely attempted to reform one aspect of society – the Church – he recognised that society's very basis was corrupt and that it had to be completely replaced. In real terms, he perhaps did not achieve much; but he saw beyond the present and aimed for the future. Read his words again – their relevance has not aged:

> Look: the origin of usury, theft and robbery lies with our lords and princes, who treat all creatures as their own: the fish in the water, the birds in the air, the plants on the earth – everything must be theirs. And on top of that, they then proclaim God's commandments to the poor and say: God has commanded that you shall not steal. But of course that does not apply to themselves. For they oppress everyone, flaying and fleecing them all, the poor peasant, the workman and all who live. But if any poor person commits the smallest crime then he must hang. And to this Doctor Liar says: Amen. It is the lords themselves who make the poor man their enemy. They refuse to remove the causes of rebellion, so how can it turn out well in the long run? And if these words make me a rabble-rouser – then so be it![3]

Chronology

For in many places . . . he has proven what kind of tree he is, for he brings forth no other fruit than murder and rebellion, and calls for the shedding of blood.

Martin Luther (1524)

(All entries relate to Thomas Müntzer, unless otherwise stated.)

December 1489?	Born in Stolberg, in the Harz
1506/1507?	Brief period of study at University of Leipzig
c. 1510/12	In Halle and Aschersleben as an assistant priest
October 1512	Enrolled at University of Frankfurt an der Oder
December 1513 or April 1514	Ordained as a priest in Halberstadt
May 1514	Given a benefice at Michaelskirche in Braunschweig
1515/16	Prefect in Cistercian nunnery in Frose
October 1517	Luther publishes his ninety-five theses in Wittenberg
Winter 1517/1518	In Wittenberg
January and June 1519	In Leipzig
April/May 1519	Deputising as preacher in Jüterbog (Brandenburg)
May/June 1519	In Orlamünde, parish of Andreas Karlstadt
June/July 1519	Johann Eck's disputation with Luther and Karlstadt in Leipzig
December 1519 to April 1520	Father Confessor in Cistercian nunnery in Beuditz
May 1520 to April 1521	Priest at the Marienkirche and Katharinenkirche in Zwickau
January 1521	Martin Luther excommunicated by Pope Leo X

16 April 1521	Müntzer leaves Zwickau
From 16 April 1521	Luther appears before Diet of Worms, then goes into hiding in the Wartburg
April/May 1521	In Bohemia (Žatec)
mid-June to early December 1521	In Prague
January to March 1522	Teaching at Petersberg monastery near Erfurt?
April 1522	Preaching sermons in Stolberg
June to September 1522	In Nordhausen
Early December 1522	Attends a disputation in Weimar
December 1522 to March 1523	Chaplain at Cistercian nunnery in Glaucha, Halle
March 1523	Takes up post as pastor in Allstedt, Saxony
April 1523	Marries Ottilie von Gersen
May 1523	Defeat of 'Knight's Revolt' in Palatinate
18 July 1523	Müntzer's *Letter to Stolberg*
Autumn 1523	Printing of *Order and Account*
September 1523	Conflict with Count Ernst of Mansfeld
November/December 1523	Printing of *Protestation or Proposition*
December 1523/January 1524	Printing of *German Church Office* and *On Fraudulent Faith*
24 March 1524	Burning of chapel at Mallerbach
End March 1524	Müntzer's son born
13 July 1524	Sermon preached before Duke Johann
15 July 1524	Oppression of Müntzer's supporters in Sangerhausen
mid-July 1524	Luther's *Letter to the Princes of Saxony*
20/22 July 1524	Printing of the *Interpretation of the Second Chapter of Daniel*
24 July 1524	Founding of Allstedt defence league
31 July/1 August 1524	Müntzer and others interviewed in Weimar
August 1524	Printing of the *German Evangelical Mass*
7 August 1524	Departs Allstedt
18 to 27 September 1524	Disturbances in Mühlhausen, Thuringia
27 September 1524	Müntzer and Pfeiffer expelled from Mühlhausen
October/November 1524	Arrives Nürnberg
2 November 1524	Printing of *An Explicit Exposure of False Faith*
Early December 1524	Departs Nürnberg

17 December 1524	Printing of *Highly Provoked Vindication*
mid-December 1524	In Basel, Switzerland
December 1524/January 1525	In Klettgau, south-west Germany
late February 1525	Return to Mühlhausen, via Fulda
28 February 1525	Installed as preacher at Marienkirche, Mühlhausen
17 March 1525	Establishment of 'Eternal Council' and 'Eternal League of God'
25/26 April 1525	Crisis in Salza – Pfeiffer takes militia there
28 April to 6 May 1525	With Pfeiffer, leads armed force around Eichsfeld
10/11 May 1525	Sets off for and arrives at Frankenhausen
15 May 1525	Battle of Frankenhausen
16/17 May 1525	Interrogation and confession at Heldrungen
27 May 1525	Executed along with Pfeiffer at Mühlhausen

Bibliography

In order that the Truth may come to light, impartial readers should read the following true lesson and decide for themselves.

Johann Agricola (1525)

Reference Editions

In German:
Thomas Müntzer Ausgabe, Kritische Gesamtausgabe: Volume 1 – Schriften, Manuskripte und Notizen (Publications, Manuscripts and Memos), ed. Armin Kohnle and Eike Wolgast, Leipzig 2017.
Thomas Müntzer Ausgabe, Kritische Gesamtausgabe: Volume 2 – Briefwechsel (Correspondence), ed. Siegfried Bräuer and Manfred Kobuch, Leipzig 2010.
Thomas Müntzer Ausgabe, Kritische Gesamtausgabe: Volume 3 – Quellen (Source Material), ed. Wieland Held and Siegfried Hoyer, Leipzig 2004.

In English:
Michael G. Baylor (trans. and ed.), *Revelation and Revolution: Basic Writings of Thomas Müntzer*, Bethlehem PA 1993.
Peter Matheson (trans. and ed.), *The Collected Works of Thomas Müntzer*, Edinburgh 1988.
Wu Ming, *Thomas Müntzer: Sermon to the Princes*, London and New York 2010 (contains several of the Michael Baylor translations).

Selected translations into English of Müntzer's works and letters are available at andydrummond.net/muentzer/muentzerwritings .html

Useful Background Reading (in English)

Michael Baylor (ed.), *The Radical Reformation*, Cambridge 1991.

Kat Hill, *Baptism, Brotherhood, and Belief in Reformation Germany: Anabaptism and Lutheranism, 1525–1585*, Oxford 2015.

Douglas Miller, *The German Peasants' War, 1524–1526*, Warwick 2023.

Lyndal Roper, *Martin Luther: Renegade and Prophet*, London 2016.

Lyndal Roper, *The German Peasants' War 1524–1526*, London 2024 (forthcoming).

E. Gordon Rupp, *Patterns of Reformation*, London 1969.

Tom Scott, *Society and Economy in Germany, 1300–1600*, Basingstoke 2002.

Tom Scott and Robert Scribner, *The German Peasants' War: A History in Documents*, New York 1991.

James M. Stayer, *The German Peasants' War and Anabaptist Community of Goods*, Montreal 1991.

Notes

Notes on the Text

1 Imperial Regimental pay-scales, 1507, cited in Doug Miller, *Frankenhausen 1525*, Seaton Burn 2017, p. 130.
2 See Peter Blickle, *The Revolution of 1525*, Baltimore 1981, p. ix.

Introduction: A Most Useful Lesson

1 *Thomas Müntzer Ausgabe, Kritische Gesamtausgabe*, Vol. 2, p. 412 (hereafter cited as 'ThMA'; see Bibliography for full details); Peter Matheson (trans. and ed.), *The Collected Works of Thomas Müntzer*, Edinburgh 1988, p. 142 (hereafter cited as 'Matheson').
2 ThMA Vol. 1, p. 422; Matheson, pp. 366–7.
3 ThMA Vol. 1, p. 200; Matheson, p. 180.
4 Philipp Melanchthon, *Die Histori Thome Muntzers* (1525). In Ludwig Fischer (ed.), *Die Lutherischen Pamphlete gegen Thomas Müntzer*, Tübingen 1976, pp. 41–2.
5 See Robert W. Scribner, *The German Reformation*, Basingstoke 1987, p. 2.

1. The End of the World

1 Annelore Franke (ed.), *Das Buch der Hundert Kapitel und der Vierzig Statuten*, Berlin (East) 1967, p. 230.
2 For more information on this, see Tom Scott, *Town, Country, and Regions in Reformation Germany*, Leiden 2005, pp. 351–9.
3 Karl Beer (ed.), *Die Reformation Kaiser Sigismunds*, Stuttgart 1933, p. 103.
4 See Tom Scott and Robert W. Scribner, *The German Peasants' War: A History in Documents*, New York 1991, p. 9.

5 For more on the relationships between landowners and peasants, see Peter Blickle, *The Revolution of 1525*, Baltimore 1981; and Scott and Scribner, *Documents*.

6 See Tom Scott, *Society and Economy in Germany, 1300–1600*, Basingstoke 2002, pp. 106–20.

7 See Scott and Scribner, *Documents*, pp. 49, 57 and 224 (Doc. 100).

8 For more on this, see Lyndal Roper, *Martin Luther: Renegade and Prophet*, London 2016, pp. 28–9.

9 In *Deutsche Reichstagsakten, Jüngere Reihe*, ed. Adolf Wrede, Gotha 1901, Vol. 3, pp. 697–8.

10 For more on this, see Scott, *Society and Economy*, passim.

11 See Scott, *Society and Economy*, p. 64.

12 For more on the social and economic background, see Scott, *Town, Country*; Scott, *Society and Economy*; Roper, *Martin Luther*; Peter Blickle, *The Revolution of 1525*.

13 See Tom Scott, *Raum und Region*, Freiburg and Munich 2021, p. 226.

14 On Joachim, see Marjorie Reeves, *The Influence of Prophecy in the Later Middle Ages*, Oxford 1969.

15 See Robert W. Scribner, *The German Reformation*, Basingstoke 1987.

16 In J. Maček, *The Hussite Movement in Bohemia*, Prague 1958, pp. 130–3.

17 For more on Hussitism and Taboritism see Malcolm D. Lambert, *Medieval Heresy*, London 1977; Maček, *Hussite Movement*; Howard Kaminsky, *A History of the Hussite Revolution*, Los Angeles 1967; M. v. Dussen and P. Soukup (eds) *A Companion to the Hussites*, Leiden 2020; T. A. Fudge (ed.), *The Crusade against Heretics in Bohemia, 1418–1437*, London 2002.

18 Martin Luther, *To the Christian Nobility of the German Nation* . . . (1520). In Martin Luther, *Gesammelte Werke*, Weimar 1883–2009, Vol. 6, p. 455.

19 Scott, *Town, Country*, p. 418.

2. The Devil Sowed His Seed

1 Letter from TM 'to his father', early 1521. *Thomas Müntzer Ausgabe, Kritische Gesamtausgabe* (hereafter cited as 'ThMA'; see Bibliography for full details), Vol. 2, p. 80; Peter Matheson (trans. and ed.), *The Collected Works of Thomas Müntzer*, Edinburgh 1988 (hereafter cited as 'Matheson'), p. 22.

2 See Hermann Goebke, 'Neue Forschungen über Thomas Müntzer bis zum Jahre 1520. Seine Abstammung und die Wurzeln seiner

religiösen, politischen und sozialen Ziele'. In *Harz-Zeitschrift* Vol. 9, Bad Harzburg 1957, pp. 1–30.

3   See Ulrich Bubenheimer, 'Thomas Müntzer und der Anfang der Reformation in Braunschweig', *Nederlands Archief voor Kerkengeschiedenis*, Vol. 65, 1985, pp. 1–30.

4   Friedrich Engels, *The Peasant War in Germany*, Moscow 1969 (first published 1850), p. 53. Engels based his work on W. Zimmermann's *Geschichte des grossen deutschen Bauernkrieges* (1843). This particular myth is also cited by Ernst Bloch in his *Thomas Münzer als Theologe der Reformation*, Munich 1921.

5   See, for example, Eric Vuillard's *La guerre des pauvres*, Paris 2019 (trans. as *The War of the Poor*, London 2021).

6   ThMA Vol. 2, p. 80; Matheson, p. 22.

7   ThMA Vol. 3, p. 271; Matheson, p. 437.

8   See Bubenheimer, *Thomas Müntzer und der Anfang*.

9   ThMA Vol. 2, pp. 4–5; Matheson, p. 8.

10 For more on this, see Friedrich Wiechert and Oskar J. Mehl, *Thomas Müntzers Deutsche Messen und Kirchenämter*, Grimmen 1937.

11 ThMA Vol. 2, pp. 14–15; Matheson, pp. 9–12.

12 ThMA Vol. 3, p. 45; Matheson, pp. 447–8.

13 Joh. Agricola, *Ein Nutzlicher Dialogus*, Wittenberg 1525. In Ludwig Fischer (ed.), *Die Lutherischen Pamphlete gegen Thomas Müntzer*, Tübingen 1976, p. 93.

14 See Ulrich Bubenheimer, *Wittenberg 1517–1522: Diskussions-, Aktionsgemeinschaft und Stadtreformation*, ed. Th. Kaufmann and A. Zorzin, Tübingen 2023, pp. 63–6.

15 See ThMA Vol. 2, p. 22; Matheson, p. 26.

16 ThMA Vol. 2, p. 19, note 1.

17 ThMA Vol. 3, pp. 45–53; Matheson, pp. 447–52.

18 See Shinzo Tanaka, 'Eine Seite der geistigen Entwicklung Thomas Müntzers', *Luther Jahrbuch*, Vol. 40, 1973, pp. 76–88.

19 Martin Luther, *Gesammelte Werke*, Weimar 1883–2009, Briefe Vol. 1, p. 392.

20 ThMA Vol. 1, pp. 487–50; Matheson, p. 442.

21 ThMA Vol. 3, pp. 54–5.

22 ThMA Vol. 2, pp. 29–30; Matheson, pp. 14–15.

23 ThMA Vol. 2, pp. 13–14; Matheson, p. 17.

24 ThMA Vol. 2, pp. 32–3; Matheson, p. 15.

25 For more on Tauler and Suso, see Steven E. Ozment, *Homo Spiritualis*, Leiden 1969; Michael G. Baylor, 'The Abyss, Detachment and Dreams: Thomas Müntzer's Reception of Medieval German Mysticism', *Medieval Mystical Theology*, Vol. 29, Issue 2, 2020, pp. 93–108.

3. Murder and Riot and Bloodshed

1   See Siegfried Bräuer and Günter Vogler, *Thomas Müntzer: Neu Ordnung Machen in der Welt*, Gütersloh 2016, p. 93.

2   For this and related information on Zwickau and its radicals, see Paul Wappler, *Thomas Müntzer in Zwickau und die 'Zwickauer Propheten'*, Zwickau 1908 (reprinted Gütersloh 1966).

3   Philip Schaff, *The New Schaff-Herzog Encyclopedia of Religious Knowledge, Volume VIII: Morality*, p. 156, last accessed at ccel. org July 2023.

4   Otto Merx, Günther Franz and Walther P. Fuchs (eds), *Akten zur Geschichte des Bauernkrieges in Mitteldeutschland*, 1934 and 1942 (reprinted Aalen 1964), Vol. 2, p. 92 (hereafter cited as 'AGBM').

5   Martin Luther, *Gesammelte Werke*, Weimar 1883–2009 (hereafter cited as 'WA'), Briefe Vol. 2, p. 346.

6   *Thomas Müntzer Ausgabe, Kritische Gesamtausgabe* (hereafter cited as 'ThMA'; see Bibliography for full details), Vol. 3, p. 56.

7   ThMA Vol. 2, pp. 38–9; Peter Matheson (trans. and ed.), *The Collected Works of Thomas Müntzer*, Edinburgh 1988 (hereafter cited as 'Matheson'), pp. 16–17.

8   ThMA Vol. 3, p. 57.

9   ThMA Vol. 3, p. 67.

10   ThMA Vol. 2, pp. 44–55; Matheson, pp. 18–22.

11   See, for example, Norman Cohn, *The Pursuit of the Millennium*, London 1993 (first published 1957), p. 237: 'As soon as Storch had enabled him to find himself, Müntzer changed his way of life, abandoning reading and the pursuit of learning.'

12   Karl G. Bretschneider (ed.), *Corpus Reformatorum*, Halle 1834, Vol. 1, p. 514.

13   In Wappler, *Thomas Müntzer in Zwickau*, pp. 81–6.

14   WA, Tischreden Vol. 1, p. 37. The accusation was first raised by an Anabaptist, Ludwig Hätzer, presumably as part of a forced confession.

15   Bretschneider, *Corpus Reformatorum*, Vol. 1, pp. 515–16.

16   See Robert W. Scribner, 'Practice and Principle in the German Towns: Preachers and People'. In *Reformation Principle and Practice: Essays in Honour of Arthur Geoffrey Dickens*, ed. P. N. Brooks, London 1980. Scribner suggests that only 8 per cent of reformed preachers had been laymen before 1517, and most were of comfortable means.

17   In August Bach (ed.), *Philipp Melanchthon*, Berlin (East) 1963, p. 164.

18   ThMA Vol. 3, pp. 86–7.

19   ThMA Vol. 2, pp. 168–9; Matheson, p. 58.

20 ThMA Vol. 2, pp. 57–8; Matheson, pp. 22–3.
21 ThMA Vol. 3, pp. 72–3.
22 ThMA Vol. 3, p. 74.
23 ThMA Vol. 2, pp. 77–8; Matheson, pp. 28–9.
24 ThMA Vol. 1, pp. 405–8; Matheson, pp. 380–3.
25 ThMA Vol. 2, p. 74; Matheson, p. 30.
26 ThMA Vol. 3, p. 90.
27 ThMA Vol. 3, pp. 82–3.
28 ThMA Vol. 2, pp. 164–5; Matheson, p. 56.

4. He Ran Away like an Arch-villain

1 *Thomas Müntzer Ausgabe, Kritische Gesamtausgabe* (hereafter cited as ThMA; see Bibliography for full details), Vol. 2, pp. 94–9; Peter Matheson (trans. and ed.), *The Collected Works of Thomas Müntzer*, Edinburgh 1988 (hereafter cited as 'Matheson'), pp. 39–40.
2 ThMA Vol. 2, pp. 92–3; Matheson, pp. 34–5.
3 ThMA Vol. 2, p. 88; Matheson, p. 33.
4 ThMA Vol. 2, pp. 81–2.
5 Karl G. Bretschneider (ed.), *Corpus Reformatorum*, Halle 1834, Vol. 1, p. 533.
6 ThMA Vol. 2, p. 84; Matheson, pp. 31–2.
7 ThMA Vol. 2, p. 86; Matheson, pp. 32–3.
8 See Paul Wappler, *Thomas Müntzer in Zwickau und die 'Zwickauer Propheten'*, Zwickau 1908 (reprinted Gütersloh 1966), pp. 40–1.
9 ThMA Vol. 2, p. 80; Matheson, p. 22.
10 ThMA Vol. 2, p. 347; Matheson, pp. 120–1.
11 ThMA Vol. 2, pp. 42–3; Matheson, pp. 453–4.
12 ThMA Vol. 2, pp. 62–5; Matheson, p. 25.
13 ThMA Vol. 1, pp. 409–10; Matheson, pp. 352–3.
14 ThMA Vol. 3, p. 105.
15 ThMA Vol. 2, pp. 102–14; Matheson, pp. 28–9.
16 For all following quotes in this chapter, see ThMA Vol. 1, pp. 418–27; Matheson, pp. 362–71.

5. Satan Wandered in the Wilderness

1 For more information on the events in Wittenberg in 1521 and 1522, see N. Müller, *Die Wittenberger Bewegung 1521–1522. Archiv für Reformationsgeschichte*, Vols 6 and 7, Leipzig 1908; James S. Preus, *Carlstadt's Ordinaciones and Luther's Liberty*,

Cambridge MA 1974; Mark U. Edwards, *Luther and the False Brethren*, Stanford 1975; Lyndal Roper, *Martin Luther: Renegade and Prophet*, London 2016.

2 Felician Gess (ed.), *Akten und Briefe zur Kirchenpolitik Herzog Georgs von Sachsen*, two volumes, Leipzig 1905/1917 (reprinted Cologne/Vienna 1985), Vol. 1, p. 210 (hereafter cited as 'ABKG').

3 Melanchthon, in Karl G. Bretschneider (ed.), *Corpus Reformatorum*, Halle 1834, Vol. 1, 1834, p. 515.

4 Melanchthon, in Bretschneider, *Corpus Reformatorum*, Vol. 1, p. 534.

5 Martin Luther, *Gesammelte Werke*, Weimar 1883–2009 (hereafter cited as 'WA'), Briefe Vol. 2, pp. 424–7.

6 *Allgemeine Deutsche Biographie*, Leipzig 1877, Vol. 4, p. 474.

7 WA, Briefe Vol. 2, pp. 474–5.

8 WA, Briefe Vol. 2, p. 493.

9 WA, Tischreden Vol. 3, p. 14.

10 See Roper, *Martin Luther*, p. 237.

11 See Ulrich Bubenheimer, *Wittenberg 1517–1522: Diskussions-, Aktionsgemeinschaft und Stadtreformation*, ed. Th. Kaufmann and A. Zorzin, Tübingen 2023, pp. 73–7.

12 *Thomas Müntzer Ausgabe, Kritische Gesamtausgabe* (hereafter cited as 'ThMA'; see Bibliography for full details), Vol. 2, pp. 116–25; Peter Matheson (trans. and ed.), *The Collected Works of Thomas Müntzer*, Edinburgh 1988 (hereafter cited as 'Matheson'), pp. 41–2.

13 ThMA Vol. 2, pp. 116–22; Matheson, pp. 42–3.

14 ThMA Vol. 2, pp. 122–5.

15 ThMA Vol. 2, p. 137; Matheson, pp. 43–6.

16 The words 'Dear . . .' to '. . . time' are in Thuringian German in the original.

17 ThMA Vol. 3, pp. 111–12.

18 ThMA Vol. 2, p. 400; Matheson, pp. 118–20.

19 ThMA Vol. 1, p. 393; Matheson, p. 344.

20 See Christian Lesser (ed.), *Historische Nachrichten von Nordhausen*, Nordhausen 1740, p. 55.

21 ThMA Vol. 2, pp. 140–1; Matheson, pp. 50–1.

22 ThMA Vol. 2, p. 144; Matheson, pp. 51–2.

23 ThMA Vol. 2, pp. 146–50; Matheson, pp. 49–50.

24 ThMA Vol. 3, p. 267; Matheson, p. 434.

25 ThMA Vol. 3, pp. 113–14; Matheson, pp. 454–5.

26 ThMA Vol. 2, pp. 150–4; Matheson, pp. 52–3.

27 ThMA Vol. 2, pp. 157–60; Matheson, pp. 54–5.

28 ThMA Vol. 2, pp. 154–7; Matheson, p. 54.

6. Satan Made Himself a Nest in Allstedt

1   See inter alia Friedrich Wiechert and Oskar J. Mehl, *Thomas Müntzers Deutsche Messen und Kirchenämter*, Grimmen 1937; Siegfried Bräuer, 'Thomas Müntzers Liedschaffen', *Luther Jahrbuch*, Vol. 41, 1974, pp. 45–102; Karl Honemeyer, *Thomas Müntzer und Martin Luther: Ihr Ringen um die Musik des Gottesdienstes*, Berlin (West) 1974; John K. Harms, 'Thomas Müntzer and His Hymns and Liturgy', *Church Music*, Vol. 77, 1977.

2   *Deutzsch kirchen ampt, Vorordnet, auffzuheben den hinterlistigen deckel unter welchem das Liecht der welt, vorhalten war . . .* In *Thomas Müntzer Ausgabe, Kritische Gesamtausgabe* (hereafter cited as 'ThMA'; see Bibliography for full details), Vol. 1, p. 5; Peter Matheson (trans. and ed.), *The Collected Works of Thomas Müntzer*, Edinburgh 1988 (hereafter cited as 'Matheson'), p. 166.

3   ThMA Vol. 1, pp. 5–6; Matheson, p. 166.

4   *Ordenung unnd rechenschafft des Tewtschen ampts zu Alstet durch die diener Gottis newlich auffgericht.* ThMA Vol. 1, pp. 188–97; Matheson, p. 170.

5   ThMA Vol. 1, p. 190; Matheson, pp. 171–2.

6   ThMA Vol. 1, p. 189; Matheson, p. 170.

7   ThMA Vol. 1, p. 7; Matheson, p. 181.

8   See Bräuer, 'Thomas Müntzers Liedschaffen', p. 101.

9   ThMA Vol. 1, p. 105.

10 ThMA Vol. 1, p. 133.

11 Emil Sehling, *Die evangelischen Kirchenordnungen des 16. Jahrhunderts*, Leipzig 1902, pp. 508–9.

12 ThMA Vol. 1, pp. 189–90; Matheson, pp. 170–1.

13 ThMA Vol. 1, p. 194; Matheson, p. 176.

14 ThMA Vol. 2, pp. 173–84; Matheson, pp. 61–4.

15 Martin Luther, *Gesammelte Werke*, Weimar 1883–2009 (hereafter cited as 'WA') Vol. 8, pp. 676–87.

16 ThMA Vol. 2, pp. 194–9; Matheson, pp. 66–7.

17 ThMA Vol. 3, p. 126.

18 ThMA Vol. 2, pp. 199–207; Matheson, pp. 67–70.

19 ThMA Vol. 1, p. 388; Matheson, p. 339.

20 Martin Luther, *Letter to Erfurt, 28 October 1525*. WA, Briefe Vol. 5, p. 591.

21 See Lyndal Roper, *Martin Luther: Renegade and Prophet*, London 2016, p. 142.

22 See 'Nikolaus_Widemar', Wikipedia (last accessed July 2023).

23 ThMA Vol. 2, p. 133; Matheson, pp. 43–6.

24 ThMA Vol. 2, p. 258; Matheson, pp. 81–2.

25 ThMA Vol. 1, p. 369; Matheson, p. 316.

26 ThMA Vol. 2, pp. 160–72; Matheson, pp. 55–9.

27 ThMA Vol. 2, p. 189; Matheson, pp. 65–6.

28 ThMA Vol. 3, pp. 132–3.

29 *Protestation odder empietung Tome Müntzers von Stolberg am Hartzs seelwarters zu Alstedt seine lere betreffende unnd tzum anfang von dem rechten Christen glawben unnd der tawffe.* ThMA Vol. 1, pp. 267–87; Matheson, pp. 188–209 and pp. 224–2.

30 See Siegfried Bräuer and Günter Vogler, *Thomas Müntzer: Neu Ordnung Machen in der Welt*, Gütersloh 2016, p. 219.

31 *Von dem getichten glawben auff nechst Protestation aussgangen.* ThMA Vol. 1, pp. 288–99; Matheson, pp. 214–25.

32 ThMA Vol. 2, p. 217; Matheson, p. 71.

33 *Deutsch Euangelisch Messze etwann durch die Bepstischen pfaffen im latein zu grossem nachteyl des Christen glaubens vor ein opffer gehandelt* . . . ThMA Vol. 1, pp. 198–266.

34 ThMA Vol. 1, p. 199; Matheson, p. 180.

35 Martin Luther, *Wider die Himmlischen Propheten* (1525). WA Vol. 18, p. 123.

7. His Face Was as Yellow as a Corpse's

1 *Thomas Müntzer Ausgabe, Kritische Gesamtausgabe* (hereafter cited as 'ThMA'; see Bibliography for full details), Vol. 2, pp. 234–9; Peter Matheson (trans. and ed.), *The Collected Works of Thomas Müntzer*, Edinburgh 1988 (hereafter cited as 'Matheson'), pp. 74–5.

2 ThMA Vol. 2, pp. 226–7; Matheson, pp. 104–7. While it is not completely certain who this visitor was, the evidence strongly suggests it was Georg Amandus.

3 Felician Gess (ed.), *Akten und Briefe zur Kirchenpolitik Herzog Georgs von Sachsen*, two volumes, Leipzig 1905/1917 (reprinted Cologne/Vienna 1985), Vol. 1, p. 72 (hereafter cited as 'ABKG').

4 Otto Merx, Günther Franz and Walther P. Fuchs (eds), *Akten zur Geschichte des Bauernkrieges in Mitteldeutschland*, 1934 and 1942 (reprinted Aalen 1964), Vol. 1, p. 634 (hereafter cited as 'AGBM').

5 ThMA Vol. 2, pp. 323–4; Matheson, pp. 103–4.

6 AGBM Vol. 2, p. 29.

7 AGBM Vol. 2, p. 186.

8 ThMA Vol. 3, p. 268; Matheson, p. 435.

9 ThMA Vol. 3, pp. 146–7.

10 ThMA Vol. 2, pp. 252–6; Matheson, p. 80.

11 ThMA Vol. 3, pp. 134–5.

12 ThMA Vol. 3, pp. 148–9.

13 Karl Förstemann, 'Urkunden zur Geschichte Thomas Müntzers und des Bauernkrieges in Thüringen 1523 bis 1525'. In *Neues Urkundenbuch zur Geschichte der evangelischen Kirchenreformation*, Vol. 1, Hamburg 1842, p. 170.

14 *Ausslegung des andern unterschyds Danielis dess propheten ...* ThMA Vol. 1, pp. 300–21; Matheson, pp. 230–52. An English translation is also available in George H. Williams, *Spiritual and Anabaptist Writers: Documents Illustrative of Radical Reformation*, London 1957. See also Michael G. Baylor (ed.), *Revelation and Revolution: Basic Writings of Thomas Müntzer*, Bethlehem PA 1993.

15 ABKG Vol. 1, p. 609.

16 ABKG Vol. 1, p. 718.

17 ThMA Vol. 2, p. 283, note 9.

18 ThMA Vol. 2, pp. 277–81; Matheson, pp. 83–5.

19 ThMA Vol. 2, pp. 281–5; Matheson, p. 85.

20 ThMA Vol. 2, p. 283; Matheson, p. 86.

21 ThMA Vol. 2, pp. 265–74; Matheson, pp. 86–91.

22 ThMA Vol. 2, pp. 311–16; Matheson, pp. 100–3.

23 ThMA Vol. 2, pp. 320–1; Matheson, pp. 101–2.

24 ThMA Vol. 2, pp. 287–92; Matheson, pp. 91–2.

25 ThMA Vol. 2, pp. 292–6; Matheson, pp. 93–4.

26 ThMA Vol. 3, pp. 142–3.

27 See Lyndal Roper, *Martin Luther: Renegade and Prophet*, London 2016, pp. 253–5.

28 AGBM Vol. 2, p. 470.

29 ThMA Vol. 2, p. 279; Matheson, p. 84.

30 ThMA Vol. 1, p. 316; Matheson, p. 246.

31 ThMA Vol. 2, pp. 316–22; Matheson, pp. 100–3.

32 ThMA Vol. 3, p. 164.

33 ThMA Vol. 3, p. 123.

34 ThMA Vol. 2, p. 386; Matheson, p. 136.

35 ThMA Vol. 2, p. 208.

36 ThMA Vol. 3, p. 139.

37 Luther, *Eyn brieff an die Fürsten zu Sachsen*. In Ludwig Fischer (ed.), *Die Lutherischen Pamphlete gegen Thomas Müntzer*, Tübingen 1976, pp. 1–12.

38 ThMA Vol. 3, p. 164.

39 ThMA Vol. 3, pp. 145–6.

40 ThMA Vol. 3, p. 160.

41 ThMA Vol. 3, pp. 175–6.

42 ThMA Vol. 2, pp. 330–5; Matheson, pp. 110–13.

8. Using God's Name, He Spoke and Acted for the Devil

1 *Thomas Müntzer Ausgabe, Kritische Gesamtausgabe* (hereafter cited as 'ThMA'; see Bibliography for full details), Vol. 1, p. 427; Peter Matheson (trans. and ed.), *The Collected Works of Thomas Müntzer*, Edinburgh 1988 (hereafter cited as 'Matheson'), p. 371.

2 ThMA Vol. 1, p. 315; Matheson, p. 245.

3 ThMA Vol. 2, pp. 52, 415; Matheson, pp. 21, 42.

4 Excluded from this analysis are the words set to music in the liturgies. For further investigations of Müntzer's vocabulary, see also, among others H. O. Spillmann, *Untersuchungen zum Wortschatz in Thomas Müntzers Deutschen Schriften*, Berlin 1971; Ingo Warnke, *Wörterbuch zu Thomas Müntzers deutschen Schriften und Briefen*, Tübingen 1993 (reprinted 2017).

5 ThMA Vol. 2, pp. 201–2; Matheson, p. 68.

6 ThMA Vol. 2, pp. 267–8; Matheson, p. 87.

7 ThMA Vol. 1, p. 335; Matheson, p. 274.

8 ThMA Vol. 2, p. 333; Matheson, pp. 110–11.

9 ThMA Vol. 2, p. 197; Matheson, p. 66.

10 ThMA Vol. 1, p. 290; Matheson, p. 214.

11 ThMA Vol. 2, pp. 240–52; Matheson, p. 76.

12 ThMA Vol. 2, pp. 324–30; Matheson, pp. 107–10.

13 ThMA Vol. 1, p. 311; Matheson, p. 241.

14 Martin Luther, *Gesammelte Werke*, Weimar 1883–2009, Briefe Vol. 2, pp. 424–8.

15 ThMA Vol. 1, p. 306; Matheson, p. 236.

16 ThMA Vol. 1, p. 333; Matheson, pp. 270–1.

17 ThMA Vol. 1, p. 422; Matheson, pp. 366–7.

18 ThMA Vol. 2, p. 202; Matheson, p. 69.

19 ThMA Vol. 2, p. 414; Matheson, p. 142.

20 ThMA Vol. 1, p. 306; Matheson, p. 235.

21 ThMA Vol. 1, p. 421; Matheson, p. 365.

22 ThMA Vol. 2, p. 197; Matheson, p. 67.

23 ThMA Vol. 2, p. 205; Matheson, pp. 69–70.

24 ThMA Vol. 2, p. 280; Matheson, p. 84.

25 ThMA Vol. 2, p. 270; Matheson, p. 87.

26 ThMA Vol. 1, p. 317; Matheson, p. 247.

27 ThMA Vol. 2, p. 331; Matheson, p. 110.

28 ThMA Vol. 2, p. 201; Matheson, p. 67.

29 ThMA Vol. 2, p. 438; Matheson, p. 148.

30 ThMA Vol. 2, p. 414; Matheson, p. 142.

31 Karl Marx, *The Eighteenth Brumaire of Louis Napoleon* (1852).

9. The Devil Never Let Him Rest

1 *Thomas Müntzer Ausgabe, Kritische Gesamtausgabe* (hereafter cited as ThMA; see Bibliography for full details), Vol. 2, p. 341; Peter Matheson (trans. and ed.), *The Collected Works of Thomas Müntzer*, Edinburgh 1988 (hereafter cited as 'Matheson'), p. 113.
2 ThMA Vol. 2, pp. 338–40; Matheson, p. 114.
3 ThMA Vol. 2, pp. 336–7; Matheson, p. 115.
4 ThMA Vol. 2, p. 343; Matheson, p. 116.
5 ThMA Vol. 2, pp. 346–7; Matheson, pp. 120–1.
6 ThMA Vol. 3, pp. 175–7.
7 *Aussgetrückte emplössung des falschen Glaubens der ungetrewen welt* . . . ThMA Vol. 1, pp. 322–75; Matheson, pp. 253–323.
8 ThMA Vol. 1, p. 324; Matheson, p. 260.
9 ThMA Vol. 1, p. 329; Matheson, p. 264.
10 ThMA Vol. 1, p. 331; Matheson, p. 268.
11 ThMA Vol. 1, p. 333; Matheson, p. 270.
12 ThMA Vol. 1, p. 335; Matheson, p. 272.
13 ThMA Vol. 1, p. 333; Matheson, p. 272.
14 ThMA Vol. 1, p. 369; Matheson, p. 316.
15 ThMA Vol. 1, pp. 339–40; Matheson, p. 278.
16 ThMA Vol. 1, p. 367; Matheson, p. 312.
17 Martin Luther, *Ein sendbrieff an die Stadt Mühlhausen* (1524). In Ludwig Fischer (ed.), *Die Lutherischen Pamphlete gegen Thomas Müntzer*, Tübingen 1976, p. 14.
18 See Günther Franz, *Der deutsche Bauernkrieg*, Bad Homburg 1969 (first published Munich 1933), p. 250. See also Manfred Bensing, *Thomas Müntzer und der Thüringer Aufstand 1525*, Berlin (East) 1966.
19 Otto Michael, *Grundbesitz und Erbzins der Bauern im Gebiet der Freien Reichsstadt Mühlhausen in Thüringen zur Bauern-kriegszeit*, Mühlhausen 1959, Appendix V.
20 Reinhold Jordan (ed.), *Chronik der Stadt Mühlhausen in Thürin-gen*, 2 vols, Mühlhausen 1900 and 1903, Vol. 1, p. 166.
21 Jordan, *Chronik der Stadt Mühlhausen*, Vol. 1, p. 186.
22 Jordan, *Chronik der Stadt Mühlhausen*, Vol. 1, p. 167.
23 Jordan, *Chronik der Stadt Mühlhausen*, Vol. 1, p. 168.
24 Jordan, *Chronik der Stadt Mühlhausen*, Vol. 1, pp. 175–6.
25 Otto Merx, Günther Franz and Walther P. Fuchs (eds), *Akten zur Geschichte des Bauernkrieges in Mitteldeutschland*, 1934 and 1942 (reprinted Aalen 1964), Vol. 2, p. 762 (hereafter cited as 'AGBM').
26 Jordan, *Chronik der Stadt Mühlhausen*, Vol. 1, p. 179.
27 ThMA Vol. 2, p. 369; Matheson, p. 133.
28 See Tom Scott and Robert W. Scribner, *The German Peasants'*

War: A History in Documents, New York 1991, pp. 103–4 (Doc. 16) (their translation taken from Matheson, pp. 455–9).

29 Jordan, *Chronik der Stadt Mühlhausen*, Vol. 1, p. 180.

30 See Siegfried Bräuer and Günter Vogler, *Thomas Müntzer: Neu Ordnung Machen in der Welt*, Gütersloh 2016, pp. 274–5.

31 AGBM Vol. 2, p. 897.

32 *Hoch verursachte Schutzrede und antwort wider das Gaistlosse Sanfft lebende fleysch zu Wittenberg* ... ThMA Vol. 1, pp. 376–98; Matheson, pp. 324–50.

33 ThMA Vol. 1, p. 378; Matheson, p. 327.

34 ThMA Vol. 1, p. 381; Matheson, p. 330.

35 ThMA Vol. 1, pp. 396–7; Matheson, p. 348.

36 ThMA Vol. 1, p. 385; Matheson, p. 335.

37 ThMA Vol. 1, p. 398; Matheson, p. 349.

38 ThMA Vol. 1, p. 384; Matheson, p. 334.

39 ThMA Vol. 1, p. 398; Matheson, p. 350.

40 ThMA Vol. 2, p. 386; Matheson, p. 136.

41 Gerhard Müller and Gottfried Seebass (eds), *Andreas Osiander, Schriften und Briefe*, Gütersloh 1975, Vol. 1, p. 257.

42 Müller and Seebass, *Andreas Osiander*, Vol. 1, pp. 261–6.

43 Müller and Seebass, *Andreas Osiander*, Vol. 1, p. 413.

44 For more on Furer, see Bräuer and Vogler, *Thomas Müntzer: Neu Ordnung Machen*, pp. 303–7.

10. His Poisonous Seed

1 See Tom Scott and Robert W. Scribner, *The German Peasants' War: A History in Documents*, New York 1991, p. 68 (Doc. 1) and p. 301 (Doc. 142).

2 More particulars on the events leading up to and during the Peasants' War of 1524–5 are to be found in Lyndal Roper, *The German Peasants' War*, London 2024; Scott and Scribner, *Documents*; Peter Blickle, *The Revolution of 1525*, Baltimore 1981.

3 See Tom Scott, *Society and Economy in Germany, 1300–1600*, Basingstoke 2002, p. 225.

4 See Scott and Scribner, *Documents*, pp. 121–2 (Doc. 25).

5 See Scott and Scribner, *Documents*, p. 69 (Doc. 1) and p. 179 (Doc. 66).

6 Scott and Scribner, *Documents*, pp. 252–7 (Doc. 125). Various English versions of the document exist online, for example 'From the Reformation to the Thirty Years War (1500–1648)', german historydocs.ghi-dc.org (last accessed July 2023).

7 See Scott and Scribner, *Documents*, pp. 130–2 (Doc. 32).

8 See Scott and Scribner, *Documents*, p. 158 (Doc. 54).

9 Luther, *Vertrag zwischen den löblichen Bund zu Schwaben etc.* in Martin Luther, *Gesammelte Werke*, Weimar 1883–2009 (hereafter cited as 'WA'), Vol. 18, pp. 342–3.

10 Luther, *Ermahnung zum Frieden*. WA Vol. 18, p. 330.

11 Philipp Melanchthon, *Wider die 12 Artikel*. In Klaus Kaczerowsky (ed.), *Flugschriften des Bauernkrieges*, Hamburg 1970, p. 127.

12 Luther, *Wider die räuberischen und mörderischen Rotten der Bauern*. WA Vol. 18, pp. 357–61.

13 See, for example, the letter from the mayor of Zwickau, dated June 1525, condemning Luther, in Scott and Scribner, *Documents*, pp. 322–4 (Doc. 157).

14 See Scott, *Society and Economy*, pp. 56–7. See also Ulrich Pfister and Georg Fertig, *The Population History of Germany*, MPIDR Working Paper WP 2010-035, at demogr.mpg.de/papers/working/wp-2010-035.pdf (last accessed July 2023).

15 Luther, *Wider die räuberischen*. WA Vol. 18, p. 357.

16 *Thomas Müntzer Ausgabe, Kritische Gesamtausgabe* (hereafter cited as 'ThMA'; see Bibliography for full details), Vol. 2, p. 385; Peter Matheson (trans. and ed.), *The Collected Works of Thomas Müntzer*, Edinburgh 1988 (hereafter cited as 'Matheson'), p. 135.

17 Ernst Staehelin (ed.), *Briefe und Akte zum Leben Oekolampads*, Leipzig 1927, Vol. 1, p. 390.

18 Staehelin, *Oekolampad*, Vol. 2, p. 21–2.

19 ThMA Vol. 2, pp. 347–66; Matheson, pp. 121–32.

20 ThMA Vol. 3, p. 266; Matheson, pp. 433–4.

21 Scott and Scribner, *Documents*, p. 253 (Doc. 125).

22 Scott and Scribner, *Documents*, pp. 136–7 (Doc. 37).

23 The '*Verfassungsentwurf*' – translated as 'Constitutional Draft' in Scott and Scribner, *Documents*, pp. 264–5 (Doc. 128).

24 ThMA Vol. 1, p. 341; Matheson, p. 280.

25 ThMA Vol. 3, p. 272; Matheson, p. 438.

26 ThMA Vol. 2, pp. 410–11; Matheson, p. 141.

27 Otto Merx, Günther Franz and Walther P. Fuchs (eds), *Akten zur Geschichte des Bauernkrieges in Mitteldeutschland*, 1934 and 1942 (reprinted Aalen 1964), Vol. 2, p. 66. It has been speculated that the brief imprisonment in Fulda took place in October/November 1524, before Müntzer even arrived in Nürnberg. See also Thomas T. Müller, *Thomas Müntzer im Bauernkrieg*, Mühlhausen 2016, pp. 22–4.

11. The Time Was Come

1 Felician Gess (ed.), *Akten und Briefe zur Kirchenpolitik Herzog Georgs von Sachsen*, two volumes, Leipzig 1905/1917 (reprinted Cologne/Vienna 1985), Vol. 2, pp. 12–13 (hereafter cited as 'ABKG').

2 Tom Scott and Robert W. Scribner, *The German Peasants' War: A History in Documents*, New York 1991, pp. 225–6 (Doc. 101).

3 Otto Merx, Günther Franz and Walther P. Fuchs (eds), *Akten zur Geschichte des Bauernkrieges in Mitteldeutschland*, 1934 and 1942 (reprinted Aalen 1964), Vol. 2, p. 66 (hereafter cited as 'AGBM')

4 Reinhold Jordan (ed.), *Chronik der Stadt Mühlhausen in Thüringen*, Mühlhausen 1900, Vol. 1, p. 182.

5 ABKG Vol. 2, p. 80.

6 ABKG Vol. 2, p. 81.

7 Scott and Scribner, *Documents*, p. 42.

8 The town magistrate, Dr Johann von Othera, quoted in AGBM Vol. 2, p. 834. The quotation is from Luke 1:52.

9 AGBM Vol. 2, p. 73.

10 *Thomas Müntzer Ausgabe, Kritische Gesamtausgabe* (hereafter cited as 'ThMA'; see Bibliography for full details), Vol. 2, pp. 391–7; Peter Matheson (trans. and ed.), *The Collected Works of Thomas Müntzer*, Edinburgh 1988 (hereafter cited as 'Matheson'), pp. 138–9.

11 ThMA Vol. 2, p. 389; Matheson, pp. 136–7.

12 AGBM Vol. 2, p. 67.

13 See ThMA Vol. 2, pp. 418–21.

14 ThMA Vol. 2, p. 403; Matheson, p. 140.

15 AGBM Vol. 2, p. 920.

16 ThMA Vol. 2, p. 430; Matheson, pp. 144–5.

17 For more detail on all this, see Thomas T. Müller, *Mörder ohne Opfer: Die Reichsstadt Mühlhausen und der Bauernkrieg in Thüringen*, Petersberg 2021, pp. 407–14.

18 ThMA Vol. 2, p. 410; Matheson, pp. 140–2.

19 See Martin Luther, *Ein schrecklicke Geschichte* (1525). In Martin Luther, *Gesammelte Werke*, Weimar 1883–2009 (hereafter cited as 'WA'), Vol. 18, pp. 362–74.

20 AGBM Vol. 2, p. 178 and p. 181.

21 See ThMA Vol. 2, p. 414, note 33; and AGBM Vol. 2, p. 758.

22 Karl Förstemann, 'Urkunden zur Geschichte Thomas Müntzers und des Bauernkrieges in Thüringen 1523 bis 1525'. In *Neues Urkundenbuch zur Geschichte der evangelischen Kirchenreformation*, Vol. 1, Hamburg 1842, p. 259; Carl Hinrichs, *Luther und Müntzer*, Berlin (East) 1962, p. 84.

23 AGBM Vol. 2, p. 163.

24 AGBM Vol. 2, p. 136.

25 See Müller, *Mörder*, pp. 383–4.

26 ThMA Vol. 2, p. 426; Matheson, pp. 143–4.

27 For more detail on this entire expedition, see Müller, *Mörder*, pp. 415–547.

28 Scott and Scribner, *Documents*, pp. 200–1 (Doc. 85).

29 Scott and Scribner, *Documents*, p. 147 (Doc. 46b).

30 AGBM Vol. 2, p. 203.

31 ThMA Vol. 2, p. 432; Matheson, pp. 145–6.

32 AGBM Vol. 2, pp. 478–80.

33 See Müller, *Mörder*, pp. 438–62.

34 Müller, *Mörder*, p. 565.

35 ABKG Vol. 2, p. 166.

36 WA, Briefe Vol. 3, p. 480.

37 ThMA Vol. 2, pp. 435–6; Matheson, pp. 146–7. Also AGBM Vol. 2, p. 230.

38 ThMA Vol. 2, pp. 439–40; Matheson, pp. 147–8.

39 ThMA Vol. 2, p. 144; Matheson, p. 150.

40 ThMA Vol. 2, p. 438; Matheson, pp. 148–9.

41 ThMA Vol. 2, p. 448; Matheson, pp. 150–1.

42 Scott and Scribner, *Documents*, p. 160 (Doc. 57); also AGBM Vol. 2, pp. 85–6.

43 ThMA Vol. 2, p. 442; Matheson, p. 149.

12. Thomas Would Catch All the Bullets in His Sleeves

1 *Thomas Müntzer Ausgabe, Kritische Gesamtausgabe* (hereafter cited as 'ThMA'; see Bibliography for full details), Vol. 2, p. 438; Peter Matheson (trans. and ed.), *The Collected Works of Thomas Müntzer*, Edinburgh 1988 (hereafter cited as 'Matheson'), pp. 148–9.

2 ThMA Vol. 2, p. 440; Matheson, pp. 147–8.

3 Otto Merx, Günther Franz and Walther P. Fuchs (eds), *Akten zur Geschichte des Bauernkrieges in Mitteldeutschland*, 1934 and 1942 (reprinted Aalen 1964), Vol. 2, pp. 249–50 (hereafter cited as 'AGBM').

4 ThMA Vol. 2, pp. 444–5. This letter was in the handwriting of Ambrosius Emmen.

5 ThMA Vol. 2, pp. 451–3; Matheson, pp. 152–4.

6 AGBM Vol. 2, pp. 202–3.

7 AGBM Vol. 2, p. 230.

8 AGBM Vol. 2, pp. 214–15.

9   AGBM Vol. 2, pp. 278–9. See also Carl Hinrichs, *Luther und Müntzer*, Berlin (East) 1962, p. 19.

10 AGBM Vol. 2, p. 230.

11 Felician Gess (ed.), *Akten und Briefe zur Kirchenpolitik Herzog Georgs von Sachsen*, two volumes, Leipzig 1905/1917 (reprinted Cologne/Vienna 1985), Vol. 2, p. 189 (hereafter cited as 'ABKG').

12 ThMA Vol. 2, p. 474.

13 ThMA Vol. 2, pp. 464–5; Matheson, pp. 156–7.

14 ThMA Vol. 2, pp. 465–73; Matheson, pp. 154–6.

15 ThMA Vol. 2, p. 479; Matheson, pp. 158–9.

16 See Siegfried Bräuer, 'Simon Hoffmann – "ein lybhaber ewangelischer warheyt"'. In U. Weiss (ed.), *Erfurt: Geschichte und Gegenwart*, Weimar 1995, pp. 297–321.

17 ThMA Vol. 3, p. 269; Matheson, p. 436.

18 ThMA Vol. 3, p. 258.

19 For more detail on troop strengths and movements at Frankenhausen, see Doug Miller, *Frankenhausen 1525*, Seaton Burn 2017.

20 Miller, *Frankenhausen*, p. 82.

21 ThMA Vol. 2, p. 488; Matheson, p. 159.

22 ThMA Vol. 2, p. 490; Matheson, pp. 159–60.

23 Philipp Melanchthon, in Ludwig Fischer (ed.), *Die Lutherischen Pamphlete gegen Thomas Müntzer*, Tübingen 1976, pp. 34–9.

24 Johann Rühel in Martin Luther, *Gesammelte Werke*, Weimar 1883–2009 (hereafter cited as 'WA'), Briefe Vol. 3, p. 510.

25 AGBM Vol. 2, p. 897.

26 WA, Briefe Vol. 3, p. 508.

27 AGBM Vol. 2, pp. 343–4.

28 Tom Scott and Robert W. Scribner, *The German Peasants' War: A History in Documents*, New York 1991.

29 See ABKG Vol. 2, p. 298; AGBM Vol. 2, p. 305 and p. 319.

30 See Miller, *Frankenhausen*, pp. 96–7.

31 ThMA Vol. 3, p. 241.

13. How God Punishes Disobedience

1   Johann Rühel in Martin Luther, *Gesammelte Werke*, Weimar 1883–2009 (hereafter cited as 'WA'), Briefe Vol. 3, p. 511.

2   Cited in Günther Franz and Paul Kirn (eds), *Thomas Müntzer: Schriften und Briefe*, Gütersloh 1968, p. 543; Peter Matheson (trans. and ed.), *The Collected Works of Thomas Müntzer*, Edinburgh 1988 (hereafter cited as 'Matheson'), p. 433.

3   For all citations from the 'Confession', *Thomas Müntzer Ausgabe, Kritische Gesamtausgabe* (hereafter cited as 'ThMA'; see Bibliography for full details), Vol. 3, pp. 266–72; Matheson, pp. 433–8.

4   See Johann Rühel in WA, Briefe Vol. 3, pp. 504–7.

5   WA, Briefe Vol. 3, p. 507.

6   ThMA Vol. 3, pp. 273–4; Matheson, pp. 439–40.

7   ThMA Vol. 2, pp. 491–504; Matheson, pp. 160–1.

8   Otto Merx, Günther Franz and Walther P. Fuchs (eds), *Akten zur Geschichte des Bauernkrieges in Mitteldeutschland*, 1934 and 1942 (reprinted Aalen 1964), Vol. 2, p. 478 and p. 479 (hereafter cited as 'AGBM').

9   AGBM Vol. 2, pp. 278–9 and p. 305.

10 ThMA Vol. 2, p. 177; Matheson, pp. 60–4.

11 Melanchthon, in Ludwig Fischer (ed.), *Die Lutherischen Pamphlete gegen Thomas Müntzer*, Tübingen 1976, p. 41.

12 AGBM Vol. 2, pp. 334–5.

13 AGBM Vol. 2, p. 383.

14 AGBM Vol. 1, Part 2, p. 385.

15 Tom Scott and Robert W. Scribner, *The German Peasants' War: A History in Documents*, New York 1991, p. 301.

16 Felician Gess (ed.), *Akten und Briefe zur Kirchenpolitik Herzog Georgs von Sachsen*, two volumes, Leipzig 1905/1917 (reprinted Cologne/Vienna 1985), Vol. 2, pp. 248–53.

17 See, for example, AGBM Vol. 2, pp. 512–28.

18 See M. Straube, 'Über Folgen der Niederlage im thüringischen Bauernkrieg'. In G. Vogler (ed.), *Bauernkrieg zwischen Harz und Thüringer Wald*, Stuttgart 2008.

19 Scott and Scribner, *Documents*, p. 169 (Doc. 62).

20 See Melanchthon, *Die Histori Thome Muntzers*, in Fischer, *Die Lutherischen Pamphlete*, p. 41. I am grateful to Peter Matheson for his suggestion that the reference may be to 2 Kings, Chapters 22 and 23.

21 See ThMA Vol. 3, p. 263.

22 WA, Tischreden Vol. 1, p. 38.

23 ThMA Vol. 2, p. 502; Matheson, pp. 160–1.

24 ThMA Vol. 2, pp. 504–5; Matheson, pp. 459–60.

25 AGBM Vol. 2, p. 666.

26 WA Vol. 18, p. 400.

14. Rebellious Violent Preachers

1   Tom Scott and Robert W. Scribner, *The German Peasants' War: A History in Documents*, New York 1991, p. 329 (Doc. 161a); also Paul Wappler, *Die Täuferbewegung in Thüringen von 1526–1584*, Jena 1913, pp. 363–4.

2   Wappler, *Täuferbewegung*, p. 364.

3   Felician Gess (ed.), *Akten und Briefe zur Kirchenpolitik Herzog*

Georgs von Sachsen, two volumes, Leipzig 1905/1917 (reprinted Cologne/Vienna 1985), Vol. 2, pp. 839–40.

4   Scott and Scribner, *Documents*, pp. 328–9 (Doc. 161a).

5   Wappler, *Täuferbewegung*, pp. 429–30.

6   Wappler, *Täuferbewegung*, p. 432.

7   Wappler, *Täuferbewegung*, pp. 155–7.

8   See Karl G. Bretschneider (ed.), *Corpus Reformatorum*, Halle 1834, Series I, Vol. 4, pp. 737–40.

9   Scott and Scribner, *Documents*, p. 331 (Doc. 162).

10 See Gerhard Zschäbitz, *Zur mitteldeutschen Wiedertäuferbewegung nach dem grossen Bauernkrieg*, Berlin (East) 1958, p. 151.

11 See Claus-Peter Clasen, *The Anabaptists in South and Central Germany, Switzerland and Austria*, Goshen 1978. Also James M. Stayer, *The German Peasants' War and Anabaptist Community of Goods*, Montreal 1991, pp. 90–2 and p. 147.

12 Zschäbitz, *Wiedertäuferbewegung*, pp. 160–1.

13 Zschäbitz, *Wiedertäuferbewegung*, pp. 155–6.

14 See Stayer, *Anabaptist Community*, pp. 150–1.

15 Scott and Scribner, *Documents*, p. 324 (Doc. 157).

16 W. Friedrich, 'Der Buchführer Johann Hergot'. In *Beiträge zur Geschichte des Buchwesens*, Leipzig 1966, Vol. 2, p. 13.

17 Otto Merx, Günther Franz, Walther P. Fuchs (eds.), *Akten zur Geschichte des Bauernkrieges in Mitteldeutschland*, 1934 and 1942 (reprinted Aalen 1964), Vol. I, p. 643 (hereafter cited as 'AGBM'), p. 643.

18 For further information on Anabaptism see C. P. Clasen, *The Anabaptists*, London 1972; H. Fast (ed.), *Der linke Flügel der Reformation*, Bremen 1962; H. J. Goertz (ed.), *Umstrittenes Taufertum*, Göttingen 1975; Kat Hill, *Baptism, Brotherhood, and Belief in Reformation Germany: Anabaptism and Lutheranism, 1525–1585*, Oxford 2015; G. Rupp, *Patterns of Reformation*, London 1969; Stayer, *Anabaptist Community*; J. M. Stayer and W. O. Packull (eds), *The Anabaptists and Thomas Müntzer*, Dubuque 1980; Zschäbitz, *Wiedertäuferbewegung*.

19 Günther Franz (ed.), *Quellen zur Geschichte des Bauernkriegs*, Munich 1963, p. 86.

20 *Thomas Müntzer Ausgabe, Kritische Gesamtausgabe* (hereafter cited as 'ThMA'; see Bibliography for full details), Vol. 3, p. 240.

21 This and the following quotes from Hut taken from Lydia Müller, *Glaubenszeugnisse oberdeutscher Taufgesinnter*, New York and London 1971 (first published 1938).

22 Wappler, *Täuferbewegung*, p. 240.

23 Wappler, *Täuferbewegung*, p. 245.

24 Wappler, *Täuferbewegung*, p. 231.

25 For more on this, see Hill, *Baptism*, pp. 204–6.

26 Wappler, *Täuferbewegung*, p. 323.
27 Zschäbitz, *Wiedertäuferbewegung*, p. 64.
28 Zschäbitz, *Wiedertäuferbewegung*, p. 58.
29 Josef Beck, *Geschichtsbücher der Wiedertäufer in Oesterreich und Ungarn 1526–1785*, Vienna 1883, pp. 49–50.
30 On Bader, see Gustav Bossert, 'Augustin Bader von Augsburg'. In *Archiv für Reformationsgeschichte*, Vol. 10, Leipzig 1913. Also Werner O. Packull, *Mysticism and the Early South-German-Austrian Anabaptist Movement 1525–1531*, Scottdale PA 1977.
31 Wappler, *Täuferbewegung*, pp. 315–16.
32 See Packull, *Mysticism*.
33 Unless otherwise noted, quotes from Denck are taken from Johann Denck, *Schriften*, ed. G. Baring and W. Fellmann, 3 vols, Gütersloh 1955–60.
34 ThMA Vol. 1, p. 335; Peter Matheson (trans. and ed.), *The Collected Works of Thomas Müntzer*, Edinburgh 1988 (hereafter cited as 'Matheson'), p. 272.
35 ThMA Vol. 1, p. 283; Matheson, p. 205.
36 See Klaus Deppermann, *Melchior Hoffman: Social Unrest and Apocalyptic Vision in the Age of Reformation*, Edinburgh 1987.
37 Wappler, *Täuferbewegung*, p. 51.
38 Wappler, *Täuferbewegung*, p. 333.
39 Wappler, *Täuferbewegung*, pp. 334–5.
40 Melchior Rinck, 'Widderlegung einer Schrift', *Mennonite Quarterly Review*, Vol. 35, Part 3, 1961, p. 215.
41 Wappler, *Täuferbewegung*, p. 231.
42 Beck, *Geschichtsbücher*, pp. 12–13.
43 Wappler, *Täuferbewegung*, p. 263.
44 AGBM Vol. 2, p. 792.
45 Wappler, *Täuferbewegung*, p. 257.
46 AGBM Vol. 2, pp. 906–7.
47 See Zschäbitz, *Wiedertäuferbewegung*, p. 149.
48 Wappler, *Täuferbewegung*, p. 265.
49 Wappler, *Täuferbewegung*, p. 425.
50 Wappler, *Täuferbewegung*, p. 429.
51 See Stayer, *Anabaptist Community*, pp. 123–38. Also Richard van Dülmen (ed.), *Das Täuferreich zu Münster*, Munich 1974; James M. Stayer, *Anabaptists and the Sword*, Lawrence KS 1976, p. 231.
52 *Eine rechte warhafftige hohe und götliche gruntliche underrichtung von der reinen forchte Gottes ann alle liebhaber der ewiger unentlicher warheit, aus Götlicher Schrifft angezeygt zum Preiss Gottes unnd heyll sines volcks in ewigkeyt* (1533).
53 See Zschäbitz, *Wiedertäuferbewegung*, pp. 144–5; also Stayer, *Anabaptists and the Sword*, pp. 203–80.

54 For evidence of the similarities between the teachings of Müntzer and those of the radicals during the English Revolution, see Christopher Hill's *The World Turned Upside Down*, London 2020.

15. The Devil in Person

1 In Ludwig Fischer (ed.), *Die Lutherischen Pamphlete gegen Thomas Müntzer*, Tübingen 1976, pp. 2–12 and 14–15.
2 Martin Luther, *Gesammelte Werke*, Weimar 1883–2009 (hereafter cited as 'WA') Vol. 18, pp. 37–125.
3 In Fischer, *Die Lutherischen Pamphlete*, pp. 18–25.
4 WA, Tischreden Vol. 1, p. 37.
5 In Fischer, *Die Lutherischen Pamphlete*, pp. 28–42.
6 In Fischer, *Die Lutherischen Pamphlete*, pp. 44–78.
7 *Thomas Müntzer Ausgabe, Kritische Gesamtausgabe* (see Bibliography for full details), Vol. 2, pp. 240–52; Peter Matheson (trans. and ed.), *The Collected Works of Thomas Müntzer*, Edinburgh 1988, pp. 76–9.
8 In Fischer, *Die Lutherischen Pamphlete*, pp. 80–95.
9 Johann Cochläus, in Klaus Kaczerowsky (ed.), *Flugschriften des Bauernkrieges*, Hamburg 1970, pp. 171–97.
10 Felician Gess (ed.), *Akten und Briefe zur Kirchenpolitik Herzog Georgs von Sachsens*, two volumes, Leipzig 1905/1917 (reprinted Cologne/Vienna 1985), Vol. 2, p. 333 (hereafter cited as 'ABKG').
11 ABKG Vol. 2, p. 483.
12 In Fischer, *Die Lutherischen Pamphlete*, pp. 97–105.
13 Bullinger, *Der Widertöuffern Ursprung, Fuergang, Secten etc*, Zurich 1560.
14 Georg T. Strobel, *Leben, Schriften und Lehren Thome Müntzers*, Nürnberg 1795.
15 Johann Friedrich Köhler, *Gallerie der neuen Propheten*, Leipzig 1799.
16 Johann K. Seidemann, *Thomas Müntzer: Eine Biographie*, Dresden 1842.
17 Wilhelm Zimmermann, *Geschichte des grossen deutschen Bauernkrieges*, Stuttgart 1841–3.
18 Friedrich Engels, *The Peasant War in Germany*, Moscow 1969 (first published 1850).
19 A. Bebel, *Der deutsche Bauernkrieg*, Brunswick 1876; K. Kautsky, *Die deutsche Reformation und Thomas Münzer*, Stuttgart 1895; E. Belfort Bax, *The Peasants' War in Germany*, London 1899; F. Mehring, *Deutsche Geschichte vom Ausgange des Mittelalters*, Berlin 1910.

20 Felician Gess (ed.), *Akten und Briefe zur Kirchenpolitik Herzog Georgs von Sachsen*, two volumes, Leipzig 1905/1917.

21 Ernst Bloch, *Thomas Münzer als Theologe der Revolution*, Munich 1921.

22 Otto Merx, Günther Franz and Walther P. Fuchs (eds), *Akten zur Geschichte des Bauernkrieges in Mitteldeutschland*, 1934 and 1942.

23 Heinrich Böhmer and Paul Kirn, *Thomas Müntzers Briefwechsel*, Leipzig 1931.

24 Friedrich Wiechert and Oskar J. Mehl, *Thomas Müntzers Deutsche Messen und Kirchenämter*, Grimmen 1937.

25 Günther Franz, *Der deutsche Bauernkrieg*, Bad Homburg 1969 (first published Munich 1933).

26 For a short political biography of Franz, see the essay by Wolfgang Behringer at uni-saarland.de/fileadmin/upload/lehrstuhl/behringer/PDF/bauernfranz.pdf (last accessed July 2023).

27 Moisei M. Smirin, *Narodnaia reformatsiia Tomasa Miuntsera*, Moscow 1947 (German trans. *Die Volksreformation des Thomas Münzer*, Berlin [East] 1952).

28 Max Steinmetz, 'Das Erbe Thomas Müntzers', *Zeitschrift für Geschichtswissenschaft*, Vol. 17, Issue 9, 1969, p. 1118.

29 See especially works by Carl Hinrichs, Alfred Meusel and Ernst Sommer; after 1956, works by Manfred Bensing, Max Steinmetz, Siegfried Bräuer and Gerhard Zschäbitz are all of considerable value.

30 See the catalogue of the Russian State Library (Rossijskaja Gosudarstvennaja Biblioteka), Moscow, Collection 218, No. 390, p. 314. Even had the SED known that Stalin had falsified his own birthdate – he was born in 1878, not 1879 – it is unlikely that their enthusiasm to send him a present of their own historical record would have been diminished.

31 See, in particular, works by E. Gordon Rupp, Hans Joachim Hillerbrand and Hans-Jürgen Goertz.

32

Period	Total	Average/year
1519–1794	433	1.57
1795–1848	127	2.35
1849–1870	37	1.68
1871–1932	276	4.45
1933–1945	81	6.23
1946–1956	109	9.90
1957–1974	400	22.22
1975–1989	1048	69.87
1990–2012	706	30.70

Figures taken from Marion Dammaschke and Günter Vogler, *Thomas-Müntzer-Bibliographie (1519–2012)*, Baden-Baden 2013. The figures from 2013 to 2023 continue the trend for the period ending in 2012.

33 Of special mention here are the works by Tom Scott, Peter Matheson, Michael Baylor and Abraham Friesen.

34 Specifically: Tom Scott, Peter Matheson, Thomas. T. Müller, Hans-Jürgen Goertz, Günter Vogler and Siegfried Bräuer.

35 Thomas T. Müller, *Mörder ohne Opfer: Die Reichsstadt Mühlhausen und der Bauernkrieg in Thüringen*, Petersberg 2021, p. 15.

36 See, as a prime recent example of uninhibited carelessness, Eric Vuillard's *La guerre des pauvres*, Paris 2019 (trans. as *The War of the Poor*, London 2021).

Conclusion

1 Martin Luther, *Gesammelte Werke*, Weimar 1883–2009, Tischreden Vol. 3, p. 406, No. 3554 (March 1537).

2 *Thomas Müntzer Ausgabe, Kritische Gesamtausgabe* (hereafter cited as 'ThMA'; see Bibliography for full details), Vol. 3, pp. 266–72; Peter Matheson (trans. and ed.), *The Collected Works of Thomas Müntzer*, Edinburgh 1988 (hereafter cited as 'Matheson'), p. 434.

3 Peter Matheson 'The Language of Thomas Müntzer'. In *Thomas Müntzer im Blick: Günter Vogler zum 90. Geburtstag*, ed. M. Dammaschke and T. T. Müller, Mühlhausen 2023, p. 130.

4 ThMA Vol. 1, p. 385; Matheson, p. 335.

Index

Index